The Book of Buechner

Frederick Buechner (circa 1995)

Frederick Buechner is one of the most significant contemporary writers of the last fifty years. Both his fiction and nonfiction writings have won acclaim, all being either directly or indirectly religious in orientation. Buechner's lucid and engaging style has made him a beloved figure who deals honestly with life while also being keenly aware of the presence of the divine in our midst.

The Book of Buechner

A Journey through His Writings

Dale Brown

Westminster John Knox Press
LOUISVILLE • LONDON

Scripture quotations from the New Revised Standard Version of the Bible are copyright © 1989 by the Division of Christian Education of the National Council of the Churches of Christ in the U.S.A. and are used by permission.

Excerpts from the following books by Frederick Buechner are used with the permission of HarperCollins Publishers: *The Book of Bebb; Brendan; The Son of Laughter; On the Road with the Archangel; The Storm: A Novel; The Magnificent Defeat; The Alphabet of Grace; The Sacred Journey; Now and Then; Wishful Thinking: A Theological ABC;* and *The Eyes of the Heart.*

Excerpts from the following books by Frederick Buechner are used with the permission of Frederick Buechner: *A Long Day's Dying; The Seasons' Difference; The Return of Ansel Gibbs;* and *The Final Beast.*

Frederick Buechner's poem "Miriam" is reprinted herein with the permission of Frederick Buechner.

Book design by Sharon Adams
Cover design by designpointinc.com
Cover photo courtesy of Frederick Buechner

First edition
Published by Westminster John Knox Press
Louisville, Kentucky

This book is printed on acid-free paper that meets the American National Standards Institute Z39.48 standard. ∞

PRINTED IN THE UNITED STATES OF AMERICA

06 07 08 09 10 11 12 13 14 15—10 9 8 7 6 5 4 3 2 1

Library of Congress Cataloging-in-Publication Data
Brown, W. Dale.
    The book of Buechner : a journey through his writings / Dale Brown.—1st ed.
        p.   cm.
    Includes bibliographical references and index.
    ISBN-13: 978-0-664-23113-2 (alk. paper)
    ISBN-10: 0-664-23113-6 (alk. paper)
    1. Buechner, Frederick, 1926– 2. Novelists, American—20th century—Biography.
I. Title
    PS3552.U35Z57   2007
    813'.54—dc22
    [B]   2006048989

For Anne and JD

Contents

Foreword

As I made my way through all these pages—it took me the better part of three days with few interruptions—it was less like reading than like listening to the voice of a friend. It must have been over twenty years ago that I first met Dale Brown during a speaking tour I made in Iowa, and though we can't have seen each other more than a dozen times since, he has become, more than anyone else I can think of, my chief promoter and advocate. He has taught my books in various of his courses at Calvin College. He has written articles about me and reviewed my books and published interviews. On two occasions, he has persuaded me to make the long trip from Rupert, Vermont, to Grand Rapids, Michigan, to address audiences, recruited by him, of no less than rock-star proportions, the last of them amounting to something like twenty-five hundred. I was aware that for some time he had also been working on a book about me, but I had no part in its composition and knew nothing about what sort of book it was until he sent me the completed typescript only a few days before I sat down to write this.

How to describe my feelings when I opened the formidable package it came in? I was enormously curious, of course. What had he said and how had he said it and what was I going to think about it? I was also touched at the thought of all the time he had spent writing it, not to mention reading and rereading all those books he was writing it about. I wondered who on earth would be interested enough to wade through it and what they would make of it if they did. I was apprehensive about what I would make of it myself. What if he said things I disagreed with? Out of the corner of my eye I was also aware of my eightieth birthday bearing down on me hard and tried not to think of *The Book of Buechner* as the gold watch presented to me at my retirement banquet, the last hurrah and final curtain call.

But within seconds of starting out on page one, all these misgivings vanished, and I found myself simply listening raptly to a discerning and sympathetic voice telling me about the books I have spent the last half century and more writing and relating them to the ups and downs, the twists and turns, of my life as I wrote them. . . .

I was only twenty when I started *A Long Day's Dying* as a senior at Princeton, and could not help wishing he hadn't spent so much time on a novel that, like the three or four following it, I would rather have had him deal with as juvenilia in some sort of concluding postscript, instead of right there at the beginning, like hanging my baby pictures in the front hall. I knew so little about almost anything when I wrote them, including who it was I was writing them for or just what it was I was trying to say to them. More importantly I hadn't yet found my own true voice as a writer. Even when I sounded good I didn't sound like me. In an effort to convince myself that writing as an occupation was as important and honorable and related to the real world as teaching school or running a business, I always used to put on a jacket and tie to work. I stood at attention, in other words. I watched my language. I watched my p's and q's. But then along came Leo Bebb heading down those urine-smelling subway stairs in a raincoat that was too small for him and a dimly Tyrolean hat, Leo Bebb who had done time on a charge of indecent exposure and spoke country English, and it was from him that I learned little by little, as I kept on writing about him, to loosen up a little—not only to sound like myself but to dare to be myself, to expose who I was, to a degree that in earlier days would have struck me as unseemly.

As Dale Brown headed on into the four Bebb books and the ones that followed it, the ones I like to believe I will be remembered by if I am remembered at all, I found myself increasingly moved—the best word I can find for it. What moved me first of all was how well I thought he'd genuinely understood both what I was trying to do in them and what I was determined to avoid doing. What I was trying to do was to be as true as I could to life as I have experienced it, including the always elusive and ambiguous experience of God, and what I was trying not to do was to preach or to make the life of faith seem any simpler and easier than I have found it to be. There are places where I found myself in disagreement with him—I think he overestimates the influence on me of Mark Twain, for instance—but by and large, it seems to me, he not only understands cerebrally what I was trying to say about the ragged, clay-footed crowd of saints and near-saints in whose company I have spent so many years of my life—Godric, Brendan, Jacob, and the rest—but has a real feeling for their oddball beauty and humanness and moments of holiness. I had the sense that, like me, he had come in some measure to love them.

The other thing that moved me was the books themselves, which in a way he gave back to me. It has been such a long time since I wrote them that I'd forgotten all sorts of things about them, just as I had more or less lost track of what was going on in my life as they first began to emerge from whatever the mystery is that books like dreams emerge from. I found myself remembering how I got so wound up in Bebb and was so afraid that something would happen to prevent my finishing with him that I literally couldn't stop writing about him but kept at it even in the tumultuous Bromley Mountain ski lodge waiting for my children to come in from the slopes; how I sat with my notebook and felt-tip pen in my lap by the little stream where Sharmy was casting for trout and based my description of Godric's Wear on the splash and glitter of it; how by some kind of magic I discovered in the ancient narratives of Genesis a world I had never even come close to glimpsing before—the blue river and swaying palms of the Black Land, the runaway camels and rutting flocks, the sound of Pharaoh's saying to Joseph on the palace terrace at sunset, "I do not fear the Gods. I feed them."

But back to that approaching birthday again. More and more often as the years go by, I think back over my all but eighty years and wonder if I have accomplished anything worthwhile during the course of them. I could have been so much braver and kinder and more unselfish. I could have been so much better a Christian, a writer, a man. But the way things turned out, I picture myself appearing before Saint Peter pretty much empty-handed except for the books. Were they worth all the time I spent on them, all the other things I neglected for them? Did they leave the world any better for having been written? What moved me most in Dale Brown's book was that he seemed to think so, and I can only hope that when the time comes, he may put in a good word for me at the fateful gates.

FREDERICK BUECHNER

(Carl) Frederick Buechner: An Annotated Chronology

July 11, 1926   Born to Carl Frederick and Katherine (Kuhn) Buechner in New York City

1928   Brother James (Jamie) born

1936   Father's suicide:

> "I suppose one way to read my whole life—my religious faith, the books I have written, the friends I have made—is as a search for him."

1937   Residence in Bermuda

1943   Graduates from Lawrenceville School (New Jersey)

1943–1944   Princeton University

1944–1946   Military service

1946   "Fat Man's Prescriptions" (poetry)

1946–1948   Princeton University (B.A. 1948)

1947   Winner, Irene Glascock Prize for Poetry

1948–1953   Teacher of English at Lawrenceville School

1950   *A Long Day's Dying*:

> ". . . to be alive was perilous."

Travel in Europe

1952   ***The Seasons' Difference***:

                    "What would you be fishing for in the sky, I wonder?"

                 "**The Tiger**" (short story in *The New Yorker*):

                    ". . . in the world we're pretty much stuck with there simply are no tigers any more."

                 Visit to George Buttrick's church in New York City

                    "Christ is crowned among tears and great laughter."

1953–1954   Lecturer at New York University

1954   Enrolls, on a Rockefeller Brothers Fellowship, at Union Theological Seminary in New York during the Golden Age of Tillich, Barth, Niebuhr, and Muilenburg

1954–1958   Works in Harlem employment clinic

1955   O. Henry Memorial Award for "The Tiger"

April 7, 1956   Marriage to Judith Merck:

                 "All measure and all language I should pass
                 Should I tell what a miracle she was." (John Donne)

1956   Four-month European tour

1958   ***The Return of Ansel Gibbs***

               B.D. from Union Theological Seminary and ordination

               Grandmother Buechner dies:

                 "Every man has his voices."

1958–1960   Chairman of department of religion, Phillips Exeter Academy

                 "My whole career is an attempt to rewrite *The Power and the Glory* in a way of mine own."

1959   First child, Katherine, born

               Richard and Hilda Rosenthal Award for *The Return of Ansel Gibbs*

1960   Second child, Dinah, born

1960–1967   School minister at Phillips Exeter Academy

1963–1964   Sabbatical in Vermont

1964   Third child, Sharman, born

1965   ***The Final Beast***
        "Mr. Buechner has put his foot in it."

1966   ***The Magnificent Defeat***
        "The sacred moments, the moments of miracle, are
        often the everyday moments."

1967   Move to Rupert, Vermont, to pursue full-time writing

1968   ***The Hungering Dark***
        ". . . in a world with God, we can never know what
        will happen."

1969   William Belden Nobel lecturer at Harvard University
        (published as *The Alphabet of Grace*)

1970   ***The Entrance to Porlock***
        "I've been waiting for the heavens to open and show
        riches."

1970   ***The Alphabet of Grace***
        ". . . there is nothing about either of us that can be
        entirely irrelevant to the other."

1971   ***Lion Country***
        "I am sure that I was, among other things, hungry for
        fortissimo."
        National Book Award nomination
        Russell Lecturer at Tufts University

1972   ***Open Heart***
        "We are all of us seeking a homeland."

1973   ***Wishful Thinking: A Theological ABC***
        "The faint glimmer on the horizon could have been
        just Disneyland."

1974   ***Love Feast***
        "... it would take God himself to sort out the tangle."
        The Faces of Jesus
        "He had a man's face, a human face."

1976   Lyman Beecher Lectures at Yale University

1977   ***Treasure Hunt***
        "WELCOME HONE"
        Telling the Truth: The Gospel in Tragedy, Comedy, and Fairy Tale
        "The gospel is bad news before it is good news."
        The Book of Bebb (tetralogy of ***Lion Country***, ***Open Heart***, ***Love Feast***, ***Treasure Hunt***)
        "Sacred Romp"
        Peculiar Treasures: A Biblical Who's Who
        "... nothing human is ever uncomplicated."

1980   ***Godric***
        "Nothing human's not a broth of false and true."
        Pulitzer Prize finalist

1982   D.D., Virginia Theological Seminary
        Archive established at Wheaton College
        The Sacred Journey (first volume of autobiography)
        "The story of any one of us is in some measure the story of us all."

1983   ***Now and Then*** (second volume of autobiography)
        "... hints of an explanation"
        Marie-Helene Davies, *Laughter in a Genevan Gown: The Works of Frederick Buechner 1970–1980*

1984   ***A Room Called Remember: Uncollected Pieces***
        "... fugitive pieces"

1987   Wheaton College speech, "Religion and Art"

   Brendan

   "Saints with feet of clay are the only subjects that interest me now."

   Christianity and Literature Belles Lettres Prize

1988   ***Whistling in the Dark: An ABC Theologized***

   ". . . to keep the spirits up while peering through the shadows for some glimmer of Meaning"

   Buechner's mother dies.

   Marjorie Casebriar McCoy, *Frederick Buechner: Novelist and Theologian of the Lost and Found*

1990   ***The Wizard's Tide*** (republished in 2006 as *The Christmas Tide*)

   "It is a mostly true story."

1991   ***Telling Secrets: A Memoir*** (third volume of autobiography)

   "I think I see patterns."

1992   ***The Clown in the Belfry: Writings on Faith and Fiction***

   ". . . a real mishmash"

   Listening to Your Life: *Daily Meditations with Frederick Buechner*

   ". . . although the night is coming, it is not darkness but light that is the end of all things."

1992   Wiersma lecturer at Calvin College

1993   ***The Son of Laughter***

   "Is his promise only a dream?"

1996   ***The Longing for Home***

   "I have to accept my homesickness as chronic and incurable."

1997   **On the Road with the Archangel**
          "I often shake with laughter."

1998   **The Storm**
          "If only."

1999   **The Eyes of the Heart: A Memoir of the Lost and
          Found** (fourth volume of autobiography)
          "I hope that it is true about God."

2001   **Speak What We Feel (Not What We Ought to Say)**
          "Fear not. Be alive. Be merciful. Be human."

2002   Victoria S. Allen, *Listening to Life: Psychology and Spirituality in the Writings of Frederick Buechner*

2004   **Beyond Words: Daily Readings in the ABC's of Faith**
          "Be alive to your life."

2006   **Secrets in the Dark**
          "I tried to be myself. I tried to be honest."

Frederick Buechner lives now on a farm in Vermont and spends the winters in Florida. He visits often with his ten grandchildren. And he writes.

First, a Word

Nothing human's not a broth of false and true.

I have spent much of my career as a teacher of literature touting those writers who plow the stony ground in the shadows cast by John Grisham, Tom Clancy, and Danielle Steele in the one field and Tim LaHaye, Jerry Jenkins, and Frank Peretti in the other. My inclinations are toward those contemporary writers who defy straightforward categorization as secular or religious, those who rest uneasily in either venue. My reading has brought me back again and again to writers who work seriously around the great fire of faith while evincing a deep regard for truth telling. Although these scribes seldom appear at the top of the bestseller lists, I have been surprised at how sizable a crowd they comprise. Though the fields they work may appear to be flinty, the soil proves again and again fertile. For many years now I have invited them to Grand Rapids for a Festival of Faith & Writing, and I have traveled the country to interview them for various publications and for my book *Of Fiction and Faith*. Although not necessarily people who practice faith via church attendance and the like, these writers work from a sophisticated awareness of fundamentally religious issues. They write of the precarious tilt between belief and unbelief, and their regard for the craft allows us to label them "literary." Most appear in the secular shops, some in the religion ones, but they are often overlooked, overwhelmed by blockbusters, page turners, celebrity exposés, and airport novels.

Festival headliners have often been familiar names—John Updike, Annie Dillard, Maya Angelou, Elie Wiesel, Joyce Carol Oates, Chaim Potok, Madeleine L'Engle, Stephen Dunn, Kaye Gibbons, Oscar Hijuelos, Donald

1

Hall. But the heart of these gatherings has usually been most obvious among lesser celebrated writers who become discoveries for conferees looking to build reading lists. Registrants trust the festivals as a resource that guides them through the perilous choices, helping them to sift the noteworthy offerings from among the thousands of books available at the Giant Discount Store, the Family Bookstore, and the mainstream mall stores like Waldenbooks, where one might find a copy of Thoreau somewhere in the far reaches, under "classics."

Because this book owes much to years of festivals, allow me to begin here by expressing my deep gratitude to Doris Betts, David James Duncan, Ernest Gaines, Jon Hassler, Robert Clark, Lee Smith, Clyde Edgerton, Denise Giardina, Will Campbell, Tim Gautreaux, Elizabeth Dewberry, Leif Enger, Anne Lamott, Silas House, Michael Malone, Katherine Paterson, Ron Hansen, and so many others for their contributions to our gatherings and for their thoughtful observations on the intersections of faith and writing. This book comes out of the grist that they have contributed over the years. I have had what Nick Carraway calls "the consoling proximity" of famous folk. I've sat in the green room with Maya Angelou, walked a trail with David James Duncan, spent an afternoon in Garrison Keillor's apartment on the west side of Central Park, shared an airport lounge with Ernest Gaines, lunched with Clyde Edgerton, breakfasted with John Updike, and had red tea in the kitchen of Jan Karon's antebellum mansion. But I come back repeatedly to the first name on my list of potential festival speakers. Frederick Buechner was the first festival invite. He was the first interview. This book is a stab at an explanation.

Most readers know the name by now and even how to pronounce it ("Beekner"). The outlines of Buechner's life—privileged beginnings, his father's suicide, the early success as a novelist, the conversion, the ordination, the speeches, the lifetime of books—are pretty firmly set in our minds. Many of us have heard Buechner's own summary of his career as "between two worlds."[1] Sometimes he talks about the suspension between the secular and religious, claiming that he is "too religious for secular readers" and "too secular for religious ones."[2] There's that poise between faith and doubt—a tension he never quite manages to dispel. As the autobiography and the nonfiction have provided a certain paradigm for understanding Buechner, the novels, too, have a story to tell. Before he preached and lectured, before he crafted essays and published memoirs, Buechner was a novelist. And a novelist he remains. The sermons, essays, and remembrances certainly elucidate the fiction. But all approaches to Buechner have to pass through the novels.

This book is a response to the questions I am frequently asked: "Why does my preacher so often cite Frederick Buechner? Why do my reader friends get so animated when Buechner's name comes up? Why should I read him? Where should I start?" And I would like to address these questions with special regard for the fiction in the Buechner corpus. What is he up to there, in the imagination and honesty of the fiction? What do the novels tell us about the developing career of Frederick Buechner? Can Buechner's career be seen as a test case for the conundrum of the believer as poet, for the challenge of integrating faith and literature?

Like C. S. Lewis, Frederick Buechner has become an oft-quoted source of pulpit anecdotes, devotional tidbits, and magazine fillers. He has even made *Reader's Digest*. Christians have gradually claimed this writer, who crossed over from the world of the New York City literati in the 1960s. In this version, Buechner is J. D. Salinger come into the fold, a modernist writer who sees the light, goes to seminary, gets himself ordained, and then devotes his writing gift to the propagation of Christian ideology. It is the Lewis model—erudite academic sheds the robes of the dons for the cloak of Christ. As usual, the story is more complicated and more interesting than the formula suggests.

Almost a century ago, H. L. Mencken rather provocatively described the role of the critic as simply providing a bridge from writer to reader:

> The function of a genuine critic of the arts is to provoke the reaction between the work of art and the spectator. The spectator, untutored, stands unmoved; he sees the work of art, but it fails to make any intelligible impression on him; if he were spontaneously sensitive to it, there would be no need for criticism. But now comes the critic with his catalysis. He makes the work of art live for the spectator; he makes the spectator live for the work of art. Out of this process comes understanding, appreciation, intelligent enjoyment—and that is precisely what the artist tried to produce.[3]

We can no longer be quite so confident about the critic's role. We have been taught to be suspicious of "impressionistic" or "appreciative" criticism.[4] We are not so glib these days as to the critic's ability to locate viable standards, and the critical enterprise has become increasingly distant and, in many instances, virtually absent from the public arena. Occasionally, however, a writer's work calls for a careful return to Mencken's unfashionable, even popular, criticism—that which leads to what he calls "intelligent enjoyment." Paul Elie's recent study of the literature and lives of

Thomas Merton, Dorothy Day, Walker Percy, and Flannery O'Connor suggests that such criticism is still tenable. Elie tells the stories of four Catholic writers in one narrative—"A journey in which art, life, and religious faith converge."[5] Elie argues that his subjects write with "a frankly religious power" (xii), a phrase that might be transported to the work of Frederick Buechner, another whose story bears telling. Serendipitously, understanding something of the significance of Buechner's life and work may turn us toward understanding the significance of our own.

Born in New York City in 1926, Buechner began with wealth and privilege. Educated in private schools and then at Princeton, he found his way to a literary career. He has produced fifteen novels, a remarkable short story, thirteen nonfiction works, five volumes of memoir, and numerous essays. Although his early fiction received the attention of such noteworthy critics as Ihab Hassan, John Aldridge, Nathan Scott, and John Gardner, and his more recent work has been championed by religious folk of many ilk, he has not been broadly heralded as an important contemporary writer. Despite his status as a finalist for both a Pulitzer Prize and a National Book Award and the impressive shelf of his work, Buechner has received limited critical attention and remains something of a niche writer despite the popular success of his first novel. The *why?* seems appropriate here. Perhaps it is the mannered style and upper-class milieu of the early novels, or maybe Buechner is simply a victim of certain shifts in literary fashion, another casualty of an age that has reduced all critical evaluation to matters of taste. Maybe his career is simply another byproduct of the information explosion, lost in the shuffle of too many books. Another possibility worth suggesting, however, relates to Buechner's penchant for introducing questions of theology in his fiction. Is it not possible that Buechner's critical standing has been clouded by contemporary standards about the decorous exercise of faith?

Buechner arrived noisily on the literary scene with the widely acclaimed *A Long Day's Dying* in 1950, but his career did not follow the path his early reviewers and critics predicted. As he continued to produce creative fiction, Buechner explored various religious bypaths, some of them dangerously close to the questions of religion. His journey took a remarkable turn with his ordination as a Presbyterian minister in 1958. The move seemed to puzzle the many critics who began to regard his work as necessarily religious since it was written by an avowedly religious man. One result has been an attempt to divide Buechner's work into phases—a sort of Saul to Paul before and after. Buechner is fond of noting that the ministry was a bad career move:

As I have long since discovered, the world is full of people—many of them I regret to say, book reviewers—who, if they hear that a minister has written a novel, feel that they know, even without reading it, what sort of novel it must be. It must be essentially a sermon with illustrations in the form of character and dialogue, and, as such, its view of life must be one-sided, simplistic, naïve, with everything subordinated to the one central business of scoring some kind of homiletical bull's eye. (*NT* 59)

Although Buechner has never pastored a church or toiled as a professional cleric, few literary critics these days discuss Buechner without alluding to his ministerial status. I remember, for example, reading a strange note in a review of *The Oxford Companion to American Literature* in which the reviewer, Alfred Kazin, commented that "an eyebrow might be raised here and there at so much space devoted to Frederick Buechner."[6] Kazin's aside is extraordinary, it seems to me, simply because Buechner's publishing record and list of honors, his place among his peers, unquestionably justify the space given him in the venerable reference book. The odd comment can be understood in the frame of suspicion that surrounds the writer who happens to be religious. Such reductive and careless categorization simply muddies the conversation.

To the charge that Buechner is tangled up in religion, I can only say, "Yes, but." Buechner is *indirectly* religious from his first novel to his most recent. His ponderings on the possibility of grace, which he offers with neither sentimentality nor simplicity, may explain both the chariness of the literary intelligentsia toward him as well as the increasing embrace of religious audiences now coming to him as they once came to Lewis. Buechner's attention to the ambiguities of human existence is the persistent chord echoing throughout his work, and the infrequent glimmering of hope is the persistent conclusion. Doubt and darkness stalk all of his major characters, and their emergence into occasional light is laced with enormous struggle. Such thematic preoccupations, when combined with Buechner's increasingly lucid and engaging style, suggest that Buechner belongs in any catalog of significant contemporary writers. In discussions of important voices in the last fifty years of American literature, Buechner deserves a place at the table, Alfred Kazin notwithstanding. Surely there's room in the canon for Frederick Buechner.

I will argue in these pages that Buechner is among the foremost of those working seriously as artists with an equal seriousness about issues of faith. He offers those flashes of insight that gifted artists walk us toward.

Buechner is the sort of artist that G. K. Chesterton had in mind when he wrote that "we have all forgotten our names" and need that rare performance via which "for one awful instant we remember that we forget."[7] Such indeed are the moments of lucidity that Buechner provides. Despite such an intrepid assertion, I do not intend to offer a simple paean of praise here. Marjorie Casebier McCoy's 1988 study, *Frederick Buechner: Novelist and Theologian of the Lost and Found*, has ably covered that territory. McCoy unabashedly confessed to being "an evangelist or apologist for Frederick Buechner."[8] My aims are more modest. I realize that Buechner's books will not be life-changing for everyone. (I recall one fellow who described Buechner's theology as "tapioca pudding.") What follows here will be an attempt to open up Buechner's words in the way that teachers of English often do such business, always with the chastening awareness that readers can read for themselves. Perhaps I can help deepen the encounter; that would be enough.

John Updike has one of his characters comment that modern novels are those books that "try to make us feel shabby."[9] If the novelistic form itself is an artifact of "a world forsaken by God,"[10] and the general tone of this past century's fiction a plunge into a heart of darkness, then Frederick Buechner is up to something decidedly off the beat. Here's where the going gets tricky, however. To say that Buechner is novelist and believer is to set up a possible misunderstanding. Buechner's books do not sit well beside the popular religious fiction that is flying out of religious bookstores and other venues these days. Buechner offers no *Smoky Mountain Sunrise* or *Love Comes Softly*, no apocalyptic thrillers or end-times blockbusters. Philip Yancey summarized Buechner's resistance to the Christian writer label:

> Buechner objects to the label "Christian novelist" often slapped on him, insisting it only applies in the sense it would apply if a physicist wrote a novel: Of course the author's outlook would suffuse the novel, and its content may well touch the field of physics, but that would hardly make it a "physics novel" any more than a novel written by a woman necessarily makes it a "women's novel."[11]

Looking for champions, Christian readers have been anxious to claim Buechner. But he doesn't make it easy. Some of his books began appearing in religiously oriented bookstores in the early 1990s, but he has never rested comfortably there.

An ordained minister in the Presbyterian Church, Buechner received letters earlier on in his career asking him to justify his ordination, letters denouncing his loyalty to a message that is honest about the darkness. He refuses to soften the picture. Skepticism, doubt, and unbelief will have their say in Buechner: "'Lord, I believe; help my unbelief' is the best any of us can do really," he repeats, and adds "but thank God it is enough."[12] Buechner believes we must tell the truth about the tragedies—the bitterness and suffering of this life—before we can move on to the comedy of redemption. The rugged terrain of that argument is the soil Buechner has been turning for his long career.

Over the years, Buechner has increasingly written about the inexplicable presence of a grace-full God, but the world over which this God presides is a tawdry one, a world of bumbling creatures and glaring imperfection. "Nothing human's not a broth of false and true," according to Buechner's flawed Saint Godric, and Godric's declaration is the key to Buechner.[13] Buechner keeps both sides in view. It was his assertion that "If there's no room for doubt, there's no room for me"[14] that made me think that somebody ought to write a book. Buechner receives more than five hundred letters a year from his committed readership, and his popularity among certain religious audiences suggests that he continues to find a constituency that values his particular take on issues of religion and appreciates his willingness to confess that "the whole business of God in my life may be something I have fabricated out of my need for solace and adventure" (*Alphabet* 42).

From *A Long Day's Dying* to *The Final Beast*, from the *Bebb* books to *The Storm*, Buechner has attempted to write novels that embrace questions of faith. He manages to discuss religious ideas—grace, sin, and spiritual longing—without becoming didactic, preachy, or one-dimensional. When asked to clarify the dichotomy between being a writer and being a cleric, Buechner refers to the essential sameness that he sees in the two professions: "People sometimes say to me, 'Why did you get out of the ministry?' I find that deeply upsetting, because I don't, in any sense, think of myself as giving up the ministry. But I do think of writing as a ministry."[15] This is the sort of proclamation, however, that again might lead to misapprehension. Buechner actually employed this theoretical notion in the production of his fiction well *before* he came to the church and ordained ministry. While his style changed as he moved through the first four novels, all of the books deal with such themes as spiritual estrangement, human fallibility, and universal isolation. Although his work of the past two decades has come to treat more openly the themes of grace and redemption, from the start he has been preoccupied with the ambiguities of faith and doubt. Although the more recent offerings may be viewed as a kind of preaching, Buechner's way of defining this sermonic attempt steers clear of mere didacticism:

I do not feel I am doing much different in my preaching and in my writing. Both are designed to illuminate what life is all about, to get people to stop and listen a little to the mystery of their own lives. The process of telling a story is something like religion if only in the sense of having a plot leading to a conclusion that makes some kind of sense.[16]

Notions of plot and providence flow at the core of Buechner's theoretical understanding of his art and provide his justification for attempting to merge religious and literary currents. He makes a similarly fundamental observation in *The Magnificent Defeat*:

The storyteller's claim, I believe, is that life has meaning—that the things that happen to people happen not just by accident like leaves being blown off a tree by the wind but that there is order and purpose deep down behind them or inside them and that they are leading us not just anywhere but somewhere. The power of stories is that they are telling us that life adds up somehow, that life itself is like a story. And this grips us and fascinates us because of the feeling it gives us that if there is meaning in any life—in Hamlet's, in Mary's, in Christ's—then there is meaning also in our lives. And if this is true, it is of enormous significance in itself, and it makes us listen to the storyteller with great intensity because in this way all his stories are about us and because it is always possible that he may give us some clue as to what the meaning of our lives is. (*MD* 60)

Observing how Buechner carries out such an idea is useful to the whole discussion of how faith and art intersect. Buechner's vision is complex, and the territory explored in his writing, as with all that writing we call literature, is the territory of the human heart in all its mystery and simplicity. The later fiction operates specifically from a perspective of faith that posits the possibility of grace amid the dark riddles of life. True enough, Buechner has become a consciously Christian writer, announcing more and more resoundingly the audacious Christian theme that beneath the dark, inexplicable, and often ambiguous superficialities of human existence is a deep and irrepressible joy. Stumbling toward such faith, humans are, as Buechner sees it, constantly startled by the comic incongruities of "crazy, holy grace."[17] With Graham Greene, Buechner believes that "Great art asserts that life means."[18] Buechner consistently looks at his own experience as stirring with "a hint of melody" (*Alphabet* 10) and writes five or six volumes of memoir with the explicit intention of encouraging readers to heed their own lives—to engage themselves in the search for plot. In *Telling Secrets*, Buechner advances the proposition that watching for plot in his own life has been "a source of both strength and fascination."[19] I suspect that readers who find solid footing in Buechner's work are responding in hope to his suggestions about the potential for meaning, a pattern, in human experience. Buechner goes at it this way:

> Since my ordination I have written consciously as a Christian, as an evangelist, or apologist, even. That does not mean that I preach in my novels, which would make for neither good novels nor good preaching. On the contrary, I lean over backwards not to. I choose as my characters (or out of my dreams do they choose me?) men and women whose feet are as much of clay as mine are, because they are the only people I can begin to understand. As a novelist no less than as a teacher, I try not to stack the deck unduly but always let doubt and darkness have their say along with faith and hope, not just because it is good apologetics—woe to him who tries to make it look simple and easy—but because to do it any other way would be to be less true to the elements of doubt and darkness that exist in myself no less than in others. I am a Christian novelist in the same sense that somebody from Boston or Chicago is an American novelist. I must be as true to my experience as a Christian as black writers to their experience as blacks or women writers to their experience as women. It is no more complicated, no more sinister than that. (*NT* 59–60)

But, of course, it is complicated, indeed. Might a believer write out of a penchant for providence, a faith in miracle, and still be regarded as a worthy peer of the literary masters of our time?

Further complicating the question of what a believing artist might produce, Buechner raises the possibility of joy—another of the reasons, no doubt, that readers are attracted to his work. (Type "Buechner" on any search engine to get some idea of how, despite relative critical obscurity, Buechner is being claimed by a burgeoning subculture.) He most commonly uses the phrase "great laughter" to describe his conversion, and one might well use the phrase as a distillation of much that he is up to in his writing.[20] It is comedy, he believes, that provides the most apt metaphor for the ultimate reaches of existence—laughter at the darkest depths of reality. Tragedy is, for Buechner, an essential metaphor but is penultimate to the comic vision of the New Testament message of joy—"These things

I have spoken to you, that my joy may be in you, and that your joy may be full"—an insight which, Buechner submits, "sums up pretty much everything."[21] In fact, Buechner conjures a phrase that might well stand as his credo: "The worst isn't the last thing about the world. It's the next to last thing" (*FB* 175). Buechner first gives these words to his disheveled minister, Theodore Nicolet, in the 1965 novel *The Final Beast* and later elaborates the point for the Lyman Beecher Lectures at Yale University in 1976. The published version of those speeches offers advice to preachers: "Preach this overwhelming of tragedy by comedy, of darkness by light, of the ordinary by the extraordinary, as the tale that is too good not to be true."[22]

So there it is: novelist and believer, a notion many might find oxymoronic. I recall an exchange, for example, between Walker Percy and Shelby Foote in which Foote took umbrage at the notion of believers producing art:

> I seriously think that no good practicing Catholic can ever be a great artist; art is by definition a product of doubt; it has to be pursued. . . . Most people think mistakenly that writers are people who have something to tell them. Nothing I think could be wronger. If I knew what I wanted to say, I wouldn't write at all. What for? Why do it, if you already know the answers? Writing is the search for answers, and the answer is in the form, the method of telling, the exploration of self, which is our only clue to reality.[23]

Percy, whose affinities on the question are rather close to Buechner's positions, actually agreed in large part with his friend. Percy concurred that the novelist is not in the business of offering answers. Discussing his Catholicism, Percy argued that "It consists . . . mainly in the deepest kind of hunch that it all works out, generally for the good (Tolson 180). In another provocative note to Foote, Percy proclaimed that "You can't get away with a Fr. Zossima these days" (Tolson 293). I suspect that Buechner would agree.

And, like Percy, Buechner rejects "Jesus is the answer" simplicity. He seems constantly surprised by American religion these days—TestaMints and megachurches. He worries about what he calls the "poison" being distributed in such places.[24] No friend of the sort of faith that begins in cocksureness, Buechner begins with "I don't know." Throughout his fiction and nonfiction, and even in the preaching, the issue of doubt is never far from the surface. In *The Magnificent Defeat*, an anthology of sermons, he claims that faith "defies logic and reason, and it breaks the laws of nature as we understand them" (*MD* 88). In fact, it is the very impossibility of proof that Buechner sees as the gap that God occupies. He believes that "God speaks to us most clearly through his silence, his absence, so that we know him best through our missing him," as he puts it (*MD* 48). The metaphor of darkness operates in much of Buechner's fiction, and he offers an explanation in *The Hungering Dark*:

> If the darkness is meant to suggest a world where nobody can see very well—either themselves, or each other, or where they are heading, or even where they are standing at the moment; if darkness is meant to convey a sense of uncertainty, of being lost, of being afraid; if darkness suggests conflict, conflict between races, between nations, between individuals each pretty much out for himself when you come right down to it; then we live in a world that knows much about darkness. Darkness is what our newspapers are about. Darkness is what our best contemporary literature is about. . . . If we are people who pray, darkness is apt to be a lot of what our prayers are about. If we are people who do not pray, it is apt to be darkness in one form or another that has stopped our mouths.[25]

Buechner's insistence on confessing the darkness puts him at odds with the usual institutional religious approaches. He has insisted throughout his career on aiming toward those readers who "more or less don't give religion the time of day."[26] Although often surprised by the readers who find their ways to his door via a wide assortment of religious backgrounds, Buechner identifies his audience as "believing unbelievers" (*HD* 15), and his message is that "God is right here in the thick of our day-by-day lives . . . trying to get messages through our blindness as we move around down here knee-deep in the fragrant muck and misery and marvel of the world" (*MD* 47). Such a line sounds a bit like Flannery O'Connor—maybe there's even a hint of a John Updike or an Annie Dillard in the phrase. But Buechner's work remains fundamentally unique in the literature of our contemporary canon.

Buechner respects the mystery. Speaking of his detractors, Buechner observes, "They want me to come out and say, 'Look, it's all true.' And of course I do believe it's true with ninety-eight percent of myself, but I want to be true to the experience of truth, which always includes the possibility that maybe you're just kidding yourself."[27] His notion of truth, then, is always poised against the possibility of error; such is the fragile balance beam on which he constantly teeters. But I wonder if this honesty isn't a large part of what has established Buechner's voice as an intriguing alternative in the scheme of contemporary literature, a voice worth hearing in both religious and secular venues?

Because he offers that rare combination of literary artist and creative believer who speaks to our longing to believe as well as to our inescapable doubts, I predict that Buechner's audience will grow in coming decades. A distinct integrity informs his writing from the first novel to the 2006 assortment, *Secrets in the Dark*, where he gathers pieces from as far back as 1959. Beside sermons from his days at Exeter, Buechner includes speeches from academic occasions over the years and essays contributed to various collections. Nearing eighty, Buechner reflects on his long career in the introduction to *Secrets in the Dark*: "Needless to say I have changed a good deal over the years just as my major themes have changed along with my way of saying things and seeing things, but by and large there is nothing in these pages that I wouldn't be willing to sign my name to still" (*Secrets* 7). Buechner here suggests a certain coherence to the career that I hope to explore in these pages. The ways and means will vary from book to book, but the core preoccupations remain much the same. Buechner has continued to offer an unblinking encounter, which, I suspect, is what we most want in those books we keep around. The best summary is again in Godric's voice, this time in Godric's last words: "All's lost. All's found" (*Godric* 171). The four words pose the Buechnerian balance, the trembling tension, in which readers are finding significant consolation and, in some instances, even a way toward faith. What follows here is an attempt to clarify how these themes emerge in more than fifty years of putting pen to paper.

Dale Brown
Bristol, Tennessee
August 2004

Notes

1. W. Dale Brown, *Of Fiction and Faith: Twelve American Writers Talk about Their Vision and Work* (Grand Rapids: Eerdmans, 1997), 33. Hereafter cited as Brown.
2. Frederick Buechner, *Now and Then* (San Francisco: Harper & Row, 1983), 108. Hereafter cited as *NT*. This is the second of Buechner's memoir volumes.
3. H. L. Mencken, "The Critic's Function," in *A Modern Book of Criticism*, ed. Ludwig Lewisohn (New York: Boni & Liveright, 1919), 171.
4. Lionel Trilling, *A Gathering of Fugitives* (London: Secker & Warburg, 1957), 137.
5. Paul Elie, *The Life You Save May Be Your Own: An American Pilgrimage* (New York: Farrar, Straus & Giroux, 2003), x.

6. Alfred Kazin, "A Cornucopia for Browsers," *New York Times Book Review*, January 29, 1984, 3, 33.

7. G. K. Chesterton, *Orthodoxy* (New York: Dodd, Mead & Co., 1943), 97. Hereafter cited as Chesterton.

8. Marjorie Casebier McCoy, *Frederick Buechner: Novelist and Theologian of the Lost and Found* (San Francisco: Harper & Row, 1988), 15. Hereafter cited as McCoy.

9. John Updike, *S.* (New York: Alfred A. Knopf, 1988), 18.

10. Georg Lukacs, *Die Theorie des Romans* (Berlin: Paul Cassirer, 1920), 84.

11. Philip Yancey, "The Reverend of Oz," *Books & Culture*, March/April 1997, 7. Hereafter cited as Yancey.

12. Frederick Buechner, *The Magnificent Defeat* (New York: Seabury Press, 1966), 35. Hereafter cited as *MD*. Buechner also makes use of this language in *The Final Beast* (53).

13. Frederick Buechner, *Godric* (New York: Atheneum, 1980), 31. Hereafter cited as *Godric*.

14. Frederick Buechner, *The Alphabet of Grace* (New York: Seabury Press, 1970), 47. Hereafter cited as *Alphabet*. These are the lines that John Irving cites in the opening pages of his novel *A Prayer for Owen Meany*. *The Alphabet of Grace* could be fairly regarded as Buechner's first foray into memoir.

15. "Door Interview: Frederick Buechner," *Wittenburg Door*, January 1980, 19. Hereafter cited as *WDoor*.

16. "Authors and Editors," *Publisher's Weekly* (March 29, 1971): 11.

17. Frederick Buechner, *The Sacred Journey* (San Francisco: Harper & Row, 1982), 46. Hereafter cited as *SJ*. This is the first of Buechner's memoir volumes.

18. Samuel Hynes, *Graham Greene: A Collection of Critical Essays* (Englewood Cliffs, NJ: Prentice-Hall, 1973), 7.

19. Frederick Buechner, *Telling Secrets: A Memoir* (San Francisco: HarperCollins, 1991), 2. Hereafter cited as *TS*. This is the third of Buechner's memoir volumes.

20. Frederick Buechner, *The Final Beast* (New York: Atheneum, 1965), 166. Hereafter cited as *FB*. See also *Alphabet* (47) and *SJ* (109).

21. Frederick Buechner, *Wishful Thinking: A Theological ABC* (New York: Harper & Row, 1973), 47. Hereafter cited as *WT*.

22. Frederick Buechner, *Telling the Truth: The Gospel as Tragedy, Comedy & Fairy Tale* (San Francisco: Harper & Row, 1977), 98. Hereafter cited as *TTT*. This is an excellent starting point for Buechner's nonfiction work.

23. Jay Tolson, ed., *The Correspondence of Shelby Foote and Walker Percy* (New York: W. W. Norton & Co., 1997), 20, 124–25. Hereafter cited as Tolson.

24. "You Can't Help but Think Eschatologically When You're My Age," *Door*, January/February 1995, 13. Hereafter cited as *Door*.

25. Frederick Buechner, *The Hungering Dark* (New York: Seabury Press, 1969), 50. Hereafter cited as *HD*.

26. Frederick Buechner, *The Eyes of the Heart: A Memoir of the Lost and Found* (San Francisco: HarperSanFrancisco, 1999), 180. Hereafter cited as *EH*. This is the fourth of Buechner's memoir volumes.

27. Quoted in Nancy Myers, "Sanctifying the Profane: Religious Themes in the Fiction of Frederick Buechner" (diss., North Texas State University, 1976), 166, 203. Hereafter cited as Myers. Myers's dissertation includes parts of an interview she did with Buechner in Hobe Sound, Florida, on March 15, 1976. Myers's dissertation is among the earliest research into Buechner's work and remains foundational in Buechner studies.

Chapter One

Writing for a Teacher

A Long Day's Dying

Whan Frederick Buechner agreed to make one of his rare public appearances for a speech in Chicago in the late 1980s, I went along to listen. I arrived early. When he came on stage to await the introduction, I noticed a white thread on the lapel of his blue blazer. When he started speaking, I forgot the thread. In the book-signing line after the lecture, I overheard the earnest expressions of gratitude, the declarations of just how much an encounter with Buechner's books had meant. When I reached the front of the procession and offered him my edition of *A Long Day's Dying*, his first book, he said, "Where'd you find this old thing?" I was to learn that Buechner characteristically dismisses his first books and explains his early success as something accidental and undeserved: "I think the success of that mannered, ancient book was a fluke, a stroke of luck, like happening to win a lottery. The success of a book is apt to have very little to do with its real worth. Look at the best-seller list."[1] On the day that Buechner's comment came to me via a letter, *Rosemary's Hip and Thigh Diet* was at the top of the bestseller list. Although it never made it to the screen, *A Long Day's Dying* was popular enough to be adapted for a movie script in 1954, and, in his subsequent career, Buechner claims to have been driven "to justify the fluke of that early and for the most part undeserved success" (*SJ* 100). Nonetheless, his debut novel continues to be among his most successful—at least in terms of sales and critical attention—"tragically enough," Buechner jokes.[2] He generally draws a boldfaced line between the first two books and the many volumes that come later. His interpreters have, unfortunately, adopted his approach. Buechner thinks of his early books as "like coming across a letter that you wrote when you were twenty-two years old." He wonders how he could have been "so

Jimmy Merrill

Buechner's grandmother's home
in Pittsburgh, Pennsylvania

Buechner's grandmother, Naya
(Antoinette Golay Kuhn)

Buechner's grandmother,
Louise Scharmann Buechner

naïve, or so dumb" (Brown 47). Stylistically stodgy and verbose, the first two novels do invite puzzlement when placed beside the later fiction, yet the preoccupations for which Buechner has come to be known are strikingly apparent in even these early books. In one of his most revealing interviews, Buechner concedes a certain importance to *A Long Day's Dying*: "I recognize in embryo there most of the themes that have concerned me both as a writer and as a human being: the isolation of the individual, and his need to be known, the failure of communication, the reality of the unseen, the subterranean presence of grace."[3]

In the fourth of his memoirs, The *Eyes of the Heart: A Memoir of the Lost and Found*, Buechner fills in the background of his first novel. His finely tuned memory conjures the beach cottage off the coast of Maine where he and his friend James Merrill, later a Pulitzer-winning poet, wrote their fledgling pieces. Both would be published by Knopf within two or three years. Buechner also whimsically recalls his first foray into trying to market his manuscript, an adventure that ended with a classic rejection letter. The New York publisher regarded the pages as "completely unpublishable" and "couldn't imagine anything" that Buechner could do to make them palatable (*EH* 34). Buechner would eventually receive an apology. The finished book he dedicated to his grandmother, Naya, the "gray gull," the family storyteller, the one who helped prop up the wounded family after Buechner's father's suicide in 1936 (*SJ* 31). Buechner adds to the tribute in *The Longing for Home* and in *The Sacred Journey* where he credits Naya for passing on to him a "taste for words" (*SJ* 64). Buechner's instinct for language even as a child was to flourish in the late 1940s as he embarked on a literary career.

Entering the scene of that long-ago summer is to imagine a time of enormous energy, a season of trying on one thing and another. Buechner poignantly records Merrill's one-sentence contribution to *A Long Day's Dying*, a sentence marvelously mimicking Buechner's then-labored style. But the significant center of these months on the beach appears in the inevitable maturing that Buechner recalls: "The selves we were beginning to grow into that summer were still in the shadowy wings awaiting their entrance cues" (*EH* 39–40). "Jimmy" and "Freddy" were discovering something of their literary selves as well as finding their ways toward the people they would become. Merrill records his take on the story in *A Different Person: A Memoir*, and Buechner remarks on their friendship in several books—both in the fiction and in the nonfiction. He remembers the days as "ringing with laughter," and one cannot help but deduce that the gentle rivalry between them contributed much to their eventual successes (*EH* 38). Buechner acknowledged as much in his contribution to Merrill's *New York Times* obituary in February of 1995, noting that "their friendly competition was an impetus for each becoming a writer."[4] Nonetheless, although they were to remain lifelong friends, Merrill and Buechner departed that fall of 1948 for very different lives. In its exploration of how lives might be lived, *A Long Day's Dying* may explain something of the divergence.

Buechner actually began writing the novel in 1946 in Bennington, Vermont, just after his Army discharge. Originally titled "A Love Story," the first draft began with the line "Tristram Bone walked like a great tired dog through the sweet kennels of the rain."[5] Buechner's scribbled note on the handwritten manuscript reads "Wow!" (Archive, IV A 1). He remembers the line as "an early and wisely discarded version."[6] The novel that appeared four years later brought Buechner the tentative praise of critics, who labeled the work "a happy portent."[7] Brook Street Press rereleased the almost-forgotten book in 2003; it will be interesting to see how a new generation of readers approaches the novel, viewing it through the lens of Buechner's long career. If the original reception was cursedly ambiguous, so is the book. Tristram Bone, the protagonist of the piece, comes close to summarizing the effect of the novel when he patronizingly addresses the woman with whom he has experienced a failure of romance, "But my dear, one can be certain of so little."[8] Such a thematic line seems incongruous with Buechner's contemporary image as among the foremost writers of the Christian novel in English. To understand something of the long view of Frederick Buechner's career, it is important to remember that he came on the literary scene in 1950 with a novel in the tradition of what we call modernism, even the most general definition of which will include an emphasis on interior consciousness, a recognition of the alienation of human beings from one another, and the positing of incompleteness as the common lot of humanity. This is the era when, as Joseph Wood Krutch announced, "skepticism has entered . . . deeply into our souls."[9] Irving Howe suggested that the general parameters of modernism include the substitution of relativism and doubt for religious conviction and moral certainty, an emphasis on the internal and subjective, an underscoring of humankind's aloneness in the universe, and a disturbing uncertainty as to the meaning of existence.[10] T. S. Eliot summarized modern literature as "a gospel of this world, and of this world alone."[11]

Many modern writers appropriate Matthew Arnold's warning:

. . . for the world, which seems
To lie before us like a land of dreams,
So various, so beautiful, so new,
Hath really neither joy, nor love, nor light,
Nor certitude, nor peace, nor help for pain.[12]

Buechner's first novel seems to weigh Arnold's contentions and find them mostly correct. *A Long Day's Dying* is well within the bounds of most definitions of modernism. One could argue that Buechner writes his first novel with an outline of the tenets of literary modernism tacked on the wall above the typewriter. In the light of Buechner's consequent career, however, the novel displays a subtle play on modernist themes, a questioning as to the ultimate adequacy of the modernist conclusions. *A Long Day's Dying* is full of questions as to how a life might be lived. One might argue that the young Buechner arranges the domestic tableau of his first novel as a test case for the years he must confront in the lifetime ahead of him. Recalling how he came to the theme of *A Long Day's Dying*, Buechner confesses: "I am sure that I chose such a melancholy theme partly because it seemed effective and fashionable, but I have no doubt that, like dreams generally, it also reflected the way I felt about at least some dimension of my own life and the lives of those around me" (*SJ* 98).

Buechner might well have used Arnold's poem as the epigraph for *A Long Day's Dying*, because the novel is clearly about the doomed attempt to wrest something like kindness or love out of an existence that refuses to yield up either. Instead, Buechner looks to John Milton's *Paradise Lost* for an epigraph and a title. Milton's words focused on the condemnation of the fallen Adam and Eve and set the forlorn tone of *A Long Day's Dying*:

But rise, let us no more contend, nor blame
Each other, blamed enough elsewhere, but strive
In offices of love how we may lighten
Each other's burden in our share of woe;
Since this day's death denounc'd, if aught I see,
Will prove no sudden, but a slow-pac'd evil,
A long day's dying to augment our pain,
And to our seed, (O hapless seed!), deriv'd.[13]

Condemned to live, the individual tries to join others against the awful reality of death but ends by merely participating with the others in the experience of death—a drawn-out affair. The only alternative is to live out the condemnation bravely, somewhat anesthetized by the slow pace of encroaching death, but never unaware of the impossibility of escape. Buechner's characters in *A Long Day's Dying* live under just such an oppressive weight. Little wonder, then, that Ihab Hassan in *Radical Innocence: The Contemporary American Novel* said that Buechner's first novel is about "the experience of nothingness."[14] It is, however, nothingness with a twist. Thirty-five years later, Buechner reflects on the conundrum of his first novel: "I was only about twenty-one when I started it. I hadn't found my own voice as a writer yet, or my own subject. Religious faith was already beginning to stir in me, I think, though in ways I didn't entirely recognize, but I wasn't ready yet to deal with it either in my writing or in my life."[15] Buechner's reflection suggests something of the subtle themes colliding in his opening salvo. He writes of absence with an unmistakable longing for presence. God has been murdered, but he is missed.

Even though *Library Journal* reviewer Shirley Barker called *A Long Day's Dying* "an ugly little story" and recommended it "for sophisticated readers only,"[16] the overwhelming conclusion was that Buechner had "arrived in superlative fashion" (Weinberger 13). The novel's central characters are upper-class easterners—wealthy people of worldly wisdom and leisure. Much of the story is filtered through the consciousness of Tristram Bone, a middle-aged bachelor whose closest relationships are with his monkey, Simon; his housekeeper, Emma Plaut; and a woman he loves, Elizabeth Poor. Elizabeth, many years a widow, moves in a circle including her son, Leander; her mother, Juliette Caven; a friend, George Motley; and Tristram. Leander, a student at an eastern college, obviously Princeton, a "sweet and dangerous hospital that nobody wants to leave," has fallen under the spell of a young teacher of English, Paul Steitler (*LDD* 73). Elizabeth's mother, generally called Maroo and modeled on Buechner's Naya, his beloved grandmother, who will show up fifty years later as a ghostly presence in his moving memoir *The Eyes of the Heart*. Maroo watches the events of her daughter's life from a distance until her daughter's crisis brings Maroo to New York City. A minor novelist and lecturer, Motley operates in the novel as an eavesdropper and a schemer who, like Tristram, feels something like love for Elizabeth.

The complications of the novel are generated by Elizabeth's third suitor, Steitler, with whom she has a night of passion while visiting Leander at the university. Also on the campus and aware of Elizabeth's indiscretion, Motley betrays her to Tristram, and, when Tristram confronts her, she lies. Her lie brings further complications and misunderstandings, inevitably eliminating the possibility of honest relationship among any of the assembled cast in the story. Tristram's simple companion, Simon, dies after mimicking his master's feigned suicide. Tristram has drawn the dull side of a straight razor across his neck in a gesture of despair; the monkey, in imitating the gesture, slices his own throat. Steitler retreats into his youthful cynicism and cleverness; the balance of the relationship between George Motley, Elizabeth, and Tristram is destroyed. As the entire group gathers around Maroo's deathbed, her hasty journey to the city having brought on a collapse, she speaks an epitaph over them all: "Everything now will be different" (*LDD* 256). But the change indicated is anything but a positive one; nothing remains except Steitler's realization of "the completeness of their isolation one from another" and the dim possibility that Leander has learned something valuable from the wreckage he has witnessed (*LDD* 253).

If the physical action of the novel swirls around Elizabeth—her pursuers, her infidelity, her falseness—the intellectual center of the story is surely Tristram Bone. Tristram presides over the narrative as a priest, a saint, a moral idealist. But even his name captures the ambiguity surrounding Tristram. His surname, "Bone," a possible allusion to the valley of dry bones of Ezekiel's vision, suggests a certain malnourishment, an impoverishment of spirit that belies his physical hugeness. "Bone" also refers to Tristram's desire to get to the heart of things, the essentials. Derived from the Latin for "sorrowful," "Tristram" ironically suggests great affairs of the heart and alludes to the story of King Arthur's gallant knight whose life is spent in desperate yearning for Iseult—a longing that is met only in death. Like the knight, Tristram will be constantly thwarted by circumstance and personal ineffectiveness. He is a strange mixture of ancient gallantry and modern futility. As Horton Davies noted in his discussion of Buechner, "Frederick Buechner and the Strange Work of Grace," Buechner never loses sight of "the ambiguities of the human condition."[17] The recognition of the mixedness and muddle of human life remains one of the hallmarks of Buechner's work throughout his career.

The opening sentence of the novel pictures Tristram, wrapped in a white robe, sitting in a barber's chair and looking at his reflection in a mirror. The reflection seems at first to be that of "a priest," and Buechner continually directs the reader to think of Tristram as a priest, particularly in the scene where Elizabeth finds herself unable to confess her infidelity to him (*LDD* 3). Troubled by the ill-defined state of his relation to Elizabeth Poor, Tristram struggles in the opening scenes of the novel to gain a clarification of that relationship. He fights against the amorphous state of human affairs, the steady dictates of time, to bring order and control to his life.

Tristram is a man of words. His awareness of "the inadequate, misleading words of others" makes him vulnerable to inaction (*LDD* 10). He is stymied by his own awareness: a priest, a knight, but impotent in both roles. Above all, Tristram longs for a world where people are kind to one another, where morality might "dictate as it chose" (*LDD* 10). The comic relief of his companion, the monkey Simon; the "overwhelming dependence" of his housekeeper, Emma; and the comfortable relationships with Elizabeth and George provide the right balance for the delicately sensitive, impressively obese, bird-watching, museum-visiting Tristram (*LDD* 39). The balance, however, is upset by Steitler's entrance into Elizabeth's life. Everything is thrown into disarray in Tristram's garden. Tristram clearly loves Elizabeth but is unable to verbalize his love. He speaks of his feelings only indirectly, metaphorically. Elizabeth senses "that he was speaking on more than one level at once, but her replies were always direct and addressed to the outer portion alone of his meaning" (*LDD* 18). Elizabeth Poor is "poor in spirit" in the worst sense of the phrase. Tristram's moral idealism runs headlong into the impulsive sexual encounter between Elizabeth and Steitler. Confronted by Tristram, Elizabeth manufactures an elaborate alibi built on the hint that Steitler has formed a homosexual liaison with Leander, a lie with which she hopes to elude Tristram's queries. The knight who is called to redress wrongs, Tristram confronts Steitler, realizes Elizabeth has lied, and struggles on to bring his world to moral attention.

Tristram's Nick Carraway–like impulse breaks most clearly in the concluding scenes of the novel when he goes to New York Central Station to meet the train carrying Maroo. Tristram is overwhelmed by the solitude and desperation he sees in the faces of the people crowding through the depot. Only the children seem in some sense alive to him. Tristram shares the angst of the crowds:

> He recognized suddenly in every face that passed him the reflection of what appeared a similar, lonely, speechless concern not with the station and the mechanics of arriving, departing, meeting someone, or saying goodbye, but with something more vital still and far beneath such minor embassies. He seemed to see in each figure that hurried by a kind of indifference to all but some secret, unexpressed care. (*LDD* 218)

Tristram, the knight errant, the idealist, wants to stop the crowds, to shout at them "to awake, take notice, awake, awake, and discover that they were men and women" (*LDD* 221). This is the futile impulse that makes of Tristram a noble, if muddled, character. Nancy Myers concluded that Tristram "is essentially a hopelessly Prufrockian figure" (Myers 15). Such a conclusion, however, misses the complexity of Tristram's character. His impotence is not that of a Prufrockian modern trapped in his own bewildering consciousness, but that of a man destined to powerlessness most particularly because of the shallowness, the spiritual vacuity of Elizabeth Poor, and the blind machinations of a cast of moral drifters. He is not a victim of his own pettiness and introspection so much as he is a victim of modern conditions. He is neither Prometheus nor Prufrock but somewhere in between—a man of considerable gifts and sensitivity rendered helpless by the collision of his own weakness with debilitating circumstance.

Although Elizabeth, like all of the characters in the novel, displays a mixed personality alternating between sensitivity and selfishness, her portrait is the least believable of the novel's assemblage of portraits. Several reviewers noted a discomfort with Elizabeth's character and some, like Theodore Kalem, claimed that the novel "just misses the final magic"[18] because of such inconsistency in characterization. Caspar Weinberger, reviewing for the *San Francisco Chronicle*, wrote that Elizabeth's eventual falsehood and her rage at Tristram "seem artificial" and out of keeping with her previous character (Weinberger 16). Although her actions are not entirely inconsonant, one wonders why Tristram would be so attracted to a woman like Elizabeth, why he would be blind to her emptiness. These are among the questions that dangle unanswered in the novel; nevertheless, Elizabeth does exemplify the vulnerability of a woman reaching middle age without props, moral or relational, to support her. Her vanity shows through in her refusal to wear the glasses that she needs to see clearly. Her self-absorption establishes her baseness and inevitably produces alienation—an idea that will increasingly preoccupy Buechner in his later fiction. Years of sexual repression explode in her passionate scene with Steitler, but even there she merely speaks in clichés like "I don't know what to believe" (*LDD* 130). Dimly aware of Tristram's complex feelings for her, she only half listens to him and feels burdened by the complication of involvement with him. She wants only an escape from any commitment, especially an escape from the tastes, needs, and awarenesses of someone like Tristram.

Tristram realizes that what matters most is not which person one loves but "whether one loved at all, and how much that love cost, and what was its reception then, that mattered" (*LDD* 159). Such a conclusion seems to be the tentative reach of Buechner's penetrating analysis of the lifestyles of his time. Elizabeth is simply not up to costly investment in the life of another. While Tristram attempts to move with distinct motives of kindness and love, Elizabeth recognizes that she has "no motive to which she might return" as she reflects upon her reasons for lying to Tristram (*LDD* 180). Her lack of clarity proves stronger than Tristram's efforts to wrest some sense from the crumbling domestic situation.

In the end, Elizabeth blames Tristram for the crisis in her life, directing her anger toward him rather than confronting her own vacuity; she whines to Tristram, "So you see what a frightful, tragic position I am in, thanks to you" (*LDD* 232). The novel ends with Elizabeth having passed from anger back into her lethargic malaise, an "absence of perceptible emotion" (*LDD* 259). Elizabeth is a blank. She does not learn. She does not grow. She has floated through her life without curiosity or vitality but in control, invulnerable and unchanging. Her misplaced rage, focused on Tristram, has its source in her being pressured for reaction; she is driven from the sheltering fortress of her floating world into the disagreeable combat of a real-life situation, not unlike the dilemma that the superficial Daisy Faye Buchanan faces with the far-too-real Jay Gatsby in Fitzgerald's novel. That Tristram would initiate such a revolution for her is something not to be endured: "Tristram, who had obliged her to face that fact [her indifference], would receive the full rush of her wrath" (*LDD* 177).

Tristram's ineffectuality derives from his idealism and his urge to be kind; Elizabeth's ineffectuality has its source in the failure of her internal character. The third character contributing to Buechner's vision of the frightening misconnections of the modern world, Paul Steitler, is ineffectual because of a youthful cynicism. Like Elizabeth, Steitler operates without a clear moral framework, and such ethical vacuity, Buechner suggests, produces chaos in people's lives. Steitler views himself as "a kind of professional corrupter of the young" (*LDD* 59):

> I teach them English is all, . . . and the pay-off they finally get to is a kind of corruption, because what they learn, when they've had the full treatment, is nothing about any particular book or any particular author or period so much as something fairly unnerving about life. . . . What they learn from me is that they're never going to have it so good again; that the great ones, the ones they read, saw it all as pretty black. I'm nothing, you see, if not trite, but what really gets me is the sense that I'm instructing a lot of beautiful, healthy children in the use of crutches, which at this point in their career is a morbid and rather pointless lesson. (*LDD* 59–60)

Steitler's words capture the ambivalence of his character and strike into something of the young Buechner himself as he looks toward his own choices—cynicism or faith, childlike romanticism or adult realism. On the surface, Steitler's pronouncements seem prescient, even brilliant; but a dark cynicism runs beneath the surface. Like most of Buechner's fully developed characters, Steitler is impossible to categorize neatly. His proclamations range from something sounding like youthful romanticism to the no-nonsense inexpressibility of the realist. He likes to think of himself as living for the moment and fashions phrases on the subject in his wooing of Elizabeth: "There will be years and years and years, and then a moment. And then years and years and years again" (*LDD* 87). Yet this same speaker of phrases, who knows just the right moment to kiss Elizabeth as they sit beside the campus lake on their evening of romance, takes offense at the suggestive tapestries and the stodgy atmosphere of the Cloisters when he goes there to meet Tristram. The cynic speaks as Steitler rejects the suggestion that the beauty and history of the place mean anything. "I don't think things work that way," he pontificates; "we're never going to have things so good" (*LDD* 199). Again the mixture; Steitler is not a particularly bad man or a particularly good one. Sometimes sophomoric, sometimes manipulative, sometimes spontaneous—just a man.

Steitler involves himself in Leander's life out of dangerous curiosity and goes so far as to read Leander's correspondence with his grandmother, Maroo. Maroo writes to Leander hoping to establish within him a bulwark against the dangers of life, longing to accustom him to the fact "that to be alive was perilous" (*LDD* 92). When Steitler writes to Maroo informing her that Leander has allowed him to read her letters and thanking her for the glimpse he has had of "so rich a garden" (*LDD* 104), Maroo senses the potential evil of the situation: "It was as if he were trying to bake her grandson into a pie of treacherous understanding" (*LDD* 103). Maroo is the first to label Steitler as Leander's "clever friend" (*LDD* 102), but Motley also recognizes Steitler's cunning (*LDD* 106), as does Elizabeth, who finally categorizes him a "clever schemer" (*LDD* 179). But Steitler is charming and wise as well—"a boy trying to talk like a teacher or, perhaps more justly . . . a teacher trying to talk like a boy" (*LDD* 61). He seduces Elizabeth even though he realizes he doesn't love her, knows that their night of passion is "something less than love" (*LDD* 206). He involves himself deeply in Leander's life from motives not entirely clear to himself, and, when accused of forming a homosexual relationship with Leander, he is staggered to realize how close the accusation comes to "the unsuspected truth about himself" (*LDD* 250). Steitler, then, is another of the novel's assembled characters who contributes, without studied villainy or clear motives, to the devastation of relationships. He is another victim of the times and the situation, knowing so much, yet possessing no moral vantage from which to act.

If *A Long Day's Dying* can be said to have a villain, however, it must surely be the voyeur, the antitype of Tristram, George Motley. As his name suggests, Motley is a combination of evasive personalities and motives. He is in some part the realist to be played off against the moral idealism of Tristram and the mixed romanticism and pragmatism of Steitler. Motley's realism differs from that of Steitler in that its aim is less philosophic and more to the main chance. Motley is the Pandarus figure of this novel, a man of internal disjunction and a type that will show up again in *The Seasons' Difference* and most strikingly in Buechner's fourth novel, *The Final Beast*. He is introduced as someone who projects one image while suggesting another. His charm, we are told, may be a "cunning disguise" and his "celebrated novels" a "childishness" (*LDD* 13). He emits "implications of a certain unnaturalness and stealth beneath his unbearably mannered exterior" (*LDD* 13). A sophisticated, somewhat weary man of the world who prides himself on seeing things as they are, Motley turns out to be wearing an elaborate disguise beneath which is weakness, vapidity, and even malice.

Early in the novel Motley joins Elizabeth and Tristram on an outing to the Cloisters, where Motley, hiding behind a pew, witnesses unseen an embarrassing encounter between Tristram and a wooden statue of a saint. Reaching out to touch the image of sainthood, Tristram accidentally catches his hand in the hand of the statue. After disentangling his hand from the trap, Tristram inexplicably kneels and utters an inarticulate prayer. Quick to report what he has seen to Elizabeth, Motley hopes "to purchase the intimacy he sought" by scheming to bring Elizabeth and himself into a special confidence (*LDD* 32).

What Motley wants of Elizabeth is not a physical relationship. Even the possibility of this is of "undeniable grotesqueness," he thinks to himself (*LDD* 109). The hint is left that Motley may be homosexual and wants of Elizabeth a special empathy or complicity. Whatever unique relationship Motley wants is threatened by Steitler's involving Elizabeth in a secret she must try to protect. The threat posed by Steitler may be part of the reason Motley betrays his suspicions to Tristram, thus setting in motion the confrontations that conclude the novel. Motley, however, is like the others in his vague understanding of motivation: "Motley was not certain himself as to why he had done it, why he had told his tale" (*LDD*

157). Again, no moral dictates, no decisive understanding between people, only a blind, dimly motivated action, producing consequences that follow like the falling of randomly arranged dominoes.

Some reviewers suggested that Leander Poor ought to be considered as the central character in the novel. Wallace Markfield, in *Commentary*, argued, for example: "Presumably, it is with Leander Poor that the novel is most concerned . . . he is threatened by the disease which destroys all those about him, a disease that has its roots in the moral emptiness of contemporary sophisticated intelligence."[19] Markfield correctly established Leander as the testing ground on which the failures of his mother and her friends will be tried, and he could have added that the young Buechner seems equally to be testing his social milieu. It is too much, however, to conclude, as did Theodore Kalem, that Leander "will escape" (Kalem 11). Leander's future is an unsettled question; we simply do not know whether knowledge of what has happened will lead Leander to genuine maturity and strength or if it will be the death of his innocence. The irresolution is, of course, part of young Buechner's idea of the modern novel. He offers no easy conclusions or clear statements regarding the future of any of the book's characters. Tristram has fought for Leander, telling Steitler that above all else "innocence must be protected" (*LDD* 201). In tones reminiscent of Nathaniel Hawthorne's Ethan Brand, Tristram warns that they dare not risk damage to Leander's innocence "for the sake of our own souls if not of those we harm" (*LDD* 201).

Two educative forces work in Leander's life: Steitler, his teacher, is the obvious force, and Maroo is the more subtle force. Steitler clearly views the college experience as a time of coming into dark knowledge. Even though Buechner gives the name "Hope" to one of the girls in the university scene, the overwhelming impact of the novel suggests that the protected Eden, the college, is just the sort of place for insidious evil to enter. Elizabeth is seduced as much by the peacefulness and beauty of the wondrous campus evening as she is by Paul Steitler. If Steitler wants an intellectual awareness for Leander, a loss of innocence enabling clear thinking in life, Maroo seems to want for him a decisive clearheadedness about relationships. She fights for Leander, "afraid for the boy as of or for nothing else" (*LDD* 92). Maybe Maroo's frantic flight to the city is more an attempt to rescue Leander than to save Elizabeth. In any case, Leander's presence is the most real to Maroo as she is dying. In her last moments, only Leander is visible to her: "And one remained. For an instant she saw him, Leander, unchanged and unchanging, unmoved, there beside her. . . . She reached out to touch him but could not" (*LDD* 267). And how are we to read such a conclusion? Has Leander, then, remained innocent? Is this positive? Or has he simply become another of the anesthetized crowd, unaware of his own somnambulance? The most one can conclude is that Buechner wants to leave such questions unanswered. We know, at least, that Maroo's journey and her subsequent death are the final gestures of despair in the novel, and Leander is inextricably bound into the fabric of the despair along with all of the others.

Finally, Emma Plaut and Tristram's comical companion, Simon, bring together the strands establishing *A Long Day's Dying* as a particularly powerful modern novel. Emma is "a servant in the old manner" (*LDD* 39). Having come from Germany some thirty years before the action of the novel, she has grown accustomed to keeping Tristram's affairs in order and has developed a deep, if unspoken, commitment to him. Buechner will elaborate on this character more completely with Irma Reinwasser in *The Final Beast*. Emma feels threatened not so much, as one might suspect, by Elizabeth Poor as by the monkey, Simon, who seems to know everything that goes on in Tristram's life. The briefest glint of humor finds its way into the novel via the interplay between Simon and Emma. This minor plot, Emma moving in the tiny world of Tristram's apartment and its residents, reflects the breakdown obvious in the communication among the major characters. Emma is full of feelings she cannot quite name. Among Simon's many names are Galahad, "the pure in heart," and the name Tristram, which he sometimes shares with his master (*LDD* 156). Simon, Tristram's alter ego, has learned to mimic Tristram's behavior and even wears cut-down versions of Tristram's evening clothes and top hat to show off for Tristram's guests. Like Tristram, Simon is trustworthy and pure, but, also like Tristram, he is inarticulate. Simon's obvious limitations combine with Emma's feelings of jealousy and her own inarticulateness to produce a minor violence—Emma strikes Simon as Tristram looks on. Tristram sees himself as the offender, and the "guilt became illogically his own" (*LDD* 240). Surely a part of the novel's thematic force swirls around this guilt of Tristram's—guilt about Emma and Simon, Steitler and Elizabeth. When, in despair at his guilt, Tristram playacts a suicide, he inadvertently causes Simon's death, an analog to the deaths of relationships among the characters in the novel.

Guilt becomes a major subject in the Buechner canon, partly, I suspect, because of his own feelings of guilt regarding his father, who committed suicide when Buechner was a child. Whether "illogical" or not, guilt can be an enervating force, and part of Tristram's loss of energy derives from his frustration that all his best efforts produce unintended results. Tris-

Buechner's father

tram's moral strength and sincerity have not been sufficient to save Simon, Elizabeth, Leander, or anyone else—not even himself. He is an ineffectual priest—the sort of figure that Buechner admires in Graham Greene's *The Power and the Glory* and the kind of character that will preoccupy Buechner in novels to follow. Echoes of Tristram will sound all the way through the *Bebb* novels to the irascible Godric and conflicted Brendan of the 1980s and in the characters of the late-career novels *Son of Laughter* and *The Storm*. By the novel's end, Tristram can see only wreckage and estrangement strewn around him. Steitler and Leander are no longer close friends; the George-Elizabeth-Tristram trio is forever changed;

Simon and Maroo are dead; and Tristram, musing on Simon's death, observes, "It's not his life I mourn, you know . . . but mine, costly and fading" (*LDD* 263).

In an earlier passage of the novel, Tristram recalls a moment when he had picked up a coin that a young lady had accidentally dropped on the sidewalk. It is one of those unconsidered moments of life perhaps, but Tristram looks back upon it as a moment where he was so graceful and effortless in retrieving the coin that he derives a sense of exultation from the memory:

> If everything else went wrong and failed there would still, triumphantly, be that; that all his life was perhaps a progression towards that moment and could descend now easily from it; that he had been created perhaps for no reason more obscure than that he might one day pick up that silver coin and return it to the young woman who had let it fall as he passed. (*LDD* 174)

Every person, I suppose, has one moment of beauty surpassing all other moments in life, and this is Tristram's. But who will know of Tristram's moment? He recalls the experience while sitting beside Elizabeth, but looking toward her, he feels deep sadness knowing that the central moment of his life "was presently and precisely incommunicable" (*LDD* 174). Wherever we go in this novel, we come back to Tristram's isolation. We leave him remembering an organ grinder: "The organ-grinder had had an organ, but he had nothing else. The organ-grinder and his organ. But nothing, no, never, nothing else" (*LDD* 257).

Early reviewers were rather too quick to point out similarities between *A Long Day's Dying* and the work of Henry James. Theodore Kalem referred to Buechner's "Mandarin" style, "a style designed to imply more than is ever said" and claimed Buechner as a "linear descendant" of Henry James (Kalem 11). The *Time* reviewer labeled Buechner's novel "almost convincing" in the "mannered, slightly effete and shimmeringly elegiac style of Henry James."[20] Ernest Jones in *The Nation* argued that *A Long Day's Dying* was for that audience which "prefers Henry James and Elizabeth Bowen to Sinclair Lewis and John O'Hara."[21] Richard Sullivan simply categorized Buechner's first novel as "a Jamesian study."[22] Later critics like Leslie Fiedler referenced Buechner's "studied Jamesian effects."[23] Such unanimity among critics may offer a nice case in point as to how the enterprise of criticism operates, or perhaps we've stumbled on a conspiracy to resurrect Henry James.

The plot really thickens when Buechner admits to never having read much James. "Despite what many reviewers assumed, I wasn't influenced by James," Buechner whimsically observes, laughing about the almost universal assumption of the critics.[24] He argues that his approach was under the influence of the prose stylists of the seventeenth century—Browne, Taylor, and Donne—for whom he had developed a deep attachment in his reading at Princeton in the late 1940s. His own testimony notwithstanding, Buechner is consistently compared to James through the early years of his career. Labels are easy to come by and almost impossible to shed. Comparisons to James can be a matter of praise or condemnation, depending on whether or not the critic is referring to what Myers called Buechner's "labyrinthine, syntactically involved style" (Myers 9) or what Nathan Scott labeled a "taut fragility of poetic form"[25] that has, in Scott's view, helped establish "a dominant mode of our fiction" (Scott 227).

The references to James are most likely reactions to the elaborate style and emphasis on character evident in *A Long Day's Dying*. Theoretically, Buechner is following James's dictates that an artist must "represent life"[26] and must have the "power to guess the unseen from the seen, to trace the implication of things, to judge the whole piece by the pattern" (James 398). In Buechner's novel, we are certainly carried into the consciousness of certain characters; it is a psychological novel, a study of the mental starts and stops of Tristram, Elizabeth, and Paul, more than it is a novel of action. Almost nothing happens in *A Long Day's Dying*. The book is about glances and guesses, inexpressible thoughts, and interior meanderings. Though Buechner will later turn to a more robust style and a concern for action, in these early days he is more like Hawthorne and James, fascinated by the implications spilling out of what we might call, in theological terms, a sin or, in psychological terms, an indiscretion.

James Wood's discussion of John Updike in *The Broken Estate* is instructive here in the distinctions drawn between a "theological" novel and a "metaphysical" one. Claiming Hawthorne for the former and Melville for the latter, Wood concluded that Updike, though "God-involved," is actually a merely theological novelist, a writer in a system, who cannot "picture absence."[27] Wood's blueprint can be fruitfully transferred to the issue of the oft-cited comparisons between James and Buechner. Although much taken with questions of good and evil, Henry James wrote within a framework hardly duplicated by any American writer since. He is a theological novelist in Wood's formulation. Buechner would be the metaphysical novelist. Allowing a certain congeniality of style between James and early Buechner, we must quickly amend the comparison by noting a distinct uncongeniality in their respective visions.

To label Buechner "Jamesian" is merely to underscore the straining toward artistry that many readers sense in this novice work. Such words do not reach to theme. Yes, the reviews were generally positive and reached a conclusion similar to that of David Daiches: "Frederick Buechner has established himself as a major literary figure."[28] Nonetheless, tones of occasional dissatisfaction rang in the most positive of the many favorable reviews of the novel. Even Daiches, for instance, noticed "excessive artfulness" occasionally breaking into the quiet power of the novel (Daiches 4). In fact, the central negative reaction to the book revolves on comments about style. *Punch* called the novel "too theoretical and immature" and claimed that it missed "real distinction in spite of its many excellent qualities."[29] Ernest Jones described the novel as "needlessly ornate" (Jones 64), and Sullivan found the work "too cold and studied" (Sullivan 4). The *Time* reviewer pointed to a prose "so self-consciously and calculatedly polished that it breaks the continuity of the novel" (*Time* 90). Criticisms such as these are valuable to illustrate Buechner's straining to write to a particular notion of what a novel ought to be.

The novel misses greatness because it is so self-conscious. The result is a bloodlessness that detracts from the powerful statements of the piece, but the novel certainly anticipates the increasingly powerful work to come. Buechner seems dreamily aware of what he might become as he paints pictures of Elizabeth, Tristram, Leander, and the others. He is much taken by thoughts of death in life in his debut novel. And such a preoccupation logically suggests thoughts of fullness of life, wakefulness, vitality, meaning, and the sort of words we might associate with Buechner's more recent work.

A further example of the straining of the first effort might be Buechner's use of the mythological story of Philomela as an allusive backdrop for *A Long Day's Dying*. Tristram, Elizabeth, George, and Paul all see the story of the ravished queen woven into the tapestries on display at the Cloisters during their visits there. The story the tapestries tell—passion, revenge, and death—is carried out in less spectacular ways in the experience of Buechner's characters. The myth, however, is unsatisfactorily integrated into the story and stands out as an attempt to provide the obligatory artfulness. John Aldridge in *After the Lost Generation* provided a complex rendering of the role of the myth in Buechner's novel but concluded that Buechner's achievement was not nearly as successful as that of T. S. Eliot in *The Waste Land*: "In Buechner's novel myth remains a static story detached from its ancient setting and applied merely as a story to a contemporary setting. It does not serve to enhance the meaning of the dilemma described in the novel but is simply a borrowed framework on which the characters and their problems are hung."[30]

It is important to remember that Buechner was in his early twenties when he produced this work—a young artist, just out of Princeton, just home from the Army, and struggling for a voice. In his own words, he was "writing for a teacher" (Myers 10). Aldridge's observations on Buechner's use of mythological materials point up the fact that Buechner in *A Long Day's Dying* is serving an apprenticeship, trying to write to some notion of how a novel should be written. In his autobiography, Buechner confesses his own discomfort with the novel: "It [*A Long Day's Dying*] was immediately a considerable success both critically and commercially despite the fact that it was very dense, static, psychological, and written in such a mannered, involuted style—the residue of my romance with the seventeenth century—that it seems outrageous when I look at it now" (*SJ* 97–98).

But even here, despite the studentlike style, Buechner's emerging voice is audible as he works with the materials of nothingness. Buechner will address the problems of style in the novels that follow *A Long Day's Dying*; his later work shows an increasing clarity of purpose and a decreasing artificiality in style. Buechner argues that the hardest thing about the writing business is finding one's voice. He knows that he had not found his voice in his earliest work. In fact, he comments in 1995 that it is only "in the last fifteen or twenty years" that he has felt himself to be writing comfortably in his own voice (*Door* 13). But what must be noted in this first novel is Buechner's fastening on the themes of his generation—loneliness, misconnection, moral emptiness, spiritual estrangement, human fallibility, and universal isolation. His novel is much in the stream of F. Scott Fitzgerald's *The Great Gatsby* and William Faulkner's *The Sound and the Fury*. Buechner shares with these writers a sense of the occasional power of individual character set against the frustration of constant misconnection and inevitable tragedy. From the first novel and throughout his writing career, Buechner deals in such emphatically modern preoccupations as the carelessness of the upper class, the problem of trying to get beyond the limitations of one's own consciousness, the inevitable doom that hangs over our every attempt at connection with others, and the devastation wrought by the manipulations of one character in the life of another. In the books to come, Buechner will continue to circle back to this sharp-edged issue of lives in collision.

As Denham Sutcliffe noted, the landscape of *A Long Day's Dying* is "a spiritual wasteland":[31]

A woman fornicates, and the issue is hatred. A man loves and the end is desolation. All this takes place in the fake medievalism of the Cloisters, the fake Gothic of the Princeton towers, the fake gentility of upper-crust New York. It takes place in a brocade of unicorns, aviaries, carven saints, and baroque prose. But it's all nastiness underneath, an image of "what it's like to be alive here now." The title, from *Paradise Lost*, might equally have come from *The Marble Faun*: we cannot sin but we destroy other Edens than our own. But nobody here cries *O felix culpa*! Nor is it hinted that the characters have come through sin to sad self-knowledge and therein found a reason for living and dying. (Sutcliffe 731)

A Long Day's Dying is the most thoroughly modern of all the books that Buechner has written. As Aldridge concluded, *A Long Day's Dying* leaves us feeling "not that life has been lived and then laboriously achieved but that life has been somehow missed" (Aldridge 219). Aldridge's analysis occasioned an interesting response from Edward Wagenknecht in 1952. Noting Aldridge's praise of Buechner and Capote, Wagenknecht lamented their work as testimony "to a widespread sickness of soul among the youngest generation of the most talented American writers which is a frightening thing."[32] In the refined worlds of Tristram and Elizabeth the reader witnesses an overwhelming helplessness with what John Maloney called "a poignant sense of man's isolation and a painful realization of our inability ever really to communicate with each other."[33] The book is about failures—failures in giving and receiving love. Ironically, the only apparently successful sexual experience of the novel is one mentioned in a brief paragraph on the occasion of Tristram's visit to an aviary. Just before his arrival, we get a glimpse of lovemaking when a youthful couple, with "the thick fragrance . . . of molasses, the mash, their desire" clinging to them, satisfy one another in a way that Tristram would probably find decidedly primitive (*LDD* 167). Buechner's Miltonic epigraph reminds us that Adam and Eve found some respite, some solace, in their relationship that softened the inevitable death that awaited them. In this novel, almost nobody finds such solace.

Visible in this malaise of disaster, however, is the Buechner to come; something stirs in his vision of nothingness. To argue that Buechner is a novelist who one day became a Christian and abruptly changed his course as a writer is to overlook the progression of his work and to ignore the preoccupation with spiritual themes even in his preconversion novels. Ihab Hassan, another critic who labeled Buechner as "a writer of distinct promise," was prescient in noticing that behind the explicit pagan mythology of the Cloisters which Buechner borrows for a framework in his bestseller is an implicit Christian system (Hassan 154). From the reminder of the fall in the Miltonic epigraph to the labeling of Elizabeth's indiscretion as "sin," Buechner is decidedly aware of Christian symbolism and ethical values.

Buechner's attention to religious themes begins well before his conversion and ordination, and *A Long Day's Dying* is about more than what *The New Yorker* reviewer called "a prize misunderstanding."[34] Daiches was the only one of the critics to note that the novel really questioned the tenets of modernism, exploring "the implications of sensibilities which operate without a clearly perceived moral base" (Daiches 4). Markfield did see that the novel was rooted in "the moral emptiness of contemporary sophisticated intelligence," but too few critics picked up on the decidedly spiritual implications of the young novelist's first effort (Markfield 391). Later critical studies began to notice the unity in the career. Myers believed that "the religious dimension of Buechner's work is present from the beginning" (Myers 8). McCoy noted "a seeking for the possibility of God present from the beginning" (McCoy 61). Of the book-length critical studies, only *Laughter in a Genevan Gown: The Works of Frederick Buechner 1970–1980* by Marie-Helene Davies overlooked the significance of the earliest novels. Even the recent, somewhat eccentric analysis by Victoria S. Allen, *Listening to Life: Psychology and Spirituality in the Writing of Frederick Buechner*, argued that the early fiction "prefigures" later work.[35]

Buechner's own summary comes in a 1981 interview with Davies. There he summarizes *A Long Day's Dying* as a novel that "sprang from . . . disgust at the emptiness of the lives of most of those he had met in the society of the rich."[36] With the chivalric Tristram, the young Buechner is weighing the alternatives available to moderns. When Tristram's kindness proves inadequate and actually contributes to the physical disasters of the novel, Simon's suicide, and Maroo's death, the reader is pulled into Tristram's sense of guilt and bewilderment.

Early in the novel, when Tristram wanders into the chapel at the Cloisters, the reader overhears his rather feeble attempts at religious expression and senses Buechner's early exploration of the religious alternative. Tristram approaches the life-size statue of the saint and reaches out toward the hand the figure holds against its chest: "He did this not altogether idly, but as a gesture with a kind of hope. The recess was empty, nor had the artist made any attempt to represent the folded palm whose outside was so painstakingly carved" (*LDD* 24). Implicit in this observation is the sense that religion, which looks so attractive on the surface, is void of reality when one peers more closely. Paul Steitler will make just such an assertion during his visit to the Cloisters. What Tristram gets for his gesture is a moment of embarrassment and panic when he realizes that his hand has become caught in the hand of the saint. In wrenching himself free, he cuts his hand and almost pulls over the statue. Nonetheless, an impulse leads Tristram to continue with the saint, to try to explain himself to this religious figure. He wants to speak his life to someone: "He felt there should be a reliable witness, impartial as a mirror, to report with overwhelming accuracy each detail not only, as he thought upon it, of his most recent encounter, but of all his experience, of Tristram Bone involved with actuality" (*LDD* 26). His kneeling, however, brings him only increasing discomfort and self-consciousness. He realizes that he is probably being "thoughtless" (*LDD* 26). He mumbles "Amen" as he leaves the chapel, but it is not the benediction of worship; it is rather an announcing of an end. The religious alternative has been irrevocably closed to Tristram.

A Long Day's Dying is the work of a skeptic, and a skeptic's voice lingers throughout Buechner's work. Buechner acknowledges his persistent skepticism everywhere in his work, often via recourse to that most foundational of biblical texts, "Lord, I believe; help my unbelief," which Buechner repeatedly contends "is the best any of us can do really" (*MD* 35, *FB* 53). Buechner thoroughly integrates his skepticism by adapting Paul Tillich's notion that doubt is not the antithesis of faith but a vital aspect of faith. Tillich will be one of Buechner's teachers in the mid-1950s, "the one who has influenced me the most perhaps."[37] The first book certainly features doubt, but the preoccupation with theological ideas is all the more striking in such a landscape. The young novelist attends to the ways of hatred and revenge, self-justification and sin, as they operate in his time and place, and, in his own way, Buechner reiterates that venerable question of American literature: "What must I do to be saved?"

If, as Ernest Jones argued, *A Long Day's Dying* is a novel that "merely labels and asserts" without ever making any definitive statement, it is because the young Buechner has no clear affirmation to make; but he is clearly longing for affirmation, and longing will remain a subject for Buechner over the decades to follow (Jones 64). Victoria Allen's brief summary of *A Long Day's Dying* came very close: "Buechner uses the metaphor of a lost paradise to describe the alienation of the modern world. As a literary modernist, he is diagnosing the problem of contemporary life that reflects his own condition."[38] Buechner's first novel is, indeed, a statement of negation. Tristram Bone, a man of great bulk and equally great need, is certainly capable of intense emotion, but, like his trained pet, he cannot speak. His loss in the course of the novel is enormous; he knows that whether he blames Elizabeth or Steitler or Motley or himself, the wreckage is complete: "If nothing else, he knew at least that, whoever the sinner, it was something like sin that had set the damaged, damaging machinery of complication in action, that both the sinner and the innocent would suffer" (*LDD* 182). *A Long Day's Dying* is preoccupied with sin and its consequences in an unredeemed and unredeemable world.

Buechner will increasingly define sin, as he does in a 1973 book *Wishful Thinking: A Theological ABC*, as "whatever you do that pushes you away from other people" (*WT* 88). Buechner describes evil as a reality that produces chaos in people's lives: "Evil is like an atomic bomb, like a mushroom. It starts with a thin stem and then enlarges. Both in the historical and the human sense, there is a reality in being possessed by demons. Evil is not only the shadow cast by light. It is vast and hideous" (Davies 69). Such an insight sounds very much like the premise of *A Long Day's Dying*, where Elizabeth's falsity mushrooms into deadly separation. Buechner's subsequent work grows from just these sorts of "wages of sin" considerations. For Tristram, Maroo's arrival means "an end of sorts, merciful, yet in its finality somehow hopeless" (*LDD* 226). For Buechner, however, this is not the end. The tragedy of Tristram is not the last word, only the next to last. The writer of *A Long Day's Dying* is a haunted man, haunted, as it seems to him in retrospect, by something unfinished about his widely praised novel.

Buechner recalls a rather strange meeting that took place shortly after the successful publication of his first book, while he was still a teacher at Lawrenceville School. Invited to lunch by one of the ministers who frequently passed through his school, Buechner was surprised by a question:

> Had I ever considered, he said, putting my gift with words to work for—God, did he say? Or the Church? Or Christ? I no longer remember how he put it exactly, and he made no great thing of it but passed on soon to other matters so that I do not to this day know whether this was what he had asked me to lunch to say or not. I no longer remember what I answered him either or what impression his words made on me except that they took me entirely by surprise. No, I must have told him. I had never considered such a thing. And that was the end of it except that out of all of the events that took place during those five years of teaching at Lawrenceville, it is one of the few that I remember distinctly, like an old photograph preserved by accident between the pages of a book. (*SJ* 101)

The "promising" young novelist, the prep-school teacher, the sophisticated socialite who had put much of himself into the portrait of Paul Steitler, the wise and weary instructor of literature, was, it seems, God-haunted from the first. Buechner even notices the irony himself as, in a softer mood, he looks back at the opening line of his ancient book:

> "The mirror reflected what seemed at first a priest," is the way the book begins, and insofar as what the mirror also reflected was an image, albeit an unconscious one, of myself, I cannot help thinking of that opening sentence as itself just such a whisper, as the faint intimation from God knows where of the direction my life was even then starting to take me. (*SJ* 96)

The world of *A Long Day's Dying* is certainly a God-forsaken one, but something of God hangs phantomlike around the edges of the narrative, ready to explode in the God-obsessed Peter Cowley of Buechner's second novel, *The Seasons' Difference*.

Notes

1. Personal correspondence, October 12, 1992.
2. Personal conversation, November 13, 2004.
3. George Garrett, "The Character of Saints," *The World & I*, www.worldandi.com, April 1993, 293. Hereafter cited as Garrett.
4. Mel Gussow, "James Merrill is Dead at 68; Elegant Poet of Love and Loss," *The New York Times*, www.nytimes.com, February 7, 1995.
5. Frederick Buechner, Box IV A 1, Wheaton College Special Collections, Wheaton, IL. Hereafter cited as Archive.
6. Personal correspondence, March 3, 2005.
7. Caspar W. Weinberger, "A Promising First Novel," *San Francisco Chronicle*, January 22, 1950, 16. Hereafter cited as Weinberger.
8. Frederick Buechner, *A Long Day's Dying* (New York: Alfred A. Knopf, 1950), 184. Hereafter cited as *LLD*.
9. Joseph Wood Krutch, *The Modern Temper* (New York: Harcourt, Brace & World, 1929), 167.
10. Irving Howe, "Introduction," in *Classics of Modern Fiction*, ed. Irving Howe, 2nd ed. (New York: Simon & Schuster, 1972), 3–12.
11. T. S. Eliot, "Religion and Literature," in *Religion and Modern Literature: Essays in Theory and Criticism*, ed. G. B. Tennyson and Edward E. Ericson Jr. (Grand Rapids: Eerdmans, 1975), 30.
12. Matthew Arnold, "Dover Beach," in *Victorian Prose and Poetry*, ed. Lionel Trilling and Harold Bloom (New York: Oxford University Press, 1973), 594.
13. John Milton, *Paradise Lost*, Book 10, ll. 958–65.
14. Ihab Hassan, *Radical Innocence: The Contemporary American Novel* (Princeton, NJ: Princeton University Press, 1961), 161. Hereafter cited as Hassan.

15. Mike Long and Jill Schreiber, "Sinners, Saints, and Life-Givers: An Interview with Frederick Buechner," *Kodon: Wheaton's Magazine of the Arts*, November 1985, 11.

16. Shirley Barker, "Fiction," *Library Journal*, January 1, 1950, 43.

17. Horton Davies, "Frederick Buechner and the Strange Workings of Grace," *Theology Today*, July 1979, 186–93. Hereafter cited as HDavies.

18. Theodore Kalem, A Novelist Who Is 'Very Nearly Right,'" *Christian Science Monitor*, January 12, 1950, 11. Hereafter cited as Kalem.

19. Wallace Markfield, "Three First Novels," *Commentary* 9 (1950): 390. Hereafter cited as Markfield.

20. *Time*, January 9, 1950, 90. Hereafter cited as *Time*.

21. Ernest Jones, "Labels and Assertions," *Nation*, January 21, 1950, 64–65. Hereafter cited as Jones.

22. Richard Sullivan, "An Excellent but Complex Study of Life," *Chicago Sunday Tribune*, January 8, 1950, 8. Hereafter cited as Sullivan.

23. Leslie Fiedler, *An End to Innocence* (New York: Stein & Day, 1972), 203.

24. Shirley and Rudy Nelson, Frederick Buechner," *Christianity & Literature* 32 (1982): 10. Hereafter cited as Nelson Interview.

25. Nathan A. Scott Jr., *The Broken Center: Studies in the Theological Horizon of Modern Literature* (New Haven, CT: Yale University Press, 1966), 227.

26. Henry James, "The Art of Fiction," in *The Portable Henry James*, ed. Morton Zabel (New York: Penguin Books, 1968), 389. Hereafter cited as James.

27. James Wood, *The Broken Estate: Essays on Literature and Belief* (New York: Modern Library, 1999), 208–9, 212.

28. David Daiches, "Widow on a College Campus," *New York Times Book Review*, January 8, 1950, 4. Hereafter cited as Daiches.

29. *Punch*, March 7, 1951, 318.

30. John W. Aldridge, *After the Lost Generation: A Critical Study of the Writers of Two Wars* (New York: McGraw-Hill, 1951), 223. Hereafter cited as Aldridge.

31. Denham Sutcliffe, "Novels of the Nebulous Self," *Kenyon Review* 12 (1950): 731. Hereafter cited as Sutcliffe.

32. Edward Wagenknecht, *Cavalcade of the American Novel* (New York: Holt, Rinehart & Winston, 1952), 454.

33. John J. Maloney, "A Miniature Work of Art, Almost Perfect," *New York Herald Tribune Book Review*, January 8, 1950.

34. *New Yorker*, January 7, 1950, 79.

35. Victoria S. Allen, *Listening to Life: Psychology and Spirituality in the Writings of Frederick Buechner* (Baltimore: American Literary Press, 2002), 51.

36. Marie-Helene Davies, *Laughter in a Genevan Gown: The Works of Frederick Buechner 1970–1980* (Grand Rapids: Eerdmans, 1983), 66. Hereafter cited as Davies.

37. Harold Fickett, "A Conversation with Frederick Buechner," *Image: A Journal of the Arts & Religion*, Spring 1989, 52. Hereafter cited as *Image*.

38. Victoria Allen, "Coming Home in the Writings of Frederick Buechner," *Christianity and the Arts*, Winter 2000, 34.

Chapter Two

Fishing for God

The Seasons' Difference

If the critical ruling on Frederick Buechner's first novel was "promising," then the second novel, *The Seasons' Difference*, was something like "promise unfulfilled." *The New Yorker* reviewer dismissed the novel as "high-flown nonsense,"[1] and the *Atlantic* critic concluded that Buechner has "nothing significant to say."[2] In his autobiography, Buechner seems anxious to skirt this period of his career. His only comment is dismissive: "a second novel . . . fared as badly as the first one had fared well" (*SJ* 107). The novel is not even mentioned by title in the memoirs, and the few references to *The Seasons' Difference* in Buechner's speeches and interviews are generally disdainful. Nancy Myers mentions Buechner's cataloging of the novel as "a bit stagey" [*sic*] and as "something I thought would be interesting to say rather than something I had really felt my way toward" (Myers 32). Buechner tells me that he has no memory of the praise the book garnered and admits that he disparages *The Seasons' Difference* simply because "it took the worst beating" of all his books (Brown 48–49). Although such observations illustrate that Buechner is aware of a certain tentativeness in his second novel, his disenchantment with *The Seasons' Difference* may have more to do with bad memories. Or does his rejection reach even deeper? After all, *A Long Day's Dying* thoroughly displeased many critics, and *The Seasons' Difference* actually garnered many positive reviews. In *The Spectator*, for example, Tangye Lean called it "one of the most distinguished novels that has recently come out of America."[3] Francis Bickley in *Punch* tagged it "a brilliant book."[4] Despite some reservations about the novel, Caspar Weinberger in the *San Francisco Chronicle*, who had praised Buechner's first novel, continued his approval: "It is not too much to say that among America's current novelists his abilities are the most obvious and his ultimate place is with the best we have produced."[5] Given the fact that the second novel was received in a way not so very different from the first one, we must consider the possibility that Buechner's dismissal of the book has its source in a personal reaction to the stunted philosophy that the novel embodies. The writer of *The Seasons' Difference* is clearly on the way to something and is, just as clearly, not yet there. Horace Gregory, in the *New York Herald Tribune*, noticed, as few other critics did, the dimension of incompleteness in the novel: "Mr. Buechner probably needs more time to complete his own vision of the world that is glimpsed in certain descriptive passages in his prose. The promise of his first book is still awaiting its fulfillment."[6] *The Seasons' Difference*, coming at a time when Buechner is trying to settle his own religious questions, is a transitional book—a novel about a young man's search for encounter with God and the effects of his search on a group of world-weary adults and coming-to-life children.

After a stint as teacher of English and assistant housemaster at Lawrenceville School in New Jersey, Buechner takes a leave in 1950 to pursue his second novel. Writing most of the manuscript at Great Milton, near Oxford, Buechner also enjoyed the benefits of travel and introductions to famous folk. Although he has little to say about the shaping forces, Buechner does feature in the novel a youngish teacher who is hefting the question: cynicism or faith? Buechner and his adjudicators mostly hold their tongues when they come to *The Seasons' Difference*. In the more than forty linear feet of holdings in the Buechner archives, only a few inches are devoted to this novel. Buechner seems to have more or less expunged it from the record. But someone should at least note that the book has real power, asks stunning questions about the efficacy of miracle and the possibilities of faith, and has to be considered another of those boldface moments in the Buechner narrative. Given his penchant for regarding human experience as hinting of pattern, Buechner will have to yield to those who want to keep his second novel in the portrait; maybe this book is more weighty than even he knows.

The assembled characters of *The Seasons' Difference* again represent the moneyed leisure class. Sam and Sara Dunn invite a young relative, Peter Cowley, to provide a summer school for children on the grounds of their sprawling vacation estate. Before the book opens, the Dunn's Oz-like retreat has been the setting for Peter Cowley's mystical experience. Peter has a vision of some indefinable sort, and the novel is a registering of the ramifications of his vague visitation for the adults and the children. Sam Dunn, the husband and father in this "household of somnambulists" (*SD* 253), falls asleep at the climactic moment of the narrative; he is defined by his languor and passivity. Locked in the complacency of his wealth and the worn weariness of his sophistication, Sam lives in a musty past peopled by Thomas Browne and other seventeenth-century writers whose words Sam frequently adapts to his own purposes, but whose passions elude him entirely. Sara Dunn, his wife, is a moderately successful sculptor, a sophisticated woman who wants to believe in Cowley's vision but has neither the faith to trust Cowley's testimony nor the strength to hold things together as the summer holiday takes a frightening turn. Julie McMoon, a grieving widow whose husband has only recently committed suicide, is a neighbor of the Dunns who sends her children to Cowley's school and, thereby, becomes involved in the events of the summer. Through the McMoons' grief, Buechner smuggles into another book the subject of suicide, the dark shadow stretching back to that November day of his tenth year when his father's suicide changed everything. Another adult visitor is Richard Lundrigan, a cynic who debunks Cowley's vision. If Cowley is something of Christ, Lundrigan is much of Judas Iscariot. Thomas Lavender, a God-haunted lunatic of a minister and Peter's spiritual advisor, joins the retreat to help Peter authenticate the vision and ends by contributing to the disasters that close out the book. Belying his name, Thomas is more believer than doubter. Another latecomer to the motley congregation is Mollie Purdue, Sara's model, who bridges the children and the adults in the novel.

Finally, the children themselves are critical: Fendall Dunn, Timmy and Daisy McMoon, George Bundle, Ellie Sonntag, Harry Fogg, and Rufus Este. Harry and Rufus are the oldest of the children and have formed a rather exclusive club, "the Uglies," as a way of identifying themselves apart from the "Persons." Persons are, by implication, those who are self-assured, who have a place in life, who know their roles and play them with confidence. Through the Uglies, Buechner will again explore his growing sense of the essential loneliness and fallibility of humanity. The memoirs make clear what some may have guessed in 1952—the original Uglies were Jimmy and Freddy, Merrill and Buechner. "An Ugly was bookish, introspective, completely nonathletic and tended to feel awkward and helpless and lost, especially on occasions when the rest of the world seemed to be having the time of their lives," Buechner recalls (*EH* 45). This connection deepens our understanding of Buechner's friendship with Merrill, of course—"at least they had each other"—but it also suggests something of the questions Buechner may well be posing for himself in the second novel as he seeks his own place (*EH* 45). Cowley's vision thrusts itself rudely into this world of intelligence and weariness, innocence and puzzledness.

Peter Cowley's vision inspires him to try to call up an encore of the miraculous moment for his doubting friends. The only way to convince his friends of the validity of his visitation is to walk them through their own miraculous display. Although the grown-ups decide to omit the children from their scheme, the children have their own ideas and enlist Mollie's aid in staging their own version of Cowley's experience. Bedecking themselves as angels and lining up on a hillside to trick the adults, the children's ruse works better than they could have hoped. The youthful trick works so well, in fact, that we are left wondering if Peter's attempted re-creation fails or not. After all, the adults do see something, if only the children. Lavender concludes that the children represent all that the adults have lost. He wants to be like them. In his attempt to enter their innocence, he first performs a startling mass marriage, wedding the children to one another in a ceremony that even they find vaguely lunatic. Finally, Lavender falls to his death from the children's treehouse, where he has fled to try to explain himself to the bewildered children after a scolding from Sara.

Lavender's plunge from the childhood play place jolts the children and the reader out of the soft shade and gentle breezes of the summer retreat and into the wintry winds of life's complexities. Bringing his no-nonsense perspective to the events of the narrative, Lundrigan summarizes:

> A man has a vision, . . . or thinks he has, and then tries to arrange another—a sort of heavenly impresario, a celestial Ziegfeld—and fails. Then another man, an old one this time and a minister, goes a little berserk and marries some children to one another. The mothers have a series of minor fits, the old man tries to climb up a tree and in the process falls and . . . breaks his neck. Dies with the children looking on.[7]

Despite all the action of accidental death, tramping around on hillsides, and games of hide-and-seek, however, the action of this novel is, as it was in *A Long Day's Dying*, interior—inside the minds of the various characters, even the cloudy and tentative minds of the children. Predictably, comparisons to Henry James and the so-called novel of character again became the standard fare in the critical response to Buechner's second novel.

As with the first novel, many readers reacted to Buechner's straining for a style. George Miles, in *Commonweal*, feared that Buechner was "suffering a Jamesian, or even a Proustian jag."[8] Reviewing for *New Republic*, Robert Phelps also made the obligatory comparison to James and concluded: "What the book is really about is Advanced Seminar English (admission by instructor's permission only)."[9] The *Library Journal* critic referred to "the arty attempt"[10] of the novel, and Robert Lowry in the *New York Times* tendered the review that stung Buechner most. After placing Buechner in "the stylish neighborhood of Henry James,"[11] Lowry branded the book "deadpan symbolic silliness" (Lowry 28). *The Antioch Review* critic summarized the general critical reaction to the style of *The Seasons' Difference*: "The style follows James, but lacks his penetration."[12] Even those readers who praised the novel did so with qualification. For example, the *Time* reviewer concluded that "His style stems from Henry James," while "his imagination makes such plodding documentarians as Norman Mailer and James Jones look like plow horses."[13] This review, although acknowledging that the novel "shimmers with frosty, neo-Jamesian elegance," finally argued that the book "breaks stride in the stretch and pulls up lame at the finish" (*Time* Review 90–91). Perhaps Buechner is less successful stylistically in his second novel, and his attempt to discuss the dilemma of a cast of thoroughly modern characters thrust into the possibility of a supernatural visitation is clouded by a prose that labors for artistry. But I cannot go as far as Myers, who said *The Seasons' Difference* was Buechner's "weakest novel" (Myers 32). I'm not so sure. Myers missed the humor, for one thing. When Buechner uses his own memories of his relationship with James Merrill to paint the comic portraits and high jinks of Rufus and Harry, the Uglies, something starts to thaw in Buechner's storytelling. And whatever we may say about style, the thematic center of the second novel dramatically opens an understanding of Buechner's career. Buechner's ruminations in *The Seasons' Difference* have inarguable weight in his personal life, as well as for the literary work that will follow over the half-century ahead.

Despite the critical demurrals, Buechner is also more successful this time in integrating the symbols that inform the narrative. The opening scene of the novel has Sam and Sara involved in a rather fanciful discussion of fishing as they watch young George Bundle cast a line into the pond. Thinking that George cannot hear them, the two adults talk first about the pleasurable feeling of the tug of a fish at the bait and then compare that tug to the pull of the wind at a kite. Extending their comparison, Sara asks, "What would you be fishing for in the sky, I wonder?" Sam answers, "Well, for God I suppose" (*SD* 5). The idea of fishing in the sky for God, of course, brings to their minds the visionary, Cousin Peter, and Sara jokes, "I can just see Peter pulling God down out of the clouds, His mouth all ragged and bleeding" (*SD* 5). The eavesdropper, Georgie, is mystified. The metaphor of God as a fish to be caught stretches in many directions through the novel—to the actual fish that George Bundle manages to drag out of the pond and to a mysterious drawing of a fish that Peter Cowley sketches in the sand during an outing at a nearby beach. The children know only that Peter's crude sketch is that of a fish with one great staring eye and a vertical inscription in Greek beneath it. Of course, "ichthus" alludes to a common Christian symbol for Christ. After one of the children has tried to wipe out Peter's drawing, "Only the word for fish remained, partially obliterated, but still decipherable" (*SD* 75). Here's Buechner, quite early on, wondering about Christ.

Although George Miles argues that such religious symbolism as the "ichthus" and the vision are not successfully folded into the book, are "quantities in a formula," the fish motif is the precise image to capture something of Peter Cowley's character and the thematic focus of the book (Miles 179). Peter is longing for an encounter with God, and he becomes something of a Christ and something of a clown to his friends and students. He is Christ in that he tries to bring a spiritual message to scoffers and unbelievers. He is a clown in his bumbling and laughable ineptitude. He is, like Graham Greene's whiskey priest, delivering a message of grace in spite of himself. It is important to note here, early on, that Greene's *The Power and the Glory* is a growing influence in Buechner's career; Buechner frequently refers to the whiskey priest as the inspiration for many of his own characters. In a letter posted on the day after Greene's death, Buechner laments, "The great Graham Greene is dead. *The Power and the Glory* will always be canonical for me, and I hope Saint Peter remembers it when Greene makes his reckoning at the gate."[14] The Greene connection is quite subtle here, but the so-called religious symbolism of *The Seasons' Difference* is much more successful than is the mythological backdrop of *A Long Day's Dying*. We get the hint in this second novel; we know this writer is up to something. At the same time, the religious inquiry is subtle, deeply woven into the fabric of the narrative.

So Peter Cowley has a vision. On one of his solitary rambles through the woods, alone with his Bible and the apple he's brought along for a snack, Peter sees something, hears something, feels something? We are never quite sure: the vision is offstage. We get only allusions to it—never a real description. The vision, it seems, is not actually the presence or even the voice of God, but an assurance "that there is a God, and that we matter to Him. Very much" (*SD* 79). Peter's response to the whole thing is childlike; he possesses something of the peculiar aliveness and sensitivity of the children he tutors. More than any of the other adults, for example, Peter is awake to the beauty of the summer retreat. He notices. Even on an outing with the children to a traveling carnival, surrounded by freaks and sordidness, Cowley experiences "an emotion like great grief or great happiness but richer than either" (*SD* 67). This Cowley, tutor and friend, saint and comedian, is vulnerable to life in a fragile, frightening way. He is a searcher after universal connection in a world of cocktail parties, spiritual weariness, and cynicism. He retains something of the puzzled innocence of the children in his quest for faith, alternately wise and foolish. Maybe Peter is a saint. Maybe he is a madman.

Peter's spiritual visitation becomes a test case for the gathered cast of the novel and, in some way, a test for readers of Buechner's novel. The question here is reminiscent of a 1988 novel by a southern writer, Peggy Payne. In her book, *Revelation*, she offers the scene of a Presbyterian minister in a staid parish, who climbs into his pulpit one Sunday to tell his congregation that God has spoken to him. When they figure out that their trusted pastor isn't speaking metaphorically, a good bit of humor and instruction breaks out. Buechner's Cowley is grandfather to Payne's cleric. What are sophisticated folk to do with this claim of miracle? Buechner wants to ask that question of his characters and readers; he seems also to be asking it of himself. When we consider Buechner's life circumstances and the literary context in which he begins his career, the question is all the more striking. Although Updike will arrive on the scene within a decade and address the debate in the form of Eccles and Kruppenbach, the ministers struggling over Harry Angstrom's soul in the first *Rabbit* novel, the general trend of the literature of the time is not about the possibility of God but about his ongoing death. Salinger and the others miss God, surely, but the generation is still a lost one; it is absence, not presence, that percolates in the literature of the midcentury.

Richard Lundrigan, of course, speaks for the absence and provides the foil to Peter's character. Ironically, Richard is nearby when Peter has his experience on the hillside. Peter tells him later that the vision was "pretty nearly gone by" before Lundrigan came on the scene (*SD* 88). Is the fact that Lundrigan sees nothing meant to demonstrate that there was nothing to see? Or is Lundrigan incapable of seeing? Or did Lundrigan, in his role as unbeliever, cause the vision to dissipate? Whatever the case, the reactions of the two men to the real or imagined vision illustrate the tension between them, as well as the thematic tensions of the book. Doubt and faith collide right here.

One of Lundrigan's functions at the gatherings of the vacationers is playing the piano to accompany their singing. Ironically, the songs he remembers best turn out to be church hymns. Lundrigan plays "Leaning on Jesus" and other such hymns from long-ago childhoods when he and the others still had ears to hear of such mysteries. During the singing, however, Lundrigan changes the lyric "leaning on the everlasting arms" to "leaning on the everlasting crutch" (*SD* 46). His impromptu revision is suggestive of his cynicism and pseudosophistication. Lundrigan is, as he admits, "outside the situation" (*SD* 182). He intimidates his friends with one of his favorite phrases—"emotional instability" (*SD* 43)—and his "weapon" of choice is the word "maturity" (*SD* 86). Julie and Sara are among the few of his friends who have learned to be unafraid of his categorizations. Most others can be silenced by the slightest threat of being judged immature by Lundrigan. Only at the end of the novel do we learn that Peter, confident that his vision at least means *something*, even if he cannot say just what, has joined the small group no longer fearful of Lundrigan's machinations. The cynic is muted, for the most part, although the issue of where Peter stands with the hard-minded Lundrigan is unresolved.

Just after Peter has arranged the restaging of the vision, he and Lundrigan are alone together at the beach. Lundrigan quizzes Peter about the vision, but the central reason for the discussion is, in Lundrigan's view, a desire to snap Peter out of it. Lundrigan, in his inquisitorial role, interprets the vision to Peter:

> You saw only what you wanted most to see. You triumphed in a dream as you hadn't been able to triumph waking. And your dream and your triumph were something you made for yourself. They came from nowhere but you—from your heart, your mind, from wherever such things are born. Call it a vision if you want, but you ought to know what it was a vision of. (*SD* 89)

Through Lundrigan, and later through Peter's own doubts, Buechner keeps alive the possibility that Peter saw only what he most longed to see. Like Julie McMoon, who during an innocent game of hide-and-seek has a frightening hallucination in which she thinks she sees her dead husband, Peter may simply be the victim of delusions and myths.

The possibility that faith is a childish longing for fairy tales becomes a consistent theme for Buechner from this novel on through his long career. Buechner's take on faith, beginning to glimmer in *The Seasons' Difference*, is an important pivot point in approaching his work. Twenty years later, in a book of sometimes side-splitting and often stunning definitions, Buechner speaks of the generally pejorative phrase "wishful thinking":

Christianity is mainly wishful thinking. Even the part about Judgment and Hell reflects the wish that somewhere the score is being kept.

Dreams are wishful thinking. Children playing at being grown-up is wishful thinking. Interplanetary travel is wishful thinking.

Sometimes the wishing is the wings the truth comes true on.

Sometimes the truth is what sets us wishing for it. (*WT* 96)

Harry J. Parker, in his unpublished thesis *The Nature of Faith in the Fiction of Frederick Buechner*, underscored the basic lack of certainty in Buechner's conception of faith, noting Buechner's preference for "faith as an experiment which becomes an experience as opposed to a series of doctrines."[15] Parker cited a Kierkegaardian influence here in Buechner's insistence that faith is risk and uncertainty. Whatever the case, we can say with certainty that the seed for Buechner's later conclusions about the essential ambiguity of faith is being sown in his second novel. To skip over *The Seasons' Difference* would be to miss so much that is vintage Buechner: the longing and the near-misses, the hints of a heavenly explanation and the harsh reminders of earthly realities, and the near saint set beside the bumbling fool—both in the same character.

Buechner often gives the last word in his novels to the representatives of realism like Lundrigan. At the close of *A Long Day's Dying*, George Motley hovers in the background unable to participate in whatever vision of life Maroo has reached at her death. In *The Final Beast*, Will Poteat, the man who insists on living in this world and no other, gets the last word, and Richard Lundrigan is the final character we hear about in *The Seasons' Difference*: "Lundrigan continued down his path" (*SD* 303), we are told in the novel's last line. The literal reference, of course, is to Lundrigan's walking away to his car to return to the city and to his normal life. Buechner seems, however, to want to leave a taste of Lundrigan's failure. Lundrigan is not significantly transformed by any of the experiences of the week. He can never quite get in tune with those who gather around the piano to sing long-lost hymns. Later novels will suggest partial redemption for the Lundrigan types, but in this novel Lundrigan is essentially unaltered; he lives on within the walls of his own limitations, acting only upon what he can see and touch.

Most of the other adults, Sara and Sam Dunn and Julie McMoon, stand somewhere between the extremes represented by Peter Cowley and Richard Lundrigan. If a major issue of the novel is the question of what constitutes faith and who is capable of faith, then these three adults are the testing area for Lundrigan's cynicism and Cowley's. Buechner himself seems to be standing beside Sara and Sam and the others, weighing the arguments for unbelief, making a choice. The big moment of the book is, of course, there on the hillside where the adults have gathered to humor Peter and witness his re-created vision. Suddenly the hillside is alive with the surprising appearance of the beautiful Mollie and the sheet-draped children, all of them off in the distance looking for all the world like angels. The sun at their backs, their presence unaccountable, they are momentarily convincing. After she has realized that "it had been only the children" (*SD* 190), Sara gives expression to her conflicted thoughts: "Surely, when the first figure in white appeared, glittering with the sun and all the green and placid beauty of sun through leaves and on grass, the very air soft as a mist with the wonder of it, there had been a moment beyond a child's contriving . . . there had been for the miracle of that instant, more by far than simply a child before them" (*SD* 190–91). Sara is called back, however, to what Lundrigan would call reality. Despite her instinct to prayer—and prayer is all over this book—Sara's maturity returns her to the sad sense that "indeed it could, the hoping heart, be deceived again and again" (*SD* 191). Sam has gone to sleep while kneeling there on the hillside, Julie has refused even to attend, afraid that Peter might be right or wrong—she cannot deal with either possibility—but Lundrigan, who had promised that there would be nothing to see, is momentarily "as moved as any of them" (*SD* 194).

Lundrigan is quick to explain his emotion to himself as owing to the beauty of the late afternoon and the successful trick of the children, but Buechner makes it increasingly clear that Lundrigan envies Peter's capacity for hope. As it turns out, Peter is not, as Lundrigan has prophesied, a lonely little man on a hillside; he is surrounded by the children, by his friends, and, most of all, by his hope. Ironically, it is Lundrigan who is lonely, Lundrigan whose angry joke—"Cowley the love-lost and Christ-bescrewed"—is ignored (*SD* 192). And it is Lundrigan who is drawn, kicking and screaming, to Peter Cowley's hope: "Whereas, Lundrigan admitted, such rational habits of mind as he himself most admired encouraged you to remain prudently within yourself where you tended always to be most alone, a hope like Cowley's, however unreasoning, drew you forward into ardent communion with whatever it was towards which you ardently hoped" (*SD* 195). But Lundrigan rejects the vision, Sara shakes herself free from the happiness it produced, Julie and Sam ignore it by simply not being there in one way or another, and only Thomas Lavender, the children, and Mollie Purdue are left to complete the verdict as to whether "something" happened or, as even Peter begins to suspect, "nothing" happened.

Mollie senses that the re-created vision, and the subsequent dominoes that fall because of it, somehow spoils what this summer retreat ought to be. She knows that "*Something* was not right" (*SD* 172). But Mollie, like almost everyone in this novel, isn't up to the implications of supernatural happenings. She has her own minor miracle in the novel, a moment when a small bird flies out of her shawl. But she doesn't really notice; she hasn't eyes for the possibilities of such a moment. By one report, Mollie leaves the scene "crying her head off" (*SD* 226). Her tears would have meant something, but, as it turns out, the tears were merely in the imagination of one of the children. Lavender, on the other hand, is a believer and then some. Like his later incarnation, Leo Bebb, he believes in "everything."[16] It is Lavender who sees that the drama comes down to a competition between Lundrigan and Cowley—"Between the ways of reason and unreason" (*SD* 262). It is Lavender who sees Lundrigan's defeat and Cowley's victory. But it is this lovely, slightly atilt Lavender who ends up dead, his memory besmirched by a reputation for a mostly harmless insanity. He is a mere clown at best, a dangerous fool at worst and incapable of carrying authoritative weight in the scheme of the novel.

Thus we are left with the children. *The Seasons' Difference* is Buechner's first attempt to write extensively about children, something he will try again in the 1990s with *The Wizard's Tide: A Story*. J. D. Scott in *The New Statesman and Nation* admired the children's portraits in the young novelist's second book, calling them "true and touching."[17] Gregory identified the children as the "true center of interest" in the story (Gregory 9). Of course, the children are remarkable in their innate gracefulness and innocence, and it is childlike innocence that Buechner means them to represent.

To call the children of this novel "true" to any real children is, however, to miss Buechner's purpose. Although no critic seems to want to say so, Buechner mainly misses fire with these strangely adult children. Their positions in the novel are posed, their lines studied and precocious. Clearly, Buechner employs the children to consider the powers and limitations of innocence and wonder. *The Seasons' Difference* is Buechner's attempt to settle religious questions; therefore, he doesn't need real children. The struggle for actual childlike voices adds to the density of the novel and to problems of voice and style. Nonetheless, the children serve well enough as a study of what happens as innocence erodes, spontaneity fails, and wonder disappears. The epigraph of the novel, from *As You Like It*, suggests the green-world escape from all but the passage of time:

> Now, my co-mates and brothers in exile,
> Hath not old custom made this life more sweet
> Than that of painted pomp? Are not these woods
> More free from peril than the envious court?
> Here feel we but the penalty of Adam,
> The seasons' difference.[18]

In a fallen world, even the Eden-like retreat is vulnerable to passing time. The children of *The Seasons' Difference* are emerging into an awareness of time, and through them Buechner considers the dubious possibility of warding off the effects of time's inevitable march.

Stacy Webb Thompson, in her unpublished dissertation, *The Rediscovery of Wonder: A Critical Introduction to the Novels of Frederick Buechner*, argued that the themes of wonder, innocence, and transformation are the central preoccupations of Buechner's work.[19] Such an assertion can, of course, be reductive in encountering the complexity of a body of writing, but Thompson's observations work nicely with *The Seasons' Difference*. Her argument that the novel is a "modern analogue" of Andrew Marvell's "The Garden" is perhaps too strongly stated, but her suggestion that Buechner is like Marvell implicitly referring to the biblical garden of Eden is helpful and essentially correct (Thompson 33).

Buechner's preoccupation with what he calls "the residue of my romance with the seventeenth century" (*SJ* 98) contributes to the cumbersome style of *A Long Day's Dying* and certainly remains visible in *The Seasons' Difference*. Buechner even expresses surprise at the critics' failure to notice the influence of Sir Thomas Browne's writings in *A Long Day's Dying* (*Chronicle* 17). In his second novel, therefore, he makes the influence more explicit through the character of Sam Dunn, who quotes Browne and the metaphysical poets and borrows from Marvell to explain his apparent sleepiness as "a green thought in a green shade" (*SD* 300). Most of this learned allusion is, however, fluff and mannerism. John Aldridge, in his commentary on *A Long Day's Dying*, argued that Buechner had written as if to "fulfill an assignment in a Creative Writing course" (Aldridge 222).

Buechner actually adopts Aldridge's summary in his own statements about the novel to Jean Ross in a 1983 interview where he comments, "In that ancient first novel, begun while I was a senior in college, I was writing in a way for a creative writing class, and I was very much on my best literary behavior in it—trying to get everything right, to show off everything I'd learned, to impress Teacher."[20] Thus Buechner confesses a preoccupation with the fashionable trends in the creative fiction of the era, as well as revealing an interesting interplay between critic and author. His attempts to write the perfect academic novel produce a coldness that largely accounts for the near miss of the first novel. Unfortunately, Aldridge's observation holds true for *The Seasons' Difference* as well. Buechner's literary exhibitionism clutters this second novel just as it clutters *A Long Day's Dying*. The importance of the second novel is, like the first, not stylistic but thematic.

One issue for Buechner in *The Seasons' Difference* is the testing of the ramifications of innocence, whether the allusion be to Marvell's garden, the land of Oz, or the garden of Eden. Sam Dunn knows that the garden of importance is the children themselves and, in an elaborate conceit, observes:

> A child, any child, is a garden, and a garden without a wall. Anything can enter there . . . and anything can depart, quite at will, as long as the wall-lessness lasts: birds and friends, secrets, hates, games, fear, and magic of all sorts—free to come and go as the wind bloweth. But then . . . after a while, not gradually so much as all of a sudden, over the course of a few days even, a wall appears, and then . . . the garden is enclosed. Whatever is there is there to stay. (*SD* 31–32)

The Seasons' Difference, then, is a study of a few days in the lives of some children with an eye to the walls appearing in their lives; it is a look at Peter Cowley's attempts to ignore the walls in his own life, at Thomas Lavender's failure to admit the reality of walls, and at the inevitable contribution to such walls by the flow of circumstance.

Thematically, *A Long Day's Dying* deals with notions of innocence, human fallibility, and the rejection of simple answers to complex human dilemmas. These themes obviously carry over into Buechner's second novel. Another echo from the first novel reverberates in thoughts about teaching, questions about the teacher as corrupter. The teacher is the one who brings sad knowledge to children. "Maybe the teacher's main business is to teach gently the inevitability of pain," Buechner observes in another place (*Belfry* 89). Thomas Lavender understands something of that when he refers to his profession as "raw and lacerating" (*SD* 132). And Richard Lundrigan rants that sad knowledge is just the thing: "I say fetter the tribe with experience beyond their grubby little years, swaddle them with knowledge of the nude and tragic as soon as you can" (*SD* 35). Another of the themes running throughout Buechner's work is precisely this romantic idea that what we call education is a generally destructive, though an inevitable and necessary invasion into innocence. As with many of his contemporaries, Buechner walks his characters through an initiation process that is often downward into complexity and irresolution. This instinct will never quite disappear in Buechner's many novels.

The Seasons' Difference is, most centrally, a homily on the New Testament dictum, "Unless you change and become like children, you will never enter the kingdom of heaven."[21] After all, the kingdom of heaven belongs to the children, and Thomas Lavender actually hauls the biblical line into his debate with the unbelievers.[22] Lavender, the wild-eyed prophet of *The Seasons' Difference*, seems to have lost his mind when he interprets the children's re-creation of Cowley's miracle as a visitation of God.

When Lundrigan disagrees by saying, "It was just the children" (*SD* 197), Lavender responds incredulously:

> *Just* the children! . . . Don't you see, don't you see! . . . A child is a miracle . . . and Peter's miracle was a child. . . . Innocence, innocence, innocence is what he was sent to say, sent mind you, and see! the sky is burning still with the truth of it. The world is too old and too wise. . . . When you know too much, you can't act anymore, because everything is too complicated then. . . . Underneath that crooked old tree a little child stood, and when I saw him I knew there had been a miracle, and I knew what the miracle meant. In that vision of candor and innocence I saw that there is no longer any room for such as you and me and that it is the children who must inherit the earth that they alone are equipped to live in with the simplicity and power to act of Jesus. (*SD* 197–98)

Lavender's voice is not Buechner's voice, of course, but through Lavender's sermon Buechner seems to consider the possibility of children as teachers. Through the character of Lavender, Buechner muses about the world being saved by seeing things "simply again and in innocence" (*SD* 126).

Buechner's ruminations here are reminiscent of those of G. K. Chesterton, who, in "The Ethics of Elfland" from *Orthodoxy*, offered a similar consideration, an image of childhood as the time of greatest spiritual richness and perception, and seems to be just the sort of thing the young novelist, Buechner, is testing in this second novel. In words with which Buechner will find consonance, Chesterton observed, "I left the fairy tales lying on the floor of the nursery, and I have not found any books so sensible since" (Chesterton 104). "We have sinned and grown old, and the Father is younger than we," Chesterton concluded (Chesterton 109). In this view, only the childlike are capable of experiencing the startling delight and wonder of life. Buechner explores this idea in *The Seasons' Difference*, often with lines from Thomas Lavender, who argues that the world is "no longer innocent enough to see things simply," and from Peter, of course, who fears that innocence would be dead in the world if not for children (*SD* 118).

Buechner will continue a preoccupation with these ideas throughout his career. Chesterton even shows up in Buechner's recent study of four writers, *Speak What We Feel (Not What We Ought to Say)*. Placing Chesterton in the company of Hopkins, Twain, and Shakespeare, Buechner underscores a kinship with Chesterton. Using Chesterton's own words about Robert Louis Stevenson, Buechner praises Chesterton's "impatient sanity . . . a shrug of skepticism about skepticism. His real distinction is that he had the sense to see that there is nothing to be done with Nothing."[23] The fact that Buechner's papers rather accidentally landed at Wheaton College, in near proximity to a center devoted to the study of Chesterton, Lewis, Tolkien, and that crowd, may be noted here as copacetic. There's more than a bit of Chesterton banging around in Buechner. Thompson went so far as to argue that wonder is the "most all-inclusive of his themes" (Thompson 21). Whether to label Buechner's preoccupation with innocence and wonder theological or romantic, biblical or Wordsworthian, is to miss his fusion; his vision partakes of both "Blessed are the pure in heart"[24] and "The Child is father of the Man."[25]

Peter Cowley accuses the adults of being incapable of spiritual insight. He scolds the adults who attend the staged visitation: "You saw nothing, and that is what you went to see!" (*SD* 217). Going further, Cowley labels them an "overeducated, ineffectual, faithless pack" (*SD* 218) and concludes:

> You were like Julie, not wanting to know one way or the other whether there really was a God, but you didn't have the strength she did to stay away. Instead you came, and only in your tepid hearts hoped you'd see nothing because life is easier that way, easier not knowing. Sam wasn't the only one because you were all asleep, and if the angel of the Lord had appeared himself with a flaming sword, you'd never have seen him because all you could see was the children, and maybe you thought they were pretty or maybe you didn't, but that was all you saw. You saw nothing, and that very fact meant nothing to you. (*SD* 218–19)

When Lundrigan challenges Peter by asking what the "nothing" should have meant, Peter flashes back that it means "you didn't look far enough" (*SD* 218). Here's the question of having eyes to see—paying attention— that runs all through the Buechner corpus.

We must question, however, if even the children have the spiritual far-sightedness that Peter touts. In the last hymnsing of the novel, the gathered cast sings, "Grant to little children/Visions bright of thee," from the hymn "Now the Day Is Over" (*SD* 278). The children have had their vision, not the one on the hillside so much as the vision of the entire summer retreat: the tension resulting from Cowley's experience, the entrance of the beautiful Mollie into their Eden when they see her posing nude for Sara, the frightful emotion of seeing their re-created vision momentarily believed by the adults, the strange wedding ceremony, and, finally, Lavender's shocking death plunge. The second chapter of *The Seasons' Difference* ends with the ominous observation: "it was already becoming evening in the woods where the children played" (*SD* 24). The double meaning of the line frames nicely with the hymn at the novel's end. "Night is drawing nigh," they sing, and some of the children know the words and are able to sing along (*SD* 277). In varying degrees, walls—complications— have been introduced into their gardens. When Lavender tells Peter that the world can be saved by returning to the innocence of childhood, Peter acknowledges the beauty of the idea, calling it a "lovely parable" (*SD* 127). Objecting, Lavender retorts, "I didn't mean it as a parable" (*SD* 127). Lavender, while sermonizing to the children about the passing of time, admits that change is inevitable but pleads with them to avoid the changes of the heart. He calls them to love only happy things and to shun "things like wisdom and death, like beauty and the past" (*SD* 232). This, for Lavender, is the essence of Christianity, to be like children and thus like Christ, who "knew about . . . complexities, but he was able to see things simply in spite of them and always spoke in the simplest terms" (*SD* 118). Lavender earnestly, fanatically, believes that childlike, Christlike innocence and simplicity can persist in the mundane. "Innocence, simplicity are not dead in the world," he preaches; we must turn to the children to know how to live (*SD* 119).

Lavender's faith in an idealized version of childhood is at the center of Buechner's considerations in *The Seasons' Difference*. Is there some way to go back, to maintain spiritual clarity, to reverse the wearisome effects of maturation, to deny the crushing reality of the seasons and their passing? Lavender's ardent faith may be attractive in the way that saints' lives are compelling. In fact, Buechner's writing career in the early 1980s features

a turn to the fictionalizing of the lives of historical saints. Buechner, ironically, in later years will play the Lavender role for his sophisticated
friends, those who regard his faith as an eccentricity.

In 1952, however, Buechner seems to conclude that Lavender is too
naive—even dangerously simple. Lavender is something like Tristram
Bone of *A Long Day's Dying*, who wanders around the Cloisters trying to
find answers in the symbolism of the tapestries. Paul Steitler brings Tristram up short when he tells him that life is just not so simple. Lavender,
too, has longed for simplicity and straightforward answers. Peter Cowley
best summarizes the final view of Lavender when he speaks his feelings
about his now dead teacher: "I'm not sure but that he wasn't the best and
wisest of us all. Wrong, wrong, but just wrong" (*SD* 281). Lavender, as
Peter finally sees, is wrong because his fanaticism dangerously ignores the
inevitable movement of time. He is wrong because he fails to understand
that the innocence of children is frail, temporary, unstudied, and unavail-
able to thoughtful adults. His wrongness, of course, produces the climactic tragedies of the novel.

The innocence of the children does not save them from the chilling end
of the retreat experience—Lavender's death, Lundrigan's recommitment
to steady cynicism, and the continuing escapism of most of the adults. In
a rather dramatic metaphor, Sara Dunn compares the children to a refrig-
erator that spends the bulk of its time with the door closed, the light off.
The children have had brief power in the novel, a miraculous moment on
a hillside, but they have returned to a semiadult world—an ever-darkening
landscape. As Lundrigan concludes, "Children don't have memories" (*SD*
263). Ellie partially proves Lundrigan's point and represents the thoughts
of the younger children when, in the last few pages of the novel, she thinks
about what it has all meant. She concludes that God must have killed
Lavender for being evil and wonders what her punishment will be for having felt happy about the marriage ceremony (*SD* 290–91). She clearly fails
to gain spiritual wisdom from Lavender's efforts at establishing a new
community based on innocence and simplicity. A light has briefly flick-
ered and darkness has returned.

The older children, Rufus and Harry, likewise reveal Lavender's failure.
Rufus and Harry are fourteen, at least three years older than any of the
other children. They are "different from the other children, but they were
very much like each other" (*SD* 18). Rufus and Harry write poetry, display
cleverness in Cowley's classroom, and spend their passing summer evalu-
ating and scrutinizing "the Persons" around them. These two precocious
adolescents have found an alliance that again alludes to Buechner's own

enduring friendship with James Merrill, the "J.I.M." to whom *The Seasons' Difference* is dedicated. Merrill and Buechner are the original Uglies, of course. The "Uglies" of *The Seasons' Difference* refers not so much to Rufus and Harry's respective physical endowments as to the central reality of their ripening years—loneliness. In defining their union, the two friends speak of Uglies as essentially isolated people who "reveal their true identity in the dark" (*SD* 50). The carnival outing gives important insight into the characters of the two older children; it is a trip deeply significant for Rufus and Harry and, unbeknownst to them, to Peter Cowley as well. While watching the obscene show at the freak's tent, Cowley thinks about one of the games the children play, Statues. The requirement of the game is to hold, as long as possible, the physical position into which you have been thrown by one of the other players. In order to win the game, one must hold the position—no matter how grotesque or uncomfortable or painful. Cowley thinks of the carnival sideshow in terms of the children's game: "It was possible for him to imagine the freaks too as having been flung forward once, albeit by a graver hand, as part of an older ritual, to flounder earthwards and be at last confronted with an even more inescapable obligation than the children's of holding the attitude, however extreme, into which they had fallen" (*SD* 62–63). Rufus and Harry joke about the freak show as the place where they most belong, and Peter Cowley, independently, reaches something of the same conclusion. Although he will eventually come to see even the freak show as "poignant and beautiful" (*SD* 62), he also holds the contrary thought of the ugliness of it all: "the ugly isolation of these creatures from one another; from a diffident humanity; from all, like life itself, that was godly too" (*SD* 63).

The carnival side show where Uglies stare at freaks and vice versa, one imagines, bespeaks Buechner's fascination with freaks. He expresses the interest in his appreciation for Diane Arbus's photography and in his reading of Flannery O'Connor's stories, which he regards as essentially discussions of freakishness.[26] Buechner avoids O'Connor's work until the mid-1980s, for fear that he might find her work too similar to his own and thus threatening. When he finally reads his first O'Connor story, Buechner discovers that O'Connor is "no threat . . . because her corner of the territory was one that no other writer in Christendom . . . could possibly work."[27] So taken with her work that he makes a pilgrimage to Milledgeville, Georgia, O'Connor's home, Buechner ultimately writes a preface for a book on O'Connor where he homes in on O'Connor's gift: "I suppose it is precisely because she has a mystic's sense of what holiness truly is that she is able to depict in such a wry and sometimes uproarious way the freakish distortions that it suffers at the hands of a mad world" (*Belfry* 69). O'Connor saw the freak as "a figure for our essential displacement."[28] That is, the freakish becomes a metaphor for all that is missing in each of us. Some thirty years before he gets to O'Connor, Buechner has arrived at an understanding of the principle that guides her work—humans in need of some sort of saving. It is in 1952 that the Catholic O'Connor publishes her first novel, *Wise Blood*. She was twenty-seven. That same year, the incipient believer, Buechner, at twenty-six, sees the publication of *The Seasons' Difference*. And maybe they do work the same field more than Buechner wants to admit.

Moreover, Peter Cowley's ambivalence at the freak show acts as a microcosm of his character throughout the novel—a wrenching combination of realist and idealist, cynic and dreamer. Rufus and Harry, on their way to adulthood, find a communion with the freaks and a reminder that the Uglies number more than two. Peter Cowley, in the same way, adds one more picture to his understanding of the vast tapestry of life. He sees his neediness in the scheme of things, and the entire novel may be viewed as Buechner's amen to Cowley's longing. The young writer is here acknowledging, in fictional clothing, his own need, his continuing ugliness.

Ugliness as a synecdoche for the estrangement of human beings from one another and from spiritual power operates thematically throughout *The Seasons' Difference*. Lavender speaks of ugliness as a human reality when he argues, "Each one of us is a child buried alive, and that is ugly" (*SD* 110). Rufus and Harry realize rejection is a part of ugliness when they describe Uglies as people who fall in love but are "never fallen in love with" (*SD* 146). They form their alliance on the basis of having increasingly encountered the hostility and loneliness of the grown-ups' world. They are, as they label themselves, poets who expect only "sadness" and isolation from their fellows—"how alone, how wise" (*SD* 241–42).

The Uglies, Rufus and Harry, are characters in transition. They represent a stage of life somewhere between the younger children and the almost-adult Mollie. In their awkward jostling toward maturity, they illustrate the gradual loss of spontaneous joyfulness and wondrous expectation. But, as they finally learn, everybody is an Ugly; everybody is debilitated by loneliness and incompleteness. The climactic message of the passing summer for Rufus and Harry occurs in the moment they realize that almost everyone is abandoned and ugly. "An Ugly," Rufus finally muses, "is somebody who knows" (*SD* 297). What the Uglies know is sadness and misconnection, and the two boys come to see that Thomas Lavender and Peter Cowley and even the other adults may be, in one way or another, Uglies too. Thus ugliness becomes another motif through which Buechner ponders the loss of innocence and another reminder of Buechner's consonance with the literary stream of his 1950s generation.

Sara's model, Mollie Perdue, offers another version of innocence in *The Seasons' Difference*. The key to Mollie is her profession. As a model she is an actress. Posing for Sara, she has learned to take on a variety of roles. As she describes it, "I've got the knack somehow of looking like whoever I'm supposed to look like" (*SD* 207). For example, when the children plot with her to stage a version of Peter's hillside experience, they assign her the chief part—that of an extraordinary angel. Posing for Sara's sculpture, *Abundance*, Mollie is a "mother-nature type" (*SD* 207). To the young spies, Rufus and Harry, who see her in one of the posing sessions, her nudity is the fulfillment of all of their adolescent fantasies of womanhood, and Mollie becomes the object of Rufus's first love—poignant and painful—a familiar story masterfully captured in Buechner's prose. In this last role she contributes to the sexual curiosity of the children and represents the further encroachment of adult complications in their lives. She is, then, prelapsarian Eve in all aspects—maternal, angelic, and sensuous. It is, however, her participation in the children's charade that produces the deepest amazement among the little vacationing community.

When Mollie assumes the mantle of innocence, she becomes precisely what Thomas Lavender has recommended for all of the adults. Mollie recognizes that, for a brief moment, the adults had seen her "as a holy saint or as an angel" (*SD* 208). Awestruck by such an idea, Mollie whispers, "for a while—that's what I was" (*SD* 208). The re-created vision, we are reminded, almost works: "No longer would it have been possible, looking at them however searchingly from without, to have distinguished between their separate attitudes of hope, alarm, or disbelief, for these had all been erased by, and generalized into, one common attitude of profound wonder" (*SD* 185–86). This transient moment of mystical insight and spiritual wonder, the possibility of the miraculous, is the first instance of what will become a preoccupation in Buechner's career.

Among the abundant examples of this aching for the extraordinary in Buechner's work, I remember his words in a letter to his grandson Benjamin, words to be read at Benjamin's twenty-first birthday party in August of 2015, which Buechner includes in *The Longing for Home*:

> We search for a good self to be and for good work to do. We search to become human in a world that tempts us always to be less than human or looks to us to be more. We search to love and be loved. And in a world where it is often hard to believe in much of anything, we search

to believe in something holy and beautiful and life-transcending that will give meaning and purpose to the lives we live.[29]

The letter powerfully summarizes much about Buechner's life and work, but the nod toward the possibility of transcendence is a pulsing beat at the core of Buechner's literary efforts.

Thomas Lavender wants to believe in transcendence and almost brings it off. Mollie Purdue also points to the possibility of the miraculous but is finally unable to achieve it in more than an ambiguous, temporary way. Shortly after the chaotic collapse of the charade, Mollie flees the retreat—partly in shame, perhaps, and partly in confusion. Before she leaves, she summarizes her involvement in Peter's dream:

> We were awful to do it maybe, and maybe I was the most awful of all. But it was almost *beautiful*, and I didn't even mind when Georgie messed things up by spinning too long and nobody could hear him. So could it be awful and beautiful both? Anyway it wasn't what Colley came to see. A vision, didn't you say, and that he really believed in it? And it was only us. Maybe if we hadn't've been there, he'd've gotten what he wanted. And maybe. . . . But this is so queer I can hardly say it. I told you I prayed that he'd get whatever he wanted, maybe he did. Maybe we were it! (*SD* 209)

Mollie asks Harry if, for at least a moment, they might not have been "more than just ourselves" (*SD* 209). Maybe there was a miracle.

Mollie, therefore, is crucial to Buechner's themes in *The Seasons' Difference*, because she is a further test of the possibilities of innocence. In terms of chronological age and temperament, Mollie is somewhere between the children and the adults. When she parodies angelic innocence in the staged vision, she almost succeeds in producing faith in herself and others. She is desperately torn between the beauty of the experience and its wrongness. When she concludes that she and the children may have been the vision Cowley so intensely sought, she repeats the word "maybe" seven times. The poised ambiguity of faith and doubt in complex mixture becomes one of Buechner's first and most enduring theological themes, his calling card for years to come. A few years later, under the tutelage of Paul Tillich at Union Theological Seminary, Buechner will find solace in Tillich's contention that doubt and faith are not opposites but are, in fact, inextricably linked. Even in this preconversion, preordination novel, *The Seasons' Difference*, Buechner explores the possibility of faith operating within doubt, somehow already prepared for Tillich's theories to come.

The issue of this novel is then more than what Thompson labels "wonder." Although Buechner is certainly intrigued by the realms of remarkable experience, the central territory of the novel is the parameters of faith. In the years following *The Seasons' Difference*, the mixture of faith and doubt in Buechner's work will coalesce around his choice of the New Testament plea, "I believe; help my unbelief,"[30] as the pivotal sentence in his own quest for faith. In his whimsical theological potpourri, Buechner concludes, "Faith can't prove a damned thing. Or a blessed thing either" (*WT* 26). He continues throughout his work to insist that "logic and plausibility are not at the heart of the matter."[31] Even in his most recent work of memoir, where he is more expressive of faith than ever before, Buechner still hedges. "I hope that it is true about God," he writes from under the weight of sadness at the death of his brother, James (*EH* 167). The mystery persists, though Buechner now confesses that it is "deeper and grander" than he has heretofore imagined (*EH* 174). One might argue that Buechner is well on his way to just such a confession in *The Seasons' Difference* as he explores the possibility that God occupies the dark gap created by our doubt.

Almost everything to come in Buechner's writing is visible as early as 1952. His style will loosen along with his tongue, but the central issues have already been posed. Something of Augustinian restlessness joins a Kierkegaardian embracing of uncertainty to produce a wishful thinking that will flower enormously in later work. As early as his second novel, Buechner is wishing for truth, longing for a way to balance unbelief and belief. Horton Davies argued that in *The Seasons' Difference* "Buechner had already envisaged all the problems involved in being a Christian apologist, even before he was ordained" (HDavies 188). At the very least we can conclude that the possibility of faith is bubbling in the longing of young Peter Cowley. Further, as Nancy Myers noted, Buechner betrays, even before his ordination, a preoccupation with the "problems that would be involved in reaching contemporary man with any kind of message that smacks of traditional religion" (Myers 36). At twenty-six, the young novelist has already touched the essential dilemma that will frame his career.

Peter Cowley, the chief character of *The Seasons' Difference*, becomes, after all, a harbinger of later Buechner heroes—Theodore Nicolet of *The Final Beast*, Leo Bebb of the *Bebb* tetralogy, and the inimitable Godric of the 1980 novel. Peter is a "magician" (*SD* 19), "a real comedian" (*SD* 242), "a celestial Ziegfeld" (*SD* 260). He combines something of the madman, the child, and the saint. Given Peter's age (around thirty) and his crusade to reform the spiritual lives of his friends, one might easily conclude that Buechner is setting up certain connections to Christ. Undoubtedly those around Peter are drawn to his hope, fall under the spell of his powerful wishful thinking. The spiritual thirst of the young author, Frederick Buechner, is on display in the questing Peter Cowley, who has had, he believes, a sign from God and desperately wants another. Confessing his doubt on the hillside where he has gathered his congregation for the re-creation, Peter prays: "I have doubted my understanding [of the vision], and I have been made by others to doubt it in ways I could never by myself have invented, but you were pleased to let me continue, despite all of this, in the conviction that I was right in what I felt my vision meant, and, believing that still, I have returned today. Let me be certain that I am not wrong" (*SD* 184). Peter wants certainty—a miraculous endorsement of his trembling conviction.

He gets, instead, a staged vision that is and is not a divine demonstration. He gets ambiguity. In Peter's concluding thoughts about his extraordinary experience and his thoughts about his personal future, Buechner sets a direction for almost everything that will follow in his literary career. Addressing the question of what he has learned, Peter summarizes:

> I believe . . . that there aren't going to be any miracles because ours is a world where they'd probably do more harm than good, where we just can't expect them to happen any more except, as if the Lord couldn't quite resist them completely, maybe once in a while when there's nobody around but some poor fool like me, some lucky, lonely fool who's not going to convince anybody. . . . But whatever my feelings used to be, I no longer believe—and that's what I had to look a lot farther to see—that miracles are our only hope or even our hope at all. What we've got already is enough. (*SD* 220–21)

Peter concludes that we do not need the extraordinary, because we have "the words and example of Christ" (*SD* 221). Buechner opens his dialogue with orthodox Christianity with these words; although Peter Cowley never arrives at a definitively Christian position, the idea is clearly under consideration for Buechner. Peter finally comes to a celebration of the "joyous possibility" of life itself (*SD* 62).

In the year following the publication of *The Seasons' Difference*, Buechner, for the first time in his life, begins to attend church. Late in 1953 he publicly proclaims himself a Christian, and in the fall of 1954 he begins his tenure as a student at Union Theological Seminary. Those critics who divide Buechner's career into "pre-Christian" and "post-Christian" phases too readily ignore the exploration of Christian ideas in the early work. To claim that Buechner was a modern novelist who, after a conversion experience, began to write Christian novels is to miss the complexity of the forces at work as early as 1952. *The Seasons' Difference*, though not in any sense a statement of orthodox Christian theology, is certainly a statement of the search for faith. The novel is the first clear summary of what John Gardner in *On Moral Fiction* called Buechner's attempt to find "a personal understanding of the orthodox answers."[32] This is not to say that the central business of *The Seasons' Difference* is the communication of a Christian message, although Gardner did want to paint Buechner with that worn brush. Myers also went too far in her assertion that the novel "deals with the problem of making the basic tenets of Christianity viable to a secular world" (Myers 34). Buechner is not yet ready for "basic tenets."

Peter Cowley comes to terms with his need for the miraculous by realizing what he really needs is a new way of seeing ordinary, commonplace reality. Buechner clings to this theme of the miraculous in the ordinary throughout his published writings and interviews, sometimes via reference to personal events that he regards as beyond ordinary and often through his reactions to biblical narratives. In a meditation on the Emmaus road events from Luke's Gospel, for example, Buechner concludes that Christ, if present anywhere, is present in "the midst":

> Jesus is apt to come . . . into the very midst of life at its most real and inescapable. Not in a blaze of unearthly light, not in the midst of a sermon, not in the throes of some kind of religious daydream, but . . . at supper time, or walking along a road. . . . He never approached from on high, but always in the midst, in the midst of people, in the midst of real life and the questions that real life asks. . . . The sacred moments, the moments of miracle, are often the everyday moments. (*MD* 87)

He further suggests in *The Alphabet of Grace* that "once in a while there is the suggestion of purpose, meaning, direction, the suggestion of plot, the suggestion that, however clumsily, your life is trying to tell you something, take you somewhere" (*Alphabet* 10). The essence of Buechner's faith, the longing for "a hint of melody," as he expresses it in *The Alphabet of Grace*, is in the formative stages in *The Seasons' Difference* (*Alphabet* 10). He believes that we "catch glimmers at least of what the saints are blinded by," and we must "go on as though something *has* happened even though we are not sure what it was or just where we are supposed to go with it" (*Alphabet* 76).

Going on through uncertainty is precisely the dilemma of Peter Cowley. He faces the decision of whether or not to act upon the dubious vision, and his Kierkegaardian commitment to try to act in spite of doubt is almost exactly the path Buechner will follow in the months after the publication of *The Seasons' Difference*. Peter's experience and his reaction to it lie at the heart of Buechner's career as a novelist. As he summarizes in a 1980 interview:

> It's sort of a continuing dim spectacle of the subterranean presence of the grace in the world that haunts me. If you look deeply enough into yourself or into the *New York Times*, there are many mysteries. And the mystery of the mysteries at the bottom of the well, at the far reach of the road, is the mystery of God, of Christ. This is what I explore as a novelist—the incredibleness of it, the spectrum of it. It seems as if maybe it isn't true . . . but, yes, maybe it is true! And the moments when it seems to be true are just staggering moments. (*WDoor* 18)

These conclusions of the older novelist and preacher can actually be seen in their budding stages in Peter Cowley. Peter plods on, despite deep awareness of his own doubt and inadequacy, despite a clear knowledge of the ambiguity in all of life—in the beauty and ugliness of the freak show, in the possibility and falsity of the vision, in the foolishness and wisdom of the quixotic Thomas Lavender, in the wonder and dullness of the children, in the comedy and tragedy that is life.

Although tragedy is plentiful in *The Seasons' Difference*, an unmistakable humor breaks in here, too—a harbinger of the Bebbish laughter to come. Rufus and Harry give Buechner space to work in the personal adventures of Jimmy and Freddy, the Huck-and-Tom sort of stories on which Buechner will elaborate in the memoirs. In the imagination and wit of the Uglies, readers get an early glimpse of Jimmy and Freddy taking on the bully in the Jigger Shop across the road from Lawrenceville School, a raucous story from *The Sacred Journey*, and another snapshot of the fledgling young writers recovering a typewriter from a flustered repairman, an anecdote from the Maine summer of 1948, recounted in *The Eyes of the Heart*. The laughter is not loosed yet; it is nonetheless beginning to brim up from somewhere deep within the young novelist.

Finally, however, it would be an enormous mistake to attempt to claim *The Seasons' Difference* as a "Christian novel." Myers's conclusion that in "*The Seasons' Difference* Buechner very tentatively offers the ways of God to secular man" works only if the emphasis is placed on "very tentatively" (Myers 52). Buechner is no Christian apologist, certainly not in these early days of his career, and maybe never. *The Seasons' Difference* is, instead, the work of an artist steeped in the conventions and conclusions of the modern novel. In this respect, the second novel is not so far from the first. Cowley's contention that the world is "sad," and his metaphorical observation that the "sad world" is like a failed party are never withdrawn. Cowley decides, "It was like a party . . . where, although no one was really enjoying himself, no one would quite say it was not a *good* party. And this was very sad" (*SD* 129). The novel is a thoroughly modern consideration of a spiritual alternative that fails to reach any settled position.

Even though Peter's world-weary pose is not entirely convincing, the outlook of *The Seasons' Difference* is indeed bleak. In the words of the hymn running through the final pages of the novel, we are reminded of the suffering of little children and the pain of watching them navigate the tempestuous shoals of experience. In the lives of Sara and the other adults, we are reminded that wonder and attentiveness, hope and passion, produce pain and suffering for the most part. We are left with overwhelming indecision and rejection—Richard Lundrigan's restored cynicism, Julie McMoon's flight, Mollie's confusion, the Dunns' attempt to forget. And we are left with death—Thomas Lavender's fall from the treehouse, reminiscent of Piggy's plummet in Golding's *The Lord of the Flies*, a book that appears almost at the same time as Buechner's, another book that offered a grim story of the death of innocence in terms far less subtle than those Buechner employs. Everything is, for Buechner, complicated, mixed, cloudy, and unresolved.

The overall power of *The Seasons' Difference*, despite its straining after style, is in the balancing of the dark vision of the debilitating results of time's march against the glimmering hopefulness of young Peter Cowley. The balance is modern in its ambiguity, of course, but is a shift from *A Long Day's Dying*. The darkness of *The Seasons' Difference* is visible even in the epigraph that speaks of the passage of time as a "penalty" for humanity (*SD* 1). The actual time frame of the novel is a mere eight days, probably an allusion to the traditional signification of completeness, the beginning of "ever after," a motif that Buechner will use in the opening volume of his own story, *The Sacred Journey*. The action of *The Seasons' Difference* is bracketed by reference to Georgie Bundle's fishing experience at the beginning and his thoughts about another fishing excursion at the end.

Lest we conclude that the return to fishing suggests total stasis or inconsequence, Buechner reminds us that the events of those days have had at least a hint of an effect. Lundrigan, taking his leave of the summer place, looks one last time at the children, "incongruously alive among all that wealth of foliage and dappled light, a part now of something else— of the city perhaps, of another season" (*SD* 298). Peter Cowley has "affected their lives" (*SD* 262). He has "set them thinking" (*SD* 262). None of the children or the adults can ever be completely as they were before this vacation.

Sara plans a picnic to try to "clear the air" and return things to "normalcy" (*SD* 265), but nothing works to reverse the ringing effects Peter, the magician, has inspired. During the singing of "Now the Day Is Over" at the end of the novel, Sara breathes a silent prayer for the assembled group: "Bless them, bless them all" (*SD* 278). The love she feels for the group has its source in Peter Cowley's example. Peter, as Sam finally realizes, has taught them to love, to suffer, and to laugh. He has, for a moment at least, shocked these sophisticated adults and their children into a flickering insight. Maybe the day is not over. By doing something so out of the ordinary, Peter has elicited what Rufus and Harry think of as "authentic responses" (*SD* 243). With the novel, Buechner seems to want to shock his readers into an authentic response, and this is certainly one of the ways in which Buechner is like his contemporary, Flannery O'Connor, who recommended distortion as a means, not to destruction, but to revelation (O'Connor 162).

Finally, *The Seasons' Difference* is Peter Cowley's, if not Buechner's, statement of faith. The ravages of time are certain and unrelieved, but fairy tales may be true as well. Sam warns Peter not to take the supposed vision so seriously:

> It's only in a fairy tale, . . . only in a story written for children, that you can trust life . . . where you're told and can be certain that if a particular thing happens or does not happen, all will be well. . . . But in the real world . . . you can't help but realize that no such promise is made. . . . In real life, Peter, you not only have to kill the dragon and set the princess free, but you may have to set a hundred other and less innocent things free too, and imprison as many more; you may have to kill more than one dragon, maybe thirteen, maybe even yourself, and even then, when you've done all of this, done it nobly and well, the whole situation may have changed. Then you may discover that all you've done was not only unnecessary but sometimes even

worse than that, sometimes even as wrong and harmful as you
thought it was right and good. (*SD* 116–17)

Such words, though spoken by Sam the sleeper, work to summarize the
tentative lessons Peter absorbs. He learns, through Lavender's death and
through personal failure, the awful dangers of rampant idealism, but he
remains God-haunted and spiritually homesick throughout the story.

Sara has warned Peter that she and the others do not want to be converted; they would "rather not know," she tells him (*SD* 175). Nonetheless, each person is caught up, one way or another, in Peter's quest.
Buechner remains a modern novelist, but the label must be qualified
somewhat after the publication of *The Seasons' Difference*. Buechner summarizes his first two novels in a 1981 interview with Marie-Helene Davies:
"*A Long Day's Dying* . . . sprang from the young man's disgust at the emptiness of the lives of most of those he had met in the society of the rich. *The
Seasons' Difference* was looking for a way out of despair" (Davies 66). Thus
Buechner's second novel looms large in his development as a writer and
as a believer.

Buechner's 1952 work does not yet meet Martin Turnell's definition of
the "truly Christian work of literature"—a work where "the writer's whole
outlook is informed by his beliefs."[33] Buechner never will do the kind of
writing suggested by Turnell. But what Buechner begins here is a preoccupation that will alter the course of his life personally and professionally.
Unsure of himself after the irresolution and hints of *The Seasons' Difference*, Buechner will try again to be the novelist his critics had expected.
The Return of Ansel Gibbs marks his effort to reestablish the promise of *A
Long Day's Dying* and to treat, for the first time, contemporary social
issues. But the issue of faith, the thematic center of *The Seasons' Difference*,
will reappear to push him toward the writing of fiction that distinctively
speaks a growing commitment to the experiment of Christian faith.

At the end of his second novel, Frederick Buechner does indeed seem
to be pondering the possibility of peering behind the curtain with which
his peers have cloaked faith. Upon learning that he and Sara and those of
their society are to be Peter's audience as he goes forward, Sam warns
Peter about what he can anticipate. Sam's cynical words can be read as
Buechner's caution to himself:

Well, I can only praise your valiance. You won't find us easy. . . . The
first time you say anything, even the glittering truth itself, so that it
sounds however remotely like a cliché, you'll lose half of us because

that's an indelicacy we can't forgive. And as soon as you start trying to appeal to our—what do they call them?—our *emotions*, you'll find the other has gone also because that's a breach of taste they simply won't be able to abide. And if we can commit a sin against arithmetic to the extent of picturing a third half, you'll have sent them packing after you've begun to speak of either the rewards of following, or the punishments of not following, your word, His word, if you prefer. (*SD* 282)

When they turn to song again in the final pages, Lundrigan tries his "crutch" for "cross" joke but gets no laugh, "no one of them attentive enough to have noticed the substitution" (*SD* 284). Does this mean Lundrigan loses? Or does it mean that the dangerous sleep of spiritual death has won the day? Something of both, perhaps. And when, at the end, Sam asks, "What will you do, Peter, when the summer's over . . . ?" (*SD* 281), one can almost hear the question, "What will you do, Fred?"

Notes

1. *New Yorker*, January 5, 1952, 73.
2. *Atlantic*, February 1952, 84–85.
3. Tangye Lean, "Fiction," *Spectator*, July 25, 1952, 142.
4. Francis Bickley, "A Second and Two Firsts," *Punch*, August 13, 1952, 241.
5. Caspar W. Weinberger, "Reviews of Six Recent Novels," *San Francisco Chronicle*, January 13, 1952, 17. Hereafter cited as *Chronicle*.
6. Horace Gregory, "Promise, Not Fulfillment," *New York Herald Tribune Book Review*, January 13, 1952, 9. Hereafter cited as Gregory.
7. Frederick Buechner, *The Seasons' Difference* (New York: Alfred A. Knopf, 1952), 260. Hereafter cited as *SD*.
8. George Miles, "Books," *Commonweal*, January 18, 1952, 379. Hereafter cited as Miles.
9. Robert Phelps, "Fiction Parade," *New Republic*, February 18, 1952, 21.
10. H. L. Roth, "Fiction," *Library Journal*, January 1, 1952, 48.
11. Robert Lowry, "The Vision on the Hill," *New York Times*, January 6, 1952, 4. Hereafter cited as Lowry.
12. *Antioch Review* 12 (1952): 238.
13. *Time*, January 7, 1952, 90–91. Hereafter cited as *Time* Review.
14. Personal correspondence, April 4, 1991.
15. Harry J. Parker, "The Nature of Faith in the Fiction of Frederick Buechner, 1965–1979" (thesis, Princeton University, 1980), 5. Hereafter cited as Parker.
16. Frederick Buechner, *The Book of Bebb* (New York: Atheneum, 1979), 143. Hereafter cited as *Bebb*.
17. J. D. Scott, "New Novels," *New Statesman and Nation*, August 23, 1952.
18. William Shakespeare, *As You Like It*, II, i, 1–6.
19. Stacy Webb Thompson, "The Rediscovery of Wonder: A Critical Introduction to the Novels of Frederick Buechner" (dissertation, Michigan State University, 1979), 2. Hereafter cited as Thompson.

20. Jean W. Ross, *Contemporary Authors*, ed. Ann Evory and Linda Metzger (Detroit: Gale Research Co., 1984), 107.
21. Matthew 18:3.
22. Matthew 19:4.
23. Frederick Buechner, *Speak What We Feel (Not What We Ought to Say)* (San Francisco: HarperSanFrancisco, 2001), 119. Hereafter cited as *Speak*.
24. Matthew 5:8.
25. William Wordsworth, "Ode: Intimations of Immortality from Recollections of Early Childhood," in *English Romantic Writers*, ed. David Perkins (New York: Harcourt, Brace, & World, 1967), 280.
26. Personal correspondence, June 26, 1986.
27. Frederick Buechner, *The Clown in the Belfry: Writings on Faith and Fiction* (San Francisco: HarperSanFrancisco, 1992), 68. Hereafter cited as *Belfry*.
28. Flannery O'Connor, *Flannery O'Connor: Mystery and Manners*, ed. Sally and Robert Fitzgerald (New York: Farrar, Straus & Giroux, 1961), 46. Hereafter cited as O'Connor.
29. Frederick Buechner, *The Longing for Home: Recollections and Reflections* (San Francisco: HarperSanFrancisco, 1996), 66–67. Hereafter cited as *Longing*. This is the fourth of Buechner's memoir volumes.
30. Mark 9:24.
31. Frederick Buechner, *Whistling in the Dark: An ABC Theologized* (San Francisco: Harper & Row, 1988), 12. Hereafter cited as *Whistling*.
32. John Gardner, *On Moral Fiction* (New York: Basic Books, 1978), 99. Hereafter cited as Gardner.
33. Martin Turnell, *Modern Literature and Christian Faith* (London: Darton, Longman & Todd, 1961), 2.

Chapter Three

Searching for a Self

The Return of Ansel Gibbs

L ong suspicious of those critical approaches that are fond of dividing
writers' careers into phases and stages—discrete, easily handled
chunks—I say, "Too easy by half." In this look at Frederick Buechner and
his books, I have tried to avoid the diminishment and destruction that
comes from parsing the career into neat categories. The cacophony of
impulses, vacillations, and rendings; the points of ease and moments of
tension; the fits and starts that mingle to make up a life and a body of work
are often blurred by tidy compartmentalization. Frederick Buechner's
life's work serves as a case in point. For example, Marie-Helene Davies
contended that Buechner's fourth novel, *The Final Beast*, is "the first" of
his "religious novels" (Davies 3). Her argument posits a moment of conversion, a movement from a first career to a second. In point of fact, Christianity bubbles throughout Buechner's preconversion novels and the
testing of faith affirmations continues in the postconversion work.

Although Buechner is popularly viewed as a converted novelist—someone who passes from a pre-Christian to a definitively Christian stance—
his early work reveals no easily traced progression to faith. Instead, we
overhear a writer in dialogue with himself on issues of religious belief. We
witness a relentless questioning, a remarkable search. Buechner's work
refuses to yield up a moment where the secular ends and the sacred begins,
and his third novel, *The Return of Ansel Gibbs*, continues in the stream of
the first two novels, mulling over religious questions, considering faith in
a world of moral ambiguity and complexity.

Buechner actually countenances no moment of conversion, only
what he calls "a slow, obscure process" (*NT* 4–5), and his career reflects
the dim process throughout. His view of history partakes of the German

71

Heilsgeschichte—sacred history or "salvation history." During his years at Union Theological Seminary, the middle years of the 1950s, Buechner's personal religious philosophy was deeply influenced by the neo-orthodox theological position, and he became familiar with such theologians as Reinhold Niebuhr and Karl Barth. From these thinkers Buechner developed an idea of God's historical presence in the history of individual lives, the possibility of pattern that he unsystematically explores in *The Seasons' Difference*, where Peter Cowley problematically tries to decipher God's message.

In 1982 Buechner will dub the first of his memoirs *The Sacred Journey*, and there he more than suggests that God speaks in human lives, even if the divine voice is faint and frequently indecipherable. In his autobiographical work Buechner looks back at his early years as a writer to reflect on how all of the voices of his life were combining to lead him to a specific spiritual commitment. Buechner uses the word "theology" in the first sentence of the first memoir (*SJ* 1). He seems to be talking about epistemology, a theory of human knowledge, how we know what we know and what the knowledge will do for us. He concludes that the writing of fiction is theological in that the writer, like the theologian,

> is examining as honestly as he can the rough-and-tumble of his own experience with all its ups and downs, its mysteries and loose ends, and expressing in logical, abstract terms the truth about human life and about God that he believes he has found implicit there. . . . if God speaks to us at all in this world, if God speaks anywhere, it is into our personal lives that he speaks. (*SJ* 1)

The "if" is important here, of course, and Buechner will persist with the subject throughout his career, a half-century wrangle over the possibility of divine involvement in human experience. Those who speak of Buechner's theological positions must consider the fundamental "if" floating there. The intermittent voice of God is the thematic center of the 1976 Lyman Beecher Lectures, which become *Telling the Truth: The Gospel in Tragedy, Comedy and Fairy Tale*, and of the memoirs. Listening for the divine voice is a controlling motif in all of Buechner's work and is at least part of what is at work in his third novel, *The Return of Ansel Gibbs*. Buechner continues his search for the meaning behind his experiences as a way to find God and, most certainly, as a way to find himself.

I have argued repeatedly in these pages that Buechner is an autobiographical novelist, that he is using the landscape of his own days and the drama of his personal questions as the very warp and woof of the fiction. Now it is time to confess: Buechner disagrees. In a 1981 interview with Shirley and Rudy Nelson, Buechner argues that he has not made much use of his own life in his fiction, except, he quips, in his "fantasy life."[1] He does go on to admit at least two thickly autobiographical passages—Nicolet's conversion in *The Final Beast* and Kuykendall, the preacher-professor from *The Return of Ansel Gibbs*—as each emerging from direct, personal experience. But no more? Our impasse on the significance of autobiography can be negotiated only via a recognition of Buechner's instinct to privacy—he is remarkably protective of the personal stories of his family and friends, for example, so he is quick to distance himself from the fiction. That's the easy answer.

The more thorny approach recognizes the mysterious business of writing novels. Is it too much to suggest that Buechner himself may not be completely sure where they come from? In an essay, "The Opening of Veins," Buechner asserts that "the only books worth reading are books written in blood" (*Belfry* 77). In *The Longing for Home*, he owns up to the possibility that his entire career has been a search for home, an attempt to fill that something missing in himself. He describes the process in that book as "simply letting an empty place open up inside myself and waiting for something to fill it" (*Longing* 22). In *The Eyes of the Heart* he claims that his method is "simply sitting back and listening to what they [his characters] were saying and watching to see what they would do next" (*EH* 84).

Buechner's novels are autobiographical in the deepest ways, not necessarily in their correlation to the actual circumstances of his life. He hints at such an understanding here and there. In an interview with Harold Fickett, for example, Buechner took a characteristic shot at *The Seasons' Difference*, calling it a "dreadful book" but then nodding toward the book's "overt" approach to a religious subject. He concluded: "I think, looking back, that there were also deeper reasons for my choice of subject. It was a kind of foreshadowing, in which perhaps I was telling myself, subconsciously, what I wanted to be about" (*Image* 55). Surely words like "foreshadowing" and references to the "subconscious" open the door to the suggestion that Buechner's work may be more autobiographical than even he knows. Victoria Allen was the one critic to underscore such a proposition: "Buechner has stated that his fiction comes from the same place dreams come from, and the underlying basis of the novel [*The Return of Ansel Gibbs*] reflects the author's pain [over his father's suicide] although he claimed it was not autobiographical" (Allen 64). Buechner's reluctance to acknowledge the connection speaks to his understanding of the complex business of tracking fact in fiction, sorting out the autobiography from the imagined story. Nonetheless, certain autobiographical passes are hard to miss in *The Return of Ansel Gibbs*.

The year following the publication of *The Seasons' Difference*, 1953, Buechner writes "The Tiger," which appeared in *The New Yorker* and was the winner of the 1955 O. Henry Memorial Award. "The Tiger," Buechner's only published short story, was written, he admits, "because *The New Yorker* printed a very bad review of one of my early books."[2] So Buechner writes the story as an exercise to prove he can write to *New Yorker* specifications, but there is more in the story than mere posing. The young hero of the Fitzgerald-like story is a man who returns to his alma mater, Princeton, to perform in the role of the tiger mascot at a football game. Slightly drunk and aware of the incongruity of the tradition that has passed from the years when real tigers were taken to games to the current practice of ludicrously outfitting a false tiger, the young man becomes depressed by the contrast between himself and a genuine tiger. For him, the contrast becomes an analogy of the difference between the twenties and the fifties: "The twenties might have roared themselves into a genuine mess, but at least they genuinely roared. The fifties were all dressed up to look like something that could roar, but nothing came out except a whimper— me."[3] At a postgame party, the still-outfitted tiger meets a young coed, a "goddess," with whom he longs for some connection (Tiger 55). He wants especially to tell her about his experience of maybe seeing an angel in a dogwood tree, an event that sounds remarkably like the vision of Peter Cowley in *The Seasons' Difference*. Before he can tell his story, he is pulled away by his drunken friends and never gets the chance to explain to her about the tiger or anything else. In melancholic tones, the story ends with his awareness of his own falsity and incompleteness: "to put it as briefly and painlessly as possible, in the world we're pretty much stuck with there simply are no tigers anymore" (Tiger 61).

The implicit longing for the real, what one might, borrowing Fitzgerald's phrase, label "romantic readiness," summarizes the period after *The Seasons' Difference*, when the young Buechner's searches take on many new forms. Buechner returns to the thematic issues of "The Tiger" in a 1965 sermon of the same title printed in *The Magnificent Defeat*, where he employs the metaphor again to make the point that "human beings as they usually exist in the world are not what they were created to be" (*MD* 91). Like Adam, who lost paradise but carried around a dim memory of it, human beings, Buechner believes, go around with a deep longing, a homesickness, a spiritual vacancy. The theme of the spiritual disjunction in the modern personality moves to the forefront of Buechner's preoccupations with *The Return of Ansel Gibbs* and will be exceedingly prominent hereafter.

A second major moment of 1953 came close to being a conversion experience, although Buechner balks at the phrase. Revisiting the experience in his memoirs, Buechner summarizes:

> The preceding year [1953] I had become in some sense a Christian, though the chances are I would have hesitated to put it like that, and I find something in that way of expressing it which even now makes me feel uncomfortable. "To become a Christian" sounds like an achievement, like becoming a millionaire. I thought of it rather, and think of it still, more as a lucky break, a step in the right direction. (*NT* 4)

Although Buechner had attended an Episcopal church during visits with his maternal grandmother and even arranged his own christening in that church at age fifteen, his religious background had been limited to little more than confirmation classes during his student years at Lawrenceville. The experience at the Madison Avenue Presbyterian Church in New York occurred in 1952, during a period when the young author had taken to filling up lonely Sundays by drifting into the church to listen to a famous preacher, George Buttrick. On one particular Sunday when Queen Elizabeth's coronation was in the news, Buttrick preached about Christ's refusal of the crown offered by Satan in the wilderness. But, Buttrick argued, "Christ is king nonetheless because he is crowned in the hearts of believers." The coronation, Buttrick said, takes place "among confession, and tears, and great laughter" (*SJ* 109). Buechner records his reaction to Buttrick's phrase in several places, this one in an interview: "For reasons I've never been able to explain, that phrase 'great laughter' absolutely decimated me. I found tears spouting from my eyes. If one were looking for the 'born-again' experience, in some funny way, this was it" (*WDoor* 17).

Buechner, however, qualifies the experience:

> To say that I was born again, to use the traditional phrase, is to say too much because I remained in most ways as self-centered and squeamish after the fact as I was before, and God knows remain so still. And in another way to say that I was born again is to say too little because there have been more than a few moments since, times when from beyond time something too precious to tell has glinted in the dusk, always just out of reach, like fireflies. (*SJ* 111)

George Buttrick

An understanding of Buechner's notion of conversion is crucial to understanding the work that will follow over the next two decades. Buechner certainly does not think of his acceptance of the tenets of Christian faith as a simple, systematic, one-step procedure. Henry Kuykendall in *The Return of Ansel Gibbs* speaks Buechner's notions on the subject: "If you tell me Christian commitment is a thing that has happened to you once and for all like some kind of spiritual plastic surgery, I say go to, go to, you're either pulling the wool over your own eyes or trying to pull it over mine."[4]

One of the first scholars to arrive on the Buechner scene, Nancy Myers focused on Buechner's rejection of neat categories and simple answers. Myers's dissertation included one of the earliest interviews with Buechner, a 1976 conversation in which he speaks of his critics' desire that he say, "Look, it's all true," and his willingness to go to "ninety-eight per cent" (Myers 166, 203). In a 1981 article, "Frederick Buechner and the Literature of Grace," Myers again cites the interview to underscore Buechner's decidedly unsystematic approach to things theological. In this version, Myers ups the percentage to "ninety-nine percent," but the sentiment still holds when she records Buechner's words: "God is too big to be expressed in our words. I'm sure He smiles at our attempts to slice things up neatly."[5] The young man who is sadly aware of freaks and fake tigers and ambiguity does not disappear with the tears shed in the Madison Avenue Presbyterian Church. It is dicey business, of course, to approach an artist's work via his or her personal story, but Buechner forces readers into just such a risk as he is so clearly using the fabric of his own experience to write his novels. The early novels clang with the ideas firing in the young writer's life, if not the actual events.

The experience in George Buttrick's church did, however, have enormous implications. Buechner's initial response, his desire "to stand up and declare myself in some intense and dramatic way" (*NT* 5), led him to enrollment, on a Rockefeller Brothers Theological Fellowship, at Union Theological Seminary. Buechner's teachers at Union were among the most distinguished theologians of the time—Paul Tillich, Reinhold Niebuhr, James Muilenburg, John Knox, Paul Scherer, and R. R. Wicks. Their era is often referred to now as Union's "Golden Age." Buechner argues that Tillich's influence was perhaps the weightiest (*Image* 52), but adds that his teachers were "alike in having a faith which continues to this day to nourish mine" (*Longing* 25). Who knows how to gauge the elusive business of influence? But some connections are inescapable and can be demonstrated. Buechner's prose style, his pedagogical theory, his theology, and his thematic preoccupations all reflect the teaching of his mentors. In *Now and Then* Buechner speaks of the novel he "put aside" for Union. He refers to "a handful of half-born characters" and "a story I had only begun to tell" in juxtaposition to his days at Union, of which he comments, "I had never spent a richer year anywhere, never been so close to total involvement in anything else" (*NT* 31).

The problem, however, is the Buechner of the mid-1950s is still divided between his call to writing and his call to ministry. "It seemed very much an either/or matter to me then," he concludes (*NT* 31). But when he thinks of the pigeonholed novel and of the possibility of "making room in it for some of the new things I had learned, some of the new people I had met," the either and the or move toward each other (*NT* 31).

Among the Union giants that Buechner will mix into the brew of the book that will eventually appear as *The Return of Ansel Gibbs* would have to be Tillich, from whom Buechner derives a version of Christian existentialism. In his 1952 book *The Courage to Be* Tillich outlined what he calls the courage of self-affirmation: "The courage to be is the ethical act in which man affirms his own being in spite of those elements of his existence which conflict with his essential self-affirmation."[6] This courage, which culminates in faith, always exists in confrontation with the possibility that life is meaningless. Therefore, doubt is an integral part of the faith system. In *The Dynamics of Faith* Tillich argued that 'There is no faith without an intrinsic "in spite of" and the courageous affirmation of oneself in the state of ultimate concern."[7] In the same text, he added, "But serious doubt is the confirmation of faith" (*Dynamics* 22). Further, Tillich, in *The Eternal Now*, argued that "we go towards something that is not yet."[8]

These three elements of Tillich's teaching—the courage to live bravely in spite of circumstance, the relation of doubt to faith, and the movement of history toward a completion—surely figure in *The Return of Ansel Gibbs* and all of Buechner's subsequent work. Ansel Gibbs is forced to deal with the failure of his past and the suspicion that he is inadequate to face the tasks ahead. He will, finally, affirm himself without losing his reservations and his doubts. In other characters of the novel—Rudy Tripp, Anne Gibbs, and Henry Kuykendall—we see a certain god-hauntedness, a hope that history is going not just anywhere but somewhere.

Marie-Helene Davies summarized Tillich's influence on Buechner by noting their similar stances on the human relationship to the divine: "Since man is always the subject as well as the object of the introvert's analysis, there is no way of getting down to the truth about oneself; therefore grace is the belief that one is accepted and pardoned and that, in relation to God, man is always wrong" (Davies 10). Thus the individual comes to God through despair and absolute conviction of personal failure to conquer life.

The cross, then, is the perfect symbol for Tillich and, later, for Buechner to capture the essence of faith that posits union with God despite the darkness of circumstance and inevitable death. The call, in the midst of alienation and estrangement, is to the acceptance of grace. As Tillich put it in *The Shaking of the Foundations*:

> Simply accept the fact that you are accepted! If that happens to us, we experience grace. After such an experience we may not be better than before, and we may not believe more than before. But everything is transformed. In that moment, grace conquers sin, and reconciliation bridges the gulf of estrangement. And nothing is demanded of this experience, no religious or moral or intellectual presupposition, nothing but acceptance.[9]

Buechner certainly does not foreground all of these conclusions in *The Return of Ansel Gibbs*, but he exhibits a preoccupation with them, the continuing struggle of a writer exploring alternatives among a world of ideas. Many of the words spoken by characters in *The Return of Ansel Gibbs* derive directly from Tillich. For example, Tillich in *The Shaking of the Foundations* said, "We possess the past by memory and the future by anticipation" (*Shaking* 35). In Buechner's novel we hear Ansel Gibbs say, "We live in memory and anticipation. The present is a kind of no man's land" (*AG* 53). Buechner was clearly paying attention in Tillich's lecture hall.

Davies nominated Karl Barth and Søren Kierkegaard as two additional major influences beginning to filter through to Buechner during his years at Union. A proponent of what has been called "crisis theology," Barth spoke of God as inexplicable in human terms. He accepted the Anselmic formula "credo ut intelligam" ("I believe in order to understand"). Further, Barth venerated Scripture as the locus of authority. The notion of faith as centrally mysterious and beyond evidence is elemental in Buechner's work from his first considerations of theological premises. Kierkegaard also spoke of the paradox that religion is not a matter of logic. As angst or anxiety is the central human reality, the individual can fight against the despair only by delving into self. The result of the introspective journey can be a breaking through into eternity. Such inner churning is the basis of a character like Peter Cowley in *The Seasons' Difference*, and Buechner's many introspective characters, who endlessly refocus on personal dilemmas as clues to universal questions, suggest something of the Kierkegaardian thesis. The eccentric Henry Kuykendall of *The Return of Ansel Gibbs* is a distillation of much of the theological bubbling of this period in Buechner's career, and Ansel Gibbs's inwardness might be aptly labeled Kierkegaardian.

Other influences of the Union period are certainly worthy of note. During these years Buechner met Agnes Sanford, a faith healer and itinerant preacher of some repute in the East. (She is the prototype for Lillian Flagg of *The Final Beast* and certainly influences the portrait of Leo Bebb of Buechner's 1970s tetralogy.) Buechner's openness to Agnes Sanford is evidence of his enormous theological range and further underscores the impossibility of trapping him in any doctrinal corner. He claims, for example, that his choice of ordination as a Presbyterian was "really almost a matter of tossing a coin,"[10] and he displays a refreshing ignorance of denominational splinterings, doctrinal disputes, and the latest fads in church growth.

To understand Buechner's ecumenicity, we need to look to James Muilenburg, Buechner's teacher in Old Testament studies at Union. Muilenburg, transformed into Kuykendall for *The Return of Ansel Gibbs*, is important, not so much for his published work, but for his intense charismatic influence upon his students. Although his name is often missing from the "influences" list, Muilenburg was the teacher to whom Buechner turned for the personal moments; it was Muilenburg, for example, who officiated at Buechner's wedding in 1956. Buechner attests to the friendship by dedicating *The Magnificent Defeat* to Muilenburg. In *Now and Then*, Buechner paints a word portrait of Muilenburg and summarizes his influence:

> But for me, as for most of us studying there in those days, there was no one on the faculty who left so powerful and lasting an impression as James Muilenburg. He was an angular man with thinning white hair, staring eyes, and a nose and chin which at times seemed so close to touching that they gave him the face of a good witch. In his introductory Old Testament course, the largest lecture hall that Union had was always packed to hear him. Students brought friends. Friends brought friends. People stood in the back when the chairs ran out. Up and down the whole length of the aisle he would stride as he chanted the war songs, the taunt songs, the dirges of ancient Israel. With his body stiff, his knees bent, his arms scarecrowed far to either side, he never merely taught the Old Testament but *was* the Old Testament. (*NT* 15)

Obviously, this powerful teacher became something of a hero figure to Buechner, who concludes his lengthy remembrance by recalling specific words of Muilenburg's lectures:

> "Every morning when you wake up," he used to say, "before you reaffirm your faith in the majesty of a loving God, before you say *I believe* for another day, read the *Daily News* with its record of the latest crimes and tragedies of mankind and then see if you can honestly say it again." He was a fool in the sense that he didn't or couldn't or wouldn't resolve, intellectualize, evade, the tensions of his faith but lived those tensions out, torn almost in two by them at times. He was a fool, I suppose, in the sense that he was an intimate of the dark, yet held fast to the light as if it were something you could hold fast to; in the sense that he wore his heart on his sleeve even though it was in some ways a broken heart; in the sense that he was as absurdly himself before the packed lecture hall as he was alone in his office; a fool in the sense that he was a child in his terrible candor. A fool, in other words, for Christ. (*NT* 16–17)

Dr. James Muilenburg

This extended picture of Muilenburg is important, not only because of his enormous influence on *The Return of Ansel Gibbs*, but also because Muilenburg was, demonstrably, the model Buechner chooses for himself. Gibbs will choose Kuykendall just as Buechner has chosen Muilenburg. Tillich and Niebuhr and others are undoubtedly central as later influences such as Kierkegaard and C. S. Lewis and Graham Greene will be, but Muilenburg contributes something of the soul to Buechner. Buechner's current popularity as a lecturer derives in part, I submit, from his internalization of Muilenburg's style and ideology. Notice in the description of Muilenburg's peculiar power the emphasis on personal honesty, willingness to be self-revealing, dedication to intense faith despite the presence of overwhelming darkness—trademarks of Buechner's own writing and preaching. Muilenburg's influence was that of a prophet, an intense, maybe even deranged, bringer of the Word. It was certainly Muilenburg whom Buechner has in mind when he alleges, "In the last analysis, I have always believed, it is not so much their subjects that the great teachers teach as it is themselves" (*NT* 12). Buechner is more romantic than analytical, more influenced by personalities than by ideas.

Another name in the Union mix would have to be Niebuhr, of whom Buechner underscores "the glittering breadth of his knowledge . . . his gift for applying the insights of the Christian faith to the whole spectrum of politics, economics, international affairs" (*NT* 13). Buechner admires Niebuhr's ability to "sniff out the irony and ambivalence of things in general" (*NT* 13), and Buechner's own career has been variously regarded for just such an ability in his own right. "I've never learned to talk about the Christian faith in the accustomed way. I've talked about it in the only way I can. In some ways it has created a dilemma for me as a writer, because my religious books are too colloquial and too secular for church people, yet too churchy for secular people," Buechner concludes (*WDoor* 18). Buechner seems to have absorbed Niebuhr's particular secular sense, but, as Horton Davies pointed out, "This is the perfect place for an innovative and imaginative apologist to be standing, between the believers and the unbelievers" (HDavies 187). Davies went on to paraphrase Buechner: he is "too religious for the sophisticated, not religious enough for the conservative and conventional" (HDavies 187). In any case, referring to Buechner as an apologist or an apostle to the cynic has become increasingly popular among his readers. Comparisons to C. S. Lewis have invariably followed in discussions of Buechner's desire to communicate intelligently a passionately held faith. Surely much of this application of faith to all of the realities of life has its source in Niebuhr's tutelage, and *The Return of Ansel Gibbs* is ample evidence of an attempt to bring Christian ideas into the arena of politics and social issues.

Buechner remembers Tillich's "depth and incisiveness" and is much taken by Tillich's contention that the assertion "God exists" is essentially metaphorical, a kind of poem (*NT* 13). The idea shows up in Buechner's attempts to connect story and religion. In a sermon anthologized in *A Room Called Remember*, Buechner venerates storytelling as vitally important "because it is a story, of course, which stands at the heart of our faith and which more perhaps than any other form of discourse speaks to our hearts and illumines our own stories"[11] (*RCR* 47). Buechner takes Tillich seriously and acknowledges his indebtedness as recently as 1999 in *The Eyes of the Heart*. His play on Tillich's premises shows up in two important essays: "Faith and Fiction," first anthologized in William Zinsser's *Spiritual Quests: The Art and Craft of Religious Writing* and later reprinted in *The Clown in the Belfry: Writings on Faith and Fiction*; and "The Speaking and Writing of Words," one of the "fugitive pieces" in *A Room Called Remember: Uncollected Pieces*. "In both faith and fiction you *fashion* out of the raw stuff of your experience," Buechner speculates in the former essay

(*Belfry* 15), and he goes on to argue for the deep connection between the pursuits of the novelist and those of the believer—both, he believes, trying to get at the plots of their lives. It is only in this sense, according to Buechner, that he can "live with the label of 'religious novelist'" (*Belfry* 16). In the latter essay, Buechner develops an argument for language itself as that which emerges out of our need to give shape and meaning to our experience. He concludes, "The ultimate purpose of language . . . is that humanity may speak with God" (*RCR* 170).

And there's *The Sacred Journey*, of course, where Buechner develops Tillich's teaching about personal story and God story, folds the notion into his very apologetic for the instinct to memoir. "We must learn to listen to the cock-crows and hammering and tick-tock of our lives for the holy and elusive word that is spoken to us out of their depths. It is the function of all great preaching, I think, and of all great art, to sharpen our hearing precisely to that end," Buechner says (*SJ* 5). Tillich argued that God may be found in the stories of our lives as in the stories of Scripture, and his young charge, Buechner, takes him at his word.

Theories of providence abound in Buechner's work after Union, even as he tries to look ahead:

> What quickens my pulse now is the stretch ahead rather than the one behind, and it is mainly for some clue to where I am going that I search through where I have been, for some hint of who I am becoming or failing to become that I delve into what used to be. I listen back to a time when nothing was much farther from my thoughts than God for an echo of the gutturals and sibilants and vowellessness by which I believe that even then God was addressing me out of my life as he addresses us all. (*SJ* 6)

Buechner justifies his preoccupation with his own story with the hope that readers might learn to better regard their own stories as a result of encountering his. It is not narcissism but a kind of instinct to testimony that drives much of Buechner's work, and so much goes back to Tillich's instruction. Buechner clearly admires as well Tillich's candor and powerful way of speaking before an audience. Like Niebuhr and Muilenburg, Tillich clearly lives in Buechner's vision of the teacher, the writer, the prophet. *The Sacred Journey*, which Reynolds Price called "detective autobiography" and "a beautifully successful experiment," is the clearest example of Tillich's impact.[12] Price concluded that Buechner's fundamental achievement in the memoir is "that he is so lucidly particular" (Price 11).

In the memoirs, Buechner finds another vein between the novels and the nonfiction, what Price labeled "intimate homiletics," to explore Tillich's theories of the enmeshment of life and theology (Price 11).

Another ingredient in the background of *The Return of Ansel Gibbs* is certainly Buechner's tenure in East Harlem as a kind of social worker and missionary. He worked in a storefront employment clinic doing fieldwork for his seminary degree. For the first time in his life, the young man from the upper classes witnesses poverty, sickness, and the smells of human suffering. In his memoirs, he writes of the difference between Harlem and the New York City of his experience: "East Harlem was another kind of city altogether—another kind of living, another kind of struggling, and with almost no beauty at all" (*NT* 24). Beyond trying to find jobs for people, Buechner handled donations made to the parish by church groups. He remembers, most particularly, boxes of used Christmas cards sent, perhaps, under the assumption that the poor people would enjoy looking at them. This episode of the secondhand greeting cards, mentioned in the memoirs, finds its way into *The Return of Ansel Gibbs*. Kuykendall rants about the secondhand Christmas cards sent to his East Harlem mission and recognizes the frustrations of the work when he observes: "Israel dies on a cross of shame and glory, and exactly three days later the tongues start wagging, the pens start scratching, the presses roll, till by now the glory's forgotten with the shame, and the cry from the cross is drowned out by the infernal clatter of typewriters" (*AG* 32). Muilenburg's voice on the limitations of the social gospel is, of course, quite plain in Kuykendall's speech, but also visible is Buechner's developing notion of how Christianity addresses the needs of people—a sense of irony. Clearly Buechner is smuggling into *The Return of Ansel Gibbs* the Harlem experience as well as the Union experience. Most specifically, Buechner uses the novel to explore some of his own motives for the Harlem work, to question whether or not he is a hypocrite. Despite doubt and indirection, Buechner found a certain inspiration and confirmation in the lives of those workers of the regular parish staff. Unlike the students who dabbled part-time in the ghetto and returned to their comfortable environments, the regular staff lived among the poor and worked with them full-time. Buechner recalls them as "closer to being saints than any other people I had ever come across" (*NT* 28). Commitment to the message of Christianity was, as the young Buechner saw, the motive force in these workers' lives. Impressed by them, yet unable to choose their path, Buechner claims to be haunted by them still (*NT* 30). He is obviously visited by these committed missionaries in the period of writing *The Return of Ansel Gibbs*. The Harlem work, with its directness and physicality—smells, despair, and decay—is, arguably, the overwhelming influence of the period. Like many writers who fear that their art is a kind of withdrawal from the action of working toward real change in their world, Buechner has had his share of doubts about his efficacy.

After a year at Union, Buechner was supposed to have decided about a career as a clergyman; at least such was the intention of the directors of the Rockefeller Brothers Fellowship. Still uncertain as to a career as a writer or as a minister, which he saw as mutually exclusive, Buechner decided to spend a year away from Union to continue his thinking about the personal implications of his commitment to Christianity and to finish a novel. The novel was *The Return of Ansel Gibbs*; the thinking continues even now. His conversion, if it can be labeled that, left him "not noticeably much godlier than I had ever been" and "far from certain even what righteousness was" (*NT* 33). This incessant wondering about Christianity, a significant part of the sabbatical year, shows up measurably in *The Return of Ansel Gibbs*, but the year's leave contributes other experiences as well, most notably a courtship and a marriage.

Buechner met Judith Friedrike Merck at a dance in the spring of 1955, and they were married in the spring of the following year. The new novel will be quietly dedicated to her. Buechner is shy about the marriage, choosing to summarize it in the memoirs by citing John Donne: "all measure, and all language, I should passe,/Should I tell what a miracle she was" (*NT* 34). Donne's poem affirms the impossibility of verbal expression of love, calling it, finally, miraculous. Buechner's regard for his marriage as profoundly important to his development as a human being sounds clearly in his summary:

> All I can say . . . is that it was within the bonds of marriage that I, for one, found a greater freedom to be and to become and to share myself than I can imagine ever having found in any other kind of relationship, and that—absurdly hopeful and poorly understood and profoundly unrealistic as the commitment was that the girl in the white dress and I made to each other in the presence, we hoped, not only of most of the people we loved best in the world, but of God as well, in whose name Dr. Muilenburg somewhat shakily blessed us—my life would have been incalculably diminished without it. (*NT* 35)

The newlyweds spent four months in Europe, mostly in Austria and England, where, among other things, Buechner finished *The Return of Ansel Gibbs*.

The completion of the novel is almost anticlimactic, given the changes and excitement of this era in Buechner's life. The book is, however, a conglomeration of all of the experiences of the period; thus some exposition of all of the background material is essential to approach an understanding of the text itself. *The Return of Ansel Gibbs* is Tillich and Muilenburg and Niebuhr, East Harlem and New York and Oxford, falling in love and making decisions about the future, and accepting adulthood. Although he made room in the novel for many of the new people he was meeting and the new things he was learning, Buechner is also returning to many of his earlier preoccupations.

He admits that he put Muilenburg and East Harlem in the story and finally, "for the first time in print, I also touched, though in considerably fictionalized terms, upon my father's suicide some twenty years earlier" (*NT* 36). The "fictionalized terms" may actually be less fictional than Buechner imagined at the time. It is instructive, for example, to set Buechner's description of his father from the various memoirs beside his fictional description of Rudy Tripp's father from *The Return of Ansel Gibbs*. The consonances are indeed remarkable. Both men suffer from an inner vacancy, both struggle with vocational and financial crises, and both leave a suicide note on the last page of *Gone with the Wind*.

Although the suicide is crucial to the plot of *The Return of Ansel Gibbs*, I suspect that Buechner cannot bring himself to look at it too directly. How else can one explain the rather strange inconsistency that the day of Rudy's father's suicide is once a Saturday (the day of Buechner's father's death) and another time a Sunday? I hazard the guess that Buechner proofed these sections carelessly as a way of avoiding a subject that he was still resolving in 1957. Although Buechner had in *A Long Day's Dying* and *The Seasons' Difference* at least considered the suicide theme, *The Return of Ansel Gibbs* marks the first of many occasions where Buechner uses the specific circumstances of his father's 1936 suicide. He speaks of the moment of his father's suicide as "the last of my childhood" (*SJ* 39). Even as a young man Buechner was still realizing the extent of his loss and dealing with the anxieties created by his father's death. Just as his courtship and marriage are translated into the relationship of Robin Tripp and Anne Gibbs in the novel, Buechner's father's suicide is translated into the suicide of Robin's father, Gibbs's best friend.

The foray into obvious autobiography turned out to be costly. Only after his mother's death in 1988 was Buechner free to tell the whole story of his third novel: "In a novel called *The Return of Ansel Gibbs* I told a very brief and fictionalized version of my father's death, and the most accurate

Buechner and his father
Circa 1920

word I can find to describe my mother's reaction to it is fury. . . . I had betrayed a sacred trust" (*TS* 10). Buechner was in his fifties before he tackled the subject again, this time in the memoir *The Sacred Journey*. Although he scrupulously omits his mother's part of the story there, he reports that he was able to tell the tale only because he "suspected that from *Ansel Gibbs* on my mother had never really read any other book I had written for fear of what she might find there" (*TS* 11). Not until his mother's death in 1988 did Buechner open up the details of his father's death, first in fictional form in *The Wizard's Tide* in 1990 and again in 1991 in *Telling Secrets: A Memoir*.

Speaking of Robin Tripp's feelings about his father's suicide in an interview with Nancy Myers, Buechner commented, "As I was writing that [*The Return of Ansel Gibbs*], I thought to myself, that is the way a man might feel, but it wasn't the way I felt myself. I am almost fifty and I still don't know what I feel about my father's death. I grieve for him. I chide him. So many things" (Myers 64). Many issues bubble in the cauldron that becomes *The Return of Ansel Gibbs*—psychological adjustment to the loss of his father, a grappling with a newly embraced faith, the teaching of theologians, the life of the poor and ministry in East Harlem, a love affair, an indecision about career, literary failures and successes, student years at Lawrenceville, and Princeton. All of this and more come together in the novel that stands as a thematic development in the heretofore popular author.

The Return of Ansel Gibbs opens with a news conference and an explanation from the central character, a public figure, a politician of sorts. Gibbs's first words are addressed to a news conference: "They say that after two years I have lost touch" (*AG* 3). Buechner, with such an observation, may be thinking of the critical reception to his earlier novels. Having been accused himself of being out of touch, of writing esoteric pedantry, his opening line suggests a renewed attempt to get in touch. The most prominent changes evident in this third novel are simplicity of style and choice of subject. As Nancy Myers notes, the novel "was well received for its timeliness and marked the beginning of a more straightforward literary style for Buechner" (Myers 3).

Buechner's central character in the novel is a man of words, a man of civilization and sophistication, a man of breeding and sensitivity. Ansel Gibbs, the VIP, has been appointed to a cabinet post by the president. The nomination precipitates a personal crisis for Gibbs, who has been in retirement for two years on his farm in Montana and now must journey to Washington for Senate hearings to confirm his appointment. Before retirement, Gibbs lived for some years in Europe and, like Henry James's

Christopher Newman or Lambert Strether, has developed a deep sense of ambiguity regarding most ethical and moral questions. The president's call and Gibbs's return to the public arena cause him to question whether or not he is indeed prepared to return to this life. One of the questions of the novel, then, is whether or not Gibbs will accept the post. A. C. Spectorsky summarized this dilemma in Gibbs's character: "Behind his demeanor of blandly impassive detachment there is a man in the throes of a crisis of conscience, of nerve, and of faith, a man involved in a searching attempt to grapple with the fundamental issues of men and morals, of civilization and government—and his involvement with them."[13]

But this is only the public side of Gibbs's quandary; he has his personal demons as well. There to meet Gibbs on his arrival in Washington are most of the novel's major cast members: his daughter, Anne; his official hostess, Louise von Louwe; and his political advisor and assistant, Porter Hoye. Another who enters soon upon Gibbs's arrival is Robin Tripp, a young television interviewer of the *60 Minutes* genre who happens to be Anne's suitor and the son of Gibbs's best friend, Rudy Tripp. Rudy has died fifteen years earlier, a suicide, and Gibbs feels responsibility for his friend's death. Henry Kuykendall, a minister to Harlem's poor and a former professor of Gibbs and Rudy Tripp at Harvard, moves in and out of the narrative in his role as mentor to both Ansel and Anne.

The crisis encounter of the novel is between Gibbs and his political antagonist, Edward Farwell. Spectorsky categorized Farwell as "an isolationist right-wing leader, spellbinder, know-nothing" (Spectorsky 31). Farwell is a Bible thumper and a flag waver, a man of one dimension and no feel for ambiguity, the sort of all-too-familiar politician who keeps showing up on the American landscape. Farwell's hatred for all that Gibbs represents emerges in their dialogue on a television program orchestrated, rather maliciously, by Robin Tripp. As *The New Yorker* reviewer noted, "The great crisis, after all, lies in the moment when Tripp feels that he has Gibbs where he wants him, while Gibbs is made not altogether painfully aware of his own vulnerability, and therefore of his own humanity."[14]

The book becomes, then, a series of trials. Gibbs is on trial with the Senate, with his daughter, with Robin Tripp, with Kuykendall, and with Farwell. Most of all, however, he is trying himself; he questions the moral base of his life, his complicity in Rudy's death, the effectuality of his liberal views, his isolation and detachment. In a note to his daughter, Gibbs proclaims: "I was made for words. I sometimes believe that I am made of words" (*AG* 246). Can the man of words ever become the man of action? Will Gibbs be able to survive the maelstrom of his doubts and bewilderments, the darkness of his personal and ethical crisis, to assume the mantle of public service? Such questions constitute the central issues of the novel.

Although most studies of Buechner's early work give short shrift to *The Return of Ansel Gibbs*, the novel actually establishes an important pivot in his career. Marie-Helene Davies summarized the novel as a "study of a politician's pangs of conscience" (Davies 63), and Nancy Myers labeled it "transitional" (Myers 52). Myers discussed *The Return of Ansel Gibbs* as the final vestige of Buechner's formative period when he searched for a literary voice, and Stacy Thompson cited the novel as "Buechner's most extended study of ambivalence" (Thompson 10).

All of these readings show up in the scene of greatest tension in *The Return of Ansel Gibbs*, the televised debate between Farwell and Gibbs. Buechner starkly juxtaposes Gibbs's ambivalence against Farwell's one-eyedness in a snapshot that captures the now familiar disputation between liberal and conservative "talking heads" on cable television. Kuykendall, watching the exchange, summarizes Gibbs's remarks as an "inveighing against a mediocrity and complacency of sentiment, the general refusal of men to admit the tragic ambivalence of a world where what looks like the holiest cause may have perdition in it and winning is often indistinguishable from losing" (*AG* 176). But Gibbs, in his almost un-American awareness of the many-sidedness of political and moral questions, finds himself stymied by that knowledge. Furthermore, his deep sense of ambiguity renders him vulnerable to such Pharisees as Farwell.

Farwell enjoys recalling for audiences an anecdote from Gibbs's early days in the wartime administration. Gibbs, supposedly in answer to a young officer's derisive question, "Well, my friend, and what are you doing to save civilization?" answers simply, "I am civilization" (*AG* 5). Gibbs, however, refuses to authenticate the story, and it becomes part of his legend, a mythological backdrop contributing to his public reputation as a political intellectual, an aristocrat of sorts. Gibbs's proclamation, whether or not he indeed said it, acts as the central image in the novel when it is transformed by a waggish cartoonist into a sketch of the evolutionary process:

> At the bottom was sketched one of the mysterious, little one-cell organisms, then the swimming things, the creeping, climbing, flying things, the mammals, monkeys, apes, until finally, way up in the top right-hand corner, you came to a spindly little caricature of Gibbs, out of whose mouth issued a cloud bearing the words: "I am civilization." (*AG* 8)

Along with Gibbs, readers know that something in the sendup is accurate. Gibbs is capable of arrogance and insensitivity. Simultaneously, however, he embodies humility and warmth. The Buechnerian mix of things works in the slippery sound bite applied to Gibbs; he is at once the best and worst of civilization.

For Farwell and his cronies, Gibbs's pronouncement encapsulates the megalomania of wealth and position: "Was this urbane, detached, and moneyed man a likely one to appoint to a Cabinet post at a time of poverty, violence, and fanaticism?" Farwell sneers (*AG* 5). Conversely, Gibbs's supporters claim the civilization comment as a rallying point. "As much as any other single man, they suggested, Ansel Gibbs indeed was civilization, was among the rarest treasures that his era had yet produced: a living proof that idealism could still flourish in out-of-the-way corners of the political scene" (*AG* 6). In his encounter with Farwell, however, Gibbs offers an explanation: "To be civilization, to be civilized, is to be aware of so many possible courses of action at any given time that no one of them ever seems to be without qualification right" (*AG* 114). That is, to be civilized is to be rendered, to some degree, helpless. The dilemma of Tristram Bone is visited upon Ansel Gibbs; how is the civilized, aware man ever to bring himself to action? Peter Cowley, too, puzzles over the question, deciding, at last, to act in spite of misgiving, doubt, and ambiguity.

At its heart, *The Return of Ansel Gibbs* is not a novel about politics, although it is remarkably prescient about our ongoing political meanderings. The novel is, instead, another consideration of the courage required to assert one's humanity in the modern world. For Ansel Gibbs, the central word is "ambivalence." Imagining, in his confrontation with Senator Farwell, a congress of planets, Gibbs postulates that the civilized nations would probably choose one of the "ultra-civilized" among them to send to a "cosmic assemblage." And what would earth's representative have to say? Gibbs concludes, "I have no idea what he would say. But . . . ambivalence. Ambivalence. If he were limited to only one word, that is the one I would suggest to him" (*AG* 114). Incensed by the shocking absence of "fixed legal and ethical principles" in Gibbs's philosophy, Farwell strenuously objects to what he sees as relativism and deluded idealism (*AG* 114–15). Farwell claims, "A man can't be many things at once." Gibbs responds: "I find him rarely capable of being less" (*AG* 115).

Forced at last to see the truth of himself, Gibbs summarizes the snares of ambivalence in a way that captures Buechner's own fears—the possibility of becoming a thoroughly modern human being and, thereby, losing all sense of spirit and conviction:

I've never shared myself. . . . I don't want to sound ridiculous or tragic, and I know I sound a little of both, but the self I've had to come to terms with alone, the self that's forced me to make this decision you're all down here to challenge me with . . . I couldn't share it even if I wanted to because it's almost without substance—like a shadow. It's not yes and not no. It doesn't love or hate, accept or reject. It sits on the sidelines. It looks on you—*even you* [Hoye, Anne, and Kuy- kendall] . . . and remains appallingly unmoved. (*AG* 276–77)

One progression, surely visible through Buechner's work, involves the increasing rejection of sterile inaction and apathy, even if the choices of action are laden with ambiguity. As Thompson concluded, "The move- ment away from ambivalence and isolation toward commitment and affir- mation noted in *The Return of Ansel Gibbs* parallels the development of Buechner fiction generally" (Thompson 14).

Norman Podhoretz, in his 1958 discussion of the modern novel, "The New Nihilism and the Novel," centered on "the loss of values"[15] as the recurring theme of the novels of the era. Including Buechner's *The Return of Ansel Gibbs* in his remarks, Podhoretz wrote:

Gibbs suffers from a certain deficiency of feeling, a certain remote- ness from the natural processes and the elemental emotions. He is almost incapable of passion (sobriety, judiciousness, detachment, moderation, tolerance being the civilized virtues), and he can no more satisfy his old teacher's demand that he become a prophet than he can prate sentimentally like the senator about Mom's apple pie. The novel raises the question of whether such a man can be relied upon to guide the fortunes of others. (Podhoretz 580–81)

Podhoretz correctly described the Ansel Gibbs of *most* of the novel, but Podhoretz neglected to stay around for Gibbs's return and thus missed the mark when he suggested that such a man cannot be relied upon. Buechner is taking Gibbs over the hard places. Gibbs must undergo transformation, must be shaken and sifted, before he can be judged worthy of his calling.

Ansel Gibbs's trial can be seen in the back story that informs the novel, the biblical narrative of King Saul and the young David. Gibbs recalls Kuykendall's lecture on the subject:

We're told, that the spirit of the Lord departed from Saul, and don't think that Saul didn't know when it happened. Oh, he'd had troubles enough already, a man born to trouble—he was too handsome, too strong to escape it—but he'd always before been sustained by the spirit of the Lord, which, contrary to popular modern opinion, isn't some kind of pious deodorant, but the terrible vitality of the Creator Himself which lacerates as it sustains, and when it departed from him, he knew it, and so did everybody else. (*AG* 59)

Ansel Gibbs, like King Saul, faces the enervation of the departed spirit. In deciding whether or not to return to the public arena, Gibbs has to learn that his spirit has departed, has to discover the weakness of his ambivalence, has to plunge deeply into the question of himself.

In this respect, the novel is a Kierkegaardian parable on the results of the introspective journey toward personal understanding and the resulting paradoxical insight into universals. Understanding, finally, the role of his gathered family and friends as they have endeavored to help him with the task of self-definition, Gibbs addresses them: "What each of you has been trying to tell me from the beginning, of course, is who I am" (*AG* 275). Therefore, questions of identity—"Who is Ansel Gibbs?" and "What will he become?"—are at the center of Buechner's third novel. Tripp's introduction to the television debate underscores the point: "What we're interested in on this show isn't the news, but the men behind the news. We don't want to know what they do, but who they are. Who is Senator Edward M. Farwell? And who is. . . . But I don't want to jump the gun on myself" (*AG* 105). Clearly, too, the spiritual seeking of the urbane, wealthy, sophisticated, verbal, and complex Gibbs reflects Buechner's own search for identity.

The essential charge against Gibbs is that he is detached—overly cerebral and cool. His critics consider him as removed from the real lives of ordinary people. Gibbs worries that they may have it right. The young novelist, Frederick Buechner, is wondering about just such questions for himself. He bluntly expresses his preoccupation with the dangers of withdrawal in *The Hungering Dark*, where he observes:

I fend off the world, I avoid getting involved with other people's needs, so that I can get ahead in the world myself. But at this deeper level, much deeper than conscience, the truth of it is that I need the world. I need the very ones that I keep at a distance. I need to love and be loved by the very ones from whom I hide myself behind this face. I need them not so that I can ease my conscience but so that I can be myself. (*HD* 22)

The dilemma Buechner expresses here reflects the plight of Ansel Gibbs, who feels alienated from his daughter and his friends, the very people he needs to support his attempted return to real life. But, like King Saul, Gibbs has been sapped and rendered indecisive by the guilts and twists of his life, and, as Thompson summarized, "Gibbs knows almost instinctively that to commit oneself wholeheartedly to *anything* is in questionable taste, quite out of keeping with the disaffiliation of a sophisticated, cosmopolitan, modern man. The gentleman has only words" (Thompson 12). Ansel's friend and aide, Porter Hoye, ironically joining Farwell as a figure who, by contrast, illuminates Gibbs's nature, twice asks Gibbs to recite the multiplication tables. Hoye explains, "I thought I would find it comforting to hear you say something in specific, concrete terms again" (*AG* 56).

In the Gibbs/Hoye relationship, Buechner reiterates the pattern of the two earlier novels—Tristram Bone/Paul Steitler and Peter Cowley/Richard Lundrigan. Buechner consistently sets the idealist against the realist, the man of words against the man of action. In dialogue with Hoye, Gibbs begins to suspect the pervasiveness of his own apathy:

> As a man grows old, he begins to lose his hair, his teeth, and his concern—for others, for the country, even for himself. He doesn't get so involved. He doesn't walk step by step through living, but begins to flap along about ten feet off the ground. He sees what's going on, mind you, but it doesn't get in his way particularly. He becomes a kind of cumbersome bird. (*AG* 54)

Gibbs is no villain. His indifference has its source in civilization and thought, words and ideas, complex motives and dim impulses of the heart. All of these combine to produce inaction and melancholy. To Farwell's accusations, Gibbs responds: "For the civilized man there aren't apt to be any absolute principles or holy causes. That's what makes civilized life possible. We may not be heroes, but by and large we're also not villains—either collectively or taken one by one. Tolerant. Ambivalent. Call us what you will" (*AG* 120).

For Farwell, of course, these are the words of "the worst kind of cynic" (*AG* 120). He charges, "You don't quite believe in what you stand for, and you don't quite disbelieve in what you're opposed to" (*AG* 120). Although a caricature of much in right-wing politics and religion, Farwell categorizes Gibbs almost correctly in many ways. He errs remarkably, however, when he labels Gibbs a "cynic." Struggling to find justification for action and explanations for his array of motives, Gibbs almost loses himself in a morass of guilt, self-pity, loneliness, and bewilderment, but he cares too much to fall into mere cynicism. Here's a novel ripe for recovering from the mothballs.

As the novel opens, Gibbs, riding into New York with Anne and Porter, thinks of Rudy Tripp. Rudy's death, fifteen years before, still haunts Gibbs. When Gibbs, forced to dismiss Rudy from his post, allows a subordinate to deliver the termination notice, Rudy senses betrayal. According to his wife, Sylvia, to whom Gibbs tries to explain himself, "It was the last, terrible straw" (*AG* 12). When Rudy Tripp kills himself, Gibbs feels implicated, and he carries a sense of responsibility through all of the years leading up to the week chronicled in the novel. Upon his arrival in the city, Gibbs learns of his daughter's friendship with Robin Tripp, Rudy's son, a startling version of Gibbs's dead friend. Gibbs's subsequent relationship with Robin, a relationship expressed in Ansel's granting of the television interview, for instance, becomes the ground for Gibbs to expiate his guilt about Rudy. Through Ansel and Robin, Buechner partially expunges his own deeply buried feelings of implication in his father's suicide. Ansel Gibbs too has delayed the closer look at his responsibility for Rudy Tripp's death. Now, with the hearings pressing, Farwell ranting, and Anne's precarious dalliance with Robin Tripp, Gibbs faces at last his possible guilt. As Thompson put it, "Ansel Gibbs is guilty, but he will atone for that guilt" (Thompson 14). Nathan Scott focused on this dimension of the novel when he summarizes Buechner's work as dwelling on "the psychological penalties exacted by loneliness and the need for love."[16]

Meeting Robin Tripp for the first time, Gibbs attempts an honest airing of his feelings about Rudy: "I've questioned how much I was to blame for his dying as he did. Don't for an instant think that because I've had other matters on my mind since, I haven't thought about it again and again. And don't think either that I haven't felt qualms about seeing you today. There's a ghost here with us, and I'm fully aware of it. I'm being candid with you" (*AG* 63). Robin responds by talking of his own feelings, as a young child, at the time of his father's suicide. Robin's reactions are Buechner's, and Robin, like Gibbs, has some ghosts to purge. He tries to gauge his reactions to Gibbs. The television program, Gibbs's trial, the central crisis of the novel, acts as a test for Robin as well as for Gibbs. The talk-show debate transforms into an inquisition through Farwell's insistent prying into the details of Gibbs's life. Gibbs finds himself confessing his possible complicity in Rudy's death to Farwell, Robin, and a television audience. At the program's end, Gibbs turns to Robin saying, "Yours is the verdict I want, Tripp" (*AG* 126). For Farwell, the verdict is "plain enough as it is" (*AG* 127). Sure that Rudy's death presents graphic evidence of Gibbs's coldness and detachment, Farwell proclaims Gibbs guilty. The press loves the scent of scandal. But Gibbs wants Robin to pronounce on the issue, and Robin agrees to do so on the next airing of the program one week later.

According to his advisers, Gibbs has committed political suicide on Tripp's show, and the week of waiting has all the signs of a wake. Tripp's reputation for hypnotizing his guests, making them say much more than they had intended, rendering them, finally, as victims, comes into play during the postprogram reactions. Gibbs's political handlers and the press corps think Robin has claimed another unfortunate sufferer. Gibbs, however, claims, "I have never been so awake" (*AG* 133), and "I don't regret a word of it" (*AG* 135). The program operates as an epiphany for Gibbs, causing him first to question, "Maybe there's snow where my heart ought to be" and thus to begin his actual return to public life (*AG* 133). Facing Robin Tripp generates a glimmer of resolve in Gibbs and leads to his declaration:

> I'm back again. Not just to this city and to you [Hoye]. Back to nothing Farwell would call the thick of things, I suppose. But at least to the thickness of things, you might say—to the solid present, what's happening right now—snow falling, this table under my hands, having a job again, or being about to. Somehow I've returned. . . . A lot of it was deciding—I told the truth about that—that I no longer had this tragedy on my conscience. The boy himself exonerated me. (*AG* 134)

The remaining pages of the novel chronicle Gibbs's working through the issues raised during his television trial, his fitness for reinvestment in life, and the implications of his return.

After fifteen years of wondering about Rudy and a possible complicity in his friend's suicide, Gibbs visits Sylvia, Robin's mother and Rudy's widow, and the actual reasons for Rudy's death emerge. More prosaic than sensational, the truth revolves upon Rudy's essential shiftlessness; undependable and married to a woman with expensive tastes, he finally shoots himself in response to the succession of failures that have comprised his life. Gibbs's misplaced guilt, evidence of sensitivity and compassion, counters Farwell's accusation of coldness. In reality, Gibbs "is seldom out of touch with the sickness in his own belly," as he admits in the first paragraph of the novel (*AG* 3). The "long shadow" (*AG* 167) of Rudy's death clings to Gibbs and Robin. As Louise von Louwe realizes, Ansel is one of those people who "live the most significant part of their lives inside there somewhere" (*AG* 238). His introspection leads him more and more deeply into himself, and what he finds there is a patchwork—a collection of appearances belied by a reality few perceive:

> In all, he was impressive in appearance, and there was a keenness and vigor about him despite the whole chart of his disorders, real and rumored, such as a silver plate in his skull with a flap of toupee to cover the scar, a brace at his back, and some vascular disturbance, an intermittent numbness of the hands and feet which necessitated hydrotherapy and a careful diet. . . . He was a handsome enough man, dear Ansel, but just imagine him at night, undoing all the straps and buckles, putting half of himself away in a dresser drawer, and then scuttling, tiny and shivering, to bed! But if that or anything like it was true, it served only to accentuate the morning miracle of reassembly, for the world found Gibbs as reassuring in his physical presence as in the attainments of his statesmanship. (*AG* 7)

With his heroism in spite of handicap, Ansel Gibbs resembles Buechner heroes to come, Theodore Nicolet of *The Final Beast*, Leo Bebb of the *Bebb* tetralogy, and the unlikely saints Godric and Brendan. Gibbs will even persist in old man Israel, Tobit, and Kenzie Maxwell in Buechner novels of the 1990s. Gibbs is the sort of character Buechner becomes increasingly fascinated by, drawn, at least in part, from Graham Greene's whiskey priest. Deeply unaware of their own heroism, partial at best in their insights and abilities, these heroes manage to go beyond what would seem to be the distinct boundaries of their personalities. Gibbs, however, regards himself as inconsequential and less than the great man others perceive him to be. In a note to Anne announcing his withdrawal from competition for the Cabinet post, a decision that he will eventually reverse, Gibbs speaks of his missed greatness and his guilt:

> A man must do the best with what he is, and even one who falls short of greatness may still greatly work for good. . . . But it's one thing to fall short of greatness—you'd have a hard time naming me six men in any given century who didn't—but to fall short of common humanity is something else again. Without flagellating myself unduly, how could I avoid, how could you or anyone else avoid, seeing that that's what I've done? What else can it mean to have a friend and not to save him, to have a daughter and not to know her, to meet a friend's son and not to trust him, to have had a wife and hardly to

remember her? In what other way do you explain a man who has lived his whole life on the blurred edge of things? (*AG* 245)

At this point in the novel, a nadir for Gibbs, he has rejected Robin's verdict: "I think in his own way he's seen what Hell looks like, and he's survived to tell the tale. Not everybody does. I admire him as much as any man I know" (*AG* 222). For the moment preferring Farwell's verdict, Gibbs must flounder through his final spiritual struggle. He recalls the words of Kuykendall, the very words Buechner heard from George Buttrick in his own moment of paradoxical breakthrough, the words that raise again the question of choosing yes or no:

> If your answer's always Yes, then you probably don't know what believing means. At least five times out of ten the answer should be No because the No is as important as the Yes, maybe more so. The No is what proves you're a man in case you should ever doubt it. And then if some morning the answer happens to be really Yes, it should be a Yes that's choked with confession and tears and . . . great laughter. Not a beatific smile, but the laughter of wonderful incredulity. (*AG* 304)

Buechner's own ruminations about the life he is living and the one he might live come very close to the surface in Gibbs's tilt with the Yes and the No.

As he edited the final drafts of *The Return of Ansel Gibbs*, Buechner was considering entering the ministry, and his central character, Gibbs, has likewise considered such a career as a young man. Kuykendall, scandalized by the thought of Gibbs becoming a cleric, discourages him, hoping Gibbs will take his gifts into the world. Kuykendall knows that Gibbs's renunciation of the world, given Gibbs's profound knowledge of it, would have made him an effective priest, but he clings to a vision of Gibbs as a prophetic figure in world affairs (*AG* 87). I have no idea if Buechner is thinking of Saint Anselm when he names his character, but the possible allusion to the eleventh-century doctor of the church, who influenced the political and religious climate of his time, is instructive in developing the complex character of Gibbs. Kuykendall will finally toast Gibbs with the words, "I drink this to you, Ansel, whoever you are, whoever you turn out to be," emphasizing the incompleteness of Gibbs's search for identity (*AG* 307).

In the last paragraph of the novel, however, Gibbs makes it clear that much has happened in his journey to self-knowledge: "You cross your fingers and hold your tongue and do what you can in the time that's left. That is the only holy cause, my dear [Anne], ambivalence be damned. And *Pronto viene*" (*AG* 308). When Gibbs pronounces, "*Pronto viene,*" he alludes to the sign, "direct and faintly scandalous," that Kuykendall has erected over the door of his inner-city mission (*AG* 13). The banner reads, in full, "*Pronto viene Jesus Cristo*" ("Come quickly Jesus Christ"). The sentiment summarizes Kuykendall's wistful longing for a positive completion of history. By returning to a specific religious phrase at the end of the novel, a phrase of vitality and hope, Buechner hints at the spiritual renewal—the conversion of Ansel Gibbs. As Nancy Myers noted, *The Return of Ansel Gibbs* is a novel "concerned with various religious themes" (Myers 61). More explicitly, the novel is concerned with specifically religious issues such as conversion, charity, faith, repentance, and, most of all, the regeneration of Ansel Gibbs.

Elizabeth Janeway, in her *New York Times* review, labeled *The Return of Ansel Gibbs* "not a successful book" because "it is conceived as a political novel when Mr. Buechner's concern is really spiritual."[17] Although she perhaps misunderstood what Buechner is up to with the political framing of Gibbs's story, Janeway did perceptively recognize the center of the novel as Buechner's spiritual preoccupation—his religious wondering. She was one of the first critics to so register the eventual focus of Buechner's novelistic career. Those critics who chided Buechner for failing to develop the political themes of *The Return of Ansel Gibbs* missed his aims in the novel. Gibbs and Farwell discuss not even one political issue. No mention is ever made of the results of the hearings to determine Gibbs's worthiness for the Cabinet post. The issues, clearly personal and spiritual, revolve in Gibbs's psyche, not in the arena of public discourse. Gibbs, "a sort of Adlai Stevenson raised-to-the-nth-degree kind of civilized man,"[18] is, no doubt, a liberal Democrat, but we never hear him articulate an opinion on a single, specific political issue.

Obviously fixated on Gibbs's moral and spiritual life, Buechner steers the novel in the direction of his own concerns—theology, relationships, and making choices. The novel does not deserve dismissal on the grounds that it fails as a book about politics and politicians, any more than Arthur Miller's *Death of a Salesman* should be criticized on grounds that it fails to include enough about sales technique and practice. Willy Loman is a salesman, but Miller's play is about more than that. Ansel Gibbs, a politician, is also a human being facing the predicament of sorting out his future. *The Return of Ansel Gibbs* becomes something of a jumble with the inclusion of the varied experiences of Buechner's life, but he, finally, wants the return of Gibbs to stand as an affirmation of possibility in life.

In his discussion of the modern novel, specifically, Stanley Elkin's *A Bad Man*, Raymond Olderman claimed that the word "possibility" became "a cause for terror" for writers of the 1950s—"terror" because it suggested that "the world is anything." Olderman concluded, "Life can still be affirmed, but laughter seems even more necessary as the ambiguities and paradoxes multiply. The man who would affirm life must pull affirmation from the very causes and roots of paradox."[19] Aware of the absence of absolutes and bereft of fixed standards, Ansel Gibbs nonetheless chooses to act. Drawing "affirmation from the very causes and roots of paradox" is precisely Gibbs's achievement.

Ihab Hassan, another critic of the fiction of the era, discussed *The Return of Ansel Gibbs* as a "decisive departure" and a book "rich in moral ambiguities." He concluded, however, that the novel suffered from Buechner's failure to unify the "political, moral, and ideological questions" of the novel (Hassan 154). Although he fell into Janeway's error of expecting the novel to be political because its hero is a politician, Hassan did include *The Return of Ansel Gibbs* in his insightful discourse on the fiction of the era. Hassan centered on the anti-hero—the Holden Caulfield look-alikes who search for a solid truth as outsiders, even as victims of society. Hassan concluded, "The problem of the antihero is essentially one of identity. His search is for existential fulfillment, that is for freedom and self-definition" (Hassan 31). Such a dilemma, of course, confronts Ansel Gibbs. Finding himself outside the active society of his time, he questions his ability to recommit himself to that society, to his family and circle of friends, and even to himself.

In his analysis of postwar American fiction, Richard Rupp got at Gibbs's essential dilemma: "If genuine celebration is rare in contemporary life, it is also rare in contemporary fiction. Nevertheless, the best of our novelists seem to move *toward* celebration, although that move is tentative, groping, and fleeting. Our most responsible fiction manifests an assent to reality, a willingness to live."[20] Rupp's contention might well serve as a summary of all three of Buechner's early attempts at the novel. Tristram Bone, having experienced betrayal and loss, must try to wrench affirmation from the personal tragedies of his life; Peter Cowley, distrusted and incomplete as a messenger of God, must attempt to act on the faint glimmer of transcendence he thinks he may have witnessed, and Ansel Gibbs, having delved into himself, breaks out with his final pronouncement: "No more words. It's a promise I've made" (*AG* 308). As Nancy Myers had it, "Gibbs' final position affirms the idea that it is the courage to become involved in a world that promises nothing that is important" (Myers 61). Later Buechner novels will be increasingly strident with this message of paradoxical affirmation in the heart of the deepest darkness.

Addressing Buechner's abandonment of the political dimensions of his novel, Myers argued that "his main concern, as usual, is the emotional and spiritual sterility of contemporary man, particularly sophisticated, educated man" (Myers 72). And, as Thompson put it, "*The Return of Ansel Gibbs* stresses the inadequacies of such symptoms of modernism as ambivalence and paralysis" (Thompson 12). Gibbs must turn to Kuykendall, a man of deep compassion for others, to find a model on which to base his new life. "Ansel Gibbs has truly returned by the end of the novel. His final speech testifies to a new direction in his life, and it makes explicit that which had previously only been implicit in Buechner's earlier novels," Thompson summarized (Thompson 13). Not remotely Christian and only subtly religious, Gibbs's conversion is to a renewed way of viewing himself and a revolutionized sense of usefulness in the world.

Therefore, a novel into which Buechner crowds his notions of conversion, his burgeoning familiarity with theology, his courtship and marriage, his teachers, his work in the inner city, and even his father's suicide, *The Return of Ansel Gibbs* becomes, at last, a statement of willingness to go on past, or in spite of, melancholy and uncertainty, a willingness to invest oneself in life. The man of words brought to a recognition of his "lapsed humanity," Gibbs thinks of himself as "the Shadow King" in "some fantastic morality play" (*AG* 271). The gathered court—"Hoye the conscience, Anne the heart, Tripp the memory"—brings him to a conclusion: "A man can get so entangled in the rhetoric of his own mind that he forgets anyone else—gets cut off even from himself. I can't thank you enough for coming. [Hoye, Anne, Tripp] I promise you that. It's made me try to remember who I am" (*AG* 271).

Gibbs journeys into self-knowledge, into a realization of human imperfection, and universal incompleteness. His resulting discovery of the workings in his own heart returns him to real life. Refusing to soften the dismal reality, Buechner returns to Kuykendall in the last pages of the novel. Kuykendall tells Gibbs about a child in his parish who has died of a rat bite (*AG* 305). Clearly reminded that he has some action to take in a world where such things happen, Gibbs announces, following Kuykendall's story, his intention to pursue the "holy cause" of doing what he can (*AG* 308). The juxtaposition of Kuykendall's narration and Gibbs's decision is not a careless one. As Robin Tripp, who distrusts those who ignore the "ugly and unpleasant" (*AG* 214–15), summarizes: "Maybe what the world needs most is somebody who knows there's no such thing as a holy cause—somebody who knows it not just cynically and hard-boiled but sweating blood and wishing to God it wasn't so but making the best of it because it is" (*AG* 257). Gibbs's decision is an expensive one, simply because he shuns the easy ways of action without thoughtfulness. His return is freighted with his poignant sense of impossibility and tragedy, and his commitment is to strain, in spite of weakness, to reach beyond them.

Knowing "every man has his voices," Ansel Gibbs catalogues his own voices—Anne, Porter, Robin, and, most of all, Henry Kuykendall (*AG* 274). Anne, "the heart," worries about being a "do-gooder" in her work with Kuykendall's mission, stews over her blooming relationship with Robin Tripp, frets about Robin's possible abuse of her father, and cares deeply about the crisis her father endures. Porter Hoye, "the conscience," aware of his dependence upon Gibbs and sensitive to the deep differences between them, plods dutifully ahead in his attempts to protect and encourage Gibbs. Robin Tripp, "the memory," who undergoes his own transformation in the novel, first thinks of himself as a "chameleon"—a collection of all the teachers and friends he has known (*AG* 202). Insecure and searching for a father to replace the dead Rudy, Robin adapts to many roles and carefully develops the art of posing. On the air, he is "Mr. Mediocrity himself"; with Gibbs, he is "the bright, promising young man" (*AG* 202). A clever and carefully disguised cynic, Robin has little use for great men or fanatical movements. Robin's one encounter with religion, a vague conversion under the direction of a female evangelist, Kitten Dory, has not settled well. He remembers her as someone who talked about "sunlight and God and a baby's smile," someone overly simplistic and ethereal (*AG* 217). But Kitten Dory still haunts Robin just as Agnes Sanford still haunts Buechner.

Although troubled by religious possibilities and, by Anne, reminded of social needs, Robin prefers down-to-earth types like his stepfather, Ed Muller. Of Muller, Robin announces, "He's worth all the rest of them put together," borrowing from Fitzgerald's Nick Carraway (*AG* 166). But even this respect is insincere, and the conniving Robin is in for a change. His growth occurs as a response to his feelings for Anne, of course, but even more as a reaction to seeing Gibbs's love for him. At one point in the novel Anne feels she must choose between Robin Tripp and her father—"a terrible choice: either to continue on her way to Tripp or to turn back even now, and go to her father" (*AG* 249). Instead, Robin and Ansel are reconciled. Each miraculously lifts and enables the other. Tripp's attempt to trip Gibbs ironically serves to inspire Gibbs's return to life, and Gibbs's

bravery in the face of guilt and inadequacy inspires Robin to the forth-
rightness he has heretofore claimed to admire. Given the depths of his
darkness, Gibbs's return generates Tripp's reconsideration of his own
identity. Tripp's new direction sounds in his respect for Gibbs, a survivor
of hell, as he puts it in his verdict.

The secondary plot of *The Return of Ansel Gibbs* revolves around Henry
Kuykendall and his Harlem mission. Kuykendall sees into the truth of
Gibbs's character when he contrasts the young Ansel with his classmate,
Rudy Tripp. Rudy's failure, as Kuykendall interprets it, is that "he had no
private home inside himself" (*AG* 40). Rudy dies and Ansel lives on
because Ansel possesses a spiritual dimension, a moral fiber, which Rudy
does not possess. In his Harvard lectures, Kuykendall had repeatedly
alluded to the Hebrew notion of names. To be given a name, he said, was
to be changed from a blob of flesh into someone—to "know who you are"
(*AG* 83). Buechner, clearly fascinated with Muilenburg's teaching about
the Jewish language, returns to the subject many years later in *Wishful
Thinking*. Noting there that the Hebrew term *dabar* means both word and
act, Buechner talks of the power of words, the connection between saying
and doing (*WT* 96). Gibbs writes in his journal, "The man of words, as
distinct from the man of action, decides to do that which he has been best
able to phrase" (*AG* 265).

Surely such an idea is in the back of Buechner's mind as Ansel Gibbs,
the man of words, tries to become a man who translates word into deed.
Kuykendall, preoccupied with Gibbs's struggle for identity, longs for Gibbs
to be a prophet: "To ask the painful question . . . and make the painful point.
To hit below the belt if that's where the blow will do the most good. More
than anything else, a prophet's supposed to know, profoundly know, the
times he lives in and to speak what seems to him the truth about them in
the most compelling way he can find, no holds barred" (*AG* 88).

Finally, Kuykendall, who had thought Gibbs might "speak the word of
judgment to this generation" (*AG* 196), must accept the reality that Gibbs
is not Jeremiah. But this acquiescence is not a surrender. "What I found
was only Ansel Gibbs. I shouldn't say only. It's not as bad as that sounds.
It's also not good. It's the way things are, that's all, and that's what we're
usually left with, hope and blubber and pray as we will," Kuykendall sums
up (*AG* 196). Kuykendall's lesson learned, that Gibbs will not save the
world but only try to save it, ironically reflects Kuykendall's own investment in the thankless ghetto work—"his fierce disheveled commitment"
(*AG* 97). The most insistent voice in Gibbs's court is Kuykendall; it is
Kuykendall who pleads with Gibbs to fulfill the dream of the prophet,

Kuykendall who charges, "Go and *be* Ansel Gibbs. Make acts your words, and speak out to the nations because that way salvation lies—not salvation for the nations, perhaps, because after all, you're only Ansel Gibbs, but certainly salvation for you" (*AG* 279). When Kuykendall, with a Hebraic ferocity, finally commissions Gibbs with the pronouncement, "Go. . . . I speak with authority" (*AG* 286), Gibbs responds. He implicitly accepts the mantle of his old teacher; he becomes, after a fashion, Kuykendall himself. Like his mentor, Gibbs abandons words with a sad knowledge of their ineffectuality, and moves ahead to act. Kuykendall inspires the fullness of time for Ansel Gibbs.

A survey of the major studies of Buechner reveals an uncertainty about just what to do with this novel of renewal and affirmation. Marie-Helene Davies mostly ignored *The Return of Ansel Gibbs*; Nancy Myers stumbled over the novel because it has not sounded the Christian chorus she hears in the later work; and Stacy Thompson mostly skipped over the novel as irrelevant to her thesis. John Aldridge, who championed Buechner's early work, dismissed *The Return of Ansel Gibbs*, placing Buechner among those writers whose "best work is behind them.[21] Buechner's interest had shifted and with it, Aldridge's approval. John Gardner displayed a fine grasp of Buechner with the observation, "The novels, properly understood, may be too much like sermons" (Gardner 99). At least Gardner saw something of the central interest evident in the changing focus from *A Long Day's Dying* to *The Return of Ansel Gibbs*. The overall critical reception of the novel featured a question mark. The book didn't match up with the earlier work and the critical expectations. The promising modern novelist has thrown a curve that disconcerts: some critics are put off, some are curious, many are dismissive. To say, as did Nancy Myers, that *The Return of Ansel Gibbs* was "well received" (Myers 3) was to miss the tones of distrust and bewilderment in the critical response.

The reception this time included a film adaptation for *Playhouse 90* in November of 1958, and a major prize, the Rosenthal Award. Buechner remembers the award dinner mostly because Truman Capote was there with his resplendent date, Marilyn Monroe.[22] But the novel fell quickly into the musty back pages of the literary scene, and the reviews more or less followed the same pattern as the general criticism. Most reviewers noticed the stylistic departures, the fresher style and voice, in *The Return of Ansel Gibbs*. The *Atlantic* reviewer noted that Buechner had become "less ornate,"[23] and R. W. Flint in *The New Republic* argued that Buechner was "shaking off" Jamesian preciosity.[24] Edwin Kennebeck in *Commonweal* tagged it the "firmest and clearest" of Buechner's work.[25] Other critics focused on Buechner's preoccupation with theological ideas. William

Hogan in the *San Francisco Chronicle* called the novel "a sermon in disguise,"[26] proposing that Kuykendall represents Christ while Porter Hoye represents Caesar, and Gibbs must choose between them. Elizabeth Janeway set up much the same equation in her review. Aldridge had heft; the idea of Buechner as sermonizer was to haunt him from this novel forward. D. L. Stevenson in *The Nation* referred to *The Return of Ansel Gibbs* as "theological musings."[27] Finally, a few reviewers discussed the book as a study of a search for identity. Coleman Rosenburger in the *New York Herald-Tribune* alluded to the novel as a detective story where the mystery is the disclosure of Gibbs's real nature.[28] The *Kirkus* reviewer spotted the theme of the book as "a problem of identity" (*Kirkus* 908), and Spectorsky concurred, "Each of Mr. Buechner's major characters, Gibbs especially, is beset by the crucial need to discover—and to face—the real, the inner self" (Spectorsky 21). Spectorsky compared the novel to "the gleam of hand-polished old silver" (Spectorsky 21), one of the more elaborate metaphorical plaudits. But no consistent pattern emerged from the reviews: many objected to the underdevelopment of the political themes, some called *The Return of Ansel Gibbs* "an important book"[29] or "a grave and beautiful book"[30] or "fiction of a high order of excellence,"[31] and others concluded that the novel was "superficial" and fraught with an "essential unreality."[32]

With *The Return of Ansel Gibbs*, Buechner moves into the rather awkward territory that he occupies still. Formally, Buechner continues in *The Return of Ansel Gibbs* to make little use of plot, relying instead upon character and psychological studies. The increased readability of the novel and the occasional intrusion of comic scenes suggest the Buechner to come, but the novel produced an ambiguous response in the critics precisely because it is such an impossible book to categorize. Labels such as "Jamesian" or "modern novel" or "Christian novel" or "sermonizer," which may serve in limited ways at one point or another in Buechner's career, simply do not apply here. Buechner has found more of his own voice, and it is the voice of questioning: What is the social responsibility of the government, the church, the individual? How does one translate theological notions into practical actions? What are the implications of embracing Christian faith?

This is not to imply that *The Return of Ansel Gibbs* is a religious treatise, although Buechner was actually trying to decide between a writing career and a ministerial one, a choice he saw as either/or, as he worked out the final pages of this novel (*Image* 47). The novel is, strictly speaking, no more religious than it is political. It is a novel, not a tract—a partial exploration of the cost of being alive. Yet, with Ansel Gibbs's affirmation, Buechner's direction is set. He will experiment and refine, but he becomes, in *The*

Return of Ansel Gibbs, as much of a Christian novelist as he will ever be. Even after his ordination, Buechner will reject the option of writing simplistic, moralistic tales. His creative fiction, throughout his career, resounds with the tones of religious exploration, hope, and even affirmation, but never with Christian dogma or piety. In Thompson's words, Buechner flirts with "the possibility that the old stories are still the truest, that there *is* a mythology which makes sense of things" (Thompson 16). Flannery O'Connor in her speech "Novelist and Believer" summarized the aim of a writer like Buechner when she spoke of the "attempt to enlarge . . . ideas of what religion is and . . . how the religious need may be expressed in the art of our time" (O'Connor 154–55). Buechner accepts the challenge of what O'Connor termed "travail with the world" (O'Connor 168).

Such a commitment carries a price: some, convinced that Buechner had "gone off the deep end," abandoned him; others began to claim him as a spokesperson for this or that Christian message. Nonetheless, he remains elusive, not a stance-taker so much as a searcher, not an ideologue so much as an ordinary human being wrestling with life, a man who wants, in Robert Adams's words, to "tell the truth in public" (Adams 205). What shines at last in *The Return of Ansel Gibbs* is what Robertson Davies, a writer Buechner much admires, called "the writer's inner struggle toward self-knowledge and self-recognition, which he manifests through his art."[33] If the result is a question, so be it. At the very least, Buechner does for his readers what great writers have always done: "He explores his own spirit to the uttermost and bodies forth what he finds in a form of art that is plain to anyone who can read it—though not necessarily to anyone who picks up his books" (R. Davies 124).

The autobiographical texture of the novels has persisted in this third attempt, yet Buechner's developing voice is somehow both freer and smarter. *The Return of Ansel Gibbs* is chock-full of pithy Buechnerisms, the aphorisms that increasingly appear in anthologies and sermons in Buechner's subsequent career. And when Gibbs fires off that Tillich line about living "in memory and anticipation" (*AG* 54), readers can sense the young author, dwelling in uncertainty still, but learning to shape something from the past as well as turning with a bit of courage toward the days ahead.

Notes

1. Shirley and Rudy Nelson, "Buechner: Novelist to 'Cultural Despisers,'" *Christianity Today* 25:10 (May 29, 1981): 44. Hereafter cited as Nelsons.
2. Kenneth L. Gibble, "Listening to My Life: An Interview with Frederick Buechner," *Christian Century*, November 16, 1983, 1042. Hereafter cited as Gibble.

3. Frederick Buechner, "The Tiger," in *Prize Stories 1955: The O. Henry Awards*, ed. Paul Engle and Hansford Martin (New York: Doubleday & Co., 1955), 58. Hereafter cited as Tiger.
4. Frederick Buechner, *The Return of Ansel Gibbs* (New York: Alfred A. Knopf, 1958), 303. Hereafter cited as *AG*.
5. Nancy Myers, "Frederick Buechner and the Literature of Grace," *Mission Journal*, May 1981, 23.
6. Paul Tillich, *The Courage to Be* (New Haven, CT: Yale University Press, 1952), 3. Hereafter cited as *Courage*.
7. Paul Tillich, *Dynamics of Faith* (New York: Harper & Row, 1957), 21. Hereafter cited as *Dynamics*.
8. Paul Tillich, *The Eternal Now* (New York: Charles Scribner's Sons, 1956), 126. Hereafter cited as *Eternal*.
9. Paul Tillich, *The Shaking of the Foundations* (New York: Charles Scribner's Sons, 1948), 162. Hereafter cited as *Shaking*.
10. Personal correspondence, November 12, 1981. Buechner makes a similar observation in the 1980 *Wittenburg Door* interview.
11. Frederick Buechner, *A Room Called Remember: Uncollected Pieces* (San Francisco: Harper & Row, 1984), 47. Hereafter cited as *RCR*.
12. Reynolds Price, "The Road to Devotion," *New York Times Book Review*, April 11, 1982, 11. Hereafter cited as Price.
13. A. C. Spectorsky, "A Crisis of Conscience," *Saturday Review*, February 15, 1958, 21. Hereafter cited as Spectorsky.
14. Anthony West, "Briefly Noted," *New Yorker*, April 12, 1958, 158.
15. Norman Podhoretz, "The New Nihilism and the Novel," *Partisan Review* 25 (1958): 576. Hereafter cited as Podhoretz.
16. Nathan A. Scott Jr., *Modern Literature and the Religious Frontier* (New York: Harper & Bros., 1958), 96.
17. Elizabeth Janeway, "Portrait of a Public Man," *New York Times Book Review*, February 16, 1958, 4.
18. *Kirkus*, December 15, 1957, 908. Hereafter cited as *Kirkus*.
19. Raymond Olderman, *Beyond the Wasteland: The American Novel in the Nineteen-Sixties* (New Haven, CT: Yale University Press, 1972), 53.
20. Richard H. Rupp, *Celebration in Postwar American Fiction 1945–1967* (Coral Gables, FL: University of Miami Press, 1970), 18. Hereafter cited as Rupp.
21. John W. Aldridge, *Time to Murder and Create: The Contemporary Novel in Crisis* (New York: David McKay Co., 1966), 140.
22. Personal correspondence, July 6, 2005.
23. *Atlantic*, March 1958, 101.
24. R. W. Flint, ". . . Ere I Forget Thee, Oh Princeton!" *New Republic*, June 23, 1958, 29.
25. Edwin Kennebeck, "Clear, Firm Work," *Commonweal*, April 11, 1958, 53.
26. William Hogan, "Triumph of the Egghead: An Analysis in Fiction," *San Francisco Chronicle*, February 27, 1958, 33.
27. D. L. Stevenson, review in *Nation*, May 10, 1958, 425.
28. Coleman Rosenberger, "Just Who Was Ansel Gibbs?" *New York Herald Tribune Book Review*, February 14, 1958, 5.
29. "On and Off the Fence," *Times Literary Supplement*, January 6, 1958, 309.

30. Robert Martin Adams, review in *Hudson Review* 11 (1958): 285.
31. Victor P. Hass, "Story of the V.I.P. Shows Skill of Uncommon Sort," *Chicago Sunday Tribune*, February 16, 1958, 3.
32. Pamela Hansford Johnson, "New Novels," *New Statesman*, June 14, 1958, 782.
33. Robertson Davies, *One Half of Robertson Davies* (New York: Penguin Books, 1978), 123. Hereafter cited as RDavies. Buechner mentions his fondness for Davies in 1983 interviews in *Radix* and *Contemporary Authors* and in several other places.

Chapter Four

Exploring Sainthood

The Final Beast

onversion and ordination move easily alongside artistic ambition as Frederick Buechner hits his stride in the 1965 novel *The Final Beast*, the work that charts the territory Buechner will explore into the 1970s and beyond. *The Final Beast* contains the fullest expression of the ideas echoing softly through the first three novels and resounding through the later work; it is the fulcrum book in the Buechner canon. Any clear understanding of Buechner's career requires a close look at this novel, the bellwether of Buechner's early career. By 1963, when he took a sabbatical to write *The Final Beast*, Buechner had settled into the routines of job and family. Through the late 1950s and early 1960s, he won awards for *The Return of Ansel Gibbs*, experienced the birth of his daughters, Katherine and Dinah, and suffered the loss of Grandmother Buechner—the citadel, the "Inspector General," one of the "giants" of his childhood—who held the family together through those perilous 1930s (*SJ* 21). Along the way too, he accepted a position as chairman of the department of religion and, later, school minister at Phillips Exeter Academy, and exercised his ordination as a Presbyterian minister through writing and preaching. *The Final Beast*, dedicated to Katherine and Dinah, emerged from a milieu of stability and evinces a growing confidence in both stylistic and thematic venues.

The novel centers on a dazed young clergyman. His wife dead in a senseless accident, Theodore Nicolet must persevere for the sake of his two young children. In spite of the cloud of bewilderment hanging over the remnant of his family, he must continue to minister to his congregation in a New England village called Myron. A year has passed since Franny's sudden and inexplicable death, but Nicolet still cannot find solid footing, still has not solved the riddle of the shopping list Franny has left behind, the

"The Moorings"
Buechner's home in Bermuda, 1937–1939

single word "beauty" not crossed off. The book opens with the bedraggled Nicolet, stretched taut by sorrow and puzzlement, hastening off in search of one of his parishioners, Rooney Vail, who has fled her husband, Clem, in apparent desperation at their failure to have children.

Soon we learn the real motive has more to do with guilt deriving from a moment of sexual indiscretion. The partner in Rooney's infidelity is Will Poteat, a local newspaper man, but Buechner only hints at this truth until the last pages, thus lending deeper currency to Poteat's own intimations in the village newspaper that Rooney and Nicolet are actually the ones involved in a tawdry affair. Maybe they have absconded together, Poteat hints. Because Poteat is in the dirt business, the reader isn't sure. Poteat's credibility is one of the mysteries that drive the narrative. Another version of Motley, Lundrigan, and Farwell, Poteat is the villain of this piece, but he is correct in his hints that Nicolet searches for Rooney from ambiguous motives.

Maybe Nicolet does love her; maybe Poteat's gossip is right on the mark. But Nicolet has other troubles, too. There's his need to escape the pressures of holding his small family together; there's the guilt he feels about his father, Roy, a distant and disturbing presence in his life; and there's the enigma of faith, the crisis of a preacher no longer sure of the message entrusted to him. Thus Nicolet's flight is a pursuit of himself as much as a search for Rooney Vail. Here's another Buechner character trying to decipher the darkest mysteries and looking for something like happiness. Rooney, the church, his father, himself—suddenly, as if in a dream, Nicolet is on the road. He catches up with Rooney at the home of a faith healer, Lillian Flagg, in an out-of-the-way, end-of-the-world sort of place, Muscadine. In this temporary retreat, Rooney has learned something of forgiveness, just as Nicolet is to learn something about joy over the course of the story.

As before, Buechner's own experience finds its way into this book—thoughts on parenting, the challenges of effective preaching, faith healers and church secretaries, preachers and teachers of English right out of Buechner's life. Even the Bermuda of his childhood is here, but the central autobiographical connection is, as with the first three novels, more about the ideas swirling than the events occurring in his life. Buechner also seems to have taken seriously his mother's anger at the autobiographical dimensions of *The Return of Ansel Gibbs*. Suicide will not be a direct subject in the new novel, although the absent father will. The pain of the lost father is buried deep in *The Final Beast*. Nicolet thinks of himself as having no father.

One tangent of his flight in the novel will take him to Roy, the father he sees maybe once a year, the father he doesn't know well at all. Nicolet thinks of Roy as a "shadow, a ghost, who must be exorcised before he could continue on his way unhaunted" (*FB* 155). Like virtually every major character in Buechner's books, Nicolet is trying to learn his own name and settle issues with a problematic father. While on the run from home and church and self, he checks into a hotel under the name Rene Laliberte, his grandfather's name, hoping that the new name might mean a new freedom, an altered destiny. In a strikingly tentative passage, we even see Nicolet press his head against his father's chest, a desperate cry for connection that goes more or less unanswered. The misconnection with Roy, clearly significant to Buechner's own story, leads to a preoccupation with guilt and forgiveness in the novel. Pardoning Roy and exonerating himself for hating Roy is a subtheme alongside Rooney's lessons in forgiveness.

Another important character is Irma Reinwasser, a more fully elaborated version of the Emma character from *A Long Day's Dying*. Nicolet's housekeeper and a survivor of a Nazi concentration camp, the haunted Irma wrongly feels that the rumors about Nicolet and Rooney are her fault; she has accidentally tipped Poteat to the potential scandal. Her public confession leads to her accidental death, the consequence of an adolescent prank executed by some well-meaning boys. Members of Nicolet's church, the boys respect Nicolet, and their misguided anger on his behalf results in a miscarried prank and a tragic conflagration in which Irma dies hideously. Irma's story is the darkest of any of Buechner's characters to this point in his career.

The Final Beast is Buechner's first novel that seems more concerned with telling a story than celebrating artistry and style, and the story told is a straightforward one of tragedy, misunderstanding, horror, and futility. Yet beneath the fabric of human weakness is a paradoxical joy that becomes a final statement of the novel. Even Poteat, the embittered gossip, the hopelessly alone, avowed enemy of Nicolet, is given laughter in the last lines of the novel. Arthur Mizener, in his *New York Times* review, noted the joy. Buechner, in Mizener's view, is attempting to arouse in his readers a sense of "the beauty and laughter underlying the filth and boredom of this world."[1] Something broods here beyond the tragedy.

Critics noticed the stylistic shifts apparent from *A Long Day's Dying* to *The Final Beast*: a freer style and an instinct for humor, although the move to a more fluid prose had begun in *The Return of Ansel Gibbs*. Nancy Myers realized that "the articulate, urbane dialogue of the characters in the early novels is replaced by colloquial, witty, often whimsical dialogue" (Myers 73). Venetia Pollock, reviewing for *Punch*, summarized the prose of *The Final Beast*: "The writing is excellent and the handling crisp."[2] Such observers underscored Buechner's move toward stylistic simplicity, but the overriding breakthrough of *The Final Beast* centered in Buechner's ambition to make the novel an arena for a religious consideration. Reviewers overwhelmingly registered the marked religious dimension of *The Final Beast*. *Time* called it a "precious pseudoreligious novel."[3] In a substantial article for *Christianity and Crisis*, Amos Wilder cited Buechner's new novel as "a good test case of whether a modern artist can make traditional Christian language palatable or effective to a general audience today."[4] Indeed, Wilder saw that Buechner was violating deeply held dogma—he was writing about religion and *not* treating his subject satirically. Among the first to forecast a potential loss of readers on both sides of the secular-religious divide, Wilder did approve of the book as the best of what a believing artist can offer. Wilder opened a conversation that continues still, a conversation audible in Tertullian's fine question, "What indeed has Athens to do with Jerusalem?" That conundrum has fueled an enduring question in both academic and popular arenas about the possible intersections of faith and literature. The central query in any approach to Frederick Buechner's work is, Can we trust a writer who is also a believer?

A. W. Phinney in the *Christian Science Monitor* categorized Buechner's "problem" in the book as a "clash between a theological point of view and an artist's."[5] Julian Moynahan, in a provocatively titled review, "Writing on Cloth Can be Tricky," concluded, "*The Final Beast* lodges itself at midpoint between the priest's and the writer's way of looking at things."[6] Arthur Mizener accused Buechner of wanting "to write a novel that not only is convincing but also justifies the ways of God to contemporary man" (Mizener 28). These reviews reflected the general reaction to *The Final Beast*: a good book perhaps, but one dabbling in the disparate arenas of religion and literature to a degree that makes critics squirm. The news of the ordination was on the streets, and the weight of this outburst of dubiety has pushed against Buechner's literary reputation since. I can't help wondering about Buechner's experience beside that of, say, Gail Godwin after *Father Melancholy's Daughter*, or John Irving after *A Prayer for Owen Meany*, or Anne Tyler after *Saint Maybe*, or John Updike after *In the Beauty of the Lilies*.

A generation later, Dan Wakefield, writing in *The New York Times Book Review*, captured Buechner's dilemma:

> From the time of my college graduation in 1955 until the 1980s, the only literary portrayals of God as a vital and natural force in the everyday lives of characters I could agree with came from Jewish writers. (I avoided Frederick Buechner on the grounds that he was a Protestant minister writing purportedly "Christian" novels, so I unfairly assumed he was some kind of propagandist, a prejudice he has suffered from widely and wrongly.)[7]

John Davenport, in *Spectator*, succinctly summarized the critical issues that emerged in Buechner's fourth novel, the issues that continue to be raised in any discussion of Buechner's literary standing: "Mr. Buechner has put his foot in it."[8] As Davenport memorably saw it, Buechner wants to write about matters of faith and theology. Davenport concluded: "He [Buechner] is a Christian. . . . He writes, this formidably austere and dedicated and most delightfully amusing man, from an unfashionable centre" (Davenport 1). In their focusing upon Buechner's supposedly unholy mixing of the literary and the religious, the critics illustrated a sensitivity to a perceived change in Buechner's aims as a novelist.

In reality, however, *The Final Beast* merely brings the earlier three novels to fruition, the heart of the matter that the reviewers and critics mostly fail to note. *The Final Beast* is neither a departure nor a new direction so much as a development, a building on what came before. Ruminating on the themes and logic of his previous work as well as upon the events of his early Christian experience, Buechner finally writes the novel he has hinted at in his first three attempts. Katherine Jackson's review in *Harper's* captured the essence of Buechner's intentions in the novel and continues to be the most nearly just of the comments made about *The Final Beast*: "This is a story that skates with daring skill and exuberant speed over the thin ice of potential blasphemy, sentimentality, and violence to emerge finally on the firm, smooth surface of honest faith and uproarious laughter."[9] The central importance of *The Final Beast* is certainly in this area of the struggle to affirm faith as emerging from doubt. Buechner has strayed into daunting territory. Ministers are OK in American literature as long as they are Elmer Gantry, a fraud, or Jim Casy, who got over it. Writing about a minister without sentiment or satire—that's just not done.

I've suggested that Buechner's central tenet—faith in the midst of overwhelming doubt, faith even within the reality of suffering, faith in spite of the mass of contradictory evidence—is reminiscent of Graham Greene, at least the Graham Greene of *The Power and the Glory*. Pursuing the parallels can be instructive for understanding Buechner's work. Buechner holds to the skepticism, maintains a commitment to ambiguity. There's that verse again looming in the background—"Lord, I believe; help my unbelief'"—the ground of Buechner's theology. According to Malcolm Muggeridge, Greene looked to the same New Testament verse as his "favorite of all texts."[10] Buechner, like Greene, refuses to minimize the actuality of the bitterness of suffering. The suspicion that incoherence is the fundamental rule of the universe is, in the view of these two writers, inherent in the human condition. At best, they say, we can hope for some glimmering moment of inspiration or intuition that hints of a larger reality—sanctity and security behind the appearance of things.

Buechner seems to have discovered this theme in *The Power and the Glory*, and the bulk of his fiction is an attempt to elaborate upon it. As Kurt Reinhardt noted, the dominant themes of Greene's novel are "isolation, decay, pain, despair."[11] But Reinhardt entitled his discussion of *The Power and the Glory* "Victory in Failure," emphasizing that the direction of the novel is toward some unquenchable hope, some spark of divinity alive in the mundane and often frightening reality of the world. This enduring sacredness within the profane is, arguably, the central motif in Buechner's fiction as well. In a 1981 interview, Buechner confesses his debt to Greene: "I sometimes think my whole literary life has been an effort to rewrite *The*

Power and the Glory in a way of my own" (Nelsons 44). Setting *The Power and the Glory* beside *The Final Beast* elucidates a shared preoccupation with the presence of a graceful God in a tawdry world, the imperfection of the bumbling creature, the message of God's paradoxical reality that brings joy in the strangest of circumstances, and the conclusion that "heaven is here." Buechner celebrates this notion in his fourth novel, a book laced with fecal imagery and the ugliness of genuine evil.

Like Greene in *The Power and the Glory*, Buechner is positing the possibility of faith and joy in a bleak world. Greene's novel introduces a protagonist who feels himself unworthy—the whiskey priest. Readers are often overwhelmed by the humanness of the unnamed priest who regards himself "unworthy of what he carried."[12] We agree. He doesn't arouse much in the way of sympathy. He is a man who needs his liquor, the father of an illegitimate child, and a priest who doubts the efficacy of his prayers. Yet, for all that, he is a priest—uncontrollably. "It's out of my power," he finishes, as if to underscore his helplessness and his call (*Power* 40). His face is "a buffoon's face, good enough for mild jokes to women, but unsuitable at the altar rail" (*Power* 59).

A failure of a priest, he paradoxically carries on in his calling: "He was a bad priest, he knew it. They had a word for his kind—a whiskey priest, but every failure dropped out of sight and mind: somewhere they accumulated in secret—the rubble of his failures. One day they would choke up, he supposed, altogether the source of grace. Until then he carried on, with spells of fear, weariness, with a shamefaced lightness of heart" (*Power* 60). The reader of Greene's novel is ceaselessly reminded of the priest's "desperate inadequacy" (*Power* 82). And to what end? Only that the priest turns out to be a kind of poet, and "a poet is the soul of his country" (*Power* 113). Despite the irony of his being a whiskey priest with a bastard child, despite his unworthiness, reluctance, doubt, and failure, the priest becomes a martyr, the reason that faith survives in his godless province. Unable to believe in God for himself, he nonetheless carries God to others and keeps the soul of his country alive. Buechner's indebtedness to Greene begins with this notion of a protagonist who is a model of human absurdity and yet stumblingly and stunningly victorious.

The Power and the Glory begins with the whiskey priest's encounter with Tench, the British dentist. Both men feel abandoned in the remote province. Greene returns repeatedly to the priest's "huge abandonment" to establish both the theme and tone of the novel. The opening pages pull the reader into the constrictive, oppressive atmosphere. The diction emphasizes desolation and death: "vultures," "carrion," and "indifference" (*Power* 1).

Missing his chance for escape because of a call to administer last rites to a parishioner, the priest is overwhelmed by a sense of his own unworthiness and a desire for freedom from the oppressive state. And with all that, there's the enormous weight of his priestly calling. Although on the run from the minions of a political revolution that has made him an outlaw, he is "the slave of his people" (*Power* 19). When the ship, his means of escape, leaves the dock, the priest "knew what it meant . . . he was abandoned" (*Power* 19).

Buechner's Nicolet also feels deeply abandoned as he begins his paradoxical flight both from and to his responsibilities. Abandoned at his wife's death, Nicolet has pressed ahead with his duties as a parent and a minister, but, with the passing of the year, something has caught up with him. In the note he leaves for Irma before his unannounced departure, Nicolet simply writes, "the time has come" (*FB* 9). Time for what? Time to grieve, perhaps, or time to try to wrest answers from his puzzlement? Irma guesses he may have gone "for the sake of God" (*FB* 13). She is right, of course; Nicolet runs to find himself and God as much as he runs in search of Rooney Vail. Like the whiskey priest whose unstudied, impulsive commitment to others makes of him, who can never absolve himself, a hero of the faith, so Nicolet, in pursuing Rooney Vail, models an unself-conscious heroism. The flight theme is reminiscent of Francis Thompson's "The Hound of Heaven," the poem from which Greene takes the first American title for *The Power and the Glory*: *The Labyrinthine Ways*. Thompson's poem stands provocatively behind both novels. Both Nicolet and the unnamed priest are hunter and hunted, seeking but also sought.

Like the whiskey priest, Nicolet exhibits deep confusion about his motives in chasing after Rooney. Aware of his inadequacy and unworthiness and sensitive to his buffoonery, Nicolet is stricken by a crisis of faith and finds himself unable to respond directly to Clem Vail's question of whether or not he believes in God. Nicolet answers, "Sometimes I believe in the hot breath down my neck" (*FB* 27). Lillian Flagg cites Buechner's favorite New Testament passage to summarize Nicolet's faith: "At first . . . believing . . . praying . . . it's all just playing a game. Quite ridiculous really, and why not? We are all quite ridiculous. . . . 'Lord, I believe. Help Thou mine unbelief.' That's it, you see. The man who said that didn't really believe very much in anything either, and it made no difference. His boy was healed. You believe in spite of not believing" (*FB* 53). Nicolet is the unwilling servant who feels sickness at the call of God: "I was glad when they said unto me, 'Let us go into the house of the Lord.' No preacher had written that. . . . I was sick to my stomach when they said unto me. . . . That was more like it" (*FB* 225). Turned nearly to dust by the call he carries, Nicolet is brother to the reluctant priest of *The Power and the Glory* who carries his priesthood like a birthmark (*Power* 41). Just as Greene's priest cannot ignore the call to serve his parish and weeps from a sense of unworthiness at the thought of such service, so Buechner's minister balks at all he senses God wants him to be. The priest and the preacher come together in their sense of deep inadequacy in their respective callings.

Further, Buechner discovers in Greene's novel an imaginative rendering of Tillich's ideas about belief in spite of doubt. In *Why Do I Write?* Greene observes, "You remember the black and white squares of Bishop Blougram's chessboard. As a novelist, I must be allowed to write from the point of view of the black square as well as of the white: doubt and even denial must be given their chance of self-expression."[13] Buechner learns from Greene the use of the most shockingly secular of situations for most strikingly unsecular observations. Using violence and distortion as a means of awakening a reader was, of course, a favorite tactic of Flannery O'Connor, who said, "I have to make the reader feel, in his bones if nowhere else, that something is going on here that counts" (O'Connor 162). In "The Fiction Writer and His Country" she added the famous lines, "You have to make your vision apparent by shock—to the hard of hearing you shout, and for the almost-blind you draw large and startling figures" (O'Connor 34).

As we have seen, Buechner claims no familiarity with O'Connor's work before 1986, but his 1983 interview in *Radix* underscores a consonance between the two in their approach to the imagined audience: "I'm still, insofar as I can imagine the audience, writing to cultured unbelievers who are interested in religion but by no means committed. To catch their attention, sometimes you have to do things that shock the committed ones a little. It is the price you pay."[14] Harold Baxter turned to the consonance for a 1983 dissertation, *Touched by Fire and Laughter: The Range of Grace in the Fiction of Flannery O'Connor and Frederick Buechner*. Baxter there argued that Buechner and O'Connor were "almost needfully linked," a phrase I take as an underscoring of their essential complementariness.[15] Horton and Marie-Helene Davies, in "The God of Storm and Stillness," compared the work of O'Connor and Buechner: "They are both prophetic voices crying in the wilderness of our modern secular society and insisting that Christ is the only oasis in that desert."[16] When Greene opines, "If you excite your audience first, you can put over what you will of horror, suffering, truth,"[17] we can almost see O'Connor and Buechner nodding in agreement.

Buechner is at home with the Catholic writers Greene and O'Connor in part because of his use of the violent and aberrant possibilities in human behavior, a technique that caused one *New York Times* book reviewer to label Buechner's method as "sanctifying the profane."[18] The technique, of course, derives from Buechner's sense of audience—he often calls his readers "religion's cultured despisers," appropriating Friedrich Schleiermacher's phrase (Nelsons 44). Buechner's novels are certainly not moralistic fables, Bunyanesque allegories, sentimental Christian meandering, or thinly disguised Christian fantasy. *The Final Beast* deals openly with sexual infidelity, aging, guilt, failure, death, and the assorted baggage of the human condition. Harry Parker, in his Princeton dissertation, referred to Buechner's insistence upon "undeniable evil" in *The Final Beast*.[19]

The reality of suffering and ambiguity in Buechner's novels is important because of the increasing tendency to categorize him as an evangelist whose appropriate place is the religious bookstore, though none of his books had shown up there by the mid-1960s. Buechner's critics have been somewhat careless in their classifications. Nancy Myers, for instance, concluded that "Buechner is unique among modern novelists in that he does not hesitate to deal with religious concepts at a time when novelists rarely deal with such concepts as if they were based on literal truths" (Myers 8). Such an observation runs the risk of transforming Buechner's work into didacticism and sentiment, ignoring the darkness and doubt from which his affirmations emerge. Even Myers, although she may mistake as a studied intention what is simply organic in Buechner, saw the unorthodoxy of Buechner's methodology: "Buechner uses four-letter words, blunt sexual references, and near-blasphemy to convey what are basically reverential religious implications. It is as if he is trying to speak to contemporary man in language and imagery with which he is familiar so that Buechner might be heard" (Myers 6). For Buechner, as he admits through Nicolet, we are all runaways, and we can never be sure of where we are running. The irreverence that Myers noted is simply Buechner's attempt to hold up a mirror instead of a message.

Buechner, then, shares with Greene a vision based on the Pauline admonition, "Remember that you were . . . separated from Christ, alienated from the commonwealth of Israel, and strangers to the covenants of promise, having no hope and without God in the world."[20] For his 1939 travel book, *The Lawless Roads*, Greene chose a lengthy epigraph from Cardinal Newman's *Apologia Pro Vita Sua*. The epigraph, which might serve as a comment on the work of both Greene and Buechner, reads in part:

> To consider the world . . . the greatness and littleness of man, his far-reaching aims, his short duration, the curtain hung over his futurity, the disappointments of life, the defeat of good, the success of evil, physical pain, mental anguish, the prevalence and intensity of sin, the

pervading idolatries, the corruptions, the dreary hopeless irreligion, that condition of the whole race, so fearfully yet exactly described in the Apostle's words, "having no hope, and without God in the world,"—all this is a vision to dizzy and appal. . . . What shall be said to this heart-piercing, reason-bewildering fact? I can only answer, that either there is no Creator, or the living society of men is in a true sense discarded from His presence. . . . And so I argue about the world;—*if* there be a God, *since* there is a God, the human race is implicated in some terrible aboriginal calamity. It is out of joint with the purposes of its Creator.[21]

Buechner follows Greene in the refusal to back off from the alienation and ambiguity of modern life—the out-of-jointness. Like the whiskey priest, Nicolet is a representative human. The unanswerable questions will prevail, and the most we can hope for is, as Greene suggested in the title of one of his short stories, "The Hint of an Explanation."

John Spurling, in his discussion of Graham Greene's career, cataloged the reaction of the Vatican to *The Power and the Glory*. Ten years after its publication, the novel was banned for being "paradoxical" and for dealing "with extraordinary circumstances."[22] Spurling concluded:

For them [the Holy Office], presumably, the faith did not shine brightly enough out of the surrounding gloom; but for non-Catholic readers it is precisely the personal, dogged, earth-bound nature of the priest's faith, the fact that the religious sense is not objectified in anything so out-of-the-way as even "a presence above a croquet lawn," which makes the book credible and sympathetic. . . . it *is* a story of heroism and it *is* a story of the Catholic faith being stronger and better than its persecutors. (Spurling 36)

The affirmation, as Kurt Reinhardt posed it, comes in understanding the whiskey priest: "He has sinned grievously again and again, broken his priestly vows, lost his human dignity, but the divine spark in him has never been quite extinguished: he has never really abandoned God and has—contrary to his own opinion—never been abandoned by Him" (Reinhardt 181). Greene's assertion, finally, is that "life *means*" (Hynes 7)—that is, human life is fraught with glimpses of a spiritual reality that give meaning to our movement through time.

Buechner works his way to a similar insight, one which can justly be labeled religious. In *The Final Beast*, Nicolet moves from the youthful experience of hearing a classmate say "Christ eats it" (*FB* 82), and being shocked into the realization that Christ does "eat it" because "it's all this world has ever given him to eat" (*FB* 83), to the final affirmation of the novel, "And God shall wipe away all tears, and there shall be no more death, neither sorrow, nor crying, neither shall there be any more pain, for the former things have passed away" (*FB* 275). Nicolet reads this text about the annihilation of the beast from Revelation over Irma's grave, and the affirmation toward which Buechner has been moving in his earlier novels reaches full expression. Suffering is not dismissed; it is, instead, juxtaposed against another possibility—hope. Although his work is more varied from book to book than Buechner's work, Greene carried this theme to many of his novels; the debate is again visible, for example, in the late fiction, *Monsignor Quixote*. Buechner carries the theme directly to his *Bebb* novels and beyond.

That Buechner clearly belongs in the company of writers such as Greene and O'Connor more than he belongs in the category of contemporary evangelicals is obvious when one listens carefully to the way Buechner discusses faith. Not only does he fail to speak with the zeal of the television preacher or write in the tones of the evangelical author, but he views faith as an intermittent possibility—something to which he aspires occasionally. In the 1969 William Belden Noble lectures at Harvard University, Buechner speaks of the doubt that haunts his work:

> In a town where there is grief and pain enough to turn the heart to stone, I have turned my back and climbed the thirteen stairs to the sheltering room. I have put a few labored and irrelevant words on paper. . . . If there is in heaven or on earth or under the earth anywhere any justification for my presence at this table in this room it is that I have something so good to say that I can be forgiven everything else if I will only say it. (*Alphabet* 99)

Buechner's vision always includes the possibility that he may be completely wrong. Suffering always has a voice. Buechner summarizes *A Final Beast* as a book in which "terrible things happen":

> A Jewish woman is crippled by torture in a Nazi concentration camp, good people die cruel and pointless deaths. And wonderful things that might happen never quite do—a young minister who believes himself to be on the verge of a religious vision ends up simply hearing the sound of two apple branches clacked together by the wind. (*NT* 60)

Buechner, of course, believes the tragic vision is penultimate, that some-thing finally glimmers through—something elusive and brief and open to question. But his work never aspires to the comfortable religious best-seller status of Bruce Barton's *The Man Nobody Knows* or Charles Sheldon's *In His Steps*, early attempts in American literature at bringing together the territory of religion and literature, or more recent religious blockbusters from writers like Janette Oke, Tim LaHaye and Jerry Jenkins, Max Lucado, Rick Warren, and Jan Karon. Buechner explores other territory and refuses to offer an unclouded spiritual vision.

One of Buechner's anthologized sermons, "To Be a Saint," alludes directly to Greene's whiskey priest, who realizes at the end of his travail that "at the end there was only one thing that counted—to be a saint" (*Power* 210). Buechner questions his readers: "What does it mean to be a saint?" He answers:

> To be a saint is to be human because we were created to be human. To be a saint is to live with courage and self-restraint, as the alcoholic priest says, but it is more than that. To be a saint is to live not with hands clenched to grasp, to strike, to hold tight to a life that is always slipping away the more tightly we hold it; but it is to live with the hands stretched out both to give and receive with gladness. To be a saint is to work and weep for the broken and suffering of the world, but it is also to be strangely light of heart in the knowledge that there is something greater than the world that mends and renews. Maybe more than anything else, to be a saint is to know joy. (*MD* 119)

The essence of Buechner's novelistic theory emerges in his interpretation of Greene's whiskey priest. Everything comes back to joy.

In the memoir *The Sacred Journey*, Buechner observes: "What Greene fathomlessly conveys is that the power and glory of God are so over-whelming that they can shine forth into the world through even such a one as this seedy, alcoholic little failure of a man who thus, less by any virtue of his own than by the sheer power of the grace within him, becomes a kind of saint in the end" (*SJ* 17). Buechner acknowledges Greene as a "tremendous influence" and *The Power and the Glory* as where he "learned that a saint is not what people normally think of—a moral exemplar." Instead, Buechner believes, the saint "can be just as seedy and hopeless as the whiskey priest" (*Image* 51). In the same interview, Buech-ner speaks of his admiration for Francois Mauriac's notion, the "subter-ranean presence of grace" as that which gives him his very subject (*Image*

51). This, of course, is the territory that Mauriac so admires in Greene. As Buechner explains, "You take seriously the brokenness of the world and the darkness and sadness and yet see in it the glimmers of the divine and salvific. Unlike a lot of 'religious writers' who won't deal with the ambiguity and the darkness—they've got to make everything sound hopeful and good and godly" (*Image* 51).

Simply put, Buechner's aim as a novelist is to demonstrate the flow of grace in a world unaware of or resistant to its operation, the grace of God in all the mire of worldly day-to-dayness. Buechner's more recent work articulates such an idea in characters like the fumbling Leo Bebb of the *Bebb* novels, in the rascal Tobit of *On the Road with the Archangel*, and the burdened Kenzie Maxwell of *The Storm*. Bebb and the others embody the proposition that grace can work in even the least likely vessels. Horton and Marie-Helene Davies called the whiskey priest the "ancestor" of Bebb (Davies and Davies 188). The working of grace also endures as the central theme in the 1980 novel about the earthy saint Godric. But *The Final Beast* clearly sets the direction and illustrates the theological basis Buechner shares with Greene. The novel stands as a thorough gloss on Buechner's career. *The Final Beast* is a first-rate starting place for novice Buechnerites, and the accessibility of the story probably influenced the decision to turn the novel into a stage production for a run in the late 1980s. The young minister of *The Final Beast*, Theodore Nicolet, is, like his counterpart the whiskey priest, a bumbling buffoon of a missionary. Nicolet moves in a world fairly reeking with the unsavory smells of corruption—gossip, infidelity, suffering, and injustice. Like the sideshow freaks in *The Seasons' Difference*, the preacher, struggling and weak, nonetheless serves as an instrument of healing for his parishioner and friend Rooney Vail. Ultimately Nicolet experiences an unspeakable joy in the unexpected and paradoxical presence of the divine in the daily drudge of his life.

But Nicolet's happy ending emerges from crises that bring him perilously close to a breakdown. His flight in search of Rooney is a longing for romantic love. His visit to his father certainly indicates a longing for family love. But the central predicament for Nicolet is his longing for God. At Union Seminary Buechner had learned from Karl Barth the significance of that "Is it true?" question. The question is, for Barth, the real weight the preacher carries to the pulpit Sunday after Sunday:

> Is it true, this talk of a loving and good God, who is more than one of the friendly idols whose rise is so easy to account for, and whose dominion is so brief? What the people want to find out and thor-

oughly understand is, *Is it true?* . . . They want to find out and thoroughly understand the answer to this one question, *Is it true?*—and not some other answer which beats about the bush.[23]

Buechner thinks about Barth's question with every sermon he writes, even now: "In all my sermons as well as in all my books, fiction and nonfiction alike, I have always tried to address it as honestly and searchingly as I know how, because it is of course my question as well as everybody else's" (*EH* 74).

In the recent collection *Secrets in the Dark* Buechner maintains that he preaches "not just to proclaim the Yes in its glory but one way or another to acknowledge and do justice to the possibility of the No."[24] Barth's question resounds in the pages of *The Final Beast*, first in the words of Nicolet's reluctant parishioner, Rooney: "There's one reason, you know, why I come dragging in there every Sunday. I just want to find out if the whole thing's true. Just *true*. . . . Either it is or it isn't, and that's the one question you avoid like death" (*FB* 28). Rooney's accusation is part of the burden Nicolet carries throughout the narrative. Feeling unworthy of his calling, he wonders if he can proclaim the absurd truth of grace and forgiveness.

Buechner returns to this central business of the preacher in his lectures on homiletics, *Telling the Truth*, where everything circles on one repeated line: "Let the preacher tell the truth" (*TTT* 23, 98). The truth to be told, however, is first of all "a tragic truth . . . that the world where God is absent is a dark and echoing emptiness." Then follows the "comic truth . . . that it is into the depths of his absence that God makes himself present." And the "overwhelming of tragedy by comedy" turns out to be the tale "too good not to be true," the greatest fairy tale of them all (*TTT* 98). Such is the consideration of faith that informs Nicolet's crisis and drives the novel.

Consistently labeled a "clown" or a "scarecrow," Theodore Nicolet views himself as unworthy and bumbles his way to heroism by becoming, in spite of himself, a channel for grace. Just as the whiskey priest has recognized that his facial expression doesn't match his vocation, the young minister, Nicolet, is told by his friend Rooney that he must never smile if he wants to pass for a priest. His smile, we are told, is "a gay, foolish smile, like a drunk's or a lover's" (*FB* 6). Further, a refrain running through the novel is Irma's resounding "*Wie man's macht, ist's falsch*" (*FB* 7, 241) which she translates for Nicolet: "Whatever you are doing, it turns out lousy" (*FB* 7). Although Irma's dictum provides satiric humor and implicates all of the characters in the novel, it most directly describes the efforts of Nicolet. Like the whiskey priest, he would just as soon abandon his vocation. When asked about the possibility of trying to leave his business behind him, Nicolet observes: "You can try like hell. . . . Hell's like what it is to try to leave my business behind. Hope-less" (*FB* 34). Nicolet stumbles through his story, dazed and disheveled, dimly realizing along the way that he is part of the "divine absurdity" (*FB* 111). His "oath and prayer" record his sense of unworthiness: "Holy God, I'm an ass" (*FB* 83).

Yet Nicolet discovers in the very midst of his imperfection and embarrassing absurdity "the great laughter—not, by some miracle, bitter, broken, but splashing like a fountain and spilling over the sides. Joy. . . . Joy, little man . . . love-sick, homesick, God-sick little man" (*FB* 166). In the sermon serving as the ringing finale for the narrative, a sermon he has been working on intermittently through the story, Nicolet proclaims:

> What's a minister like me even but God's pimp, maybe half in love with the flesh he's peddling but only half? What's any one of you? Beloved, don't believe I preach the best without knowing the worst, that's all I mean. I know it, beloved—a flop of a son, comedian of a priest. But the worst isn't the last thing about the world. It's the next to last thing. The last thing is the best. It's the power from on high that comes into the world, that wells up from the rock-bottom worst of the world like a hidden spring. Can you believe it? The last, best thing is the laughing deep in the hearts of the saints, sometimes our hearts even. Yes. You are terribly loved and forgiven. Yes. You are healed. All is well. (*FB* 174–75)

So Nicolet runs after Rooney to get away from his parishioners, himself, and even God, but he finds, at the end of his flight, that even in his slapstick world there resides a kind of magic and that "all the lost things are found" (*FB* 241).

The theme of joy and magic behind the surface of things shines through most dramatically in the humor of *The Final Beast*. Where the first three novels had been somewhat stodgy, the fourth novel offers numerous examples of the comic. When Nicolet's daughter Cornelia begins her nightly prayer "Our Father who aren't in Heaven," instead of "Our Father who art," Irma imagines "both God and Nicolet laughing" (*FB* 13–14). Nicolet frequently invokes Harold to protect his children after Cornelia has mistaken the phrase "hallowed be Thy name" for "Harold be Thy name" (*FB* 33). Speaking to a bus driver about the untimely death of his wife, Nicolet's sad joke is that only Harold can understand it. Asked who Harold is, Nicolet responds, "He runs a dancing school" (*FB* 35). Part of the way Nicolet sets about finding the dance is through whimsy, playfulness, and

laughter, through his capacity as a clown. As a young man, Nicolet has visited a monastery where he thought his questions might be answered. In
The Sacred Journey, Buechner describes his own anticlimactic visit to a
monastery where he found pretty much what Nicolet finds (*SJ* 123–24).
Nicolet describes the monks as tight-lipped: "They would only nod and
smile as though it was some joke too rich for the telling" (*FB* 85). It is the
joke that the young preacher pursues throughout the novel, the joke that
sometimes breaks out in laughter but more often lurks in silence.

Buechner even plays out his own conversion experience in George Buttrick's church by making it parallel to Nicolet's conversion. It was, of
course, the phrase "great laughter," the possibility of joy spilling into life,
to which Buechner had responded. The same phrase awakens Nicolet, and
he recalls the moment as he faces the current crisis in his life and ministry
(*FB* 166). He concludes, finally, that all of them—his daughters, Irma,
Rooney, Poteat, his parishioners—are a "slapstick family" (*FB* 272).
Maybe even Roy would be in the group if Nicolet had a chance to recon-
sider his list. And Nicolet does intuitively recognize that his success as a
preacher has its source in a "curious lightness of heart": "a way he had in
the pulpit of smiling sometimes as though he knew beyond all doubt a
hilarious secret which was that the glory he was proclaiming either really
was, or really was not, true, but that in either case it was a cause for light-
heartedness: life was a joke too terrible or too wonderful to take any other
way" (*FB* 193).

At the heart of everything, a joke, and, of course, a joke can be cruel as
well as funny. Irma dies as a consequence of a joke; Nicolet finds a way to
live by finding his way to the biggest joke of all. Buechner has turned
Robert Frost's celebrated prayer on its head. Frost loved to open lectures
with the prayer, "Forgive, O Lord, my jokes on Thee,/And I'll forgive
Thy great big one on me."[25] The final joke, for Buechner, is not the victory of the darkness but its banishment.

As in the earlier novels, Buechner has a bit of fun with names here, a
character named "Pure" of all things and a daughter named Cornelia, an
echo of another name big in Buechner's repertoire, Shakespeare's Cordelia. Cornelia's nickname, "Pie Face," illustrates Buechner's consistent
emphasis on the inseparable mix of slapstick and tragedy, but the suggestion that Nicolet's travail in some way recalls Lear's tribulation in Shakespeare's play fits well with Buechner's reading of the great tragedy, one of
his favorite texts.

In the 1977 Lyman Beecher Lectures at Yale University, Buechner
speaks of *King Lear*:

> I think of *King Lear* especially with its tragic vision of a world in which the good and bad alike go down to dusty and, it would seem, equally meaningless death with no God to intervene on their behalf, and yet with its vision of a world in which the naked and helpless ones, the victims and fools, become at least truly alive before they die and thus touch however briefly on something that lies beyond the power of death. (*TTT* 44)

Buechner's reading of *King Lear* shows up in the Yale lectures, where he calls the play "one of the mightiest of all preachments" (*TTT* 4), and in the *Bebb* novels, where we overhear the drama being taught in a high school classroom.

Buechner has returned recently to *King Lear* in *Speak What We Feel*, looking to Shakespeare's masterpiece as the place where he learns a most significant lesson on the business of tragedy and comedy:

> What Shakespeare asks of his audience is a suspension not only of disbelief—and belief along with it—but of the inclination to view life as either tragic or comic, or as sometimes one and sometimes the other. Life is continually both at once is what his obedience to time's sadness led him to say, and what he *felt* about it and opened his veins to make his audience feel along with him was that it was precisely that quality that constituted the richness of it, and the terror of it, and the heartbreaking beauty of it. (*Speak* 153)

Buechner holds consistently to the affirmation of joy and laughter as in balance with the catharsis of suffering. Theodore Nicolet has suffered a lost wife, an almost lost father, and a threatened ministry, but his wit and his uncanny capacity for joy point toward salvation and account for much that is humorous in the novel. Buechner thus makes the point that alongside tragedy is comedy "unpredictable, free, hilarious, like God's grace" (HDavies 190).

James Woelfel's summary of Buechner's career, based primarily on a reading of the *Bebb* novels, highlighted the "inseparable mix of the ridiculous and the sublime, the absurd and the gracious, the accidental and the providential."[26] Woelfel's conclusion serves well as a statement of the importance of comedy, which emerges as a crucial motif in *The Final Beast*: "In the final analysis, however, it is comedy that provides the most adequate metaphor for the ultimate state of things—for the great laughter at the dark depths of reality" (Woelfel 286).

Although critics are quick to notice the new emphasis on humor in *The Final Beast*, not all of them are happy about it. Joseph Dewey, for example, in a vitriolic aside in *The Hollins Critic*, rejected Buechner's work as "agenda fiction, temple rhetoric from an ordained minister."[27] It turns out that Dewey, an archmaterialist, is most offended by "that celebration, the sheer audacity of the obligation of joy, that has distinguished Buechner's fiction and that, curiously, has all but banished it from the scope of academic analysis" (Dewey 2). Dewey's definition allows for no happy endings; his literary landscape is a barren one—only dark days allowed. Maxwell Perkins, the editor for Hemingway, Fitzgerald, and Wolfe, has a good bit to answer for, indeed.[28] Chad Wriglesworth identifies Dewey's complaint as deriving from a misunderstanding of the angle from which Buechner works.[29] Not the propagandist Dewey assumed, Buechner lets his characters loose in much the same way as any other novelist might. What Dewey really stalled on is simply an agenda he cannot swallow, the indefinable quality of a word like joy.

"Joy" is a conversation stopper. How to measure? How to test? Joy is the ultimate *deus ex machina*, and a writer who believes in such foolishness has put himself beyond the pale of research and analysis. Although such rules did not apply in the cases of Bunyan, Milton, or Donne, the strictures have come to be vigorously defended these days. One need only look at the phenomenon of the American Booksellers Association versus the Christian Booksellers Association or the mainstream bookstore versus the family bookstore to understand something of the divide. C. S. Lewis addressed the issue in a letter in which he observed that "one of the minor rewards of conversion is to be able to see at last the real point of all the old literature which we are brought up to read with the point left out."[30] I remember a conference presentation on O'Connor in which the speaker boasted of teaching O'Connor sans the religious, which struck me as the cart without the horse, the automobile without the engine. She told us that the class worked out fine. Jenny Franchot argued that religion is the "invisible domain" in American literary studies.[31] She has a point. Such wariness of religion speaks to our fearfulness of the subject and goes some way toward explaining what has happened to Buechner, especially in the academy. Buechner insists on miracle and mystery as legitimate concerns for a novelist. He cozied up to the door in *The Seasons' Difference* and *The Return of Ansel Gibbs*. In *The Final Beast* he barges through.

Nancy Myers sensed the religion winds blowing through *The Final Beast*. First labeling the novel "whimsical and parabolic," she went on to cite Buechner's words to her in an interview where he speaks of his encounter with Agnes Sanford, the model for Lillian Flagg in *The Final Beast* (Myers 74). Buechner notes the acquaintance as "really a turning point" (Myers 80). In his autobiography, Buechner alludes to Sanford's sincerity and "earthy sense of humor" (*NT* 61). He recalls much of her teaching on prayer and seems particularly attracted to her view that all that matters is faith—one must pray through disbelief. Sanford called them "Fairy-tale prayers," and Buechner credits her with first speaking to him of the joyfulness of faith (*NT* 63). Agnes Sanford contributed to Buechner's growing sense of the connection between joy and grace, a connection he had intuitively felt since his conversion, and this is another of those echoes in Buechner that remind readers of another reluctant convert, C. S. Lewis. Buechner and Lewis share a belief in the possibility of joy. The longing for joy is for them, in part, proof of its possibility, just as the fact of hunger suggests the reality of food. In *The Final Beast* Buechner pulls together his reading of Graham Greene, his conversion, and his reaction to the faith healer, Agnes Sanford.

Furthermore, Buechner turns up the laugh meter. Arthur Mizener pointed to the humor in the novel in such passages as when a parishioner comments to Nicolet: "I've never gone in too much for the Holy Ghost," and Nicolet responds, "Well, I'm sure the feeling's mutual" (*FB* 27). Mizener concluded, "This is not merely funny. It is a precise expression of Nicolet's particular sense of the holiness, the awfulness, and the gaiety of God" (Mizener 5). Margaret Wimsatt, in her 1972 discussion of the Buechner corpus, rightly argued that Buechner's themes have changed little over the course of his career. The development she noticed is that "Buechner has learned that people can save, as well as destroy, one another."[32] Marie-Helene Davies concluded her discussion of Buechner: "He writes like a man who has brushed away his tears to recall the great laughter at the heart of the universe and to live in 'Eternity's Sunrise'" (Davies 192). The cheerfulness and laughter emerge most markedly with *The Final Beast*, the story of a beleaguered man who has lost much and stands on the verge of losing everything, yet manages to see the laughter in it all.

Buechner eventually codifies his theory of great cheerfulness by comparing the gospel to a magnificent fairy tale. In the Beecher Lectures, later published as *Telling the Truth: The Gospel in Tragedy, Comedy, and Fairy Tale*, Buechner summarizes the hypothesis on which much of his later work will rest:

> But the whole point of the fairy tale of the Gospel is, of course, that he [Christ] is king in spite of everything. The frog turns out to be the

prince, the ugly duckling the swan. . . . There is no less danger and darkness in the Gospel than in the Brothers Grimm, but beyond and above all there is the joy of it, this tale of a light breaking into the world that not even the darkness can overcome. (*TTT* 90)

Attempting to clarify his notion of the link between fairy tale and gospel in a 1979 interview, Buechner adds, "Then we come to the Gospel, where it's the Pharisees, the good ones, who turn out to be the villains. It's the whores and tax collectors who turn out to be the good ones. Just as in fairy tales, there is the impossible happy ending when Cinderella does marry the prince" (*WDoor* 21). Buechner frequently refers to the parables as jokes, stories with a "sad fun about them" (*WT* 66). The laughter of *The Final Beast*, Nicolet's inexplicable joy, derives from the affirmation of the happy ending. "With parables and jokes both, if you've got to have it explained, don't bother" (*WT* 67), Buechner concludes.

Thus Buechner makes explicit what Greene suggests in *The Power and the Glory*. Both novels are based on the Pauline premise that "all have sinned and fallen short of the glory of God"[33] in combination with the Pauline conclusion that despite one's failure, or perhaps through one's failure, it is possible to come to "overwhelming victory."[34] Augustine in *The Confessions* summarized this basic tenet of Christianity by focusing first on his personal insignificance and sin, calling himself "dust and ashes."[35] Moving further, Augustine described his conversion as love piercing his heart like an arrow and ended by celebrating a joy that follows the suffering of unworthiness (Augustine 206). Such is precisely the motivating force in the Buechner canon. A summary sentence of the idea in Buechner's own words is spoken by Godric, the besmirched saint of the 1980 novel: "What's lost is nothing to what's found, and all the death that ever was, set next to life, would scarcely fill a cup" (*Godric* 96). Buechner seems to regard this sentence as a credo and repeats it as a summary of the second volume of his memoirs, *Now and Then*, as if to say that everything comes together for him in the Christian view that life holds possibilities surpassing the realities of suffering, failure, and death.

For Buechner then, the preacher, or the novelist, is the steward of the wildest mystery of them all and must speak truthfully the tragic as well as the comic truth. Theologically, Buechner believes that the "good news" of the New Testament gospel is bad news first—news that humans are crippled, thwarted, limited. Tragedy. Then, of course, comes the message of grace—the creatures are loved anyway. This is the comedy, the good news. The ultimate message is that all things are possible with God—the news of fairy tale. Taken together, these three become the base of the theological ladder for Buechner, and his writing is an attempt to incarnate the notion. Now the question again: Does such a formula, drifting there in Buechner's prose, negate somehow the importance of his work? I have certainly outlined here an agenda-drivenness in Buechner's novels. And where is that writer who works without agenda? If Buechner can be dismissed on such grounds, almost everybody goes with him.

Therefore, I return to Greene and Buechner for those instructive conjunctions—their shared views of human possibility in tension with their conviction of humankind's gloomy actuality. They finally come together in their faith in regeneration; they each reach toward the sacred in the profane. They share the conclusion that despite being abandoned in a world reveling in insanity, humans can still aspire, through homesickness and longing, to a glimpse of the eternal. Again, such an idea found succinct presentation in the words of Augustine: "You have made us for yourself, and our heart is restless until it rests in you" (Augustine 43).

In his memoirs Buechner reveals another source of influence that finds its way into his fourth novel—a childhood fascination with fantasy stories and fairy tales. Forced by a serious illness to spend the better part of a year confined in bed, Buechner discovers the Oz books:

> During the period that I was in bed, I lived, as much as I could be said to live anywhere, not in the United States of America but in the Land of Oz. One Oz book after another I read or had read to me until the world where animals can speak, and magic is common as grass, and no one dies, was so much more real to me than the world of my own room that if I had had occasion to be homesick then, it would have been Oz, not home, that I would have been homesick for as in a way I am homesick for it still. (*SJ* 14–15)

Buechner's fascination with *Sehnsucht* or longing or *Angst* is reminiscent of Malcolm Muggeridge's description of homesickness in *Jesus Rediscovered*, C. S. Lewis's account of his childhood in *Surprised by Joy*, and G. K. Chesterton's observations in *Orthodoxy* about the superiority of fairy tales and the divine quality of childlikeness. Buechner's awakening has much in common with these others; he came more or less reluctantly to faith, and he came in search of laughter, the laughter he first heard in the fantasy stories of his youth. Buechner expresses his fictional tribute to the Oz stories in *The Entrance to Porlock*, a thinly veiled twentieth-century version of the travelers on the yellow brick road, published five years after *The Final*

Beast. The Oz character leaving the deepest impression, however, is King Rinkitink. Rinkitink's white pearl speaks a wisdom Buechner regards as timeless: "Never question the truth of what you fail to understand, for the world is filled with wonders" (*SJ* 16). Buechner confesses that he has been haunted by Rinkitink, who shows up for him as Samuel Pickwick, as the Emperor Claudius, as the mysterious Sunday in Chesterton's *The Man Who Was Thursday*, and, of course, as the whiskey priest.

In *The Alphabet of Grace* Buechner offers an analysis of the connections between his childhood love of fantasy and the development of his personal religious views that can serve as a commentary on his theory of fiction:

> Fatherless at ten, I may simply have dreamed some kind of father into some kind of life somewhere else. I have always loved fairy tales and to this day read E. Nesbit and the Oz books, Andrew Lang and the Narnia books and Tolkien with more intensity than I read almost anything else. And I believe in magic or want to. I want flying saucers to be true, and I want life to exist on Mars, and I dream of a heaven where old friends meet and old enemies embrace one another and weep. . . . All of which is to say I am a congenital believer, a helpless hungerer after the marvelous as solace and adventure and escape. I am also a fabricator, and I am willing to believe that the whole business of God in my life may be something I have fabricated out of my need for solace and adventure. (*Alphabet* 41–42)

This is the sort of admission that gets Buechner into trouble with the believer side of his audience, but he refuses to back away from it.

True enough, for Buechner the believer, innate human homesickness or "hunger for the marvelous" is met by the biblical story and by the Christian faith with their affirmations of the mysterious incarnational activity of God. Buechner's fiction, then, is intensely preoccupied with the hidden complexities, mixed motives, coincidences, might-have-beens, and ambiguities of human behavior. His apparent aim is to set human reality against a background of human longing, emphasizing, above all else, transcendence—the comic vision. Ultimately, Greene and Buechner share a belief that the sense of the sacred, an irrepressible intuition in the human personality, empowers humans to find joy. The reluctant priest of *The Power and the Glory* keeps saying to the peasants, "Above all remember this—heaven is here," and tries to believe such an incredible thing himself (*Power* 70). As R. W. B. Lewis noted, this was Greene's recurrent theme—"natural ugliness is touched by grace."[36] The priest becomes the symbol of God's unlikely presence in the most unexpected of places. To build a world where God is eliminated, as the Mexican government in Greene's novel is attempting to do, is to destroy the human.

In Greene's view, humans are inextricably linked to something of God. The priest is overwhelmed by the mystery:

> But at the centre of his own faith there always stood the convincing mystery—that we were made in God's image. God was the parent, but He was also the policeman, the criminal, the priest, the maniac, and the judge. Something resembling God dangled from the gibbet or went into odd attitudes before the bullets in a prison yard or con-torted itself like a camel in the attitude of sex. (*Power* 101)

The essence for Greene is that one can never eliminate God without elim-inating oneself as well. This message, carried by a not very impressive priest in a poverty-stricken province, is that God's love is something sensed only fleetingly. The glaring lucidity of those moments may even frighten us, Greene intimates, but such moments nonetheless furnish meaning in life and give validity to human suffering and endurance. Humankind can-not recover Eden and must, therefore, come to terms with having lost Eden—terms that include a homesickness in the heart. Moments come, however, when the reality of Eden shines painfully and gloriously through, as when the whiskey priest feels a paradoxical lightness of heart, a "moment of exhilaration" (*Power* 59), or when Nicolet looks at the crowd huddled about Irma's grave in the last pages of *The Final Beast* and thinks: "They were all of them more than they were, angels standing in the rain" (*FB* 275), all of them bearing, Buechner likes to say, "the fingerprint of God."[37]

The fact that Buechner bases faith not on dogma or tradition but on the subjective movements of the heart may go some way in explaining the sometimes cold reception he would see from an orthodox Christian audi-ence beginning in the 1950s and stretching into the 1990s. Buechner feels that faith is more often registered by a quickening of the pulse than by an intellectual response to creeds and formulas. "Religion starts, as Frost said poems do, with a lump in the throat—to put it mildly—or with a bush going up in flames, a rain of flowers, a dove coming down out of the sky," Buechner writes (*WT* 65). Again, Buechner, who will end *The Final Beast* in "a rain of flowers," expresses this theological notion in ways that echo Greene. The most characteristic picture of Greene's whiskey priest shows the priest with his mouth open, staring, bewildered—a "look of vacancy" (*Power* 13). With the takeover of the revolutionary government and the resulting outlawing of religion, the priest finally realizes that "there had never been a home" (*Power* 11). That is, the priest is moving through his life as an alien, an alien not just in this obscure Mexican province, but an alien in some deeper spiritual sense.

Nicolet too is an alien who increasingly realizes that "the best can never be"—at least in *this* world (*FB* 187). Nicolet summarizes his yearning: "While his contemporaries dreamed of their heart's desire, he had dreamed of a time beyond desire, of resting secure and dry at last on the other side of the treacherous river. . . . He had learned to be world-weary before he had learned anything very much about the world" (*FB* 187). Tristram Bone's pining for communication and relationship in *A Long Day's Dying*, Peter Cowley's yearning for an endorsement of his vision in *The Seasons' Difference*, and Ansel Gibbs's aching to know himself in *The Return of Ansel Gibbs* become a more thoroughly theological notion in Buechner's fourth novel. Allusions to vacancy, homesickness, and longing are oft-repeated refrains in Buechner. In *The Return of Ansel Gibbs*, for example, Buechner uses the word "astonishment" to summarize what Rudy's father died of (*AG* 41). In *Now and Then*, Buechner confesses that he thought of the word as he wondered about describing what his own father had died of. He now wishes he had used the word "homesickness" instead (*NT* 36). Homesickness will perk throughout the *Bebb* novels in the 1970s and into the more recent stories of Tobit and Kenzie, and it is his longing for a place he has never seen except in dreams that awakens in Nicolet the suspicion that, if he could but peel back reality, the dance at the heart of things would shine forth—that longing itself is, somehow, evidence of God, a hint of home. "I think the dance must go on back there," Nicolet muses, "way down deep at the heart of space, where being comes from. . . . There's dancing there" (*FB* 182). This intimation of the dance brings Nicolet to the conclusion that "The whole bloody earth is holy ground" and thus to a realization of joy—an epiphany. The intimation is, of course, transient, fleeting (*FB* 183).

Nicolet knows that "If we saw any more of the dance than we do, it would kill us sure" (*FB* 182). Greene's priest labels this intimation as "God's love" and reaches similar conclusions: "I don't say the heart doesn't feel a taste of it, but what a taste. The smallest glass of love mixed with a pint pot of ditch-water. We wouldn't recognize that love. It might even look like hate. It would be enough to scare us—God's love. . . . Oh, a man like me would run a mile to get away if he felt that love around" (*Power* 199–200). Nonetheless, it is this love, or the yearning for it, that makes the whiskey priest a saint. Greene's priest and Buechner's young minister have eyes for

God. The priest moves toward a kind of saintly suicide, and Nicolet follows "the deep magic and laughter of God" through the tangle of his life to come to terms with irresolution and incompleteness (*FB* 234). Neither writer is glib about faith. Greene chooses lines from Dryden as the epigraph for *The Power and the Glory*: "Th' inclosure narrow'd; the sagacious power / Of hounds and death drew nearer every hour" (*Power* 6). The tightening trap and the ghastly death hover oppressively throughout the novel, and Greene refuses to alleviate their reality by resorting to pious gibberish.

Buechner chooses a similar epigraph for *The Final Beast*, from Stephen Crane's "The Black Riders":

> Then from the far caverns
> Of dead sins
> Came monsters, livid with desire.
> They fought,
> Wrangled over the world,
> A morsel.
> But of all the sadness this was sad—
> A woman's arms tried to shield
> The head of a sleeping man
> From the jaws of the final beast. (*FB* 1)

Like Greene, Buechner is much aware of inescapable sadness. He chooses one of American literature's most grim voices for the opening emotions of his story, and *The Final Beast* neither denies nor ignores the sadness. Buechner does, however, turn Crane's depiction of the finality and senselessness of it all on its head when Nicolet, in the last pages of the novel, opens his Bible to Revelation for his text at Irma's funeral. Nicolet reads first from Revelation 19:20 where the "beast was taken" and "cast alive into the lake of fire" and with him all of those deluded by Satan and his minions (*FB* 275). Then Nicolet turns to a more traditional funeral text, Revelation 21:4: "And God shall wipe away all tears, and there shall be no more death, neither sorrow, nor crying, neither shall there be any more pain, for the former things have passed away" (*FB* 275). None of Nicolet's disheveled listeners object as he preaches hope while standing there in the rain over the grave of one whose life has been absurdly full of sorrow. Nicolet's final sermon is not exactly a packaged answer, but Buechner more than hints, finally, that homesickness does, indeed, hint of home.

The Final Beast is a novel about faith as, in one way or another, the earlier novels have been, but it is also a novel of rich ambiguity, terrible suffering, and alarming inhumanity. Labeling a novelist is, of course, serious, if risky, business, and hard categorizations often impede any full understanding of an author's work. The tag "humorist," for example, early on attached to Mark Twain, has required careful reexamination to allow a more complete understanding of Twain's work. In Buechner's case, the "religious novelist" pigeonholing has dramatically affected a career. Marie-Helene Davies summarized the general critical response to *The Final Beast*: "Critics resented the fact that it was overtly Christian and ruled out Buechner as a novelist, thus creating a schism in his personality as a novelist and a Christian" (Davies 64). The improvident labeling of *The Final Beast* as "overtly Christian" marks a period of tension between Buechner and his critics. Clearly offended by reviews of *The Final Beast*, Buechner speaks of the novel in his memoirs as "in some ways a departure," but declaims the tendency of the critics to dismiss him casually as a sermonizer (*NT* 58). In an interview at the 2004 Festival of Faith & Writing, Buechner again referred to the "stupid move" of ordination that brought him the mixed regard of critics, but paradoxically gave him his "passion," his inspiration. He cites Truman Capote's line—"That's not writing; that's typing"—to describe his aversion to Christian bookstore fare and underscores his dread of the label "Christian novelist" as it implies a writer trying "to score some sort of homiletical bulls eye."[38] Buechner insists, "I write not as a propagandist but as an artist," but his saying so doesn't make the criticism go away (*NT* 59).

With *The Final Beast*, Buechner begins to face the dilemma infecting his critical standing even now—how to reconcile the double vocation of writer and clergyperson, how to live in the two worlds that have become so sharply divided in our time. Nonetheless, because of his deep investment in *The Final Beast*, an investment both literary and autobiographical, Buechner found the reviews of the novel deeply hurtful. Myers called *The Final Beast* Buechner's "most autobiographical novel," and the novel certainly contains a frank working through of Buechner's personal approach to faith, a study of his early thoughts about ministry, and a revelation of his ideas on family and personal relationships (Myers 3). To have such a work dismissed by critics was, in some way, to have his interpretation of his life experiences dismissed as well. Davies insisted that Buechner, "both clergyman and novelist, had suffered from our modern narrowness" (Davies ix). Suggesting that writers who split their focus can expect a lukewarm reception, Davies overlooked such writers as T. S. Eliot and Wallace Stevens, who maintain high standing despite double vocations, but she certainly hit on a sensitivity of modern critics to the mingling of the fields of religion and literature. With the publication of *The Final Beast*, Buechner was relegated to a place outside the mainstream of American literature and suffered a chilling descent in terms of critical reputation. The unwarranted categorization of Buechner as a one-eyed Christian novelist has, unfortunately, produced neglect and misunderstanding of his work.

In recent years, Buechner has reluctantly accepted the labels "Christian novelist" and "apologist," but only after a careful explanation of what such designations mean for him. It is not, he insists, the careful smuggling of theological ideas. He gets at what it is best, ironically, when he talks about preaching. In the early 1980s Buechner taught a course in preaching at Harvard Divinity School. Recounting the experience in his memoirs, he speaks of what he learned:

> I had never understood so clearly before what preaching is to me. Basically, it is to proclaim a Mystery before which, before whom, even our most exalted ideas turn to straw. It is to proclaim this Mystery with a passion that ideas alone have little to do with. It is to try to put the Gospel into words not the way you would compose an essay but the way you would write a poem or a love letter—putting your heart into it, your own excitement, most of all your own life. (*TS* 61)

I take Buechner at his word here, that preaching and novel writing are both chiefly about paying attention to one's life, and the best summary for the messages of both is "Mystery." Such a theory explains both the autobiographical dimension of Buechner's work and the unique theological stance embodied in the fiction particularly. Buechner elaborates these ideas in a 1985 speech at Wheaton College arguing that faith always emerges from the shabbiness and ups and downs of our day-to-day experience, and this faith is always encapsulated in story—the story of our lives. The best way to discuss such faith, he argues, is in narrative.[39] In *A Room Called Remember* Buechner adds that "literature is a metaphor for a writer's experience" (*RCR* 180). Therefore, Buechner's notion of his business as a writer merges with his ideas about the apologist's task, in that both are called to be true to the story of their lives—both the belief and the unbelief. Such a position stands far from the stance of the propagandist who views fiction as an opportunity to smuggle across a premise, and explains something of the distance between Buechner and popular family bookstore fiction from Frank Peretti, Tim LaHaye and Jerry Jenkins, and their ilk.

Buechner fuses the religious and the literary because he believes both are, at the core, simply story. In a 1992 speech Buechner speaks of the essential conjunction of faith and art, "twin versions of the human spirit." He talks of how art calls us to attention and goes on to suggest that the greatest of all commandments has to do with paying attention to God and to our neighbor. Concluding that "the greatest tragedy of them all is not to be present in our own lives,"[40] Buechner argues that art and faith share this call to regard personal story. In *Whistling in the Dark* Buechner marshals Emily Dickinson to his side: "'Consider the lilies of the field' was the only commandment she never broke. She could have done a lot worse. Consider the lilies. It is the *sine qua non* of art and religion both," Buechner writes (*Whistling* 16). Thus the conclusion that *The Final Beast* is "a ministerial sort of novel, a melodrama with theological overtones about two kinds of love—sacred and profane"[41] failed to see with depth into Buechner's aims, served to discourage Buechner as an artist, and severely restricted his audience.

Buechner's reputation suffers from a stigma similar to that which has, to some degree, surrounded the work of Catholic artists such as Flannery O'Connor or J. F. Powers and more recently Jon Hassler and Ron Hansen. The same reproach has influenced the critical acceptance of some part of the literary output of C. S. Lewis and Graham Greene. Many of the writers speaking at the biennial Festival of Faith & Writing express their fear at the stigma of being labeled religious in some way. Tim Gautreaux, Mary Hood, Doris Betts, and Michael Malone are among the many names that come to mind on the question. They have learned to tip-toe carefully around the explosive issue of didacticism. Any work that is plainly Christian will fail to appeal to a contemporary secular readership that has come to expect unhappiness as the central thematic force in its literature. On the other hand, some writers are dubiously regarded in the Christian camp because of their refusal to be sufficiently happy.

Despite the reservations and reproaches of critics, however, the voice of *The Final Beast* registers a certain culmination for Buechner—the achieving of the philosophic base he finds most palatable to his gifts. More finely tuned than in the earlier novels, his prose revolves upon "the possibility of being born again,"[42] which is, as Gerald Weales rightly concluded, the subject of all of the early novels. The fine-tuning occurs within the context of Buechner's becoming more comfortable in his ministerial vocation and within the context of his reading of Graham Greene, an author with whom Buechner displays a broad affinity.

During the early 1960s, while teaching at Phillips Exeter Academy, Buechner first turned to such texts as *The Power and the Glory* "to put flesh on the theological bones" for his students (*NT* 48). In *Now and Then*,

Buechner describes the 1950s at Exeter as "the period of the *nego*," the student who was "negative, against, anti, just about everything" (*NT* 43–44). In his 2006 collection, *Secrets in the Dark*, Buechner recalls the challenge: "They slouched in the pews and stared up at the ceiling. I tried every way I could think of to catch their attention and make them listen," Buechner remembers. "I avoided traditional religious language and imagery as much as possible as well as the kind of fuzziness, bombast, and sentimentality that preachers are apt to resort to when all else fails," he adds by way of introduction to the sermons that he has culled from those years for inclusion in the new book (*Secrets* 1–2). The Exeter years provided a significant apprenticeship, and when Buechner comes to *The Final Beast*, he forgoes writing for critics, teachers, and an imagined novel-reading public. Now he simply develops his own burgeoning ideas of faith into a fictional form.

The Final Beast is Buechner's tentative acceptance of the mantle of apologist and his response to Tillich's challenge to make "the message [gospel] heard and seen, and then either rejected or accepted."[43] With the novel Buechner enters the company of such writers as Flannery O'Connor and Walker Percy, drawing deeply from the well of theological waters, but still offering complicated and truthful narrative.

The Final Beast stands in a long line of American novels about preachers. From Hawthorne's Dimmesdale to Twain's con-men evangelists, from Theron Ware to Elmer Gantry, from Howell's *Leatherwood God* to Caldwell's *Journeyman*, from Steinbeck's Jim Casy to Updike's Thomas Marshfield, versions of the preacher echo through our literature. Buechner's Nicolet is a mixture of many of the others; he is sensitive, aware of the temptation to duplicity, and freighted with guilt. Ironically, however, Nicolet may be most like Jim Casy of *The Grapes of Wrath*, since both characters become less important than the idea they represent; their characters give expression to the centrality of an idea. Casy's death, of course, is a martyrdom for a political ideology. Nicolet, conversely, lives through a spiritual and emotional martyrdom for a religious idea. Through Nicolet's survival and victory, Buechner inculcates the notion that "There is a God right here in the thick of our day-by-day lives who may not be writing messages about himself in the stars but who in one way or another is trying to get messages through our blindness" (*MD* 47).

Philip Yancey insisted that Buechner's thoughts on faith in his novels can only be described as "muted" (Yancey 7). I suppose that's true, but Buechner does finally accept the role of message bearer. Like his Nicolet, like the whiskey priest, however, he does so grudgingly and with qualification. It must not be forgotten that much of the message is indeed dark. However, when he comes to *The Final Beast*, Buechner chooses to write through the darkness to an affirmation of light. Speaking of his first thoughts about the writing of the book, he observes:

> Sin is easier to write about than grace, I suppose, because the territory is so familiar. . . . I was too occupied with my job [at Phillips Exeter] to think much about the next novel I myself might write, but it occurred to me that, if and when the time ever came, it would be the presence of God rather than his absence that I would write about, of death and dark and despair as not the last reality but only the next to last. (*NT* 49)

It is just such an intention that the early novels have pointed to, and with *The Final Beast* Buechner achieves his central aim of writing about the victory of grace.

Now this is tricky territory, and several contemporary writers have tried to make hay from the supposition that sinfulness alone doesn't make the story. I've mentioned Jan Karon and Jon Hassler. I could add Philip Gulley, Janette Oke, or Ann Ross. I actually admire the dream. I think Franco Zeffirelli's Pope Innocent had it right—"In our preoccupation with original sin, we have forgotten original innocence," he says in Zeffirelli's film of the life of Francis of Assisi, *Brother Sun, Sister Moon*.[44] It is a line worthy of a pope. Some of these writers are up to something potent in their attempts to write about the elusive business of goodness. But it is territory for very brave folk or very foolish ones.

Confronted with the phrase "Christian writer," Annie Dillard mumbled, "That's a death knell."[45] Doris Betts claimed that the word "Christian" there "spoils to a rancid adjective."[46] Garrison Keillor gave me a funny look, and Ernest Gaines fidgeted and changed the subject. I recall David Guterson's epigraph from *Snow Falling on Cedars*: "Harmony, like a following breeze at sea, is the exception."[47]

Buechner summarizes it in "The Opening of Veins," where he refers to popular book fare: "With a few happy exceptions, I am suspicious of writers whose books end up in the paperback sections of drug stores and supermarkets and B. Daltons throughout the universe because my guess is that they have written not what they believe is true but only what they believe will wash" (*Belfry* 81). Buechner insists that most of our lives simply cannot be reduced to obvious shades of black and white. Buechner writes in the voice of one trying to keep the tension in both sides of the phrase "Christian novelist." He writes of answers, surely, but of questions, too. In the back and forth is the honesty and the umph.

If referring to *The Final Beast* as a "theological novel" means that the book deals with such themes as forgiveness, servanthood, sin, grace, conversion, joy, then the label is apt. But employing such a designation must not be allowed to obscure the reality that the novel is another Buechnerian consideration of heroism, a search for the salvation possibilities in the dilemma of contemporary life. Although the novel, like Greene's *The Power and the Glory*, does emerge from what might be called a thesis, theological themes do not overwhelm the narrative; religious ideas are subordinated to the successful rehabilitation of Theodore Nicolet. His story emerges in the way all good novels develop: driven by the characters, not by the ideas. Nicolet, with a paradoxical mix of sadness and joy, rejoins his community, becomes the reinvigorated voice to his congregation, and learns of a power hinting at meaning in life. The affirmation progressing from Peter Cowley's obstinate clinging to his vision and Ansel Gibbs's decision to return to life reaches a new pinnacle with Nicolet's heroism.

Ironically, Irma's funeral provides the circumstance for Nicolet's return to his people. Her life having been filled with misfortune and disconnection, Irma dies as a consequence of thoughtlessness and misunderstanding, her death as senseless as much of her life. Buechner relentlessly insists that a message of grace and affirmation must emerge from the suffering and injustice of real life. He cites the Buddha's notion that "suffering is the undercurrent and bedrock of life" as a way of pointing to the role that pain fills in any theory of joy (*Belfry* 91). Buechner's perspective on faith, if it is to be clinically labeled, must be termed existential. Harry Parker, one who has tried to codify Buechner's theology, summarized:

> In essence, faith for Buechner is three-fold. In addition to the Tillichian notion of faith as the courage to be, faith is also existential. The way that it combines Kierkegaard's notion of a risk with the idea of faith as a process, not a possession, and the concept that the sense of God's presence is never absolutely certain further substantiate this existential concern. Finally, faith has a Pauline basis rediscovered by Martin Luther. It is a trust and confidence in God. (Parker 16)

Parker was right to see Tillich's influence in Buechner's work. Nicolet, for example, exemplifies what Tillich called the "courage . . . rooted in the God who appears when God has disappeared in the anxiety of doubt" (*Courage* 190). Clearly, too, Buechner views conversion or faith as a pro-

gressive unfolding, accepting the biblical summary of faith as "the substance of things hoped for, the evidence of things not seen."[48] Yet any theological summary of *The Final Beast* seems sterile and incomplete. In the
attempt to touch Buechner's goals as a writer, theological formulations are
less and less helpful. He remains, as he has been from his first novel, elusive to the doctrinal corner or the theological position. Whatever Nicolet finds of God, he finds in an orchard where he hears the sound of
branches knocking together and imbues the sound with meaning. He is
more like Peter Cowley, a bit of a mystic, than he is like a theologian—
more likely to discover spiritual meaning in the home of a faith healer than
in his study among tomes of systematic theology.

Moreover, to argue that Buechner, with *The Final Beast*, became a "theological novelist" is to overlook the continuity of his thought as it has
evolved from the first novel. He began as a modern novelist with a yearning to explore matters of faith, and, as Stacy Thompson noted in her discussion of *The Final Beast*, "symptoms of modernism remain."[49] She caught
the changes: "The irony and ambiguity of the early novels are still evident
in his later works. The implication that the inadequacies of modernism can
be overcome is perhaps itself the most radical element of Buechner's later
fiction, child as it is of modernism" (Thompson 44). Like Graham Greene,
who keeps taut the tension between the hunted priest and the nameless
Lieutenant, the hunter, between this world and the spiritual world, Buechner maintains the tension within one character, Theodore Nicolet.

Nothing in *The Final Beast* is completely new for Buechner. Even
though he references new subjects, managing, for example, to crowd
echoes of the Holocaust into this narrative, the book remains, like the earlier ones, a product of a modern insight. Like his contemporaries Flannery O'Connor, J. F. Powers, Graham Greene, and Elie Wiesel, however,
Buechner does come to reject an entirely secular framework. The possibility of a larger world of spiritual potentials is at the heart of *The Final
Beast*, but this is not so much new, as Myers and others suggested, as it is
an elaboration, a development (Myers 74). Buechner has clearly hinted in
his earliest work that the futility of modernism may not be the last thing;
in *The Final Beast*, his hints move closer to proclamation.

Therefore, the novel points the way to all that will follow for Buechner—a more thorough immersion in religious thought, a studied attempt
to suggest the presence of grace in a tawdry world, and a desire to jar readers and listeners into a consideration of spiritual possibilities. He affirms
in a way reminiscent of Elie Wiesel, another contemporary writing out of
a context of darkness in search of a higher vision. In *The Oath* Wiesel

advised: "Thus, what is essential is to live to the limit. Let your words be shouts or silence but nothing else, nothing in between. Let your desire be absolute and your wait as well, for all yearning contains a yearning for God and every wait is a wait for God."[50] *The Final Beast* reverberates with such a vision of the longing for God. Buechner's novel works as a Christian novel only in the most unconventional sense. It is, more profoundly, a novel posing a survival that leads to victory.

The final message, then, in the novel with theological overtones as offered by the unlikely pair Greene and Buechner, proclaims grace as operative in the day-to-dayness of existence. Tying Buechner to Greene, as I have done here, may lead to the suspicion that Buechner's work is derivative, but *The Final Beast* is not a simple reworking of *The Power and the Glory*. Buechner has, indeed, revisited Greene's book in a way of his own. Nonetheless, the whiskey priest's dictum, "Above all remember this—heaven is here" (*Power* 70), finally summarizes both novels. And because "heaven is here," sainthood is possible, anything is possible. Both Greene and Buechner graphically express a belief that the world is a dark place, indeed, and they body forth characters who have more than a usual portion of human impotence; but beyond human inadequacy they find faith, grace, and absurd joy. As Irma Reinwasser has it, "*Wir sind alle Schweine*" (*FB* 222). Humankind's "swinehood," for Buechner and Greene, is not, however, the last thing, only the next to last thing. We are left again with those "angels standing in the rain" (*FB* 175).

A comparison of these single texts of the two writers yields, finally, a glimpse of what the so-called Christian novelist is up to. Associating Buechner's work with the more familiar work of Graham Greene shows how Buechner has reshaped Greene with great fecundity. Such a comparison also elucidates the preoccupations of the so-called theological novelist, a fascination with the central elements of Christian thought—the possibility of faith, the state of humankind, the presence of dancing at the heart of things. *The Final Beast* illustrates Buechner's working through the issue of his personal faith toward his summary in the Yale lectures, where he calls for preaching of "the overwhelming of tragedy by comedy, of darkness by light, of the ordinary by the extraordinary, as the tale that is too good not to be true because to dismiss it as untrue is to dismiss along with it that catch of the breath, that beat and lifting of the heart near to or even accompanied by tears, which I believe is the deepest intuition of truth that we have" (*TTT* 98).

"Is it just mumbo-jumbo, Nick?" Rooney wants to know (*FB* 97). This time the answer is still, "Maybe." But it is also, "Maybe not."

Notes

1. Arthur Mizener, "Dancing Angels and a Gay God," *New York Times Book Review*, January 24, 1965, 5.
2. Venetia Pollack, "New Novels," *Punch*, June 30, 1965, 976.
3. *Time*, February 5, 1965, 114.
4. Amos N. Wilder, "Strategies of the Christian Artist," *Christianity and Crisis*, May 3, 1965.
5. A. W. Phinney, *Christian Science Monitor*, February 18, 1965, 5.
6. Julian Moynahan, "Writing on Cloth Can Be Tricky," *Book Week*, February 14, 1965, 6.
7. Dan Wakefield, "And Now, A Word from Our Creator," *New York Times*, February 12, 1989.
8. John Davenport, "Buechner's Fourth," *Spectator*, June 11, 1965, 763. Hereafter cited as Davenport.
9. Katherine Gauss Jackson, book review, *Harper's*, March 1965, 159–60.
10. Malcolm Muggeridge, "The Last Days of Christendom," *Atlantic Monthly*, September 20, 1982, 166.
11. Kurt F. Reinhardt, *The Theological Novel of Modern Europe* (New York: Frederick Ungar Publishing Co., 1969), 177. Hereafter cited as Reinhardt.
12. Graham Greene, *The Power and the Glory* (London: Penguin, 1940), 19. Hereafter cited as *Power*.
13. Graham Greene, "Why I Write?" in *Religion and Modern Literature: Essays in Theory and Criticism*, ed. G. B. Tennyson and Edward E. Ericson Jr. (Grand Rapids: Eerdmans, 1975), 337.
14. "A Conscious Remembering: An Interview with Frederick Buechner," *Radix*, July/August 1983, 7. Hereafter cited as *Radix*.
15. Harold Jason Baxter, "Touched by Fire and Laughter: The Range of Grace in the Fiction of Flannery O'Connor and Frederick Buechner" (diss., Florida State University, 1983), 7.
16. Horton and Marie-Helene Davies, "The God of Storm and Stillness: The Fiction of Flannery O'Connor and Frederick Buechner," *Religion in Life*, Summer 1979, 188. Hereafter cited as Davies and Davies.
17. Graham Greene in *Graham Greene: A Collection of Critical Essays*, ed. Samuel Hynes (Englewood Cliffs, NJ: Prentice-Hall, 1973), 1. Hereafter cited as Hynes.
18. Cynthia Ozick, "Open Heart," *New York Times Book Review*, June 11, 1972, 36.
19. Harry J. Parker III, "The Nature of Faith in the Fiction of Frederick Buechner, 1965–1979" (thesis, Princeton University, 1980), 19. Hereafter cited as Parker.
20. Ephesians 2:12.
21. John Henry Cardinal Newman, *Apologia Pro Vita Sua* (New York: Image Books, 1956), 320–21.
22. John Spurling, *Graham Greene* (London: Methuen, 1983), 36. Hereafter cited as Spurling.
23. Karl Barth, *The Word of God and the Word of Man* (Gloucester, MA: Peter Smith, 1978), 108. Hereafter cited as Barth.
24. Frederick Buechner, *Secrets in the Dark* (San Francisco: HarperSanFrancisco, 2006), 5. Hereafter cited as *Secrets*.
25. Robert Frost, untitled poem, in *In the Clearing* (New York: Holt, Rinehart & Winston, 1962), 39.

26. James Woelfel, "Frederick Buechner: The Novelist as Theologian," *Theology Today* 40 (October 1983): 286. Hereafter cited as Woelfel.

27. Joseph Dewey, "Wrestling with Angels: The (Im)Possibility of Joy in the Fiction of Frederick Buechner," *Hollins Critic* 36.5 (1999): 2. Hereafter cited as Dewey.

28. The sentence was supposedly spoken by a professor witnessing a campus riot in the 1960s. The implication is that Maxwell Perkins, editor to Hemingway, Wolfe, Fitzgerald, and the rest, by providing much of the then current curriculum, was somehow to blame for the breakdown in the system.

29. Chad Wriglesworth, "George A. Buttrick and Frederick Buechner: Messengers of Reconciling Laughter," *Christianity & Literature* 53 (2003): 70.

30. C. S. Lewis, *The Collected Letters of C. S. Lewis*, vol. 2, *Books, Broadcasts and the War, 1931–1949*, ed. Walter Hoopes (San Francisco: HarperSanFrancisco, 2004), 467.

31. Jenny Franchot, "Invisible Domain: Religion and American Literary Studies," *American Literature* 67 (1995): 833–42.

32. Margaret Wimsatt, "A Novelist for the New Church?" *America*, October 7, 1972, 262. Hereafter cited as Wimsatt.

33. Romans 3:23.

34. Romans 8:37.

35. Augustine, *The Confessions of Saint Augustine*, ed. John K. Ryan (Garden City, NY: Image Books, 1960), 46. Hereafter cited as Augustine.

36. R. W. B. Lewis, "The Trilogy," in *Graham Greene: A Collection of Critical Essays*, ed. Samuel Hynes (Englewood Cliffs, NJ: Prentice-Hall), 60.

37. Frederick Buechner, "Religion and Art," speech in Grand Rapids, MI, April 29, 1992.

38. Frederick Buechner, "Career Reflections," speech at Calvin College, Grand Rapids, MI, April 24, 2004.

39. Frederick Buechner, "The Speaking and Writing of Words," speech at Wheaton College, Wheaton, IL, October 3, 1985.

40. Frederick Buechner, "Religion and Art," speech at Calvin College, Grand Rapids, MI, April 29, 1992.

41. *Newsweek*, January 25, 1965, 92.

42. Gerald Weales, "Going His Own Way," *Reporter*, September 9, 1965, 46.

43. Paul Tillich, *The Theology of Culture* (New York: Oxford University Press, 1959), 201.

44. *Brother Sun, Sister Moon*, Paramount Pictures, 1972.

45. Personal conversation, April 13, 1996.

46. Personal conversation, August 8, 1992.

47. David Guterson, *Snow Falling on Cedars* (New York: Vintage Contemporaries, 1995), xiv.

48. Hebrews 11:1 KJV.

49. Stacy Webb Thompson, "The Rediscovery of Wonder: A Critical Introduction to the Novels of Frederick Buechner" (diss., Michigan State University, 1979), 44. Hereafter cited as Thompson.

50. Elie Wiesel, *The Oath* (New York: Avon Books, 1973), 198.

Chapter Five

Preaching in Oz

The Entrance to Porlock

Beyond Nancy Myers's foundational work and the various dissertations and critical studies I have mentioned in these pages, the two most striking approaches to Buechner are Joseph Dewey's "Wrestling with Angels," a 1999 voice I included in the discussion of *The Final Beast*, and an essay by Chris Anderson, "The Very Style of Faith: Frederick Buechner as Homilist and Essayist," in *Christianity & Literature*. Anderson's 1989 essay, essentially a defense of Buechner's talent for addressing "questions of faith without foolishness,"[1] acknowledged the angle of vision, the attempt to produce novelistic worlds as seen through the prism of Christian faith, that has defined Buechner's career, especially since 1980 or so. But Anderson believed that Buechner's stories "do justice to the complexity and ambiguity of experience," thus contrasting Buechner with contemporary purveyors of religion (Anderson 17). Anderson concluded that Buechner has pulled off a remarkable feat in walking the tightrope over the abyss of didacticism. Even in the explicitly faith-centered work, the sermon collections and autobiographical volumes, Anderson noticed that Buechner seems always about the business of undoing the cliché (Anderson 15). Anderson has the theological acumen to explicate Buechner's notions of religious experience and analyzes how one might legitimately tell the story of God-encounter. Noting that Buechner was "not yet part of the contemporary canon" Anderson seemed to be wondering at the exclusion (Anderson 8). Anderson's bewilderment is to the point, especially since Buechner has been perceptively registering human experience, telling the truth, for more than a half century.

Buechner has done what Ron Hansen, another contemporary novelist who toils in the vineyard of faith and fiction, argued a writer who is a believer must do:

A faith-inspired fiction squarely faces the imponderables of life, and in the fiction writer's radical self-confrontation may even confess to desolation and doubt. Such fiction is instinctive rather than conformist, intuitive rather than calculated; it features vital characters rather than comforting types, offers freedom and anomaly rather than foregone conclusions, invites thoughtfulness not through rational argument, but through asking the right questions.[2]

Hansen wrote his essay "Faith and Fiction" in part as a defense of work that operates out of a belief system, I suppose, but much of what Hansen offers in defining the writer who is believer could be said of any good writer. He talks of a special attentiveness to humanity, for example, and a deep regard for the details of nature. But Hansen was remarkably on his guard against "the shoehorning of religious belief" (Hansen 25). His condemnation of Christian bookstore fiction was vitriolic:

So-called Christian fiction is often in fact pallid allegory, or a form of sermonizing, or is a reduction into formula, providing first-century, Pauline solutions to over-simplified problems, sometimes yielding to a Manichean dualism wherein good and evil are plainly at war, or offering as Christianity conservative politics. We cannot call a fiction Christian just because there is no irreligion in it, no skepticism, nothing to cause offense. (Hansen 25–26)

Hansen's argument positing the authentic "faith-inspired" writer over and against the "so-called" version could well have Frederick Buechner in mind. Who can doubt that Buechner exemplifies Hansen's writer of "the imponderables" or that Buechner would be saying amen to Hansen's diatribe?

Ten years after Anderson, however, and Hansen's definitions notwithstanding, Joseph Dewey offered a remarkable demurral. Without mentioning Anderson or any other critical studies of Buechner's work, Dewey testified that "happening upon Frederick Buechner's fictions in these latter days of the twentieth century is rather like coming upon a herd of unicorns in a busy city park, there in plain sight, something marvelous yet oddly ignored"; like Anderson, Dewey noticed that Buechner is strangely marginalized (Dewey 2). While vaguely admiring Buechner, Dewey went on to explain the neglect that has surrounded Buechner's work as inevitable, because Buechner has violated that most basic premise of our artistic culture—he writes out of belief in an active supernatural presence.

Dewey's prose is shimmering, his argument lucid, and his conclusions devastating for anyone arguing for Buechner's inclusion in the canon of American literature.

Dewey even identified the very moment when Buechner goes beyond the pale. Although he is critical of a certain fancifulness, an instinct for otherness, in *A Long Day's Dying*, Dewey surmised that the problem really reared its head in a serious way in *The Final Beast*. Citing the scene where Theodore Nicolet has reached a breaking point, Dewey recognized the character's longing for a Damascus-road experience. Having been coached by Lillian Flagg, Nicolet manages to utter, "Please come," and, after a pause, he adds, "Jesus" (*FB* 176). And then:

> Two apple branches struck each other with the limber clack of wood on wood. That was all—a tick-tock rattle of branches—but then a fierce lurch of excitement . . . it was an agony of gladness and beauty falling wild and soft like rain. Just clack-clack, but praise him. . . . Maybe all his journeying . . . had been only to bring him here to hear two branches hit each other twice like that. (*FB* 177–78)

Buechner confesses, in his lectures at Harvard in 1969, later published as *The Alphabet of Grace*, that the branch-knocking moment is autobiography in a "quite direct" way, but Dewey found the whole business a stumbling block, nonetheless (*Alphabet* 7).

Offended by what he sees as a collision with certainty, Dewey viewed the scene as *the* moment of Buechner's crossing over, offering, Dewey argued, "a narrative that here admits . . . the sure presence of God" (Dewey 8). This supposed embrace of the otherworldly was, for Dewey, the end of the line. From that point on, we can admire Buechner's work in the same way that we admire exotic fish in an aquarium, forever outside, excluded from their experience. Dewey traced Buechner's supposed solecism in a pattern through four novels—from *A Long Day's Dying* to *The Final Beast* and on to *Lion Country* and *Godric*—claiming that Buechner's increasing obsession with the vertical, with the possibility of spiritual connection, leads to a repudiation of the horizontal and, most significantly, abandons readers along the way. We simply cannot go where Buechner's visions take him. "Clack-clack" is the end of Buechner's fiction.

Dewey is not to be ignored; I think he was dead wrong. But he was so winningly wrong. He mistook a character in *The Final Beast*, Lillian Flagg, and her belief in certainty as evidence of a narrative statement about certainty. He ignored Nicolet's waffling on the meaning of the branches clacking together, and he misread dreams, imaginings, and considered possibilities as paranormal interventions. He needed to read more of Buechner before classifying him so narrowly. Despite his misaligning Buechner with novels of affirmation like Dickens's *A Christmas Carol*, Dewey did understand "the heavy responsibility of joy" that resonates in Buechner's work (Dewey 3). Chiding Buechner, Dewey argued that even Christians have long been known by their capacity for waiting:

> In the nearly two millennia since the apostles stared as Christ vanished into the chalk-white vacancy of the Bethany skies, Christians have engaged their deity only in an elaborate hide and seek that valorizes the work of prayerful waiting. Christians rest (un)easily within familiar paradoxes: God speaks, they argue, in silences or in codes they cannot break; they find confirmation in doubt; they are empowered by helplessness; they touch presence in absence.... What Christians know of certainty is how to live without it. (Dewey 3)

Then comes Buechner offering work "where God steps so boldly, so unironically into the narrative line" (Dewey 3).

Thus Buechner, according to Dewey, violated even the tentativeness of historical Christianity. Even if the contention were true, Dewey's outrage is as interesting as the argument. He simply could not brook this fussing about with the holy. In his frustration, Dewey sounds like the speaker in Stephen Dunn's poem "At the Smithville Methodist Church." The narrator of Dunn's poem is suffering through his daughter's attendance at an evangelical vacation Bible school event. He'd thought his daughter, a child of her time, would already have learned to think of Jesus "like Lincoln or Thomas Jefferson," someone "sufficiently dead," and he was torn by the fact that he "hadn't a story nearly as good."[3] Like Dunn, Dewey was impressed by the story. Fascinated by Buechner's admittedly mesmerizing and well-fashioned stories, Dewey stared into the aquarium with something like amazement: "The rarest aquarium fish reminds us of the highest possibility of the world we share.... Buechner's splendid affirmation makes valuable, makes significant our struggles without, even against certainty. His confirmation confers significance on our doubt, his joy confers significance on our sorrow, indeed creates the context for it" (Dewey 17). So Dewey acknowledged the human longing for joy, for Eden, as he grumbled that Buechner serves only to remind us of all we cannot have. Buechner merely accentuates our sad knowledge of how far-fetched our dreaming can be. Dewey concluded that Buechner merely reminds readers of a nagging thirst that can never be quenched.

There is some fiction by Christians for whom Dewey's conclusions would work. They will not work for Buechner, however. Joy for Buechner is never tantamount to certainty. Chris Anderson acknowledged the "evangelical industry" where "complex religious ideas are reduced to the pleasant images of easy slogans. . . . More and more the Christian comedy is transformed into a sitcom" (Anderson 7). But Anderson rightly placed Buechner well outside this evangelical industry: "At a time when religious discourse has become intellectually impoverished and increasingly dogmatic, Buechner has maintained a tentative, self-dramatizing, literary form of religious persuasion" (Anderson 8). Focusing on the possibility of God in everyday existence as "the recurring theme" of Buechner's work, Anderson cited Buechner's own qualification of the assertion: God's "words to us are always veiled, subtle, cryptic, so that it is left to us to delve their meaning, to fill in the vowels, for ourselves, by means of all the faith and imagination we can muster" (*SJ* 4). Buechner adds in that same context that God may speak, but that trying to express what God is speaking "is as precarious a business as to try to express the meaning of the sound of rain on the roof or the spectacle of the setting sun" (*SJ* 4). Already, Buechner's position seems more complicated than Dewey would have it, more in line with that Christian tradition which acknowledges mystery and waits in incompleteness.

Buechner proposes that our attraction to story has to do with our longing for plot, not just in our reading, but in our lives. So he tells us a story about a weak-kneed preacher who kneels in a field to ask for a miracle. And he gets a clack or two. What Anderson understood and Dewey did not understand is that the meaning of such a story is "not something we can detach from it and fix discursively" (Anderson 11). The character in the story, at least momentarily, believes he may have had some confirmation of God's presence. The reader is offered several possible explanations for Nicolet's miracle, just as Buechner always insists that his predilection for joy, even "the whole business of God in my life may be something I have fabricated out of my need for solace and adventure" (*Alphabet* 42). Huckleberry Finn has a change of heart; Nick Carraway sees the worth of the gangster, Gatsby; Holden Caulfield misses the phonies and slobs; Nicolet prays and hears something—writers are always asking us to believe much, even to stretch our imaginations to see something of the hopeless and madcap multiplicity of things.

The key in Buechner is what Anderson called "tentativeness and open-endedness" (13). Anderson concluded:

> Throughout his writing Buechner insists that the texts of our experience, though complex and elusive, are not entirely arbitrary, inaccessible to interpretation. For him meaning does happen—in the very thick of things, out of the very thick of things—and through intuition and reason and faith we are able to apprehend a possible coherence. What distinguishes Buechner as a novelist is that he dramatizes moments of joy and, possibly, of grace at a time when most contemporary novelists take as a given that life is either random and meaningless or that whatever meaning it does have is the result of human endeavor alone. (Anderson 19)

The banging of these branches can be variously read. A consideration of what such noises might mean becomes all the more interesting in our time when we display a fervent faith in this world while also displaying a passionate loyalty to almost every imaginable kind of other world—the material versus the spiritual in everyday collision. Buechner is simply not easily captured in one position or another; his take on faith opens in many directions. Buechner's work resists the easy classification, and his metaphors leave a good bit of space in which to wonder.

I have taken time here to play out the debate between Dewey and Anderson as a way of dramatizing that central question in Buechner: what are we to do with this business of joy? When critics responding to *The Final Beast* shouted about the novels a minister might write, Buechner pulled back. Novels reacting to critics are always tricky. I think, for example, of Clyde Edgerton's *Killer-Diller*. So anxious to address the critics of his first novel, *Raney*, Edgerton loses something in the sequel. Buechner writes *The Entrance to Porlock* to those who thought *The Final Beast* was Christian propaganda. He wants to say, "Put my foot in it, eh?" Twice in *The Alphabet of Grace* Buechner mentions "cloudy novels" and "cloudy rhetoric" as he discusses the writing he is toiling over at the time (*Alphabet* 75, 22). *The Entrance to Porlock* is that novel, and it is cloudy indeed. Although replete with Buechner's usual considerations, this novel turns everything fifteen degrees, considers from a new angle. That's the first thing to say about Buechner's fifth novel.

I must add something about context. *The Entrance to Porlock* (1970) is Buechner's first novel that sits easily alongside his nonfiction of the late 1960s and early 1970s. *The Magnificent Defeat* appears in 1967, then *The Hungering Dark* in 1969. Both are collections of sermons. Then in 1970 there's *The Alphabet of Grace*, really Buechner's first run at memoir, the record of his speeches at Harvard in 1969 on the potential connections between fiction, autobiography, and theology. In 1973 Buechner will produce *Wishful Thinking*. Out of this cauldron of many words comes the fifth novel, *The Entrance to Porlock*, one that is deeply informed by the several manuscript piles deranging Buechner's work table as the 1960s wind down.

Before we turn to the novel, then, a detour into one of the nonfictions may prove productive. Surely *The Alphabet of Grace* is a turning point in Buechner's career, even if—like *Peculiar Treasures*, *Wishful Thinking*, and *Whistling in the Dark*—it is nearly impossible to classify. The collection of the Harvard lectures might be called Buechner's practice memoir, a loosening of the tongue, a first draft of the life he will tell in many volumes beginning in the 1980s. The lectures are, in part, a reaction to critics, a way of talking about the reading of experience, and certainly a reflection on the novel he was laboring over at the time. Buechner advises that we approach *The Alphabet of Grace* as "graffiti"—"longings and loves," "grievances and indecencies," all "scratched up in public" with the aim of motivating readers to meditate privately on their own longings (*Alphabet* viii). He traces the hints of meaning in one prosaic day of his life as an invitation to readers to trace their own days. Such is the precise technique that Buechner will later employ to justify the writing of memoir, but here the attention to his day is an address to the question the critics asked about Theodore Nicolet's story: how can a grown-up man, a talented writer and thinker, someone witnessing the muddle of wars and disasters at a particularly violent moment in human history, talk about miracle with a straight face?

So Buechner gets right to business by reiterating Nicolet's maybe-miracle, actually lifting the experience that so mortified Dewey straight out of *The Final Beast*. Then Buechner claims the experience as his own. As usual, he is quick to qualify; he refers to the "glimmering through of grace" as "obscure" (*Alphabet* 8). Nonetheless, he really seems to want to insist on "a hint of melody," a miraculous tune heard only in brief snatches and sounding dimly as from a long distance (*Alphabet* 10). "The invisible manifests itself in the visible," he maintains, and he turns to, of all things, the alphabet, "alphabetic drab," for his metaphor (*Alphabet* 11). The supernatural becomes known, if at all, in the very natural, the common, the everyday. And Buechner goes on to risk himself as the example of how the miraculous might appear in the mundane. As Mary Shideler put it, the book offers "much to delight and enliven."[4] I'd say that the delight is in the enormous chance that Buechner takes in writing of miracle, and the enlivening comes with the vitality, the universality, of the question. We have, most of us, crossed our fingers a time or two.

Buechner summarizes his subject in *The Alphabet of Grace* via an acknowledgment of those rare moments when meaning breaks through: "once in a while there is the suggestion of a purpose, meaning, direction, the suggestion of a plot, the suggestion that, however clumsily, your life is trying to tell you something, take you somewhere" (*Alphabet* 10). In the two sermon collections that come out in the years just before *The Alphabet of Grace* and *The Entrance to Porlock*, Buechner's favorite texts turn out to be stories of miracles at Emmaus and Cana, parables about treasures in fields and priceless pearls, and references to the spiritual superiority of children. All the Buechner themes are there in *The Magnificent Defeat*, dedicated to his teacher, James Muilenburg, and in *The Hungering Dark*, dedicated to his students at Phillips Exeter Academy, where he labored as school minister to translate religious ideas for reluctant audiences during the first half of the 1960s. But those books are sermons—didacticism allowed—not lectures at Harvard.

In *The Alphabet of Grace*, Buechner engages himself in a crucial dialogue in an imagined encounter with a ghostly interlocutor. He muses about the novels he has written as perhaps veering away from "the real nub of the matter" and wonders aloud if this time he might just "give it to them straight" (*Alphabet* 46). And the inquisitor's question is a familiar one: "Have you ever had what you yourself consider a genuine, self-authenticating religious experience?" (*Alphabet* 47). This is, of course the question at the center of *The Final Beast*. It is the question haunting Buechner as he turns to the new novel. And it is the question that will tremble to the surface from this point on in Buechner's books. Buechner's answer is not the resounding yes Dewey and others might have led us to expect:

> Not the least of my problems is that I can hardly even imagine what kind of an experience a genuine, self-authenticating religious experience would be. Without somehow destroying me in the process, how could God reveal himself in a way that would leave no room for doubt? If there were no room for doubt, there would be no room for me. (*Alphabet* 47)

We've heard it before. Theodore Nicolet was fond of just such proclamations. Even in this nonfiction, Buechner seems to want to insist that it is the longing he is sure of. The rest is in shadow.

Much of the coloration of this era in Buechner's career comes from the drama of the times themselves—not good times for writers of books. I think of Ernest Gaines, holed up in San Francisco and writing novels during those bursting 1960s, his friends on the front lines of the freedom marches and perplexed by his, to them, irrelevant pursuits. Buechner too faces a sense of irrelevance. He talks in *The Alphabet of Grace* of the world's pain, of the "muddy deaths in Viet Nam," and of his doubts about whether or not he has anything to offer in such a maelstrom (*Alphabet* 93). The world was burning, and Buechner wonders if it really needed "another lecture" or "another book" (*Alphabet* 62). The lecture in question is *The Alphabet of Grace*, dedicated to his daughter, Sharman, and full of personal tours into a day in the life of the Buechners; the book is *The Entrance to Porlock*, a tour of the lives of a fictional family. But in both renditions there pulses the common question of what it all might mean.

At forty-three and at a critical point in his career, Buechner decides to be more elliptical this time. This novel is more about ghosts than spirits, more about dreams than miracles, but he confesses his aims in the lectures running alongside the novel:

> Religion as a word points essentially, I think, to that area of human experience where in one way or another man happens upon mystery as summons to pilgrimage, a come-ye-all; where he is led to suspect the reality of splendors that he cannot name; where he senses meaning no less overwhelming because they can only be hinted at in myths and rituals, in foolish, left-handed games and cloudy novels; where in great laughter perhaps and certain silences he glimpses a destination that he can never know fully until he reaches it. (*Alphabet* 75)

The Alphabet of Grace clarifies much about the novel-in-progress. We see, for example, how autobiography finds its way into the fiction when Buechner mentions an October when he opened the front door to the golds and browns of leaves blowing in on the hallway carpet, a scene he plops over into *The Entrance to Porlock*. The novel will, once again, involve a suicide, as Buechner revisits that sad episode of 1936. Oz is here in a distinct form as Buechner demonstrates again his love for Baum, the Chestertonian instinct I've already noted. Buechner even offers his own summary of the novel in *The Alphabet of Grace*: "The old man is the Tin Woodman who lacks a heart, one son is the Cowardly Lion who lacks courage, the other son is the Scarecrow who lacks a brain, and the grandson is the child who wants to go home but does not know where home is" (*Alphabet* 85). Although Buechner admits that his main character runs away with the novel "in ways other than those I had in mind for him" (*Alphabet* 83), he does divulge that the old man of the novel is his own creation. Buechner talks of the audacity and potential foolishness of his godlike attempts to manipulate the lives of his characters and wonders if the coming book is worth the trouble: "If there is in heaven or earth or under the earth any-where any justification for my presence at this table in this room it is that I have something so good to say that I can be forgiven everything else if I will only say it. I must believe that I have some such thing to say. I do not always believe it" (*Alphabet* 99).

The Alphabet of Grace ends with a return to the old Barthian question: "Is it true?" The novel that emerges in the swirl of the speeches and the news of 1970 is just another way to ask the ancient question and to answer, "Just maybe it is true" (*Alphabet* 100). Sure enough, Buechner goes at the question in a new way this time—more Oz than Emmaus—plenty of visions and dreams and maybe even a miracle or two, but decidedly earthly miracles this time.

Most of the heavyweight critics have departed the Buechner band-wagon by the time *The Entrance to Porlock* comes along. Those climbing on tend to be more interested in the religious than the literary, and Buechner feeds the fire with the forays into essays on religious subjects and the sermon collections. The critical summaries generally nodded back to the work of the 1950s, noted a break in Buechner's career at *The Final Beast*, and focused on the supposed Christian content of the 1970s work. Significantly, however, many of the major critics who had written on the earlier novels ignored Buechner's work of the 1970s, having apparently given him over to the popular reviewers and the journals of religion. But being on the short list for a Pulitzer Prize for the 1980 *Godric* returned Buechner to the critical spotlight, and more recent books—*Brendan*, *The Son of Laughter*, *On the Road with the Archangel*, and *The Storm*—will keep him there. *The Entrance to Porlock* is probably Buechner's most neglected book; it anticipates the more celebrated *Bebb* stories and stands crazily jux-taposed to the more noticed *The Final Beast*, but somehow *The Entrance to Porlock* gets passed over. Throughout these fluctuations of critical regard or critical silence, Buechner has simply carried on with the big idea that runs like a steady current through his career—the possibility of joy in the midst of puzzling reality.

While rereading *The Entrance to Porlock*, I wondered if I might be the only person on the planet visiting that aged volume, a book without any edges. William Pritchard labeled the novel as "often dazzling"[5] but also believed that "Buechner was mainly interested in a cleverly-turned book" (Pritchard 169). Strangely enough, both comments are close to the mark; unevenness haunts this book. Writing in the *Southwest Review* in 1983,

Rudolph Nelson noted that "*The Entrance to Porlock* included no mention whatever of explicitly religious ideas or experiences. But the concerns are still no less ultimate, however nonreligious the language."[6] Somehow the attempt to avoid the religious quagmire ends in another sort of difficulty. Peter Sourian in his analysis for the *New York Times Book Review* referred to the "highly self-conscious writing" as that which "strikingly heightens our sense of what is going on" and also constitutes "an annoying distraction."[7] Although a surprising number of critics missed the Oz motif, they nonetheless sensed the parable. What the *Christian Century* called a "gem,"[8] *Choice* called "too patently symbolic."[9] The *Virginia Quarterly Review* talked of a "reliance on obscurity for its own sake."[10] The dependence on the Oz motif, the fear of the Christian fires, and the troubles of the times all connive to return us to the Jamesian density of the early novels.

Buechner's style on the cusp of the 1970s merits some analysis, as the four *Bebb* novels bear the marks of his instinct for dreams, rampant allusions, and the occasional detour into a self-conscious artfulness. Buechner's penchant for the shaggy dog story, resolution derailed by forays into dreams, and references to Prometheus and Ariel and J. D. Salinger may contribute to the cloudiness that Buechner himself felt hovering over *The Entrance to Porlock*. The technique will be less distracting in the *Bebb* novels, because they do not have the burden of a formula in the way *The Entrance to Porlock* does. The box into which this novel has to fit is Oz, and the reminders of the tale behind the tale disturb both the realism and the pace of the narrative. Sometimes it is the preciosity of one character or another that doesn't quite work; sometimes it is the method of introducing a symbol, say a painting, and delaying the details of the canvas for a few pages and the application to the theme of the novel for still a few pages more. Artful, yes, but somehow too convoluted for the story trying to emerge here, too stylish, perhaps, for the times. Although dreams and allusions will continue to circulate in the *Bebb* books, the overall pace there will be snappier, the narrative less self-conscious, and the feel more relaxed. But for now, Oz has him cornered.

Buechner is sticking with fantasy tales this time, but care must be taken to see just what Oz and the rest mean to him. In a brief essay "Rinkitink in Oz," included in *The Longing for Home*, Buechner underscores his view of an implicit connection between the land of Oz and the realms of Christian theology. Borrowing Tolkien's notion of "*eucatastrophe*," the surprising bend toward the happy ending that we expect in fairy tales, Buechner argues that "Baum never wrote a book with more laughter and goodness in it than *Rinkitink*, but the evil that also stalks its pages is too humanly believable and close to home to shrug off" (*Longing* 75). The Oz world contains the mixture of good and evil that Buechner sees in every direction. In another essay in *A Longing for Home* Buechner confesses, "Like the majority of humankind, I don't know much about wholeness at first hand" (*Longing* 105). The title of that essay, "The Journey toward Wholeness," suggests something of what Buechner learns in Oz and rediscovers in Christian faith. None of the Oz travelers is whole, of course, and Buechner will build his Oz novel on that presupposition—a bunch of ragtag, inept, and devastatingly incomplete travelers on their way to something like wholeness, a small hint of affirmation. That's a story for which Buechner feels great fondness. Perhaps the distance between Oz and Christianity is, in the broadest outlines, not so far. Of Rinkitink, Buechner concludes, "No danger or defeat can keep him down for long, and if idiocy is one thing to call it, the peace that passeth all understanding is another" (*Longing* 73).

All is not well with the country as Buechner struggles through *The Entrance to Porlock*. All is not well with the family, with the career, with you name it. But all will be well. Buechner insists. The new novel comes along in the context of Buechner's attempts at opening his life in an entirely new way to listeners of his *The Alphabet of Grace*. He has spent years now thinking about how to freshen religious language and ideas—first for his charges at Exeter and later for his readers. Many of the passages of *The Alphabet of Grace* and *The Entrance to Porlock* will actually show up in edited forms in *Wishful Thinking: A Theological ABC*. When Buechner talks about mysticism in *The Alphabet of Grace*, for example, he says "religion is mystical" and goes on to argue that religion starts, "as Frost says poems do, with a lump in the throat, to put it mildly, or with the bush going up in flames . . ." (*Alphabet* 75). He will use almost exactly that same language and those same examples to define "mysticism" in *Wishful Thinking* (*WT* 64–65). So *The Entrance to Porlock* is not a retirement from the battle of trying to produce literature within a context of faith; it is, instead, another way of going at the project.

Another novel dedicated to one of his teachers, this time to Gerrish Thurber, one of his mentors at Lawrenceville, *The Entrance to Porlock* has that "to a teacher" feel again in some ways. And the usual suspects are here—Shakespeare, Greene, and Twain brooding behind the Oz motif. But it is finally like all the other books, a wondering about where one might find the quenching of a spiritual thirst. In a speech anthologized in *The Clown in the Belfry*, "The Emerald City: A Commencement Address," Buechner confirms his belief that "we're all of us Tin Woodsmen, of course, just as we're all of us Scarecrows and Cowardly Lions, too. We all have our moments of feeling out of place and left out" (*Belfry* 63). We are still in the territory of the Uglies trying to find the way toward home. The old man of this new novel, aware that his grandson wants to go home, will realize that "his reason for going was . . . to find out where home was."[11]

Margaret Wimsatt properly identified grace as the "ongoing motif" in Buechner's writing. Wimsatt concluded:

> But the gift of grace is not to be commanded or commandeered, perhaps not to be desired by the rest of us. It is a condition of open-ness to all the worlds, and in the Buechner *corpus* it descends on (*inter alios*) an English teacher [*The Book of Bebb*], a former professor of Old Testament history now working in the New York slums [*The Return of Ansel Gibbs*], a faith healer [*The Final Beast*], and a quack doctor [*The Entrance to Porlock*]. (Wimsatt 261)

Wimsatt saw that Buechner has not remarkably diverged over the years; his work, she argued, "forms a consistent opus" (Wimsatt 262). Although he develops a less encumbered style and allows humor more place in his novels, Buechner's search for the presence of God in human experience continues to be the unifying theme of all of his work—the homiletics and the fiction. Wimsatt went too far, however, in aligning Buechner with John Bunyan and suggesting that Buechner was a novelist of the church (Wimsatt 261). She wanted to claim Buechner for the stained-glass, Sunday morning crowd, but he is a rough fit. A careful look at the context in which Buechner places his religious language reveals just how rough. Much turns, for example, on Buechner's understanding of grace.

For Buechner, grace is not, at first, a theological tenet as much as it is theological wishful thinking—hopefulness—another way to put the possibility of joy business. He defines this sort of grace by offering examples: "A good sleep is grace and so are good dreams. Most tears are grace. The smell of rain is grace. Somebody loving you is grace. Loving somebody is grace" (*WT* 33–34). Defining grace, the theological term, he adds: "The grace of God means something like: Here is your life. You might never have been, but you are because the party wouldn't have been complete without you. Here is the world. Beautiful and terrible things will happen. Don't be afraid. I am with you. Nothing can ever separate us. It's for you I created the universe" (*WT* 34). Thus Buechner decides upon a relatively secular view of grace; his characters search for a hint of meaning in life, the happy ending of the fairy tale, as much as they search for religious union with God. In this regard, Buechner might be categorized as a humanist or a secular optimist as much as a Christian preacher. His notion of grace deals not so much with the specifically Christian idea of prevenient or saving grace as with a variety of common grace. (This is one of the reasons that Buechner has an increasing popularity among those who have dropped out of various fundamentalist persuasions, as evidenced by his appearance in such journals as *The Wittenburg Door, Christianity Today*, and *Mission Journal.*)

Buechner's notion of universal grace is nowhere more evident than in his attitude toward the Christian doctrine of hell. He claims that "the bottomless pit is not really bottomless" and argues, Dante notwithstanding, that hope exists even in hell. Suggesting there is no length to which God will not go to extend grace, Buechner concludes: "Maybe not even Old Scratch will be able to hold out against him forever" (*WT* 37–38). But even in discussing such a distinctly doctrinal issue, Buechner speaks whimsically; he assiduously avoids the righteous tones and dogmatic positions of the televangelist and other public purveyors of religiosity. In the novels he prefers to hint of possibilities in life rather than to forge overt theological statements.

Buechner's reading of *The Brothers Karamazov*, for example, clearly suggests his own aims as a novelist. Claiming Dostoevsky's masterpiece is a "single metaphor" (*RCR* 180) for the question of God's existence, Buechner argues that all worthy literature acts as a metaphor for a writer's struggles with central questions of truth. Citing Anthony Trollope, of whom he declares "there is no greater writer in English" (*RCR* 179), Buechner points to Trollope's stated desire to teach the virtues of nobility, honesty, courage, and truth.[12] Trollope even confessed to thinking of himself "as a preacher of sermons" (Trollope 124). Buechner responds favorably to Trollope's audacious claim:

> Words like Trollope's are in many ways out of fashion now. . . . For a novelist to speak of himself as a preacher of sermons puts everybody off. But when Trollope . . . says that the calling of a writer is to teach virtue and nobility, and when he expresses the hope that people will learn from his words that true manliness, true humanness, is to be found not in falseness and flashiness but in truth and a gentle spirit, that is something else again. (*RCR* 179)

Many writers such as Trollope and others of his general era—Samuel Richardson, Fanny Burney, and Jane Austen—aim at encouraging readers to positive, hopeful lives. (Ian Watt claims that Richardson "was conspicuously successful in carrying his moral and religious aims into the fashionable and predominantly secular field of fiction."[13]) Buechner's work reveals a consonance with those works of fiction inspiring readers to reach through the muddle of life to a vision of hopefulness. Buechner, in fact, meets the criterion outlined in Gardner's *On Moral Fiction*, "presenting valid models for imitation, eternal verities worth keeping in mind, and a benevolent vision of the possible which can inspire and incite human beings toward virtue, toward life affirmation as opposed to destruction or indifference" (Gardner 18).

Believing that words can never embody theological truth, Buechner views the novel as a metaphor of one individual's grappling with issues of truth. In a 1985 speech, "The Truth of Story," Buechner explains his tentativeness about creeds, doctrines, and theological positions by focusing on Christ's contention: "I am the way, the truth, the life."[14] Christ refuses to hold forth an ethical system or a church or a religion as truth, says Buechner, but points instead to himself—to the shifting, elusive story of his own life.[15] Thus Jesus keeps silent before Pilate's questioning, because truth can never be captured in words. Buechner's conception of his work as a novelist partakes of this notion of truth. He underscores the unpredictability of truth—truth somehow complexly wrapped up in the stories of individual lives, in autobiography. The novelist, finally, is the memoirist, the register of occasional glimpses of truth in his own experience. Buechner plays both sides of the religious/secular vision and, finally, cannot be trapped on either side. His Christianity remains unorthodox; his fiction, like the truth it metaphorically embodies, remains elusive.

In fact, *The Entrance to Porlock* features religion less than any other Buechner book. The novel contains no discussion of religious ideas, involves no specifically theological material, and steers away from the Christian overtones of *The Final Beast*. Buechner's silence on the religious front derives in part from his reaction to the critical response to *The Final Beast*. He says as much in an interview with Shirley and Rudy Nelson:

> When *The Final Beast* came out, a number of reviewers, having heard that I'd recently been ordained, attacked me, I felt, not for the book I'd actually written but for the book they assumed I must have written because I was now a minister. Whether the book was good or bad, the point is that it wasn't the kind of pietistic pap they charged it with being. So part of what I was doing in *Porlock* was to steer clear of anything overtly religious in hopes that maybe the reviewers would deal

Buechner's home in Rupert, Vermont

View from Buechner's study

with me again like any other writer. Its plot and characters are largely based on *The Wizard of Oz*, and the book is religious in much the way that wonderful tale is—by implication and indirection. (Nelson Interview 11–12)

Buechner probably admits more here than he realizes about his sensitivity to the critics and about his notions of how a believer might approach the art of the novel, but he sharply clarifies the history of *The Entrance to Porlock*.

Returning to the model of *The Return of Ansel Gibbs* for his fifth novel, Buechner keeps the religious element on low. Marie-Helene Davies even went so far as to say "the Christian hid behind the novelist" in *The Entrance to Porlock* (Davies 64). I prefer the idea that Buechner comes at the faith issues from a different direction this time. Theological issues are deeply cloaked in this tribute to *Oz*, but it would be a mistake to assume that *The Entrance to Porlock* is not the book that Buechner wanted to write. Surely Buechner believes in Oz almost as much as he believes in Christ, and his fifth novel is a thoroughgoing statement of Buechner's notions of universal grace. Further, as Buechner tells Nancy Myers, the painful birth of the novel was part of his reaction to the social unrest and assassinations of the late 1960s. Calling the novel a "strangled book," Buechner says that he felt "if there was one thing the world didn't need, it was another book" (Myers 99).

In 1967 Buechner left Phillips Exeter Academy for a farmhouse and a career as a full-time writer in Rupert, Vermont. The move reflected the fulfillment of a dream, but *The Entrance to Porlock* reveals the uncertainty and struggle precipitated by the decision. He made the move, and "the writing didn't come" (Myers 99). These months are, nonetheless, pivotal in Buechner's development toward that career theme that defines so much of his work since the 1970s—"listen to your life" as he puts it (*NT* 87)—a notion that emerges in stark form as Buechner nears the end of *The Entrance to Porlock*.

In the memoirs, Buechner claims the novel was born "by Caesarian section" (*NT* 81). Recalling the novel with some of the same shudders he usually reserves for *The Seasons' Difference*, Buechner talks of the struggle, the "grim throes" of a novel that came painfully (*NT* 83). Confessing that the novel is "symbolic autobiography," Buechner recalls the laborious effort the book required and the feeling that he had written himself "into a blank wall" (*NT* 81). He adds, "I had lived myself into a blank wall too," and the novel partakes of the turmoil of this period in his life. Summarizing his situation, Buechner concludes, "I was a minister without a church, a teacher without students, a writer without a subject. I looked to my wife and daughters for more than any human being can give to another. I felt like a rat in a trap, and the trap I was in was myself and the new life I had chosen" (*NT* 82). But the desperation of this period in Buechner's life has been taken by Myers and Davies as an indication that *The Entrance to Porlock* is an aberration, a temporary setback in the development of a Christian writer.

On the contrary, the novel clearly posits one side of Buechner's preoccupations—his belief that the searches of life may end in a deepening self-knowledge, and he looks to fairy tale, Oz, more than to Christianity as a way to explore the idea. In a time of personal doubt and change, Buechner, perhaps in an attempt to clarify his own situation, goes back to the thematic center of *The Return of Ansel Gibbs*, the search for identity. The search is not the orthodox Christian pursuit of Christ but a longing for self-identity and richness of experience. *The Entrance to Porlock*, consistent with the fabric of Buechner's entire career, centers on the quest for meaning and ends by sounding what R. W. Henderson called "a faintly affirmative note."[16] Henderson's observation might accurately describe all of Buechner's fiction.

The protagonist of *The Entrance to Porlock* is an eighty-year-old eccentric, Peter Ringkoping. Buechner summarizes the character: "An old man who runs a secondhand bookstore on a mountain like ours in Vermont sees the ghosts of dead writers whose books he sells, sees glimpses of a shimmering reality within reality, and in the process, loses touch with his family" (*NT* 81). In *The Alphabet of Grace*, Buechner speaks of the character emerging in the manuscript pushed to the far side of the desk:

> I am writing about an old man who exists only in my mind. I have put him together out of scraps and pieces, most of them forgotten. There's some of Mark Twain in him, the old Mark they brought back in a wheel chair from Bermuda to die at Stormfield. There's some of the old man Isak from Bergman's *Wild Strawberries* in him. . . . There's some of an old German cousin in him who looked like the Kaiser. (*Alphabet* 82–83)

Peter Ringkoping is Peter Cowley grown old—a believer in the possibility of mystical visions—and Buechner refuses the writerly cliché that Peter creates himself. Although accepting responsibility for the creation, Buechner does admit that he is surprised by Peter's occasional tears and his tendency to be "crustier and more remote" than Buechner had imagined he would be (*Alphabet* 83).

Like Theodore Nicolet, Peter Ringkoping searches for meaning behind the appearances of things. He thinks there may be fire at the heart of it all, and mightn't we read "fire" to mean "meaning"? Estranged from his family by his own self-preoccupation, Peter longs to know them better, as he longs to know himself. Peter is the Tin Man in search of a heart. His middle-aged sons, Nels and Tommy, and his nineteen-year-old grandson, Tip, will join Peter on his journey to a community for the mentally handicapped run by a friend from years long past, Hans Strasser. Making preparations for his death, Peter intends to donate a sizable tract of land on Tinmouth Mountain, "Shangri-La," to Strasser and wants to visit Strasser's community before completing the transaction (*Porlock* 22). The family opposes the deal, fearing that, nearing eighty, Peter has finally gone round the bend. So the boys go along to protect Peter and to protect themselves as well. Nels, the older of Peter's two sons, is a rigid headmaster of a boys' preparatory school, unmarried and obsessed with the fear of having a heart attack. He is the cowardly lion. Tommy is the irresponsible and insecure practical joker, the scarecrow seeking a brain, his eyes always watering from what may be, he thinks, an allergy to himself (*Porlock* 15). Tip, Tommy's son, has inherited his grandfather's mysticism and introspection, and is Dorothy seeking a home. His forehead prematurely creased by worry lines, Tip just wants to get home, and he joins the journey as a way of finding out "where home was" (*Porlock* 67). This group travels the "yellow dirt road" (*Porlock* 33) to Strasser's retreat, thinking, as Peter puts it, "Maybe Strasser's the one who will help" (*Porlock* 96). They journey to the answer man, the guru, in search of inspiration, hoping to come to terms with themselves. The only other characters in the novel are Peter's nearly blind, death-haunted wife, Sarah; Tommy's desperate wife, Alice, who protects her Lear-like father-in-law from the raging storms; and the cast of discarded folks in Strasser's menagerie.

The collective quest of the travelers—the facing of personal failures, old age, death, personal identity, and collapsed relationships—is obviously a kind of religious quest. Peter, the descendant of Theodore Nicolet, believes that reality may lie just under the surface of life and can, perhaps, be discovered by slipping a thumbnail under and peeling back the surface, like lifting a label from an envelope. Peter learns, finally, that the key to life is in one's relationships, and he experiences a moment of fulfillment at the end of the novel when he identifies with one of the damaged boys and finds "just as he least expected it, his thumbnail had slipped under and pulled back the air" (*Porlock* 256). Peter, like Eliot's Prufrock, "had never heard a human voice . . . only the echoes of voices. He had never seen a human face—only the shadows of strangers" (*Porlock* 132). Too fascinated by that "somewhere beyond his watching," Peter has failed to see the people and places right in front of him. Even his boys and his wife, Sarah, have gone unnoticed in the daze of Peter's misspent life. He has watched, but he hasn't seen—precisely the theme that Buechner tears into in *The Alphabet of Grace*. But Peter does figure out some of the riddle in the novel; his moment arrives when a simple-minded "boy's face was itself a door that opened. . . . The secret panel slid back on a treasure" (*Porlock* 256).

Ironically, the scene from the unnamed boy's life that the door opens on is a scene from Buechner's own life—the haunting snapshot of his grandmother and mother trying to revive his dead father on the November morning of Buechner's childhood. Although, out of deference to his mother, the reference is more oblique now, almost buried, Buechner still smuggles the story in as testimony to the pain he cannot shed, as the best example he can think of as to what we might see if we could truly have glimpses into one another's lives. The curmudgeon Peter, surrounded by his dysfunctional family, thinking that his life has been a mostly misfire affair, in some odd way anticipates the ebullient Leo Bebb of the novels to follow in the decade after *The Entrance to Porlock*. Peter, like Leo, is a crank of the highest order, and they are both trying to peel back the layers to find out what, if anything, is at the core. Like Leo Bebb, Peter is part mind reader, part mystic, part idealist. His grandson is reminded of Buffalo Bill or maybe "a retired general" when he sees Peter all dressed up for the journey (*Porlock* 33). Readers encounter Peter in a way not unlike the way his own family encounters him—via guesses and imaginings.

Peter's eldest son, Nels, joins the trip while mulling the suspension of a student, Davey Mullavey, who has been caught seeking a hallucinatory experience with a prescription drug. Nels's philosophy requires that he be strict with Mullavey, and Nels clashes with one of his teachers, Walter Penrose, who encourages leniency in the Mullavey case. Penrose is one of those teachers with whom the boys identify, one who treats the boys as friends. Such a teaching philosophy is anathema to Nels; he believes "You drew a line and held them to it" (*Porlock* 108). The crisis for Nels comes when Mullavey, anticipating banishment and disgrace, hangs himself. Nels finds his courage when, still on the pilgrimage with his family, he is informed of Mullavey's death and asked what he had decided to do about the expulsion. Tempted to lie, take the easy way out, Nels tells the truth that he had indeed decided to expel the boy.

Nonetheless Nels is deeply changed by the student's death and finds courage to face his own mortality as a consequence of what he sees as a kind of bravery in Mullavey. When Nels asks himself what the Davy Mullaveys of the world were "looking for that the world did not provide," Buechner seems to be asking the question of the 1960s (*Porlock* 112). Nels rejects his own thoughts of possible complicity in Davy Mullavey's demise, but a gradual sense of responsibility settles over him. He is the elder brother, serious to a fault, grimly subservient to the rules, giving his life to his school, "born with a dagger in his teeth" (*Porlock* 18). But his nickname at Putnam School is "Bunny," and his timorousness is evidenced by his constant sense of some impending disaster. If Peter lives in the mists of dreams and ghosts, Nels lives with his hand on his chest, constantly dreaming of death as a way of holding death at bay. Cynical and practical in a Poteat/Lundrigan/Motley sort of way, Nels will come to a dramatic moment when "a landscape that he had not seen before came alive" (*Porlock* 208). That's as far as Nels will get, but the journey is miles and miles.

Tommy is the younger brother, the prodigal, "born with an arrow through his head" (*Porlock* 18). He deals with his longing and incompleteness by retreating into a life of slapstick, a running litany of punning and trying to ignore the straw that holds him together. Nels tells him that he lacks confidence and cannot be taken seriously (*Porlock* 104); he is "the man of a thousand faces" who has "forgotten his own" (*Porlock* 166). The man with a child's name, Tommy, also matures in the course of the story. His growth is evident in two scenes—instances where he acquires a brain or, more to the point, learns to accept his own inevitable death and thereby accept his own maturity as an adult.

Along the road to Strasser's community, the travelers stop to rest, and Tommy spots a crow standing in the distance. In a scene that Buechner wrote before he had a book to put it in (*Alphabet* 86), Tommy grabs his rifle and aims at the crow. In a strangely suspended moment, Tommy, the scarecrow, and the "dapper little funeral of a bird" stand staring at one another (*Porlock* 135). Finally, Tommy shoots the bird, but the crow flies straight toward Tommy before it dies and falls at Tommy's feet. Surprisingly, Tommy gets down on his knees, picks up the dead crow, and touching it to his cheek says, "Old Croaker, old squawker" (*Porlock* 135). The crow undoubtedly represents the darkness and death to which Tommy is becoming reconciled. Later, at the retreat, Tommy tears his clothes while walking in the woods. The inmates of Strasser's home carry Tommy into a workshop where he is "stitched up." His "stuffing" generates new life for Tommy, and even Nels notices that Tommy forsakes his usual clownishness.

Finally, Tommy sees that the "last joke was that there was no joke" (*Por-lock* 243); he learns to hold his tongue, and when Strasser offers to prepare a place for the family to spend the night so they can avoid a long drive home in the dark, it is Tommy who declines, saying, "But darkness gives us back the day again. . . . We have nothing to fear from the darkness" (*Porlock* 262–63). He has made his peace with death and with himself.

Tip, the grandson, whose name summarizes his incompleteness, faces the wars of adolescence; he is "looking for an escape into the world" (*Por-lock* 186). Buechner considered writing the novel from the point of view of Tip, the boy who goes on the journey "to find out where home was" (*Porlock* 67), and Buechner will turn to first-person narration with his next novel, *Lion Country*. Instead, this time Buechner gathers in Tip all of the longing and bewilderment of the searcher "looking always for something not to be found" (*Porlock* 119). Even at the end of the novel, when Strasser tells Tip, "You're the one I know least," Tip responds, "Same here . . . I'm the one I know least" (*Porlock* 266). Tip is at the wheel when the travelers start their journey back home, but he is still looking for a way out of words, an opening into Porlock.

Tip may be the character most anticipatory of Antonio Parr in the Bebb novels to follow soon. Full of homesickness for a place he's seen only in dreams, Tip cannot confess his love to Libba Vann. He has more than a little Holden Caulfield in him. Like Holden, Tip is developing X-ray eyes, yearning to "see through other's eyes" (*Porlock* 116). When his grandfather asks him if he's hungry, Tip answers, "You don't know the half of it" (*Porlock* 118), and he wants to tell Peter about this gnawing at the soul. But the old man already knows, of course. Tip is straining to figure out what the older folks are thinking, trying to see into himself, bewildered and aware mostly of absence and misunderstanding for most of the novel.

Buechner's title derives from Coleridge's whimsical report of the composition of "Kubla Khan," in which the poet, eagerly penning the poem that had come to him in a dream, was interrupted by the visitor from Porlock, the village nearby. Porlock is the dull surface of things, and Tip, like his grandfather, is hoping for something beneath the surface. Porlock, as Buechner uses the term, points to "the tension between everyday reality and the reality of dreams, of imagination" (*NT* 81). Further, Porlock, in the immediate context of the novel, is the name of a horse that has formerly been assigned to one of the stalls in Peter Ringkoping's barn, the barn he has converted into a bookstore. Peter maintains the stalls and uses them to section off his thirty-five thousand volumes. Porlock's old stall becomes the drama section, history is in Daisy's former stall, and fiction is in Sam's. Old Peter, musing late one night in the bookstore, thinks he has glimpsed the ghost of Shakespeare in the drama section. Peter even becomes something of a celebrity when he publishes a moderately successful book, *Doorways in the Air*, about the experience. Peter declares, "I've had my glimpses now and again," but he is increasingly cynical in his old age that he has had no more than intimations and hints (*Porlock* 29). When Tommy tells him, "You've had your ghosts at least," Peter responds, "Just shadows" (*Porlock* 94). On the way to Strasser's Pilgrim Village, Peter, half-dreaming of his death, feels that "there were no doorways in the air," fears that "life opened up to endless vacancy" (*Porlock* 126). Here's the doubt that has haunted Tristram Bone, Peter Cowley, Theodore Nicolet, Ansel Gibbs, and the others.

Peter finally overcomes his despair by accepting incompleteness, what Lear calls the "mystery of things" (V, ii, 16). As we have seen, Buechner calls *King Lear* "one of the mightiest of all preachments,"[17] and Lear's cry of "mystery" echoes throughout *The Entrance to Porlock*; Davy Mullavey searches for the mystery in "an ounce or two of his asthmatic abracadabra" (*Porlock* 112), Nels ponders the mystery of his own weakness, and Tommy explores the mystery of his thoughtlessness. Finally, however, it is Tip who is preoccupied with "the mystery within himself" (*Porlock* 57).

Tip promises to follow the path of his grandfather through a life of alternating intimations and doubts to a final reconciliation with the mysteries, but the affirmation is a mere hint—no ringing finale this time. Tip carries on a copious, diarylike correspondence with Libba Vann, a young girl who works in his grandfather's house. Of course, Tip has not declared his feelings to Libba and will not mail the letter he writes to her during the journey to Strasser's community. In the letter, however, Tip reveals his fascination with the same questions that haunt Peter Ringkoping:

> I am alone and in great danger, Libba Vann. I am at the entrance to Porlock. . . . Blessed are the poor in spirit, for they shall see Porlock. Porlock, you may remember, is where the poetry and drama are. . . . Porlock is where the shadows are thickest. Porlock is where Grandfather saw Shakespeare. Porlock is where the secret is both known and told, and it is the place I visit often in my dreams. . . . Am I in danger, or is the secret of Porlock that there is no secret? (*Porlock* 183–84)

Tip probably finds less of himself than Peter and the others find of themselves, but Tip certainly learns something from his grandfather's conclusions:

> My life has been a pilgrimage in search of a land beyond the land I
> knew, and as for the land I knew, I mislaid it somewhere, like a collar
> button . . . a wedding ring. The land beyond—the land of heart's
> desire—I never found. You might as well know it. Not because it
> wasn't there all along, for all I know, but because I had no heart to
> find it with, to desire it properly. (*Porlock* 249)

Such is the thematic center of the novel. Searching for explanations to the
bewilderment of their lives, the travelers find glimmers of answers inside
themselves.

Strasser, of course, is the reluctant wizard who steers the way. The wizard figure pops up here and there in Buechner's career. In "The Emerald
City: A Commencement Address," for example, Buechner records his
attraction to Oz and to the wizard in particular: "In the ordinary abracadabra, presto-changeo sense of the word, the Wizard of Oz is not a wizard at all. But in another sense, he is not only a very great wizard indeed
but the worker of magic which no one should be allowed to graduate from
anywhere without knowing about" (*Belfry* 60).

Through Strasser, Buechner weaves into *The Entrance to Porlock* themes
related to his growing theological vocabulary—loss of innocence, the
attainment of full humanity, and the presence of grace. When the
Ringkopings are touring Strasser's village, he tells them of the absence of
"sexual ripeness" in the "unfinished" victims of Down syndrome. Emphasizing the innocence, Strasser adds, "a mongol has no fear of death," and
"it is almost impossible to anger him" (*Porlock* 216–17). The visiting family, beset by precisely such fears as the fear of death, angry at life's tricks,
and, especially for Tip, painfully aware of puzzling sexuality, begins to see
Strasser's patients as Eden dwellers. Summarizing the state of one of
Strasser's patients, Peter says, "He lives in Paradise," and Tommy quips
"Where do I sign up?" (*Porlock* 217). Strasser responds: "For us it is too
late for Paradise. . . . We have come along too far. The mongol is the raw
clay we are all of us molded out of, but we have been molded now and
glazed and baked in the oven. He alone comes to remind us of our original being. It is why mongols have started being born, I think. They are
messages to us from a world that we've lost" (*Porlock* 218).

Like the children of *The Seasons' Difference*, the weak-minded are innocent, but for all who grow normally to maturity, the innocence is sadly,
inevitably, and irretrievably lost.

Growth toward the fullness of human possibility is anything but
inevitable. Strasser's wizardry comes down to hints and intimations. He

confesses his own weakness when he acknowledges that all his life he's "been waiting for the heavens to open up and show riches" (*Porlock* 247). What he's gotten is "a puff of wind and a few raindrops" (*Porlock* 248). Nonetheless, he speaks a kind of wisdom that turns out to be enough: "Life does not end. . . . It keeps pushing up in new ways out of new deaths" (*Porlock* 179). Thus Buechner arrives at the mixture that will circulate in his work in dramatic ways from this point on.

Back at home, Alice has begun to fret about her fragile husband and his entourage. Fearing that some accident has befallen Peter and the others, she makes her own pilgrimage to Strasser's village, and she convinces Sarah to join her for the harried drive. Arriving in Strasser's realm, Alice almost immediately begins pouring out her sadness to Strasser, who—it is hinted—may have been her lover in bygone days. Their relationship is one of the mysteries of the text. Strasser responds by talking to Alice about his years of work, informed by a philosophy that he jokes about: "Sometimes I make a little joke about mankind. Man, I say, is the missing link between the ape and the human being. Here, our work is to help the ones who are a little more like apes to become a little more like humans. . . . I see by your face I do not have to tell you that being human can be very painful" (*Porlock* 175–76). Buechner probably derives this emphasis from Tillich, who argued that modern life deprives us of our "united, centered personality" (*Eternal* 152) and concluded that one must have the courage to affirm "one's essential nature" (*Courage* 4). The wizard's ultimate advice is not something translatable into words; it is something about a peace beyond understanding (*Porlock* 182).

Therefore, Buechner can say that his central message, as a preacher and a novelist, is "Listen to your life" (Gibble 1043). In other places, Buechner calls the process "a conscious remembering" (*Radix* 8), and feels that deep awareness of one's humanity leads first to a fuller participation in life and finally to the possibility of seeing beyond life. In a 1969 sermon Buechner asserts: "I believe that by God's grace it is our destiny, in this life or in whatever life awaits us, to discover the face of our inmost being, to become at last and at great cost who we truly are" (*HD* 23). A decade later, in a sermon about *The Wizard of Oz*, Buechner points out that the travelers in Baum's story already had in them what they traveled to find and concludes, "We want very much what these three wanted, and that is to become fully men, to become fully persons. And we want it for the same reason that they wanted it, because as things stand now we know that we are only partly men, partly persons" (*MD* 55). Buechner summarizes Strasser's importance in *The Entrance to Porlock* when he comments on the novel in his memoirs: "The Wizard is an Austrian who runs a community for the mentally and emotionally disturbed, and it is in their relationship to him that they all move at least a step closer to finding what is missing in themselves" (*NT* 81). Strasser's final gesture in the novel is to return to Peter the land that the old man has given him—the acres on Tinmouth Mountain. In returning the land, Strasser offers the commentary: "I give the land back, Peter Ringkoping. The golden mountain is yours again. Excuse me, that is not correct. The golden mountain is yours for the first time. Nothing can ever really be yours, you know, until you get it as a gift" (*Porlock* 269).

The Entrance to Porlock stands, finally, as another discussion of the gift of grace. Far from being anomalous in the Buechner canon, the novel distinctly communicates the same craving for hope that has been at the center of the earlier work. Strasser captures the hope when he tells the visitors that although "everybody is drowning," a little child may yet show them the way (*Porlock* 189). Eventually Peter's interaction with one of the mentally challenged residents does, indeed, fuel a kind of salvation for him, though this book keeps its distance from all things religious. The most specific expression of religious hope comes in the form of a formulaic exchange when Strasser jokingly tells Alice, who is going off to rest because of a headache, "*Requiescat in pace*" and one of the patients adds, "*In spe resurrectionis*" [in hope of resurrection] (*Porlock* 196). Hope is just a clichéd religious litany stuck somewhere in the memory.

Although Buechner avoids explicit religious conclusions in *The Entrance to Porlock*, the novel is replete with the small affirmation, the half-step progress toward understanding one's place in life. The novel is, as Diana Loercher recognized, "more parable than story."[18] The parable is the chronicle of a journey, of course, and the reader walks beside the Ringkopings toward their lesson that answers are elusive at best and may never come. The most they can do is try to be all that a tin man, a scarecrow, a cowardly lion, and a homesick waif can be, and in their better moments they sense that this may well be enough after all. As Buechner puts it in his *Oz* sermon, one may not reach home "but the place through which we must pass if ever we are to reach home at last" (*MD* 56). It is the journeying, not the arriving, that matters finally.

The Entrance to Porlock, then, is important not so much for the humor and whimsicality that set it apart, along with *The Final Beast*, from the first three novels, but for its fablelike reworking of the pilgrimage theme to which Buechner will return with remarkable success in *Godric*. Nancy Myers, for example, missed the larger point of consonance in her insistence that these two novels represented a new direction and a "loosening up the tongue" (Myers 117). Instead, *The Entrance to Porlock* is another way of exploring the possibilities of grace, the truth of fairy tale. Stacy Thompson caught the most surprising aspect of the novel by noting what Buechner might have done:

> How easily the disabilities and abnormalities of the villagers could be used to develop the kinds of themes we expect from and find in much contemporary American fiction: isolation, incommunicability, hopelessness. It is important to note that for Buechner they become instead the sources of wonder and transformation, love and affirmation. (Thompson 127)

Thompson's direction was the most insightful approach to Buechner's fiction. It hearkens to the standard set by John Gardner, who, though he mistakenly feared that Buechner had become overly loyal to a Christian message, argued for fiction that "clarifies life, establishes models of human action, casts nets toward the future, carefully judges our right and wrong directions, celebrates and mourns" (Gardner 100). *The Entrance to Porlock* offers no baptisms, no tearful confessions at church altars, no orthodox sermons, and nothing remotely akin to a specific Christian teaching. As he has in all of the early work, Buechner explores the longing of the soul.

Buechner is, then, a novelist of the spirit—never a novelist of the church. James Woelfel succinctly described the thread running through *The Final Beast* to *The Entrance to Porlock*:

> In *Porlock* as in the earlier novels, Buechner paints on a small canvas, exploring the personal hungerings for meaning and love and the complex and fragile relationships among a small group of people bound together by ties of family and friendship. And as in *The Final Beast*, there is grace too at the end for each of the protagonists through their visit to Strasser's community—but again as a "now and then" of healing and renewal in the midst of life's complexities. (Woelfel 285)

The miracle this time is just a maybe ghost in a used bookstore on a night full of dozing and dreams. Peter's book on the subject, *Doorways in the Air*, may be "autobiography or fairy tale," as Peter is not sure of "any difference between them" (*Porlock* 54–55). Buechner's signature doubleness persists here as when Strasser points to the scribbles of the patients he calls pilgrims, noticing one "I hate you, Hans," and another "I love you, Hans" (*Porlock* 174–75). Strasser explains that both proclamations were written by the same person. And there is no refuge in orthodoxy. Peter's briefly famous book is called religious by some. But Nels realizes "it was no religion a man could get hold of; it showed no way, pointed to no truth, urged no life" (*Porlock* 197). Despite his penchant for magic, Peter has no taste for church. Buechner stays far away from the stained glass this time. The only sermon is something about paying attention, and the only conclusions circle on the long-shot possibility of quenching those deepest, inexpressible human longings: "Porlock," Tip concludes, "is where the shadows are thickest" (*Porlock* 183). With his fifth novel, Buechner nonetheless reiterates his belief that reality, though puzzling and difficult, is fraught with meaning, and he continues the premise into the *Bebb* tetralogy that will occupy him for most of the 1970s.

Notes

1. Chris Anderson, "The Very Style of Faith: Frederick Buechner as Homilist and Essayist," *Christianity & Literature* 38, no. 2 (Winter 1989): 19. Hereafter cited as Anderson.
2. Ron Hansen, *A Stay against Confusion: Essays on Faith and Fiction* (New York: Harper-Collins, 2001), 26. Hereafter cited as Hansen.
3. Stephen Dunn, "At the Smithville Methodist Church," *Local Time* (New York: William Morrow, 1986), 53–55.
4. Mary McDermott Shideler, "Honest and Sensitive," *Christian Century*, October 21, 1970, 1263.
5. William Pritchard, "Senses of Reality," *Hudson Review*, Spring 1970, 169. Hereafter cited as Pritchard.
6. Rudolph L. Nelson, "The Doors of Perception: Mystical Experience in Buechner's Fiction," *Southwest Review*, Summer 1983, 270.
7. Peter Sourian, *New York Times Book Review*, February 1, 1970.
8. *Christian Century*, April, 1, 1970.
9. *Choice*, October 1970.
10. *Virginia Quarterly Review*, Spring 1970.
11. Frederick Buechner, *The Entrance to Porlock* (New York: Atheneum, 1970), 67. Hereafter cited as *Porlock*.
12. Anthony Trollope, *An Autobiography* (New York: Oxford University Press, 1947), 124. Hereafter cited as Trollope.
13. Ian Watt, *The Rise of the Novel* (Harmondsworth, Middlesex, England: Penguin, 1957), 56.
14. John 14:6.
15. Frederick Buechner, "The Truth of Story," speech at Wheaton College, October 4, 1985.
16. R. W. Henderson, book review, *Library Journal*, January 15, 1970, 95.
17. Frederick Buechner, *Telling the Truth: The Gospel in Tragedy, Comedy, and Fairy Tale* (San Francisco: Harper & Row, 1977), 4.
18. Diana Loercher, book review, *Christian Science Monitor*, February 5, 1970, 11.

Chapter Six

Listening for the Lone Ranger

The Book of Bebb

M ost readers coming to the *Bebb* novels after a chronological reading of Buechner's earlier work would notice departures: a freer
style, coarse language, sexual scenes reminiscent of John Updike's novels
of the same era, topical references, outrageous characters, punchy puns,
and a first-person narrator. The editors at Atheneum predicted a breakthrough with these novels that fill Buechner's 1970s. Because they were
"racy and fun and colorful things happen in them," Buechner notes,
expectations ran high (Brown 34). Buechner even invested his royalties in
the publicity campaign, but "it didn't make any difference at all," he says
with a shake of his head; "the same faithful group went out and bought
them" (Brown 34). Buechner's own supposition about the miscalculation
returns to the ordination-as-culprit premise, though I'd be hard pressed
to believe that any uninformed readers of *The Book of Bebb* imagined that
a minister was pulling the strings behind the curtain. I'll concede, however, that reviews about the perils of writing on cloth were no doubt having their effect by now, at least at bookstore cash registers. In reviews and
critical pieces from the mid-1960s forward, Buechner the novelist was
consistently associated with Buechner the minister. The insidious suggestion that the one calling precluded the other must have cost Buechner
some readers in one venue, though the mix of novelist and believer would
eventually cultivate new readers in another venue. *The Book of Bebb* comes
along in the gap.

The four novels—*Lion Country* (1971), *Open Heart* (1972), *Love Feast*
(1974), and *Treasure Hunt* (1977)—tell one periodic tale of Antonio Parr's
involvement in the life of Leo Bebb, itinerant preacher, diploma salesman,
ex-convict, saint, and/or hypocrite. Or do the novels chronicle the story

of Bebb's involvement in Antonio's life? In 1979 Buechner edited the four novels, gathering them into one volume, significantly dubbed *The Book of Bebb*. Although Antonio Parr narrates the stories, and the reader sees the landscapes of the novels through Antonio's eyes, Bebb broods over the narrative throughout; the novels are his even when he exists only as a memory on Tono's fuzzy home-movie reels. Because Leo Bebb is, ostensibly, a man of the cloth, Buechner can comfortably interweave religious rhetoric, biblical allusions, and theological considerations, as he has in *The Final Beast*.

Bebb is anything but a typical clergyman, however, and *The Book of Bebb* emphatically is not a collection of religious novels. Although some critics tried to categorize the novels as "essentially religious" (Myers 133), the novels are religious only in their implications and suggestions, never directly. Theodore Nicolet, despite his introspection and doubt, is a staunchly orthodox minister beside Leo Bebb, the colorful and controversial preacher of the tetralogy. They both wear robes when they preach, but the comparison stops there. Again, Buechner's approach can be labeled "religious" only if one stretches the word beyond its typical connotations. *The Book of Bebb* continues with the questions dominating all of Buechner's work: belief versus unbelief, the ambiguities of life, the nature of sin, human lostness, spiritual homesickness, the quest for self-identity, the need for self-revelation, the search for meaning, and the possibility of joy. The fabric of the work stretches somewhat, but it is very much the same fabric. Cynthia Ozick labeled the books "God-hungry comic novels,"[1] and she is on the right path. Again, although God is argued for and argued against, he is never absent. But the question of God finally goes unsettled. Buechner refuses to smuggle in a conventional religious conclusion; he simply reports, instead, a faith struggle—a delicately balanced statement of affirmation and doubt, another book that raises intriguing questions.

Bebb is where I came in. From behind the counter of Shirley's Old Book Shop in Springfield, Missouri, Shirley pointed out the gaudy, bright yellow and orange, omnibus edition of the novels that she'd set back for me. She had already affixed my name via a paper clipped to the spine. It was the price that appealed—$4.60 even with tax included—and Shirley had guessed right about me before. I had no idea how to pronounce "Buechner," but the investment seemed safe enough—four novels after all. So I entered the world of Leo Bebb, a shady preacher, in the early 1980s, when we'd been hearing about one shady preacher after another. Although Leo's shades were different from mine, his failures had a ring I'd heard. Along with weak and marvelous Leo came Antonio Parr, a lost sort of fellow, also someone I knew. I had long been wary of identifying with characters in books, and the Lion Country featured in this book was unlike any place I'd ever visited, but the story of Leo and Tono was strangely captivating. I was well along in *Lion Country* when I realized that it might be my book—not the best book I had ever read, but my book nonetheless. I suspect many readers come to Buechner by similar routes.

I would have been amazed at the time to hear that the author of these raucous novels was a Presbyterian minister, but I did, even then, sense a subterranean something in the quickly turning pages. Something stirred in Buechner's brew, something about the reality of suffering and the legitimacy of doubt in marvelous counterpoise with the subtle sense that lives just might be going somewhere and not just anywhere. This writer was obviously curious about the possibility of life with a plot line, even as he was conspicuously honest about the elusive details, the sharp outlines of what that plot might be.

I would learn later that by the 1970s Buechner was becoming increasingly celebrated within the Christian subculture that was meeting him via such books as *The Magnificent Defeat*, *The Hungering Dark*, and *The Alphabet of Grace*. His name was beginning to circulate in pulpits, and invitations to lecture here or preach there arrived more often at his Vermont home. In the midst of a busy schedule of writing, speaking, and keeping up with a bustling family, the *Bebb* stories emerge.

The germ came during a visit to a barbershop where Buechner came across a *Life* magazine exposé of the Reverend Doctor Herman Keck Jr. of Calvary Grace Christian Church in Fort Lauderdale, Florida. Famous for his advertisement, "Answer God's call—start preaching today," and for the mail-order theology degrees he dispensed to all who could pay the fees, Keck was lampooned in a lengthy feature by Bill Bruns.[2] Buechner was fascinated, and *Bebb* was born. The character inspired by the magazine article quickly took on "a life of his own" in Buechner's imagination, as Buechner puts it in an interview with Em Griffin.[3] What was so fetching about the con man? Buechner hints that perhaps the contrast between himself and Bebb formed the core of his attraction to Bebb's tale: "Bebb was strong in most places where I was weak, and mad as a hatter in most places where I was all too sane. Bebb took terrible risks with his life where I hung back with mine and hoped no one would notice" (Griffin 4). More than ever before, Buechner's writing process will be, as George Garrett summarized, "less of invention than of discovery" (Garrett 295). And the unfolding story of Leo Bebb is a query into saintliness and villainy in an inseparable jumble. James Buie noted that "Buechner has never been able to create a completely evil character."[4] His villains heretofore—Motley, Lundrigan, Farwell, Poteat, and their ilk—generally get out of their scrapes with at least a slight shift toward the light. Maybe this time Buechner has found a bona fide villain in the nasty piece of work, Herman Keck, the inspiration for Leo Bebb.

A finalist for the 1971 National Book Award, *Lion Country* was finished within three months of that haircut. The writing came more easily, more pleasurably, than with any previous book, an amazing contrast to the struggle that attended *The Entrance to Porlock* (*NT* 97). In his introduction to the collected *Bebb* novels, Buechner remembers them as "the great romance of my life." He views the story as "a kind of love letter" (*Bebb* viii) and dedicates the books to family and friends—the third to his mother— as if to underscore his fondness for the novels. In a letter at the time of the paperback edition of the collection, he concludes, "if Leo was to disappear from print, I was afraid that I myself would no longer cast a shadow or find anybody much looking back at me from the bathroom mirror."[5] He summarizes his feelings about the books in the words of a hymn: "Apart from who the characters are and the places they go and the things they do, there is the sense of what the old hymn quaveringly addresses as 'O love that will not let me go,' the sense of an ultimate depth to things that is not finally indifferent to whether people sink or swim but endlessly if always hiddenly refuses to abandon them" (*Bebb* ix). Buechner views his entanglement in the life of Leo Bebb as a kind of blessing, an education that holds him for most of a decade.

Lion Country

Antonio Parr, the Nick Carraway–like narrator of *Lion Country*, is a sometime teacher of English, a dabbler in sculpture, and a would-be writer. Having moved from his "teaching period" to his "scrap-iron period" and anticipating his "writing period" (*Bebb* 5), Tono responds to an advertisement, "Put yourself on God's payroll—go to work for Jesus now" (*Bebb* 4). (Buechner is obviously a better adman than Reverend Keck.) When he receives his diploma and ordination papers from the Church of Holy Love, Inc., Tono arranges an interview with the Reverend Leo Bebb, the mastermind behind the mail-order business. Having learned that Bebb has been arrested at least once, Tono targets Bebb's nefarious dealings for a "journalistic exposé" (*Bebb* 35). Looking back, he describes his intentions:

Put yourself on God's payroll: this burning bush tucked in among the hemorrhoid cures and dashboard Virgins and neckties that glowed in the dark. At every level I could have been held accountable on, it struck me as inspired rascality ripe for my exposing—except that I can believe now that in some subterranean way I may have been interested not only in exposing it but also perhaps in, shall we say, sampling it. (*Bebb* 5)

Like Nick Carraway, who has his thirtieth birthday during the course of Fitzgerald's *The Great Gatsby*, Antonio Parr, at thirty-four and unattached, is "hungry for fortissimo" (*Bebb* 6). He is an around-par sort of fellow—trapped in the ordinary, beset by averageness, nearly destroyed by the run of the mill. Meeting Bebb in New York City, Antonio is confirmed in his commitment to the exposé, even as he is vaguely impressed by the verve, the zip, of the bustling Bebb. Yet Tono is no forceful, heroic righter of wrongs. Good at spotting foulness, Tono is really not so good at setting anything right. Truth be told, no Buechner character to this point has been more full of longing, more incomplete, than Tono, though he is certainly brother to Tip Ringkoping, Theodore Nicolet, and Peter Cowley.

The usually subtle Fitzgeraldian influence is more pronounced this time as Buechner tries his hand at first-person narration. Writing in *The Atlantic* in 1979, Benjamin DeMott offered one of the few substantial looks at the tetralogy, which he compared to *The Great Gatsby*, in that *Bebb* has "two centers—not merely the major Bebb but the minor Antonio."[6] Despite certain moral reservations about Gatsby's character, Fitzgerald's Nick tells the story of the larger-than-life Jay Gatsby; Nick becomes the keeper of secrets for Gatsby and others in the famous book. Tono too, alternately attracted to and disgusted by Leo Bebb, surprisingly becomes one of those in whom people invest their secrets, one who tells other's stories, one in search of a hero (*Bebb* 88). At the beginning of *Lion Country*, Tono suffers from a deep malaise; his twin sister, Miriam, is dying, and his one relationship, a sober friendship with the stolid Ellie, is passionless. He almost envies his sister who is about to escape life, and he has dreams of "unutterable sadness" (*Bebb* 26). Spiritually exhausted, he comes to Bebb, the "charlatan priest," another version of Greene's whiskey priest (*Bebb* 15). Through the lens of his own persistent longing and intractable cynicism, Tono observes Bebb's apparent phoniness. He begins to visualize Bebb as a symbol of "the bankruptcy of God" (*Bebb* 18), a target on which Tono can vent his anger and despair. So the lapsed Catholic, Tono, travels to

Armadillo, Florida, to gather background for his exposé. There he meets Laverne Brown, Bebb's sexless assistant; Sharon, Bebb's voluptuous, adopted daughter; and Lucille, Bebb's wife, a wobbly alcoholic grieving over some not-yet-told past. As he becomes increasingly entangled in these lives, like none he's ever known, Tono gradually forgets about the sensational article he had planned to write.

Other characters introduced in *Lion Country* and more or less involved throughout the tetralogy are Charlie Blaine, his sister Miriam's hypochondriac ex-husband; Chris and Tony, Miriam's sons; and Herman Redpath, the eccentric Indian who may turn out to be Bebb's golden angel, his financial sugar daddy, in the mail-order divinity school diploma business. The plot is more straightforward than in any previous Buechner effort, and the book somehow more transparent. Some of the change may actually be registered in Buechner's move from the working title, *The Harrowing*—a serious if not daunting appellation—to the more accessible *Lion Country*. In notes written almost exactly one year after Buechner came across the Keck article and included in the Wheaton archives, Buechner acknowledges that *Lion Country* "is different from any other novel I've written" (Archive, IV A 5). He speaks about the pace of the writing and the joyousness of the labor, as well as suggesting a difference in the way his own life comes into the narrative. The characters, he says, "are not people I've known in my life except for a minor detail here and there but people from some deep and hitherto hidden part of whoever I am" (Archive, IV A 5). *Lion Country*, he concludes, was "on the house," a book he thinks of as the one he just had in him (Archive, IV A 5).

The novel that Buechner calls a love letter begins with Leo Bebb quoting Scripture while his fluttering eyelid gives him away. He seems almost to be winking. Primed for the betrayer role, Antonio Parr recognizes a con man when he sees one. Setting aside his novel writing period, the restless Antonio sets out to spill the beans, tell the truth, about the raincoat-clad suspicious character that is Bebb. "Welded to nothing," Tono has only Tom, his imperturbable pet cat; Ellie, the spinsterish girlfriend; and Miriam, his dying twin (*Bebb* 6). His dark view of life evinces itself in his exchanges with Miriam, who thinks of her death as, perhaps, "doors opening," a phrase that echoes back to *The Entrance to Porlock* (*Bebb* 8). She can't get over the idea that she may be "*going* someplace," she confesses (*Bebb* 8). The Antonio of the opening pages sees life through his sister's pain, fears that she is being delivered into nothing, and sees his own days as vacancy. So why not allow Bebb to ordain him? Symbolic of the great fraud that is life, Bebb is a perfect target for the cynical Mr. Parr, or is he now the Reverend Parr?

Learning that Bebb has a criminal record only fuels the fire for Antonio's mission to Florida. Leaving the sterility of his life with Ellie and Tom in chilly New York City, he takes the train to Armadillo, Florida—southern voices, oranges, sun, and the "charlatan priest," Leo Bebb (*Bebb* 15). Surprisingly, however, the betrayer, Tono, feels oddly betrayed to learn that Leo Bebb indeed is not what he pretends to be. Armadillo is more shabby than Tono could have imagined, the perfect setting for a slimy operation like Bebb's. But how to explain Antonio's disappointment? If Bebb were a real priest, maybe an explanation would be forthcoming for the deaths of Antonio's parents when he was only twelve, maybe Miriam would recover from the cancer devastating her body, maybe Tono would have something to believe: "He *should* have been able to help. He should have been *real*. And if he had been real—the more I think about it, the more I believe this may have been the real nub of it—then I would also have been real" (*Bebb* 19). A lapsed Catholic, Tono has learned to hold eternal questions at bay, but Miriam's slow diminishment toward death has him rattled. Watching her decline is like revisiting *Romeo and Juliet* and "allowing yourself for a moment to hope that somehow this time Juliet will wake up from Friar Lawrence's potion before Romeo swallows his death" (*Bebb* 21). Thus the cynical Antonio dreams of miracles as he bids goodbye to his sister. They talk of her ex-husband, Charlie Blaine, bland Charlie, of whom Miriam comments, "Someday they'll have to come wake him up to tell him he's dead" (*Bebb* 22). Such is the death-in-life hollowness that Antonio is fleeing as he boards the southbound train, which provides a between-worlds transition to the unsafe, unpredictable, slapstick world of Armadillo. Carrying his "unutterable sadness" (*Bebb* 26), an ungodly weight, Tono arrives in Florida to glorious warmth and a "sense of promise" (*Bebb* 28). Maybe it is just the sweet southern sounds, maybe it is that this Judas has an uncommon capacity for hope, but Tono finds himself feeling like a "child getting out of his last class on the last day of school" (*Bebb* 28). Almost immediately, Tono's plans for exploding Bebb's sordid kingdom begin to waver. Maybe Bebb has reasons for his nefariousness—a childhood of poverty and deprivation? Besides, what's the big deal about selling diplomas anyway? Tono is almost able to admit to himself that the real reason he's journeyed to Bebb's world is the "hoping against all reason" that Bebb may be able to "cast a holy spell" on Tono's weary existence (*Bebb* 29).

Armadillo turns out to be an unlikely town for a prophet—like Nazareth in that respect. In the muddle of the begrimed junkyard of a place, Tono finds his way to Bebb's church, "the Mother church" as Bebb calls it, between a souvenir shop and a barbershop, an eyesore featuring a life-sized cross made of frosted glass and lit from the inside (*Bebb* 31). In the neon glow, passersby can read "HOLY" on the vertical piece and "LOVE" on the horizontal piece. The words share the O with a heart shape preceding LOVE to balance it all out. Tono believes the whole thing is "not unlike the trademark stamped on Bayer aspirin tablets" (*Bebb* 31). Inside the forty-folding-chair storefront sort of affair that passes for Bebb's church, Tono notices a rug of the kind usually associated with tourist fare—Elvis and sunsets. But this rug features a picture of Christ himself, looking "a little like Charlton Heston" and staring off toward a hot-air register (*Bebb* 32). Who knows why Christ averts his eyes? Maybe he is simply embarrassed by the spectacle of Holy Love.

This is Buechner's first real chance to satirize Bebb's version of religion—the sentimental, superstitious, downright tacky variety of the Christian faith visible up and down America's highways and cable television channels. Somewhere in his spotty past, Bebb was even a Bible salesman, a specter that conjures up a Flannery O'Connor story or a televangelist pulpit-pounder. Bebb's sort of tawdry preachers are easy marks. Oddly enough, however, Buechner's camera goes to Tono, the agnostic, who suddenly finds himself wanting to pray, wondering if Miriam's approaching death, maybe death itself, is "just a complicated misunderstanding" (*Bebb* 33). Here too Tono reflects on the possible meaning of his journey to Armadillo, dimly considering the prospect that this wild flight to Florida might be a real journey to somewhere, somewhere important.

On this point, Benjamin DeMott made another contribution to opening up *The Book of Bebb*:

> In the age of H. L. Mencken and Sinclair Lewis, the approved line of approach to lives like Bebb's was satiric. (Meet shoddy, small-time Leo, cynical exploiter of innocence and gullibility, representative citizen of the Boobocracy. Meet him and scorn him.) But nowadays, obviously other options are open. *The Book of Bebb* acknowledges the sordidness and meanness of scale of episodes in the life story it recounts. But its tone is closer to panegyric than to satire, and its narrator presents the evangelist ex-con not as a maniac but as manna. (DeMott 89)

The question keeps bobbing back to the surface for Buechner. Is it possible that the unlikeliest of vessels, the obvious shyster, that round ball of contradictions and failings, could function as an instrument of grace? Marie-Helene Davies tried to locate Leo Bebb in a theological frame:

Buechner adheres to the Calvinist belief that God is totally other than man; in his eyes man is sinful and no man can escape from his compulsion to do evil, except by the grace of God. Ministers, being human, are only poor forked animals, or dirty windows to be bleached by the light of God's sun. But since they are committed Christian witnesses, they point to a reality that lies beyond them, by which others may gain *Sehnsucht*, or longing for God.[7]

Davies's metaphors mixed, but the point is that Bebb-types give evidence of spiritual possibilities, not, as Davies had it, because they are "committed," but in spite of themselves, whatever they are. If there's a chance that Leo Bebb turns out to be more than he knew, maybe there's hope for Tono, and Buechner, and us.

Lion Country takes a surprising twist when Tono's mission turns from unmasking Bebb to breaking through to God. His fruitless prayers interrupted, the only response a rumble from the air duct, Tono looks up into the glittering false teeth smile of the assistant pastor, Laverne Brown. Bebb's right-hand man, or more accurately his lackey, Brownie manages to win Tono to "Bebb's sordid little team" (*Bebb* 38), even if Tono only figures it out later. Brownie calls him "dear" and refers to Jesus as "G. Zuss" (*Bebb* 36). The reader keeps thinking that Tono will explode in laughter and the whole charade will collapse. But no. Brownie teaches exegesis and New Testament background at Bebb's Gospel Faith College, so we get to hear several of his rollicking sermons. As Buechner was thinking his way toward biblical retellings at the time, Brownie's sermons could almost be outtakes from such 1970s books as *Wishful Thinking* and *Peculiar Treasures*. Brownie claims that Christ's rejection of the Syrophoenician woman in the seventh chapter of Mark, for example, has been popularly misinterpreted because of a translation problem. That line about casting bread to the dogs, Brownie concludes, is more accurately understood if we substitute "Poochie" for "dog." "It was just his little joke—using a pet name like that," Brownie argues and takes a good bit of the edge off a disquieting scripture (*Bebb* 36–37).

Brownie has a way around a whole pile of troubling scriptures, but when Tono confronts him with "*Eli, Eli, lama sabachthani*" [My God, my God, why have you forsaken me?], which Tono interprets as "calling God a sonofabitch for running out on him," Brownie looks "old and confused" and admits, "No dear, those terrible words mean just what they say" (*Bebb* 37). Still wondering about the "truer reason" for his journey to Armadillo, Tono identifies with the sense of abandonment in Christ's desperate words and warms to at least the one truth that Brownie has told him (*Bebb* 38). Brownie is one of the characters here who seems so outrageously drawn as to be ludicrous. He must have been on the minds of those critics who talk about *Lion Country* as beyond the realms of realism. But one need only visit up and down the radio dial in many parts of this country to see how Buechner is on to something with Brownie—a cartoonish figure, no doubt, but one that gets close to the truth, as cartoons often do.

At the manse Tono meets the blurry Lucille, sloshed on Tropicanas, her alcoholic brew of choice, and bearing the brunt of living with Bebb, the clergyman who "runs into outer-space people all over the place" (*Bebb* 42) and may be, according to his wife, "from outer space himself" (*Bebb* 43). Here Buechner sharpens *Lion Country* into a detective story—Tono's investigation into Bebb's soiled past, the mystery of Sharon, who seems out of focus in this strange picture, the enigmatic loyalty of Brownie, the obvious despair of Lucille. Tono wakes the next morning to Bebb himself standing at the foot of the Magic Fingers bed in the sleazy Salamander Motel. Bebb has let himself in for fear that Tono "might be dead" (*Bebb* 56), and of course this is just what Tono has been fearing for himself. Is it too much to say that some sort of rebirth occurs in this unlikeliest of places? Bebb seems to read Antonio's mind as he brings up the troubling question of motive. "Why did you want to be ordained?" he asks Tono, and it is clear now that the exposé is no longer the first thing on Tono's mind (*Bebb* 59). Roger Dionne's review of the tetralogy for the *Los Angeles Times* dubbed Buechner as "one of the most underrated novelists writing today" and suggested that the power of the tetralogy revolved on Tono's gradual realization that "Bebb is far better and more real than he himself is."[8] Still waffling on his opinion of Bebb at this point in the narrative, Tono is escorted back to the manse in Leo's large-finned convertible replete with "a plastic Jesus on the dashboard" (*Bebb* 59).

If the journalistic plot hasn't already backfired, it will now; Tono is about to meet Sharon. Their meeting is not unlike that one in Buechner's short story "The Tiger," where the narrator spies the goddess. To the backdrop of the Big Bopper tune "Chantilly Lace" and the not-so-subtle line, "Oh, Baby, you know what I like," Sharon climbs into the convertible beside the stunned Tono (*Bebb* 62). Buechner's touch here is masterful as he forces readers to fill in the omitted lyrics, a risk that would have worked well, at least, for readers coming to the novel in the 1970s. Radio blaring, Sharon, Tono, and Leo are off to Lion Country, a tourist trap where captive lions roam over palm-treed acres surrounded by a fence. Visitors drive through to spy on the lions from the safety of cars provided by the management, and Leo finds it the perfect place for unwinding. Something is already working loose ("like a long-neck goose") in Tono, who has spent most of his life, as Bebb intuits, "tied up in knots" (*Bebb* 63). Amid allusions to Christians among lions and Tono's sudden insight that he is in a cage *with* the lions and, for most of his life, in a cage *like* the lions, Leo Bebb climbs out of the safety of the car to snap a picture of a lion for the struck-dumb Tono. The message is plain: take a chance, "go on outside where the sunshine is" (*Bebb* 66). The significance is not lost on Tono, and something is starting to brew between Bebb's daughter and the muckraker. Tono's enthrallment with this Daniel of a Bebb now has entirely new dimensions. And how much of this is orchestrated by Leo Bebb? How much is orchestrated by God? Or is there orchestration at all?

But one thing does lead to another—that much we can say—and Tono will wonder about the possible pattern behind it all. Sharon winds up in the Magic Fingers bed, a scene that must certainly have turned the heads of those who had Buechner lined up for the Christian bookstore market. In the intimacy of the Salamander and Tono's unmade bed, we learn more: Brownie may or may not drink after-shave; Bebb has been in jail for exposing himself to children, but he may have been framed; Lucille and Bebb had a child long ago who may have been killed by Lucille; and Tono has placed his life in the hands of Bebb's beautiful daughter. Tono can only quote John Donne—"O my America! My new-found land"—to try to explain the inexplicable joy of his union with Sharon (*Bebb* 76). (Buechner will resort to the same source for language about his own love in *Now and Then*, a memoir dedicated to his wife, Judith.) Changed by lions—the wild ones and Leo, the wildest one of all—caught up in the lives of the evangelist and his motley crew, Tono has forgotten about New York City, his girlfriend, his sister, his cat. But the sexual repast with Sharon is far from casual, even if this is 1970.

Tono is connected and beginning to see that, though he came on the scene to expose Bebb, it is Antonio Parr who is increasingly being exposed. Who knows what might have happened next? But Tono is called away; Miriam needs him to help arrange a last visit with her children, and Tono has to scurry back to the city and the dying he's pushed to the back burner. He remembers to take a coat, as it is November back there in the city and still November in his soul too, we suspect. But a certain transformation registers as Tono finds himself in a pastoral role with his sister, counseling her in a way that surprises even him. Back in that Nick Carraway position, he listens to Miriam's confession that she's lied to her own children, tried to protect them from the horrors of her plunge toward death, to spare them the ugly truth of her brittle bones. Tono offers what can only be called a religious consolation, a dream about Christ in "a blaze of light," a vision of the possibility that Miriam is headed off on her best journey yet (*Bebb* 88). Surprised at the power of his own sermon, Tono must be wondering if Bebb's signed diploma has had some salutary effect already. Tono also has his own confessions to make, this time to Charlie Blaine: "Everybody's scared to death of something, and you just happened to be scared to death of death," he tells Charlie. Then he adds, "For me it's life" (*Bebb* 84–85). And Miriam's last words to her son, Tony, Antonio's name-sake, reinforces that other Buechner preoccupation, paying attention. "Now you stay awake, Tony," she tells him. "You just keep your eyes open and stay awake" (*Bebb* 89).

Homesick for Armadillo, of all places, Tono hurries back to Sharon and finds the whole place in a dither over the arrival of Herman Redpath, the potential donor, the source of enough oil money to prop up Bebb's cottage industry for years to come. Bebb spills a good many beans in this section of the narrative, and Buechner crowds in details that will be useful for the three books to follow. Leo Bebb takes his place alongside that Elmer Gantryish crowd of American literature's preachers. He is "chief among sinners," he claims, quoting Paul (*Bebb* 92). He admits a fondness for the big car, the luxury that Herman Redpath's bundle might provide. But he also speaks of exposing his deepest self to God's love, a perilous and powerful possibility. Like Greene's whiskey priest, Leo Bebb wants to open himself completely before God. He wants to lay bare his sin and guilt, and Antonio is caught up in the drama.

We also learn that Brownie's loyalty derives from his belief that Bebb has raised him from the dead some years before in Knoxville, Tennessee. And Buechner is not speaking metaphorically this time. From Bebb's point of view, however, the resurrection isn't all the way accomplished. Brownie is one of those people who, as Bebb puts it, "hold their own past against themselves till it gets where they can't break loose out of it any more" (*Bebb* 94). You can guess whom Tono thinks about when Bebb utters that. Surely resurrection is in Tono's mind—resurrection for Miriam, yes, and for himself too. As with almost everything in Bebb's astonishing biography, readers are left to decide for themselves, sharing Tono's bewilderment as the stories pile up—aliens and miracles, Brownie as Lazarus and Bebb as the strangest G. Zuss ever to come down the pike. Maybe Brownie was just knocked into a coma by that electrical current in Tennessee. Maybe he was dead, indeed.

Buechner pulls the book together quickly from here. Herman Redpath is flying in to be ordained, a process he sees as a way to reinvigorate his sexual potency now that he has passed eighty. Of course, Herman is drawn to Tono, but Tono nearly runs out of words to describe the wizened Indian and the menagerie he flies in for the ordination ceremony. As to what happens at the service, who can really say? Sharon and Tono miss it entirely, otherwise involved in Sharon's bedroom at the manse. According to some witnesses, when Bebb lifts his hands for the final blessing, his white robe opens in a most conspicuous and unfortunate place and "the rabbit pulled white and squirming out of the magician's darkness" emerges to bring the ceremony to a chaotic end (*Bebb* 112). Leo Bebb's own words, however, may explain something of the events that bring down the curtain: "Time comes a man wants to be known for what he is, the bad with the good of him, the weakness with the strength. He wants to lay the whole shebang out in the light of day where the sun can get at it and folks can see all the shameful, hurtful parts of him same as the other parts that's decent and straight" (*Bebb* 113). In the novel to follow, *Open Heart*, this desire to be known will persist as something Buechner conjures with, but for now Holy Love Church is a goner. Bebb takes refuge from a possible legal prosecution by heading off to Herman Redpath's ranch in Houston. Herman thinks the laying on of hands may have worked; the rest doesn't matter to him. Tono's vacation in Bebb's crazy world is cut short again by the news that Miriam is dying. Our last glimpse of Bebb, before he hotfoots it to Texas, comes in the flickering light of the neon sign at Holy Love. He has lost "some of the bounce," Tono notices, but we suspect he still has some oomph left as we hear him sing "Rock of Ages" in his "1930s radio voice" (*Bebb* 114). "Nothing in my hand I bring," he sings, and the joke is not entirely lost.

The minister hired for Miriam's funeral service chooses Psalm 51 for a text: "Make me to hear joy and gladness that the bones which thou hast broken may rejoice" (*Bebb* 217). Tono first thinks about how inappropriate the words are as he has watched as Miriam's bones have indeed broken during the progress of her disease. The idea that God was breaking those bones is, well, just too much for Tono. Rethinking his reaction, Tono ponders the end of the sentence, concluding, "if the last word was really going to be one of rejoicing, I could forgive him almost anything" (*Bebb* 118). The "him" is God, of course, and the peace that Tono makes here, although partial and tentative, is something like spiritual peace nonetheless. Saying farewell to Miriam and Tom takes only another few

days, and Tono is off to Houston at Bebb's invitation, and "on such slen-
der threads hang the destinies of men and nations" (*Bebb* 122).

Although most readers probably anticipate something of a happy ending
here, Buechner makes room for a certain doubleness in the final paragraphs:

> For me, *Lion Country* was a good dream, and I've never enjoyed
> myself more than during the time I was dreaming it. Sad things hap-
> pen in it, to be sure. A young woman dies a hard death. A baby is mur-
> dered. The boy gets the girl in the end, but he loses something too.
> And although Bebb stays out of jail for the time being, he still doesn't
> by a long shot make it to Lion Country. But it was a good dream for
> me anyway because I loved the people who wandered through it, and
> because there were happy things and funny things that happened to
> them along with the sad things, and when I woke up, I was glad I'd
> dreamed it and rather sorry to be awake again. (Archive, IV A 5)

Tono and Sharon are married by an Episcopal priest on the Redpath
ranch. Tono gets some release from the loss of his twin when, in a dream,
Miriam tells him how good it feels to have shed the white cast that had
held her together in her last months (*Bebb* 123). Sharon calls him "Bopper" now and sometimes "Bop." "Bip" is her nickname for Bebb, so maybe
Antonio has a new twin. Bip and Bop.

Tono has learned that "a distaste for dying is twin to a taste for living,"
and when Miriam's boys move in to stretch out his family, Tono seems destined to something like maturity—maybe even wisdom (*Bebb* 128).
Although he claims to still be "a fool and a coward," another of the many
"lost persons," the reader knows that the Antonio of the last page is a
much different man from the one who boarded that train at Penn Station
a few months before (*Bebb* 128). Writing in *America* just after the sequel
to *Lion Country* had appeared, Margaret Wimsatt argued that Tono had
become "wiser and kinder" as a result of his encounter with Bebb (Wimsatt 262). Like Lear, who, according to one of Tono's students, undergoes
a transformation toward kindness, Antonio learns to look at the world
with, if not new, at least changing eyes (*Bebb* 177). Although there's less
drift in him now, we sense that Bebb isn't finished with him yet, any more
than he's finished with Buechner.

Among the many achievements of what turns out to be only the first of
four forays into Bebb's world, the real tour de force of *Lion Country* is in
the narrative voice. Buechner's experiment with the first-person narrator
is remarkably successful. William Pritchard follows DeMott in under-

scoring the Nick Carraway connection. Pritchard said "there are worse voices to give in to" and labels the novel a "powerful and beautiful creation."[9] The trick is the same one Mark Twain uses in *The Adventures of Huckleberry Finn*—the narrator knows less than the reader. Just as certain jokes and insights pass through the youthful narrator of Twain's masterpiece, so Buechner winks and nods to the reader, often over Tono's head or behind his back. Readers suspect that Tono is being converted to Bebb's energy if not his theology, for example, long before Tono figures it out—if he *ever* figures it out. Most of the reviewers caught the freshening breeze that accompanied Buechner's stylistic changes. Wimsatt noticed that "cheerfulness and comedy have broken in" (Wimsatt 262), but she also saw that, despite the signal new directions, Buechner's books still comprised "a consistent opus," adding that "the change of pace does not reflect a change of theme" (Wimsatt 262).

Several of the critics guessed at the Greene connections and thus felt the tug of the theological undertow. Woelfel suggested that, in spite of everything, Bebb is a channel of grace "to fill up empty lives" (Woelfel 287). Rosemary Deen contended that Buechner was here refusing "to make religious truth remote."[10] Wimsatt called Bebb an "unlikely saint" (Wimsatt 261). Guy Davenport's take in the *New York Times Book Review* invoked the word "parable"[11] but only after letting it be known that Buechner was a Presbyterian minister. (Davenport had already begun banging that drum five years before.) John Skow underscored the unrealism of *Lion Country* in his *Time* review. He liked the book but noted that "disbelief is not suspended."[12] Some critics are nasty: Kurt Hoeksema labeled the entire *Bebb* collection as "portraying confusion,"[13] *Choice* called it "sentimental,"[14] and David Littlejohn in *Saturday Review* went for the jugular with a reference to "the author's tiresomely clever voice."[15] The general drift, however, was extremely positive. P. A. Doyle even tagged *Lion Country* as "O'Connor-like,"[16] and Deen concluded that Buechner had come up with a "masterful creation of the improbable genuineness of a latter-day apostle, a tarnished Daniel among the Babylonian lions" (Deen 388).

The critics coming along with the benefit of years of commentary on the tetralogy also wanted to claim much for the *Bebb* books. Marie-Helene Davies argued that in them Buechner "regained the courage to be himself as both Christian and artist" (Davies 64). I'm not convinced he'd ever lost his courage. As we have seen, *The Final Beast* carves out the territory of faith and fiction in dramatic ways. Victoria Allen saw the two main characters of the tetralogy as "dual sides of Buechner, the intuitive writer, who in creating them is living out unconscious parts of himself. Parr and Bebb represent the psychological and spiritual struggles going on inside their author. Because Buechner is the skeptic and the true believer, he is able to laugh and cry with both" (Allen 79). Maybe. But this would be to ignore Bebb's doubts and Tono's persistent believing in spite of himself. McCoy emphasized how Bebb got hold of Buechner, and she resorted to words like "saltier," "funnier," and "easier" to describe what happens in *Lion Country* and in the revisitations to follow (McCoy 96). McCoy said that *Bebb* launched Buechner into his "most creative period" (McCoy 68).

I'd say that he's been pretty creative before 1970, but he does himself underscore something special about these novels. In the memoirs, *Bebb* gets particular attention:

> For the first time I felt free to be funny in ways that I hadn't felt comfortable being in print before, to let some of my saltier-tongued characters use language that before had struck me as less than seemly in a serious work of fiction, to wander off into quirkish reminiscences and observations that weren't always directly related to my central purpose. There was all of that to help make my writer's task an excitement and a delight instead of a burden to labor under. . . . But there was also something more than just that, and what it was, supremely and without any question, was Bebb himself. When I reached the final page of *Lion Country*, I tried my hand at a few other things, but it wasn't long before I started a second novel about him called *Open Heart*, and then *Love Feast*, and then *Treasure Hunt*, none of them ever quite the joy-rides that *Lion Country* had been but all of them written because I couldn't help myself, because I missed Bebb too much to let him go, or because—whatever it may mean to say so—Bebb would not let me go. (*NT* 98–99)

Among the meanings of Buechner's love affair with these novels may be that he had reached that stage in his career where his writerly gifts have marvelously joined with a crystalline articulation of his underlying propositions. *The Book of Bebb* avoids excessive artfulness and autobiography in dramatic ways, given Buechner's previous record, and Buechner acknowledges the stylistic venture into first person, that "Antonio Parr as a narrator was a little bit like Nick Carraway as a narrator. Both are detached and yet involved, and both have elegiac tones to their voices" (Brown 46). To be fair, Buechner also insists on the Greene influence, this time emphasizing style—"a dying fall—sentences almost end that way with three nouns at the end . . . sort of bump, bump, bump" (Myers 147). But the brew is really still thick with the familiar set of Buechner questions.

As the *Bebb* stories burst forth in the years after *Lion Country*, Buechner continues to heft the themes that will carry him to the masterpiece to come at the beginning of the next decade. The lostness and longing established in the Antonio Parr character, a constant in Buechner's fiction, will persist in the books to follow. There's also the failed priest line that runs and runs through the work, that notion Buechner so admires in Greene, the idea that God may use figures as ludicrous as the whiskey priest, Antonio Parr, Leo Bebb, and more. Theological questions perk on: What is the nature of sin, repentance, and forgiveness? Is religious faith possible in a world of craziness and bewilderment? Is God at work somewhere inside the obstacles with which most of us struggle? This last question, of course, more or less encapsulates the rest. Does human experience embody some observable pattern that would assure us of the presence of a God who is out and about to bless? Even in the bawdy romp that is *Bebb*, the big question endures. Leo and Tono and the assembled cast of misfits will continue to kick this can around for hundreds of pages, and the most we can say is that it is one thing to believe in a plot, a pattern, and quite another to be able to say what that plot, that pattern, is. Buechner's art hinges on the gap between belief and sight.

Open Heart

The sequel to *Lion Country* jumps right in on the religious questions, opening with Bebb's words shouted over a corpse: "Get up, Herman Redpath," and we pause at the outset to see if this is a replay of Brownie's rumored resurrection in Knoxville (*Bebb* 131). Perhaps we will get to see the miracle this time, we will know for sure. But, no, Bebb seems to be speaking metaphorically, urging Herman on his way into a new life, and we are off on another romp with Bebb, who *believes* Herman is going somewhere; and with Tono, who *hopes* Herman is going somewhere. *Open Heart* begins with death and no resurrection, and Tono has surely carried something of both to the circus of a funeral in Houston. Things aren't going well with Sharon. Tono needs to talk with Bebb.

Although Buechner returns to the story within a year of *Lion Country*, five years have passed in the narrative of Tono's life. Sharon and Tono now have a child, Bill, and strains have begun to develop. Tono comes to Houston "homesick for life" (*Bebb* 136); he is in most ways the same character we knew before, even though he has settled into a teaching job in Connecticut and taken on the guardianship of Miriam's boys—Tony and Chris. He still tries to assemble his sculpture in a shed off the garage, but "the Thing," as he calls it, won't quite mesh (*Bebb* 141). It is like his life—holding together but lacking coherence. He also continues to be alternately fascinated by and repulsed with Bebb, and when Bebb tells Tono that Herman Redpath is being born again in death, Tono offers a cryptic remark suggesting just how remarkable Bebb's belief is. "Listen," Bebb responds, "That's not even half of what I believe." Tono asks, "What else do you believe?" and Bebb's answer—"I believe everything"—strikes Tono with its "classic grandeur," its "sheer magnitude." After a silence, Tono offers, "You make it sound almost easy," to which Leo responds, "It's hard as hell" (*Bebb* 143). Bebb's faith proclamation and the subsequent admission of the difficulty implicit in maintaining such faith establish the essential contrast between Bebb and Tono. Furthermore, belief and doubt set up as the fundamental thematic tension driving the *Bebb* novels. Buechner is finding his métier.

Whatever was happy about the ending of *Lion Country* has become considerably muted in the interval. Sharon is a woman of the 1970s—yoga, speed-reading, guitar lessons. Tony is "a raging jock," Chris is "bookish as distinct from bright," and Tono is teaching "sixteen year olds *Cry the Beloved Country* and how to identify iambic pentameter and what was wrong with 'like a cigarette should'" (*Bebb* 144). If Bebb is right and "sin is life wasted," then there's a good bit of waste in Tono's world and a good bit of rescue in order (*Bebb* 147). The plot of *Open Heart* stirs most dramatically at the outset when Herman Redpath's $100,000 bequest to Leo Bebb makes it possible for the Bebbs to relocate to Connecticut where, having turned Holy Love Church over to Brownie, Leo can concentrate on founding a new church. Open Heart Church features a reprise of the Holy Love sign, this time with OPEN on the crosspiece beside a heart shape, then HEART on the vertical piece, sharing the E to make a cross. The gaudy neon cross this time bedecks a barn on Bebb's rented property near Tono and Sharon, outside Sutton, Connecticut. Maybe he goes north, as he allows, because that's where the money and the power reside—and "the great whore" (*Bebb* 154) too, even though Leo is southern through and through, right down to his pronouncing "amen with a long a" (*Bebb* 203). Maybe the move is just another desperate reach for "a clean slate"—"starting out fresh with nothing except Jesus" (*Bebb* 164). Maybe Bip just knows that he's needed in Connecticut. Tono awaits Bebb's arrival in a house where something has gone wrong, though he only feels the absence, knows there's bad news in the offing. Tono's world is full of dark silences, sudden outbursts, and bewildering broodings. Brimful of plans and projects, Leo Bebb sweeps in, a W. C. Fields presence. Things promise to percolate now.

Open Heart gives Lucille more time on stage than she had in *Lion Country*, at least for the time that there's anything of Lucille to be on stage. We hear a good bit more of her theories about Bebb as a space traveler, about the lost baby that she has indeed murdered in a drunken stupor, about her puzzling entanglement in the life of Bebb. Lucille even gets her own chapter, a wide-ranging collage of notes bequeathed to Tono, which he reads during the desperate search for Lucille, who inexplicably disappears right in the middle of one of Bebb's sermons at Open Heart. Tono makes his way through her tortuous ramble before they find what's left of Lucille, her body at the funeral parlor in Houston where she has fled to commit suicide to the sound of Brownie reading Scripture.

The notes reveal an obsession with Bebb's frequent recourse to a promise of something beyond this vale of tears and Lucille's struggle to believe that she can overcome her guilt. She reports that Bebb had been nicknamed "Blinky" as a child because of his uncontrollable eyelid. Bebb has assured her that "everybody has parts like that they don't have any control over" (*Bebb* 218). But she is less sanguine than Bebb about her sinfulness. To his claim, "we are all washed clean in the Blood of the Lamb," Lucille responds, "the only thing I've been washed in is the shit of the horse" (*Bebb* 219). Thus Buechner returns to the fecal imagery of *The Final Beast* to make a wrenching statement about Lucille's inability to go on. The Tropicanas won't drown it anymore. "She's got so she can't stand light any more," Bebb mourns, as he deploys the troops to look for her with her sunglasses, and we suspect it is more than daylight he's talking about. With Lucille's death, Bebb himself becomes almost human. Less sure of himself, almost morose in his lostness, the Leo Bebb of *Open Heart* is a much sadder version than heretofore, more than ever acquainted with the darkness. He will come to realize the heartbreaking truth that he is "not anybody's number one person anymore" (*Bebb* 270).

And the wretchedness is multiplied by other revelations. Lucille has marched out just as Bebb preaches about his homesickness for "someplace else far, far away" (*Bebb* 174). Lucille finds a way to settle her own homesickness. Tono is still trying to solve his desperate lostness when he learns that the elephant he's been tiptoeing around in his own house is Sharon's infidelity. She and Tony, her nephew, have begun an affair, as Tono will come to understand, because they long to give some shape to things where only chaos seems to rule (*Bebb* 262). Shaken, Antonio goes on teaching Shakespeare, helping with the search for Lucille and, later, with the distressing arrangements to be made, all the while knowing that literally everything hangs in the balance. The Shakespeare is *King Lear*, the play that Buechner revisits periodically in such books as *Telling the Truth* and *Speak What We Feel*. One particular class produces a memorable moment, unscripted and nearly inexpressible. Antonio ad-libs a question about Lear's prayer for the "poor naked wretches." At Antonio's question, "Who are these poor naked wretches," the classroom wag blurts, "We are" (*Bebb* 179). And nobody laughs.

Wretchedness holds this narrative together like glue. When Tony starts working his way toward unburdening himself, Antonio shudders; "although I still didn't know what he was leading up to, I already knew in some queer way that it was the saddest thing I'd ever heard," he laments (*Bebb* 184). The questions of *Open Heart* are about whether or not Bebb can swallow the death of Lucille: Will Tono's marriage founder on the rocks of betrayal? Does any of this mean anything in the larger scheme of things? Or is there any blueprint at all? Like Tono's unfinished sculpture, maybe life is a random mess of misconnection.

Tony and Sharon have become "lovers by accident rather than by design" (*Bebb* 185), and this novel is full of random tragedy and what-ifs. Open Heart Church struggles from day one, almost as if it has gone unblessed, unnoticed by the object of its worship. Lucille's grisly demise fits no pattern anyone can see, and even Bebb is unable to pull a rabbit out of this hat. Pointing toward her coffin, Bebb despairs, "All [that] is left of Lucille Yancey's that poor shell that used to hold a life in it. She's in that box if you want to know where she is. She's a empty box inside that box" (*Bebb* 238). Oddly trying to comfort Tony after the terrible truth about the affair spills out, Antonio tells him, "Things happen, that's all" (*Bebb* 186). The patternlessness leaves Tono spiritually winded: "I am thirty-nine years old and my wife has been screwed by my nephew and my hairline is receding and for the first time in my life I can believe that someday I'm going to get old and die" (*Bebb* 189).

We are a long way from the laughter of *Lion Country*. But *Open Heart* will ask what we are to do with emptiness and loss. Tono thinks he may have his own affair. He makes a trip to the city and manages a meeting with his former girlfriend, Ellie Pierce. But only failure emerges from his vision of opening his heart to Ellie: "Ellie never found out what was in my heart, and I never found out what was in hers" (*Bebb* 196). Then, while waiting for the train home, Tono runs into Laura Fleishman, one of his students and an occasional visitor to his dreams. Another maybe moment follows, an elaboration of two possibilities—one a visit to a hotel and the other an innocent cold drink in the station bar. Readers are left with both versions for a time but suspect, before we learn the truth, that it was the bar and not the bed, and another nonhappening turns out to be a happening. His mobile still unfinished, Tono juggles his anger and Bebb's tragedy and his desire to run from it all. But he stays. He stays for the funeral, where for a breathless moment we wonder if Bebb might raise Lucille from the dead. But God misses another chance. Lucille's suicide is different from Buechner's many takes on the subject in his more-than-twenty-year career up to this novel. Her last words, "Read me about Jesus, Brownie," jar against the image of her slit wrists and the blood pumping as she sways to her death in a rocking chair. And Buechner veers dramatically away. We flit back to Connecticut in something like emotional shock.

Connecticut offers little respite. Tono resorts to Matthew Arnold: "For here we are as on a darkling plain. Swept by confused alarms of struggle and flight" (*Bebb* 246); and Sharon complains of their house as the place where all the shipwrecks are washing up (*Bebb* 244). Tono impulsively responds to her question with his own: "Are we washed up too?" (*Bebb* 243). Like the man "who happens to scratch his ear at an auction," Tono knows that he is suddenly exposed, "could be taken for everything" (*Bebb* 245). Forgiveness and repentance circulate in a wordless way, and the marriage is patched and caulked, though the damage is still obvious to anyone who is really looking. Sharon concedes that they've "come one hell of a long way from the Salamander Motel," and the reader suspects that they have a ways to go yet (*Bebb* 245). But the forgiveness and renewal is real enough as Buechner seems to want to believe in the possibility that, even here, the news can sometimes be good news.

More craziness ensues. What was Bebb doing in the night when he shows up in Chris's room in nothing but a bathrobe? Was he really just laying his hands on Chris in prayer? And what of Clarence Golden, the character who flits at the edges of this narrative, shadowing the shadowy Bebb? Although we will learn that Fats Golden was Bebb's cellmate in those five years Bebb was locked up, the puzzle of why Golden is hanging around is variously explained. Maybe he is there to blackmail Bebb, expose the exposer. Or is he there as a disciple? Lucille has accounted him as one of Bebb's space visitors. Maybe he is an angel, she thinks. Tono is disappointed to learn the more prosaic truth that Golden is just one more troubled character in this cast of eccentrics. And then there's Gertrude Conover, the theosophist, another version of Agnes Sanford, who shows up in the last pages as Bebb's new love, though it is a love destined to be platonic. A vigorous seventy-five-year-old with blue hair and money, Gertrude hooks up with Tono, Sharon, and Leo on a trip to Europe that aims toward bringing peace to the nearly shattered bunch. Golden fills in a good many blanks, becomes another way that we learn the real story of Leo Bebb, "the whole bare-ass truth and nothing but the truth" (*Bebb* 254). Bebb begins to recover by thinking up a ministry aimed at "young folks" (*Bebb* 257), and readers can feel another novel looming, this one based in part on what Buechner must have been reading about in those early 1970s—a Jesus movement. "They're the hope of the world," Leo preaches, "and most of the time they don't even know their tail from first base" (*Bebb* 257). Bebb plans "to bring the gospel of Jesus straight to the Pepsi generation," so Buechner must this time have been thinking already about the more to come (*Bebb* 258). But first a journey to the old country that *may be* a beginning.

Tono never quite seems to figure out that Leo has orchestrated the trip, not just as a way to deal with his own grief over Lucille, but also as a chance for Sharon and Tono to right their listing ship. Abandoning the speed-reading and the swami, Anita Steen, who seems to have a prurient interest in her student, Sharon agrees to the vacation to be funded by Herman Redpath's dollars. Some of the secrets stay secret as Tono wonders what Sharon really knows "about herself, about me, about the whole comic strip of things that as far as I know may be running serially somewhere" (*Bebb* 260). One more time, Tono pauses over providence. Remembering a childhood game in which he and Miriam would exchange haphazard scrawls, daring each other to make a picture from the scribbles, Tono explains, "The trick was to make it look like *something*" (*Bebb* 260–61). That's the conundrum of Tono's life—how to turn the Thing into *something*, how to turn his life into *something*.

And the trip yields more grace than we could have guessed. Bebb is reinvigorated by Gertrude, who believes Bebb is the reincarnation of her ancient Egyptian lover, and the unlikely travelers do indeed arrive somewhere. Buechner almost enters the narrative through Tono's summarizing considerations of whether or not the events of his story have a shape. Tono notes that authors implicitly make the point "that for good or ill events have a shape" (*Bebb* 268), while his life has been more like episode following episode "without ever getting anyplace in particular" (*Bebb* 268). Then, in response to Tono's statement "You're a long way from home," Sharon returns, "You're my home," and I suspect that episode makes some sense in the design of things, at least as Antonio Parr sees it (*Bebb* 268). Gertrude Conover summarizes: "Everything's got to do with everything else. Everything fits in somewhere, and there's no power in heaven or earth that can upset the balance" (*Bebb* 273). Listening to the ceremony that will send Herman Redpath on his way in the early pages of the novel, Tono wonders if there is a pattern to it. Finally, he decides, "either there is no pattern at all or a pattern so vast and simple nobody can figure it out" (*Bebb* 134). Facing everything that's out of kilter in the world, Buechner, now halfway through the tetralogy, seems still to want to believe that Gertrude has it right, that the plot exists even if we cannot quite decipher it.

Here's a place where Buechner might have crossed over into Christian bookshop fare, but he pulls back into mystery. In *Whistling in the Dark*, Buechner talks about the problem of apologetics, the need to reduce issues of faith "to a defendable size." The problem, as Buechner sees it, "is that by and large logic and plausibility are not the heart of the matter" (*Whistling* 12). Despite his commitment to be true to the indecipherable, there's still enough laughter here to hear by. As Paul Theroux concluded in his *Book World* review, *Open Heart* stands as "comedy of the most serious sort."[17]

Much of *Open Heart* is a simple backdrop for Tono's musings about Bebb's beliefs and his own. Sure, there's the story line—what will happen in the lives of these people we've come to know? But there's that overriding and deeper puzzle—does Bebb really believe the outlandish claims he makes? Can Tono believe them? Can anybody? Even with all he knows about Bebb's sordid past and questionable present, Tono's fascination with Bebb has already been transformed into friendship and loyalty in the second book of the tetralogy. Leo isn't up for sainthood yet, but his crooked ways are looking straighter than we once thought they were. Like Steinbeck's Jim Casy, Bebb has a sexual weakness, but his charisma, like Casy's, appears to overwhelm the failing. Tono knows Bebb is "full of beans and bounce. . . . He is a supersalesman for Jesus" (*Bebb* 165).

With his trick eyelid, wrinkled clothes, and outrageous mannerisms, Bebb is several times described as Happy Hooligan. The counterfeit is evident, yet Tono senses something beyond hypocrisy in Bebb's words, something about being born again. Bebb's words mystify Tono, and the puzzle holds him to attention. Buechner seems to have been well along in *Lion Country* before the multiple dimensions of Leo Bebb began to dawn on him. "I had another kind of character in mind entirely when I started. In his tight-fitting raincoat and Tyrolean hat, he simply turned out to be the person he was in the journey of writing those books. I didn't expect him," Buechner confesses (*Belfry* 19). Tono will increasingly lean toward Bebb from this point on in the tetralogy, trying to catch his real name being spoken or hoping to hear some confirmation of his deepest wishes about life. When Leo preaches a sermon about the parable of the great feast and argues "there's no strangers" in the kingdom of heaven, Tono will be genuinely stirred by the possibility of balm for his unrest (*Bebb* 306). Buechner manages to take readers along on Tono's journey as he readjusts his feelings toward Bebb. Bebb has forgiven Lucille after all, and Bebb loves Sharon indeed. He did stand up to those lions, and his faith does sometimes ring with an enviable simplicity. Neither Tono's skepticism nor the reader's doubts entirely dissipate. There's always enough of a wink to keep us guessing, but the movement of the novels is toward transformation.

Another of Bebb's sermons, the one that struck a note Lucille could leave on, takes as its text Paul's words to the Ephesians about being a prisoner of Jesus Christ: "Saint Paul means this whole planet's my prison because I don't belong to this planet. I'm down here just for your sake same as Jesus was. That's all. I belong to someplace else far, far away. Sometimes I get homesick for it something wicked" (*Bebb* 174). Bebb goes on to make a transition connecting Paul's restlessness to a longing in the hearts of all people, and Brownie summarizes: "We are all of us seeking a homeland . . . though we have only seen and embraced it from afar. We are all of us strangers and pilgrims on the earth" (*Bebb* 228). Tono, whose pilgrimage carries through the four novels and whose loneliness echoes throughout the narrative, cannot denounce Bebb for fear that, crazy as it all seems, Bebb might be right. It is Augustine played out in a 1970s New England soap opera—hearts longing for rest, indeed (Augustine 3).

Love Feast

The European trip was to be about healing and recovery, gathering new energy for a renewed run, but *Love Feast* opens under the same ominous clouds that dominate the last pages of *Open Heart*. Whether the vacation worked or not, things are falling apart at home. The picaresque story continues from sequel to trilogy, carrying on the chronicles of Tono and those of Bebb, their sometimes crossing, their many divergences. Reviewer Roger Sale, keeping careful watch as the *Bebb* books appeared, offered useful insight—"In *Lion Country* Antonio is pretty much just there to observe, in *Open Heart* he moves nicely into the story, in *Love Feast* he is suddenly asked to become a full-fledged human being, which is a terrible fate for someone born to be a comic seeing eye."[18] Sale understood that the gist of the third installment of the *Bebb* books rested on a decreasing detachment in Tono, a shift in which Tono's role began to submerge even the ebullient Bebb. Michael Mewshaw in the *New York Times Book Review* went so far as to suggest that the trilogy "chronicles the decline of his [Tono's] cynicism and his awakening, if not conversion, to religious experience."[19]

If Mewshaw is right, I wonder if any reader could guess it from the opening scenes of *Love Feast*.

Buechner leaves no interval between novels this time. He has produced *Wishful Thinking: A Theological ABC* in the year before *Love Feast*, a whimsical volume capturing his position in the title. "Christianity," Buechner summarizes, "is mainly wishful thinking" (*WT* 96). Excerpted in *Reader's Digest* in 1972, the tart definitions and theological turns increased Buechner's notoriety, as did in 1973 *The Faces of Jesus*, Buechner's single foray into the coffee-table genre and an invitation to revisit renditions of the face of Christ, to see his face, perhaps, as "a face we somehow belong to . . . the face of Jesus as the face of our own secret and innermost destiny."[20] Despite the several irons in various fires, however, Buechner seems to have been wondering about Bebb and Tono and the others. He returns us to Connecticut with some speed. We walk in on Tono reviewing his vacation video, and there's Bebb at the Eiffel Tower. The screen fills with Bebb inadvertently dropping his ice cream cone from the viewing platform. As the scoop of ice cream plops from strut to strut on its slow journey downward—"a pink blob of spit"—Bebb turns the accident into a sermonic metaphor. "It's got a long way to go before it makes the City of Lights," Bebb comments. And then he adds, "We all of us do" (*Bebb* 280). And we are back in Bebb country. They had, as Tono puts it, "limped to Europe for repairs." Although the dead "are harder to get away from than the living" and "there was no getting away from any of the things we were trying to get away from."

Tono thinks that "somehow the trip worked anyhow" (*Bebb* 281). Tono has seldom been more wrong. Dropping Gertrude Conover in London, Sharon, Tono, and Bebb arrive in Connecticut to the smoldering ruins of Open Heart. What's become of Clarence Golden, who was living in the place before the fire? Bebb shrivels at the ruin of his ministry, soon heading back to Houston and Brownie. "But his heart wasn't in any of it," Tono tells us, meaning that, even back at Holy Love, Bebb is restless and lost (*Bebb* 287). Soon enough, Leo is off to Gertrude Conover's Princeton estate, Revonoc—Conover spelled backwards—suggesting the doubleness of this strange woman. Formerly Ptah-sitti and Uttu in Pharaoh's Egypt, according to Gertrude, at least, Leo and Gertrude will spend several years traveling, doing what rich people do. Although the cosmic couple drops by Sutton now and again for a visit with Tono, Sharon, and the children, Tono sees Bebb as "diminished" and watches the changes with "a sense of disillusion." Tono and Sharon are "haunted by the Bebb he used to be" (*Bebb* 288–89).

Maybe it is still Bebb's story, but he is offstage now, and Tono has no recourse but to deal with his worsening crisis alone. We know it is the marriage, of course, even before Tono talks of "the knowledge that for better or worse something was coming to an end between us" (*Bebb* 285). The trip, the fire, and Bebb's departure have only delayed the inevitable realization that deathliness has crept in somewhere. Tono says, "Something was rumbling in the hot air ducts. We went through the motions of our life together much as usual, Sharon and I, but I sensed in the background, dimly, we were perhaps also going through the motions of our death together" (*Bebb* 285–86). The infidelity, the unspoken bitterness and guilt, have taken their toll.

Anita Steen is back in the picture, a competitor for Sharon's romantic attention, Tono thinks. Sharon and Anita have opened a health food shop, and the business keeps Sharon busy. The marriage devolves into pain and silence before Sharon finally gives him a "line to leave on"—"Why don't you get your balls out of here" (*Bebb* 293). "At loose ends himself," Bebb is distressed by the news of the separation and offers prayer in which, Tono suspects, Bebb "must have risked a spiritual hernia," given the dimensions of this mess (*Bebb* 296). Sharon has her moment of harsh truthfulness when she bursts into Bebb's prayer with a malediction of her own. "Bip," she interrupts, "I might as well lay it on the line. Whoever you think you're talking to, I've never seen him or heard him or felt him, and I've never tasted or smelled him either. As far as I'm concerned, you've just been beating your gums" (*Bebb* 297). Tono sees that Sharon's doubt is a harder pill for Bebb to swallow than even Lucille's death or those five years in prison. It is Bebb's "bleakest hour" (*Bebb* 297). Tono has moved into a boarding house, ironically just down the hall from his nephew, the boy-man, Tony, who has cuckolded him; Sharon is falling to pieces—no hope at her core; and Bebb is helpless before the collapse. The separation settling in like drying cement, it is left to Gertrude Conover to save Bebb, at least, from "the dark night of his soul" (*Bebb* 297).

By the time Buechner gets to *Love Feast* in 1974, *Time* and *Newsweek* have each run lengthy features on the Jesus Revolution phenomenon sweeping the country. Buechner turns to current events in a way that makes *Love Feast* his most topical novel to date. Bebb confesses his homesickness to Gertrude, describing a malady more spiritual than physical, but Gertrude has a practical remedy. Her brilliant suggestion that Bebb put on a Thanksgiving dinner for Princeton students reminds Tono of her belief "that there is no such thing as chance" (*Bebb* 298). Returning to his interest in this generation of young folk so different from anything he has ever imagined, Reverend Bebb decides to take up Gertrude Conover's challenge. Their carefully worded invitation, posted here and there on campus, goes mostly unheeded. A dozen or so students straggle into Revonoc, where a feast has been prepared for something more like two hundred.

What to do? It is the Bebb of *Lion Country* who saves this day as he rises to preach the parable of the great feast from Luke. Who but Bebb would finish the sermon by sending forth his ragtag bunch into the highways and byways to recruit diners? Even the aimless Tono, down from Sutton for want of anyplace else to go, heads into the streets wondering "How did you invite people to a parable?" (*Bebb* 303). And it works. In fact, Tono snags the biggest fish, one Nancy Oglethorpe, who will become a leader of the movement spawned by the Thanksgiving gathering. Nancy's response to Tono's invitation—"This is positively providential"—suggests something of her role from the first moment (*Bebb* 304). She becomes the recruiter and the public relations staff for Bebb's revival, which is about to sweep through Princeton. A combination of the sensitivity sessions and spiritual outpourings of the era, Bebb's jamboree-like worship promotes free-for-all confession, and a new take on the kingdom of heaven as a place where frightened and lonely people, the displaced and the hopeless, can find a home. Imagine middle-aged, bald Bebb, in his "Gent's furnishings suit with all four points showing from his breast pocket" (*Bebb* 408), holding forth for the "Peter, Paul, and Mary" crowd, and you've captured a bit of the hilarious incongruity that drives this part of Buechner's story. Few American writers have tackled this era beyond Vietnam and Watergate; the so-called Jesus Revolution has become a footnote. But Buechner makes use of the months of idealism that boasted religious revival, public baptisms, and celebrity conversions. Bebb's love feasts feature sacramental potato chips and kisses of peace, religious practices sure to run into trouble somewhere. But Bebb is renewed by the outbreak, the crusade "to make Princeton, New Jersey, one big love feast for Jesus" (*Bebb* 316). Tono will mostly watch from afar, sometimes amazed, mostly caught in the web of his own decline into despondency.

Bebb is up now, but Tono is down. Back in Sutton, Tono feels insubstantial, a ghost, though "more haunted than haunting" (*Bebb* 311). He lectures his students on irony but winds up communicating only a bitter joke about inner and outer meaning. He is the English teacher as corrupter that we heard about all the way back in *A Long Day's Dying*. "Once you get reading and writing out of the way," Tono concludes, "I suppose what you teach children in English class is, God help you, yourself," echoing what Buechner says of his own teachers in the memoirs (*Bebb* 313).

Buechner has thought about teaching from both sides via his mentors at Union and his charges at Lawrenceville, and what he has learned often finds its way into Antonio Parr's thoughts on the profession.

But what Tono is teaching these days is mostly death, and he approaches his nadir in this third novel of the tetralogy. Tono's plunge into palpable despair takes place in, of all places, a dentist's chair. To be fair, he carries a good bit of pain to the appointment. He's just learned that Tony has returned to Sharon's bed. Anita Steen wasn't the problem after all. The anticipated pain at the hands of the dentist is "a kind of rehearsal," he thinks, "for the final pain" (*Bebb* 316). Tono is turning everything into death. In another of the coincidences that pile up in the tetralogy, Tono's partner in pain that day, the hygienist, is none other than his dream girl, Laura Fleishman. It is partly the coincidences that suggest parable in this novel. Among other things, Laura and Tono share a fondness for the line from *King Lear*—"The worst returns to laughter" (*Bebb* 271, 317). In a letter to Tono in *Open Heart*, Laura interprets the line as meaning "it's always darkest just before dawn" (*Bebb* 271). In *Love Feast* she resurrects Shakespeare's words in a bootless attempt to cheer the cheerless Tono. The sentiment, of course, has considerable weight for Buechner. One might even argue that the principle is central to everything he has written. But this time, he pulls it inside out. Dark days are dead ahead.

And Bebb is no help. Fleeing his neurotic housemate, Metzger, another frightened and alienated character—Metzger too often practices his emergency signal, three knocks on the wall, just in case of the heart attack that he's sure is on the way—Tono heads back to Revonoc and away from it all. He is fleeing, Tony too, of course—and Bill and Anita and his classroom full of irony and Sharon and himself. On the short trip, Tono remembers his "poor young father who died before I got around to knowing who he was," and we can hear Buechner in that mix (*Bebb* 320). In the subsequent paragraph, Tono confesses that he "needed to see Bebb, needed to have someone I could talk to about Sharon" (*Bebb* 320). Is it too much to suggest that Bebb has become his father figure? But the irony this time is Bebb's not noticing Tono's need.

Bebb is caught up in his own drama. Nancy Oglethorpe and Bebb's Jesus freaks have begun to garner detractors. The "Here's to Jesus" crowd includes some down-and-outers, some hippies, some bright-faced boys and girls, some of this, and some of that (*Bebb* 324), and the school fathers are beginning to squirm. Bebb's particular nemesis is a history professor, Virgil Roebuck, who has a word for the love feasters: "Every place I look I don't see Jesus," he rages (*Bebb* 324). Roebuck's special ire is reserved for

Bebb's talk of miracles, since Roebuck's son, a hopeless invalid, has apparently gone untended by God. Almost everyone in the tetralogy has good reasons for bitterness toward God. What that anger does to the angry ones is part of what Buechner is up to in the *Bebb* books. Bebb presses on, despite Roebuck's hostility, admonishing his followers: "But until you lay your cards on the table and level with him, they're the great gulf fixed between you. It's only when you tell it to Jesus like it is that they become the Golden Gate Bridge" (*Bebb* 325). Tono participates in the mass confessions, drawing Nancy Oglethorpe as his partner, but he heads back to Sutton decidedly unpeaceful. And now Christmas.

A brief visit to Sharon at the health food store adds other dimensions to Bebb's problems. Sharon has heard that the IRS is investigating Bebb, because he has had a bit of a lark on his tax form, filling in his first name as "Jesus" and his last name as "I am the first and the last, says the Lord" (*Bebb* 330). Under "wages," Bebb has put down "The wages of sin is death" (*Bebb* 330). Talk of Bebb's difficulties meanders to talk of Sharon's own troubles as the holiday season presses on them. She's been thinking about her unknown parents, her mysterious adoptive father, about those five years away, and all she doesn't know about herself. But Tono leaves the store wondering what Bebb penciled in for "Number of Dependents." Tono guesses, "I suppose what Bebb put down was Everybody. For myself I would have put down Nobody" (*Bebb* 332). He wants to tell Sharon that he is moving back home, but there's not enough of him to move. It is "death that was real," he concludes, "my life the echo" (*Bebb* 332).

If Bebb can't help, maybe Brownie is the next best thing, so Tono heads for a Texas Christmas with Brownie and the Redpath Indians and into one of the weirdest episodes of his life. Brownie at least asks about things with Sharon and waxes Augustinian with his advice. Tono has asked him about this peace business that Brownie has posited at the end of restlessness. Brownie echoes his earlier observations on the subject, saying, "Whatever peace is, we know it best from the empty place in our hearts where it's supposed to be. Until we find it, dear, we're all strangers and pilgrims on earth" (*Bebb* 336). Tono answers, "I hope you find it, Brownie," and the irony is mostly missing (*Bebb* 336). The rest of Tono's retreat to Open Heart is a hallucinatory experience brought on by a puff or two on John Turtle's pipe. John Turtle is one of the Indians, the joking cousin, who drifts in and out of the narrative and in and out of Tono's dreams. The dream this time goes all the way back to Lion Country, the zoolike world Tono visited six or so years before with Leo Bebb and Sharon. In the vision he meets Miriam, Lucille, and Herman Redpath. The dead seem mostly

OK; they've found a place. That Tono has not is emphasized in the last scene of the dream. Finding a silver dollar, Tono realizes that something is written there:

> What was written on it wasn't Antonio Parr or Tono or Bopper or Sir or any of the other names I've been called by various people at various times in my life, and yet it was my name. It was a name so secret that I wouldn't tell it even if I remembered it, and I don't remember it. But if anyone were ever to show up and call me by it, I'd recognize it in a second, and the chances are that if the person who called me by it gave me the signal, I'd follow him to the ends of the earth. (*Bebb* 342)

The strongest version yet of Tono's longing, his poignant search for someone, registers here in lines that again conjure the Chestertonian idea that we move about in forgetfulness. Tono's essential dilemma is that he cannot find Sharon until he finds himself. And he cannot find himself until he finds someone or something he cannot name.

Sharon heads back to Florida, and Tony's report—"She just needed somebody to hang onto"—does nothing to cheer Tono (*Bebb* 345). We are led to wonder if Sharon might be bound for Lucille's kind of end, but Tono is too curled in on his own darkness to notice. Suddenly Bebb shows up to report that "The fat's in the fire" (*Bebb* 346). The IRS is closing in, and academe, uncomfortable with "the language of the sawdust trail," has blocked university facilities to Bebb's madcap congregation (*Bebb* 348). Roebuck is the villain of that piece, of course. Accusing Bebb of "ignoring all the shit in the world" and offering "fairy tales about Heaven," Roebuck has spelled out the intellectuals' charges against Bebb. Bebb's answer takes us back to the fecal imagery of *The Final Beast* and Buechner's talk of the same in *The Sacred Journey*: "Roebuck, you think I don't know about shit? What you've been telling me about isn't even a millionth part of all the shit there is" (*Bebb* 351). In the Nicolet novel, of course, Nick is stunned by the charge that "Christ eats it," a moment alluded to in the first of the memoirs as well (*FB* 82, *SJ* 94). Nick's response, that "Christ does eat it, of course. . . . Because it's all this world has ever given him to eat" (*FB* 82–83), more or less prefigures Leo Bebb's retort to Roebuck, "I'm full of it too, Roebuck. I'm not denying it. And you're full of it. It's the shit in us is part of what makes us brothers, you and me" (*Bebb* 352). Old Godric will make much of the world-as-shit analogy as well; "jakes" he'll call it, referring to outhouses and what happens there (*Godric* 6). Buechner finds multiple synonyms for dross. And the dross is heavy on

Roebuck, heavy on Bebb. "The night is dark, Virgil Roebuck, and home's a long way off for both of us," Bebb tells him (*Bebb* 353). And there's more. That fire at Open Heart probably wasn't an accident. The insurance company is investigating an arson charge—only a matter of time before they learn that Golden's prison time was for firebugging.

"Thus the woes of Leo Bebb," Tono says, and somehow Tono adds all of this to his own list as he heads off to Laura Fleishman's house and the rock bottom of his despair at last. When Tono winds up in bed with Laura, he has come to the end of hope. Their union is more about desolation than love, more about homelessness and longing, sex without much in the way of joy. The whole scene reeks of sadness, in fact, and Tono admits that they "were just keeping alive" (*Bebb* 363). Tono even remembers a word he's run across in a *Times* article, "decathexis," defined as "an emotional detachment from life" (*Bebb* 364). Whatever it is, decathexis descends on Tono at Laura's door. He has crossed over into a bleakness from which there may be no way back. "There was nothing I had to let go that I hadn't let go already," he finishes (*Bebb* 364). Nothing matters.

Bebb's troubles explode in a protest march on the university and end with a riot that makes Bebb a fugitive. The school newspaper reports the wild events, even transcribing a good bit of the sermon that Bebb plunges on with after the amplification system gives out—"hushed Gospelese" the writer calls it, and adds, "You could have heard a pone drop" (*Bebb* 373). There's the confrontation with the Atheists for Democratic Action. They chant, "God is dead," while the "Bebbites battle back with God is Good to the same beat'" (*Bebb* 373). For the reader, a tour of the early 1970s— Jesus Freaks. For the student reporter, who witnesses the scene, a "sacramental orgy" (*Bebb* 374). For Bebb, the end of another run. Antonio even shows up in the newspaper report. In the ruins of Bebb's wacky experiment among flower children and outcasts, in the outrageous denouement, Tono strikes an entirely serious note by quoting Robert Browning as a tribute to Bebb:

> We that had loved him so, followed him, honored him,
> Lived in his mild and magnificent eye,
> Learned his great language, caught his clear accents,
> Made him our pattern to live and to die. (*Bebb* 375)

Tono's paean sounds almost like a funeral ode, a broad hint at least that we may well be on our way to just that. We can almost see Bebb's wink. Tono probably gives away more than he knows with his homage to Bebb.

His ardent testimony here is one of the few times in the tetralogy that Tono actually articulates his feelings for Leo Bebb; one could say that Leo has become something of a hero for Tono by now.

Predictably enough, Bebb's travails bring Sharon back from Florida and maybe back to Tono. Trying to find their ways back to each other, they listen for news of Bebb. The house still beset by emptiness, the unfinished mobile now closer to the compost heap in the backyard, Tono and Sharon nonetheless find a "kind of stopgap peace together" (*Bebb* 383). They've been here before, of course. Maybe it is just their bodies reuniting, but we suspect that some river has been recrossed, some evil done away with. It is Golden, mostly forgotten by now, who shows up to lead them to a clandestine rendezvous with Bebb, somewhere in the bowels of a warehouse, Bull's International Storage, in New York City. Sharon will be the one to interpret Bebb's words, although Tono is there beside her when Bebb comes clean: "Sharon, honey, I'm through hiding. There is nothing hid which shall not be manifested nor anything kept secret but that it shall come abroad" (*Bebb* 386). Bebb's penultimate confession is not to a fear of the IRS, Roebuck, the arson investigators, or Princeton University. "It's the darkness in here I'm scared of," he tells Tono, "tapping his chest. . . . The shameful things a man does with his life. The shameful things don't nobody know about but him" (*Bebb* 387).

Sharon realizes that Bebb is saying goodbye. Looking back on it, Tono admits he should have heard it. Leo makes a clean breast of it: "I've burned all my bridges. Up's the only place I got left" (*Bebb* 389). The final speeches of the Reverend Leo Bebb indeed light the way to the story of that scalawag Saint Godric, the subject of the novel to come in the next decade. After speaking of shame, Bebb turns to doubt: "The Apostle Paul wrote faith is the evidence of things not seen. Now if the only evidence a man's got is something he can't see, you can't blame him if sometimes he—when a thing's not out there where you can see it, sometimes you have a hard time believing it's there" (*Bebb* 390). When Golden tags it "a fifty-fifty chance," Bebb responds, "It's a chance you got to take" (*Bebb* 390).

Curiously enough, it is Sharon who quizzes Bebb at the end, Sharon who has declared her unbelief, Sharon who has been trapped in her murky prison while Tono walked us through his dark night. She pushes Bebb about his willingness to bet everything on that chance: "Would you bet your tail, Bip?" (*Bebb* 390), she asks. Bebb's answer? "I'll just have to say, Savior, let thy grace be sufficient," he responds. "Jesus, take, pity on this wore-out tail of mine that's all I got left to bet with" (*Bebb* 390). Bebb has just one more prayer left. After admonishing Sharon and Tono to be unafraid, he finally offers a bit of marital advice. Admitting that he connived their courtship long ago, he tells them to "stay put because if you don't, you'll spend the rest of your life looking to find each other in the face of strangers" (*Bebb* 393). Bebb tells them what they suspected, but his explanation hits hard. "Antonio," Bebb says, "first time I laid eyes on you, I could see you were right for each other. You were a tree without apples. Sharon, she was apples without a tree" (*Bebb* 393). Their reunion is consolidated in Bebb's telling them what they already intuit about themselves.

At the end Bebb even wants to explain his arrest in Miami—a "crazy chance" he calls what happened there, and sees it in the context of this desire to be known, his instinct to confession (*Bebb* 394). Tono and Golden are still there, but Bebb's words seem directed mostly to Sharon, who needs to solve the riddle of herself, find out if things can be made right. Even as Leo Bebb prays his last prayer, we can sense another book on the horizon, this one to solve the mysteries of Sharon's life that Bebb has somehow touched on but left unanswered in *Love Feast*. The prayer is simple enough—"Come, Lord Jesus"—but Bebb figures "it put pretty much the whole thing in a nutshell" (*Bebb* 395). Bebb's last words.

The final chapter of the novel takes us to Bebb's funeral. The rites are a mostly private affair as they are held in the potato field where Golden has crashed the stolen biplane he and Bebb were using to drop balloons and take "a parting shot" at Princeton on the day of a citywide celebration. The plane circles the town for almost an hour, plenty of time for Roebuck and the rest to see the streaming banners, "HERE'S TO JESUS" and "HERE'S TO YOU" (*Bebb* 399). Brownie and John Turtle come in from Houston for the funeral service; Gertrude and Charlie Blaine and even Anita Steen show up. Sharon and the boys are there. Brownie does the honors, beginning the ceremony with "I am the resurrection and the life" (*Bebb* 401), and Tono wishes someone had seen a parachute. There's a bit of talk about alternate theories of the crash, since no trace of either Bebb's body or Golden's can be found anywhere in that potato field. But lots of people on the ground saw the plane in flames before the nosedive, and "the fire was so intense and its destruction so complete that some said it could have been caused only by somebody's soaking the crate in gasoline and then touching it off with a match" (*Bebb* 401). Parting shot indeed.

The wrapping-up takes a mere two pages. As Bebb has prophesied, Sharon is indeed pregnant and gives birth to a daughter, Lucy, named for Lucille, and Tono has to live with the question of whether the baby is his or Tony's—one more weight on the fragile recommitment. A year later,

Tony marries Laura Fleishman, with Tono beside him as best man. Tono expresses something of the incredulity readers might feel at this: "it would take God himself to sort out the tangle" (*Bebb* 403). Tono's tongue-in-cheek observation pretty well speaks for *Love Feast*, as well as for the book that will finish the stories of Tono, Leo, Sharon, and the rest.

We go toward *Treasure Hunt* assured, at least, that Tono is back from death. Although he thinks it may be his youth that ended during this phase of the story, his "capacity for ignoring irony," his "taste for certain flavors of hope," he promises himself "no decathexis" (*Bebb* 404). Horton Davies emphasized the resplendent "Christian charity," the compassion that reflects "the image of God beneath the filth and the recriminations, the foulness and the failures," as central to *The Book of Bebb*.[21] No doubt, Tono has learned much about mercy by observing Leo. Even if we have little reason to believe Tono to be a new man, he is convincing this time:

> Out of the wreckage of things I picked up a kind of marriage again, a daughter who by one route or another at least has my blood in her veins, a capacity if not for rising above irony like the saints, at least living it out with something like grace, with the suspicion if not the certainty that maybe the dark and hurtful shadows all things cast are only shadows. (*Bebb* 404)

"Suspicion" and "not certainty"—another way for Buechner to slip in his central formulation on faith. Bebb's last words are lifted from the next-to-last sentence of the Bible, of course, the part of the prayer that ends with "The grace of our Lord Jesus Christ be with you all."[22] Something like grace presides over the brief space between books three and four, but it is not the sort of grace that brings us to our knees. Sharon and Tono search for a more or less secular calm in the tempest that has been their marriage. Bebb's words are still back there somewhere, but nobody here is heading out to church on Sunday.

Treasure Hunt

Treasure Hunt manages to resurrect Leo Bebb. There are the audio tapes of his sermons that Gertrude listens to in the opening pages, Tono's frequent dreams featuring Bebb, a Bebb impersonator par excellence, and Sharon's inquiry into the final mysteries of Bebb as a doorway into the mysteries of herself. The wackiest of the four novels, *Treasure Hunt* makes the Princeton love feasts look sedate. Many of the same reviewers lined up for this fourth visit to Bebbland—Pritchard, Wimsatt, Skow, Doyle, and Davenport—most of them still fans, and all of them noticing that *Treasure Hunt* turns up the antic-meter by a full notch or more. The *Library Journal* reviewer caught the drift:

> There's a little of everything here: UFO's, life rays, and karmic fields; philosophy and theosophy; Messiahs that run the gamut from Christ to the Lone Ranger. . . . *Treasure Hunt* is a rare find, a serious novel that never seems serious. Buechner laces his sermons with humor, with irony, even with fantasy. In this journey south, it's hard to tell the homilies from the grits.[23]

Although I might object to this talk of sermons, that "homilies and grits" phrase is just too good to pass up, and it indeed captures something of a book "awash with similes," according to the *New York Times Book Review*. *Treasure Hunt* is Buechner at his adventurous extreme, off on a riotous jaunt in several directions at once. Christopher Lehmann-Haupt's review of *Love Feast* for the *New York Times* actually raised the question about how all this works. Although he praised Buechner as "technically accomplished," he suggested that "the contrast between the serious and the absurd serves to underline the meaning of both *Love Feast* and the trilogy as a whole." Lehmann-Haupt found the effect somewhat jarring. "I can't get in touch with their deeper motivations," he concluded of the characters of the trilogy.[24]

If the reader cannot quite go along for a ride that seems more fantastic than actual, the view from the stands is entertaining enough. Maybe comedy is the way to talk about religious questions; Buechner seems to be thinking so here and will codify the idea in his Yale lectures *Telling the Truth: The Gospel in Tragedy, Comedy, and Fairy Tale*, which appear in book form in the same year as *Treasure Hunt*. Despite the distancing factor of absurdist comedy, Tono continues to be just normal enough to invite something like identification. Bebb is gone, and boy, is he missed! Gertrude Conover mourns the fact that Bebb "took a lot of the action with him when he checked out," and Tono can only agree.

It is soupy summer as the last of the *Bebb* novels opens on Gertrude, Tono, and Sharon dreamily listening to a recording of Leo Bebb. The evangelist who has gone out in a fireball of martyrdom still has a certain power. Tono can almost see Leo poring over some sermon ideas, dictating a few letters that will never be sent, and then springing the news of a surprising inheritance that will send the trio off on a pilgrimage into the mystery of Bebb. As in *The Entrance to Porlock*, the travelers in *Treasure Hunt* will finally, however, be in search of themselves. When Bebb's recorded voice talks about "Life with a capital L" in a sermon that explicates Christ's parable of the treasure hidden in a field, readers can imagine Tono becoming a bit more awake (*Bebb* 409). Capital letter life is just the sort of treasure Tono has been hunting for from the beginning. Tono hopes for revelations on the tape, explanations about Bebb's last flight, perhaps, or something about that dark deed in Miami that landed Bebb in prison. What he gets is Bebb's confession:

> All my life I wanted to do something big for Jesus only nothing I ever did amounted to scratch. Could be the best thing I ever did for him was back when I was on the road selling Bibles where folks could read up on him for theirselves, but that wasn't big enough to suit me. I wanted to be up there in the head office—gospel-preaching, healing, revivals, the whole shebang. Talk about your missions, I set up Gospel Faith College and put in paid ads all over creation. "Put yourself on God's payroll," they said. "Go to work for Jesus now." A racket? . . . Listen, was it a racket Jesus saying lay down your fishpole? . . . I ordained anybody answered that ad and sent in his love offering. Gospel Faith's still in business, but it's small potatoes. Everything I ever did, it was small potatoes. I'm a small potato man my own self, and that's the truth of it. (*Bebb* 412)

Bebb's confession precedes the commissioning of his little band of disciples. As if from the grave, Bebb talks of his birthplace, Poinsett, South Carolina, and of a house he owns there. The house he bequeaths to Tono and Sharon, along with the fateful charge that they "do something nice with old place. And I want you to do it for Jesus" (*Bebb* 413). All three are crying before the tape ends, enough longing to go around.

Gertrude really muddies the water when she explains that Bebb himself directed her to the tape. For a while we hold our breath, thinking maybe Bebb did walk away from that potato field. Maybe Gertrude has had a particularly vivid dream. Maybe Bebb, reincarnated, is trying to send her messages. Gertrude, remember, is like Bebb in that she can believe almost anything. She believes in divine wisdom, theosophy, and she'll take it where she can get it. Mission delivered, the novel begins in a dream that will set the atmosphere for the whole trip. It is Tono's dream, of course, a dream in which he is digging a hole that just keeps filling back up. He asks Bebb for help with his Sisyphean task, but Bebb just walks away. There beside him in a yellow raincoat, Sharon observes, "You're just digging your own grave" (*Bebb* 417). Even a rocket scientist could interpret that dream. Tony is still "hungry for fortissimo" (*Bebb* 6), defined by his longing and his search.

So off he goes to recruit Brownie to help with "the Jesus part" (*Bebb* 417). In a turn that would have been tough to predict, Brownie has had his own problems since Bebb's demise—he has lost his faith. Brownie, who could once turn even the most ominous Scripture into pure treacle, can barely hold himself together these days. (Bebb jokes that Brownie could "make the book of Job sound like a Mother's Day card" [*Bebb* 492].) It is like losing a child, he concludes, and the burden of hiding it from his congregation is palpable. Remarkably, Tono plays the pastor here, tries to comfort Brownie, but Brownie responds, "Scripture says where your treasure is, there shall your heart be also. The trouble is my treasure's turned out to be a bad check. Spiritually speaking, I don't have a nickel left to my name" (*Bebb* 424). The similes do pile up, all to the effect that Brownie is done with G. Zuss or G. Zuss is done with him. Pastor Parr tells him, "you need to stop taking your spiritual temperature all the time," the pot calling the kettle black, I'd say (*Bebb* 424), but nothing works until Tono hints that the real reason for the southward journey may be to find Bebb himself, Bebb alive and in need of his disciples. Brownie eventually signs on for the treasure hunt, hoping "to stumble on something down there" (*Bebb* 425). Brownie goes to try to recover faith, Tono goes looking for faith, and Sharon goes to "have a look for myself" (*Bebb* 426). Her declaration cuts brilliantly in two—she's going to do family research, and she's going in search of herself. The treasure hunt is on, and the treasures in question cut in many directions, but all seem to end up having to do with spiritual treasure, with meaning, with the filling of some empty space. Another motley crowd heads out on the road to Oz as Buechner turns to his favored pilgrimage motif. Nobody has much to lose, anyway.

Buechner conjures up the ancient nursery rhyme about the dog and the cat and the rat and the rest to muse again about the possibility of pattern, the one-thing-leading-to-anotherness of the adventure (*Bebb* 426). Farewells in Sutton allow time for musings on the cracked plate of a marriage that has been "glued together again," and we have a sense of the fragility that still hangs over the house. And guess who comes along to care for the children while Tono and Sharon are on pilgrimage? Sure enough, Tony and Laura. In the evening before the travelers depart, we get an enchanting fantasy of might-have-beens as Tony holds the daughter, Lucy, who may be his, and Tono beholds the woman, Laura, who might have been his. Role reversals give way to goodbyes, and Buechner moves in close when Tono bids farewell to Bill—"If you really stopped to think about it, I don't suppose you would ever say it" (*Bebb* 430). Buechner's father didn't say it on that Saturday long ago, and Buechner seems to be thinking about it in now-and-then moments like these.

Gertrude proposes that they drive to Poinsett, taking in tourist sights along the way; their chauffeur is Callaway, who appeared briefly in *Love Feast* and is to have a larger role in *Treasure Hunt*. A handsome black man who speaks a language all his own, Callaway was, according to Gertrude, a pharaoh in some past incarnation. Callaway is also "the canary in the coal mine" (*Bebb* 462), because his nosebleeds supposedly indicate the presence of Leo Bebb. Brownie is to meet up with the odd little covey of pilgrims in Poinsett, but the whole thing is held together by a dead man. Gertrude goes on about Bebb as an "eternal sightseer" and "an always-returner" in language that Buechner first seems to chide and then seems to associate with Christ. Gertrude offers the opinion that "every time Bebb turned up, he made it a red-letter life," surely a glance toward the words of Christ in the New Testament (*Bebb* 432). Then she explains, "As long as there's anybody left to return to down here, Leo Bebb will always return to them. Return *for* them might be a better way of putting it" (*Bebb* 433). Gertrude's rather syncretistic theology frequently threatens to morph into a version of Leo's Bible-belt fundamentalism. At a stop to visit the Library of Congress, Tono thinks he sees Leo wandering the stacks and pauses to feel the pain of Bebb's absence. Tono notes that when Bebb was around, "There was more of you to feel with" (*Bebb* 434).

But Poinsett is where the action is. Not the site of anyone's imaginings, Poinsett, pronounced "Points," seems an unlikely place for a treasure of any sort (*Bebb* 438). "No wonder Bebb hightailed it out of here first chance he got," Sharon jokes. Then she adds, "Jesus" (*Bebb* 436). And the home place turns out to be occupied as well as haunted. The sign on the door reads "UFORIUM," and now the fun really begins.

Sharon recognizes the Bebbsian flavor of this museum of moon artifacts and gathering place for witnesses to alien visitations, and readers catch a whiff of another popular pursuit of the 1970s. The cast of *The Book of Bebb* is now complete, with Bertha and Babe Bebb and this new faith that has remarkable affinities with the sawdust-aisle version Leo has promoted. Bertha wears a wig and speaks in questions. She asks if Leo has "passed" and seems interested in Sharon, but she's a shadowy presence at first, meek and overwhelmed by the brother of Leo Bebb, the *twin* brother of Leo Bebb (*Bebb* 442). Buechner seems to have decided about Leo's resurrection—whether it was to be actual or metaphorical—as he was in the process of writing *Treasure Hunt*, and Babe provides one of those instances when we think Leo may have survived to make it back home to Points. In March of 1976, while at work on *Treasure Hunt*, Buechner tells Nancy Myers that "Bebb may or may not appear alive" in the new book (Myers 198–99). The book comes out in 1977, and Buechner seems to have concluded that Bebb would have more power in the dreams than in the flesh—a bit like Christ, I suppose. But Babe is Bebb "if you didn't look too hard—Bebb in a fright wig, Bebb having gained a few pounds and aged a few years" (*Bebb* 443). Poinsett is Leo Bebb's past, the secret he's buried beneath all the others. Babe says, "He was a bag stuffed full of times he didn't talk about," but it turns out that Babe and Leo have been estranged for most of their lifetimes (*Bebb* 444). Gertrude wants to believe in Babe's faith in space visitors—"the hope of the world come true" (*Bebb* 445), but Sharon recognizes that "It's Bip all over with the Gospel left out" (*Bebb* 447). And Tono adds, "I'd never been persuaded even by Bebb's eloquence that the Gospel was for me, but when it was left out, I missed it" (*Bebb* 447). Like Gertrude, Babe offers flavors that interest Tono, a 1970s pastiche—a little Eastern this and a little science fiction that—but it is Leo whom Tono keeps leaning back toward.

Nonetheless, Babe has remarkable powers. He almost speaks Tono's name, for one thing, almost knows him as he pronounces Tono "all wore out" (*Bebb* 448). Babe's summary bespeaks a prescience that goes back to Leo's early appraisals of Tono as "tied up in knots" (*Bebb* 63), and a dam breaks somewhere. Tono lets us know that he's been keeping up a brave front, "making the best of things because you can no longer make the most of them" (*Bebb* 448). The longing is never far from the surface through all five hundred and more pages of the orange and yellow book. Jarred by Babe's insight, Tono is ready to leave well enough alone and head back north. Sharon, on the other hand, wants her birthright. Babe and Bertha have to go—for Jesus. The specter of the almost-Leo and the apologetic Bertha, the why of the trip to Poinsett, Tony and Sharon back there in the Sutton house, and lectures about irony—public and private, inner and outer, doubleness—swirl together in *Treasure Hunt* to the point that "things both were what they seemed and yet were something else too" (*Bebb* 451). Through Tono, Buechner ruminates on the meaning or nonmeaning beneath the mysteries. Poinsett will bring us to the points.

While Buechner was churning on the *Bebb* books through the 1970s, Hal Lindsay was riding the crest of his bestseller *The Late, Great Planet Earth*. The apocalyptic thriller sold fifteen million copies. Now available for one cent via the Internet, the rapture book must have been somewhere in Buechner's mind as he painted the portrait of Babe Bebb. Among the many things Babe believes is a space-traveler version of the rapture. He tells Tono, "Someday Jesus'll climb out of a saucer. Sunshine in his hair. Gather his own up just like it says. Only he's a spaceman, that's what" (*Bebb* 458). Babe's theories are progressive. And lunatic. The two at once. Like the readers, the pilgrims have to decide what to make of Babe's religion—profound or comical or both. Gertrude can swallow a lot of it. Brownie likes the flavor too. Sharon has long ago learned to avoid climbing out on these kinds of limbs, and Tono is withholding judgment, at least until he can arrange for one of Babe's readings, a combination of psychic mumbo jumbo, hypnosis, and telekinesis that helps Babe support his Uforium.

With his inimitable ability to see everything from skewed angles, Brownie fits Babe's machinations into a larger frame by suggesting that the UFOs are one of the signs of the end times. "When the end is coming, you can expect many peculiar things to start to happen," according to Brownie (*Bebb* 455). Babe's visitors are much divided on his claims, though I'm guessing they would agree on "peculiar." Gertrude believes with the ease of a sparrow lifting off a window sill, Brownie wants to believe, the wistful Tono cannot silence the voice telling him that Babe's notions are crazy beyond belief, and Sharon is the tough unbeliever. "Well I heard it, but I can't believe it," Sharon offers, as they talk of Babe's claim that extraterrestrials speak to him via transistors planted in his molars. "I can't even believe Babe believes it," she adds (*Bebb* 455). Tensions have thickened by now. Babe is not to be so easily evicted from his homeplace. Bertha is apparently known in the neighborhood for her sporadic rampages and vandalism. Brownie is falling under Babe's spell, which threatens to divide the troops. Callaway is hanging around Bertha, and that looks like trouble coming. Gertrude is trying to organize a search for the reincarnated Bebb, who must be, she thinks, a child born around Poinsett in the last year or so. Even Tono is vulnerable to Babe's stunning imitation of Leo. When Babe, with Leo's voice, tells Tono to "hold on to Jesus, boy," Tono recognizes that he is, like Sharon, an "orphan"—"for a moment there Babe was my father and my mother both, and I would have followed him to the ends of the earth" (*Bebb* 459). The moment will pass, but things are getting downright thorny.

Babe tries to convince Tono that he and Bert "thought the world" of Leo, but Tono senses the whole thing is more complicated than that. Chewing over Leo's strange bequest and a good many more unspoken currents, Babe muses, "Death leaves a awful mess." Then, after a pause, he adds, "Hell, so does life," and we probably inch a bit closer to the truth

(*Bebb* 458–59). The baby search turns up Leo Bebb—Gertrude thinks so anyway. Even without Callaway's nosebleeds, Gertrude leads them to Jimmy Bob Luby "in skimpy shorts that his diapers hung down out of and a washed-out Donald Duck shirt that didn't quite cover his belly" (*Bebb* 464). The unimaginably pitiable child is made all the more so by the fact that he is blind, but Gertrude is undeterred: "I know it's the one," she concludes (*Bebb* 464).

When Tono snaps, more than a reader or two probably shout "Hurrah." His tolerance has reached something of a limit as he watches Gertrude with the baby. "As she looked down at that poor, starch-fed child in her lap whose diapers I could tell even at that range were in desperate need of changing, what she saw was a bodhisattva because that was a more manageable sight to see" (*Bebb* 465). Tono's tantrum features a shrill statement of unbelief, "When you're dead, you're dead. Christ. Bebb's dead. That's not Bebb that's crapped in his pants because the dead can't crap any more. People don't get to come back, and flying saucers haven't landed, and let's get the hell out of here" (*Bebb* 405). Tono makes good sense, of course, and we more or less expect his to be the final word. But Buechner always has a trick up his sleeve. The camera swings back to Gertrude. "What you say may be true, Antonio. We won't know till the curtain comes down on the last act. But in the meantime I'll tell you what I feel. . . . I'd rather be wrong about all those things I believe in and more or less alive and interested than right as rain and bored half to death," she finishes (*Bebb* 405). Considerable wind comes out of Antonio's sails. He cries. Antonio weeps infrequently enough to cause us to pay special attention to what is moving him. This time he cries over his unbelief, because he "couldn't believe it was Bebb" (*Bebb* 405). Tono's low point in *Treasure Hunt* relates not so much to physical circumstance as to ideas. The marriage is hanging together, but the issue of faith remains.

Reflecting on his tirade, Tono quietly confirms his unbelief:

Bebb was dead, I had said to Gertrude Conover in my moment of exasperation, and Jesus was dead, and though the exasperation was long since gone, the fact was with me still. The dead didn't care whether you did something nice for them or not, and there in that shadowy, wall-to-wall cave with my bourbon and ginger in my hand and vacation in my heart, I didn't much care that they didn't care. (*Bebb* 466)

Several mysteries circulate in the novel, but the central one, the same one that has stirred throughout the tetralogy, is whether or not Tono will be able to climb out of the dark stasis of his unbelief. Will he climb out of this muddy hole? Will he be lifted out? Or will he simply find what rest he can in the rain and the muck?

After a dust-up over a dead chicken—apparently Bertha has gone berserk again—Tono heads off to bed thinking about this strange world in which he's landed, but it is Leo who invades his dreams. Margaret Wimsatt was one of those critics who praised Buechner's penchant for recording dreams: "Memories and visions are what he does best."[25] I see her point, though it often seems to me that the dreams intrude, thus delaying the plot, and actually function to separate the reader from the life of the novel, as dreams and visions are, like miracles, intensely personal. Nonetheless, Tono's dream here works not just to revitalize Tono but also to suggest something of where Buechner is to go from here. Tono dreams of "The Venerable Bebb" (*Bebb* 468).

Jumbled memories of a Catholic childhood percolate in Tono's long night as he considers the likelihood that Bebb might be a saint. All the way back at the beginning, Tono has pondered Bebb's claim that there's "a priest in all of us" (*Bebb* 86). Forced again to the question of Bebb's priestly attributes, and to recollections of talk about saints in his Catholic childhood, Tono conjures up the qualifications: "reputation for sanctity, the heroic quality of your virtues, and a few blue-chip miracles" (*Bebb* 468). Tono admits that "the sanctity of Bebb was like a fish I was trying to hook" (*Bebb* 469). Somehow it matters, this business of Bebb as saint-in-the-making. Tono argues with himself: "God knows there had been other saints before him who were queer as Dick's hatband." He proceeds to a list of "flagpole sitters, leper-lovers, middle-aged celibates in barbed wire underwear, virgins floating in the air like birthday balloons, grown men preaching to yellow-bellied sapsuckers or naked and cruciform in subzero cells." He concludes, "So why not Bebb with his penchant for baring something maybe not all that unlike his soul?" (*Bebb* 469). There's the "fiery martyrdom" on Bebb's side of the ledger, of course, and Tono's sure knowledge that "there was hardly anything worth believing that Bebb did not believe" (*Bebb* 469). And there's that Knoxville resurrection to set beside Herman Redpath's revived potency and the few tottering steps of Professor Virgil Roebuck's son when Bebb maybe healed him back at the final Princeton love feast.

But the real heft of Tono's tangled vision comes in the word that Bebb delivers in the middle of it. "There's dark and shameful things a man keeps hid that if he don't get them out into the sunshine they'll drag him into the dark," Leo claims (*Bebb* 470). In some ways the central line of the four texts, Leo's words not only explain his terrible moment in Miami and the central premise of his ministry, but they also explain why he has brought his family and followers to Poinsett. The stark sentence also stands close to the center of something that happens in Tono. His night of visions and visitations ends with an imagined letter to Leo. After he has tried speaking words—"Old friend" . . . "old father" . . . "old fart"—Tono drafts a letter, "Dear Bip, Even if you never worked a miracle, you were a miracle, and that's what counts" (*Bebb* 470–71). When Sharon announces, "Rise and shine, Bopper. It's time to get up" (*Bebb* 471), we can almost see Tono scrambling upward out of more than merely a bed.

Within a few paragraphs, when Bertha wants to show "her treasure" to Sharon, Tono whispers, "Where her treasure is, there shall her heart be also." Just in case we missed it, Sharon responds, "That's Scripture" (*Bebb* 472). Pastor Parr with the ready verse; not Bebb, not even Brownie, but Tono. Has Tono become Leo in some way? Could the tight-fisted, fearful, ever tentative skeptic, Tono, find his way to the kind of beans that Leo was full of? Bertha's treasure turns out to be her heart, sure enough, and Leo's checkered past is coming up fast. In the meantime, Brownie has had Babe's "life-ray" treatment. Brought to tears by the fact that Babe called him "Laverne," his true name, Brownie has found life again, not to mention the side effects—new teeth stirring beneath his gums to render the false ones redundant (*Bebb* 474–75). The teeth are the proof that Babe's theories can somehow be stirred in with Leo's religious stew to come up with enough to live on. Tono places Brownie's conversion beside Gertrude's theories, appraising them as part of "the metaphysical ride" of his pilgrimage to Poinsett and finds them inadequate (*Bebb* 477). Tono and Brownie have their talk hanging in the air above Poinsett on a carnival ride at the county fair. But they are brought back to earth soon enough, back from spiritual meanderings to the practical problems. Bertha has disappeared.

Although Buechner has occasionally ventured into the territory of the daily newspapers of his own time, touching on several topics of the decade in the *Bebb* tetralogy, he seems relatively uncomfortable with the huge subject of the time—race. Julian Moynahan, whose review of *The Final Beast* was substantial, offered a less than scintillating consideration of *Treasure Hunt*. Moynahan took Buechner to task for "comically picturesque American Indians," labeling Buechner's portraits as "a lapse of taste."[26] I am somewhat surprised that more critics didn't challenge Buechner's treatment of the inmates of Strasser's asylum in *The Entrance to Porlock* or dispute his verging toward stereotypes in several passages of the *Bebb* tetralogy. There are the aforementioned Indians, often seen as unruly children with bewildering superstitions and bizarre folkways, and there's Callaway, who speaks in a dialect that threatens to reduce him to foot-shuffling cliché. Callaway is as close as he will get to the largest racial and social questions of the 1970s, and, though Buechner skates clear, the whole business seems a bit forced in this context. Babe several times refers to Callaway as "boy," and Babe certainly stands for a stereotypical racism haunting the country still (*Bebb* 478, 479). The story Babe tries to sell is that Callaway has accosted Bertha, and anonymous notes and ugly threats follow as Callaway is evicted from the motel room he's been sharing with Brownie.

Tono recognizes that this is just Babe's last-ditch effort to get this bunch of interlopers out of his hair, and Babe's villainy raises questions about his credibility all along. He is "both what you could see he was and also what you could not see he was" (*Bebb* 485). Buechner is clearly arriving at that theme, that "broth of false and true" that he will pick up again within a year or two (*Godric* 31). All this time we thought Leo was to be the villain, and now it turns out to be Leo's buried secret, his evil twin, who is to play the role. In the final confrontation between Babe and Tono, Babe modulates into Leo's voice to assure Tono that "Everything's going to wind up making sense" (*Bebb* 487). We've seen the last of Leo Bebb, but we haven't heard the last of his voice or the end of his sentiments. Tono doubts the messenger, but he likes the message. It is the same kind of message Buechner will seek out again in the memoir *Telling Secrets*, where he will play Tono's role as Buechner's long-dead father tells him that "Everything is going to be all right" (*TS* 100). Babe is the one speaking here, but Tono's conversation is with Leo.

When the voice proclaims, "God shall wipe away all tears," Tono retorts, "Jesus, Bip, don't think I wouldn't believe it if I could" (*Bebb* 488). When Leo responds via Babe, "Antonio, you'll believe it when it comes," Tono lets it all go:

> "Oh shit, Bip"—shit not as an expletive but as a cry of longing and despair that welled up not just out of Callaway's getting screwed but out of the whole world's getting screwed, out of all sadness, failure, loss. . . . everybody was included in my excremental lament. . . . "He's been coming two thousand years, Bip, and he hasn't made it yet." (*Bebb* 488)

Bebb only responds with "Hi-yo Silver" and a riff on the *William Tell Overture* (*Bebb* 488). With the Lone Ranger planted in his head by Leo/Babe's humming, Tono ponders the meaning of the parable. Is the Lone Ranger

Christ and Leo his faithful friend, *Kemo Sabe*? Or is Tono to be *Kemo Sabe* and Leo the masked hero? Tono could be Tonto, I suppose; he is clearly enough Sancho to Bebb's Don Quixote, Nick Carraway to Bebb's Gatsby. When the ufologist is finished with him, Tono has come about as close as he will get to conversion in these novels. He almost catches the sound of his name, almost comes to terms with the life he has hugged to himself all these years, almost believes he can escape that hole he's been digging.

The new Tono helps us into a flurry of revelations. Disguised as Bertha, Babe has been terrorizing the neighborhood to make certain that Bertha will be ostracized by the townsfolk. His distrust of her, his venom, goes all the way back to Leo, of course. Most readers will have guessed that Sharon is not the adopted child of Leo Bebb but the natural one. And Bertha is her mother, the mother who has become overweight, silent, and ugly under the cloud of her guilt. One of the treasures in Bertha's suitcase is Leo's letter detailing the transfer of Bertha's love child, her source of shame, to Lucille and Leo after the death of their own child. We are to the bottom of Leo's secrets at last. The unveilings shed new light on everything for Sharon and for Antonio too. Tono has moved from Jimmy Bob Luby to the life-ray to the Lone Ranger and now recognizes in himself "a kind of panicky openness to almost any possibility, which I suspect must be, if not the same thing as what people like Bebb would call faith, at least its kissing cousin" (*Bebb* 501). It is an openness that came via dreams, and Tono concludes that "we are often closer to the truth in dreams than anywhere else" (*Bebb* 501). Tono's faith is not the same as Bebb's variety; let's be clear about that. Anyone trying to turn the *Bebb* novels into anything like an orthodox Christian statement has read very poorly. Tono finds enough of something to live by, and that's something, "a little touch of Leo in the night," maybe, as Gertrude puts it (*Bebb* 505).

Much of the humor of *Treasure Hunt* is of the darker sort, the "secret source of humor" being "sadness in the human heart," if Mark Twain had it right.[27] Poor Brownie feeling for those teeth, abandoning his false ones and, with them, the smile that has defined him for five hundred pages, has had his battle with the silence of God. He has listened hard and heard nothing. And his new faith in Babe starts to look tenuous. When Babe spews his final poison in the closing pages, poison that is the sad product of his years of hatred for his brother, he casts down the gauntlet for both Brownie and Tono. "There's miseries in this world enough to make a stone weep," Babe decrees, and goes on to list a good many of them. Brownie weeps as Babe repeats just what Tono has himself confessed—he'd believe it if he could. "Leo was all the time preaching hold tight to Jesus, hold tight to Jesus," Babe complains. "It's like a drowning man holding tight to water," Babe finishes (*Bebb* 515). Brownie is winded. Now Babe lets Tono "have it" (*Bebb* 515). "Father, Son, and Holy Smoke, you ever laid eyes on that crowd, Antonio Parr?" (*Bebb* 515), Babe asks. Most everything hinges on Tono's answer, his opportunity to be Peter or Judas or just some ordinary chump trying to sneak through. He thinks out an answer—"I know what I've looked at but not what I've seen"—good as far as it goes (*Bebb* 515). It has that tentativeness, can go either way. But what he says is nothing. As with Jesus before Pilate, it is the silence that speaks. Gertrude tries with words. "The Mystery is deep and holy, and you have baby eyes that see only the nasty surfaces of things and the shiny toys in the sky," she tells Babe (*Bebb* 516). But the silence works better. In the scuffle that follows, Brownie falls dead. His last word may have been "dear" (*Bebb* 518).

It is a heart attack that fells Brownie, though the dramatic reversals in his faith life must have had a good bit to do with his death. "He'd had Bebb shot out from under him and then Jesus. He'd given up Holy Love because he couldn't make the rough places of Scripture smooth anymore even for himself. . . . Then he'd latched on to Babe only to discover the terrible truth about him," Tono figures (*Bebb* 520). Ruin is all over the stage as Sharon realizes that the whole terrible drama of her parents' lives was about guilt, a remorse so deep that it covered everything, a ruinous blanket. Babe has spent a lifetime wreaking vengeance, Bertha a lifetime of shameful hiddenness, Sharon a lifetime of bewilderment, and then there's Leo. Sharon explains, "I don't think he ever got over it. I think every crazy, half-ass thing he ever did was on account of it. . . . He was trying to get it out where somebody could tell him it wouldn't count against him forever" (*Bebb* 523).

Like its predecessors, *Treasure Hunt* is much about the inevitability of brokenness, but this time Buechner seems to direct us toward the central question: forgiveness or nastiness? Do we find ways to live *in spite of* instead of *in spite*? Such is Tono's question, too. Tony and Laura wait back in Sutton, and the glue has still been drying on Tono and Sharon's reunion during the road trip to Poinsett. Can he have faith in his marriage again? In himself? In some kind of God out there prowling in and out of his life to coax him toward laughter?

Several of the 1971 reviews of *Lion Country* appeared alongside reviews of the new Walker Percy novel, *Love in the Ruins*, published at about the same time. Also featuring a lapsed Catholic, Percy's novel tackled metaphysical questions via subtle routes and suggestiveness, in ways that invite comparison to Buechner's approach. Percy argued that "the novel is at its best when the story bears some relation of truth to one's own story."[28]

Despite topical references and moments of stunning insight into the realities of our day-to-day landscapes, the *Bebb* novels mostly inhabit a land readers can only laugh and cry and shake our heads over. Central characters like Babe, Bertha, Gertrude, Brownie, and Leo, of course, are drawn so large as to become caricatures, oversized versions of people we've known perhaps, but so outsized as to force us to keep our distance. Poinsett, like Armadillo, is just a bit out of reach. But that's the outward dimension of these novels, and what Percy really means is that the truly good novels are those where "the reader is affirmed in his deepest and most inward experience" (Percy 358). We turn to Huckleberry Finn or Hester Prynne or Holden Caulfield or Antonio Parr, not so much because we identify with the outward circumstances of their lives, but because we recognize their inward battles. We recognize the battles because they are our battles too.

Percy's words on the subject appeared in his 1987 speech "Morality and Religion," in which he specifically considered the problem of the novelist as believer. Recognizing the train wreck that any novel that "sets out to be uplifting" would be, Percy went on to argue that a believer-novelist can, nonetheless, tell the truth (Percy 362). "Bad books always lie," he concluded: "They lie most of all about the human condition, so that one never recognizes oneself, the deepest part of oneself, in a bad book" (Percy 364). The truth we are after, Percy believed, is "a deeper truth about the way things are, the way people are . . . a truth about the human condition . . . a truth of such an order, both old and new, that one recognizes oneself in it. Therein lies the pleasure" (Percy 365–66). I am convinced that the joy-jaunt of a journey that *The Book of Bebb* provides is tied up in the way Buechner gets to those inward, universal questions, successfully connecting them to the reader's own metaphysical puzzlements. His allusions more private school than not, his references more *New York Times* than not, his scenes more incredible than not, Buechner nonetheless manages to pull his readers into connection, inner connection.

The possibility of faith remains the persistent theme of Buechner's work. The *Bebb* novels reinforce Buechner's assumptions that humankind, lost and desperate, searches for meaning and self-identity, desires to be fully known, and can arrive, through the paradox of simultaneous belief and unbelief, at a perception of grace. Horton Davies pointed out that the reader never really knows if Bebb's exhibitionism is deliberate or accidental; Buechner refuses to solve the mystery (HDavies 192). Is Bebb a fraud or an innocent or, as is more likely, an ambiguous combination of belief and unbelief? As it turns out, Bebb's authenticity—like the whiskey priest's, like Nicolet's—is far less important than what happens through him. Bebb is, as the Gospel writer has it, "the Word made flesh,"[29] and Leo Bebb is flesh indeed. Bebb's message, as Woelfel summarized, comprises "a gospel of pure, unbounded love undergirded by a profound and graphic sense of human pain and tragedy" (Woelfel 287). One critic even labeled the *Bebb* books "unorthodox inspiration," a phrase that captured something of the achievement Buechner pulls off here.[30]

The preoccupation with Bebb as a vessel of message, along with the vivid characterizations of the *Bebb* novels, has invited comparisons to Flannery O'Connor. Buechner's repeated use of ambiguous protagonists as channels of grace suggests Graham Greene, J. F. Powers, and Robertson Davies. John Skow's 1972 *Time* article compared Buechner to Peter DeVries,[31] and there's the Fitzgerald aura I've mentioned several times. I've also mentioned a handful of writers with whom Buechner shares the believer-as-writer project. Thompson suggested that Buechner be placed with his contemporaries Saul Bellow and John Updike in his rendering of "ordinary human experience" as a key to ultimate significance (Thompson 157). I'm not sure that I would designate the experience of the *Bebb* books as "ordinary," but Buechner's work does display a distinct consonance with the work of many writers of his generation. That said, he remains distinctly apart from these writers, some of whom he claims never to have read. He didn't come to O'Connor until the mid-1980s, well after Bebb was loose in the world. Buechner was the first to point me to the connections between O'Connor and Diane Arbus, suggesting that O'Connor's stories have "the same power and limitations" as Arbus's photographs of freaks,[32] so he certainly understands what O'Connor was up to with her theory of the grotesque, may have even been up to the same business in the *Bebb* chronicles. Although he admires Walker Percy's "way with words," Buechner finds Percy somewhat "barren and unconvincing."[33] Less allegorical than O'Connor and more affirmative than Percy, Buechner is singular in his certainty about uncertainty. With Leo Bebb, Buechner has been practicing for Godric, both of them characters of more saintliness than either of them imagine and both, in most ways, lost in a dark wood. Godric will think of life as "a tune that ends before you've heard it out," another of those Buechnerisms that work well as summary lines (*Godric* 51).

Unbelief certainly has its say in the tetralogy. If we work toward anything here, it is not uplift and consolation; no smuggled-in moral or bold-faced lesson will wrap up the story of Antonio Parr, Leo Bebb, and the others. When Babe summarizes Sharon's story as "got in shame and born to grief," he has it mostly right (*Bebb* 517). But when she orders him out of her kitchen, some reversal begins. Thinking that Buechner has found his villain at last, we more or less expect Babe to slink off into the night, lucky to have escaped prosecution for one of his many crimes and deceptions. For Jesus and Leo Bebb, Sharon decides to move the Lubys into her house. Bertha will be going on to Connecticut and a new life with her new-found daughter. But we should be ready for the Buechner rug pulling by now. As Babe walks toward his car to leave, Bertha hurries to his side; he "doesn't have anybody," she cries, and we are forced to rethink the whole Babe business—maybe there's hope for him as well (*Bebb* 525). We leave Poinsett with a view of Jimmy Bob and his family, rescued from their trailer-park nightmare, as they wave the pilgrims goodbye. When Gertrude offers, "Well, there is nothing nicer you could have done for Jesus than that," Tono adds, "Maybe that's who that was out there with his rubber pants filled" (*Bebb* 527). Just the sort of thing Leo would have said. Tono has one last visitation on the journey home. In a hotel in Charlottesville, he dreams of Babe and Leo in a boat that each of them is trying to row. Of course, they are working against each other, so the boat only goes in circles—the long-known incompleteness, the waste, the ugliness. Buechner is stunningly honest about the mire. Tono's skepticism slips here and there but stays pretty much healthy all the journey along. Yet *The Book of Bebb* is not awash with cynicism and doom. Buechner manages a middle ground, what Ozick calls "sanctifying the profane" (Ozick 36).

Lion Country more or less begins with a song on a car radio, and Buechner circles back now to another such song. Tony Orlando and Dawn have the tune of the summer, "Tie a Yellow Ribbon Round the Old Oak Tree," the song that pulls the weary bunch toward home and a lawn bedecked by yellow ribbons, yellow toilet paper, and a sign hanging on Tono's infamous mobile: "The sign on it said WELCOME HONE, that last little leg of the M missing because my son Bill either didn't remember about it or had run out of steam by then stringing all that toilet paper around. It seemed oddly fitting. It was good to get home, but it was home with something missing or out of whack about it" (*Bebb* 529).

We are there at last, but just where are we? Tono pauses to think of Brownie and what-ifs and might-have-beens before returning to the oddly appropriate sign: "WELCOME HONE the sign said, and I can't help thinking again of Gideon and Barak, of Samson and David and all the rest of the crowd that I had mentioned to Brownie once, who, because some small but crucial thing was missing, kept looking for it come hell or high water wherever they went till their eyes were dim and their arches fallen"

(*Bebb* 529). So Tono's story is ours, after all. It is Gideon and David. It is Babe and Gertrude, and "Jimmy Bob Luby's father even, with the mean-looking, caved-in upper lip—who knows what far bank he wades toward in his dreams" (*Bebb* 530). There's mercy enough to go around, and maybe transformation too, as Tono brings us up to date. "I leave HONE to teach track and irony to the young only to come back again to make amends if I can, to make peace, make love when I can," he says (*Bebb* 530). The slight melancholy, the wistfulness, mixes still with the promise to get up and keep moving, if not charging, forward.

But there's more than that. Buechner takes the novel at last to a line from *King Lear* that plays prominently in *Telling the Truth: The Gospel in Tragedy, Comedy, and Fairy Tale*. (The line will also show up in the title of Buechner's 2001 book, *Speak What We Feel [Not What We Ought to Say]: Reflections on Literature and Faith*.) Tono tells us that he's tried to tell the truth in this account of his life, accurately recording "the weight of this sad time," as Shakespeare's Edgar puts it, to say what he feels at all costs (*Bebb* 530). In the maelstrom of these lives destroyed and those hanging by threads of one sort or another, Tono feels the absence, the something "that is always missing" (*Bebb* 530). He's not even sure that he has "ever seen it even from afar," and he is enough like most of us that he "can hear a dim humming in the tracks," the press of age coming on and questions still unanswered (*Bebb* 530). Buechner could have ended with that, I suppose—Marvell, Shakespeare, and trying without quite enough light to see by. But Tono has one more truth to tell; he also hears "something else" at the core of his search. Not "'Hi-yo Silver. Away' echoing across the lonely sage, perhaps, "but the faint chunk-chunk of my own moccasin heart, of the Tonto afoot in the dusk of me somewhere who . . . whispers '*Kemo Sabe*' every once in a while to what may or may not be only a silvery trick of the fading light" (*Bebb* 530). The commitment in the last scene of *Love Feast*—to "living it out with something like grace"—endures to the final feeling of *Treasure Hunt* (*Bebb* 404). The homesickness, the tentativeness, the "may or may not" persists to the end and pushes forward into *Godric*, now on the horizon. But maybe Leo Bebb did something big for Jesus after all.

Notes

1. Cynthia Ozick, "Open Heart," *New York Times Book Review*, June 11, 1972, 4. Hereafter cited as Ozick.
2. Bill Bruns, "Instant-minister Racket," *Life*, November 14, 1969, 67–78.
3. Em Griffin, "An Afternoon with Frederick Buechner," *Wheaton Alumni*, September/October 1983, 4. Hereafter cited as Griffin.

4. James Buie, "Buechner," *Books & Religion* 16, no. 1 (Winter 1989): 18. Hereafter cited as Buie.

5. Personal correspondence, May 19, 1990.

6. Benjamin DeMott, "The World according to Bebb," *Atlantic*, September 1979, 89. Hereafter cited as DeMott.

7. Marie-Helene Davies, "Fools for Christ's Sake: A Study of Clerical Figures in DeVries, Updike and Buechner," *Thalia* 6, no. 1 (1983): 67.

8. Roger Dionne, "Novel Lists," *Los Angeles Times*, November 11, 1979, 14.

9. William Pritchard, "Stranger than Truth," *Hudson Review* 24, no. 2 (Summer 1971): 362.

10. Rosemary F. Deen, *Commonweal* 94 (July 23, 1971): 388. Hereafter cited as Deen.

11. Guy Davenport, "*Lion Country*," *New York Times Book Review*, February 14, 1971, 7.

12. John C. Skow, *Time*, April 12, 1971, 84.

13. Kurt Hoeksema, "Bebb Revisited," *Cornerstone* 20, no. 95 (1979): 18.

14. Steven Kroll, *Choice* 8 (September 1971): 829.

15. David Littlejohn, *Saturday Review* 54 (February 20, 1971): 35.

16. Paul A. Doyle, *Best Sellers* 30 (March 1, 1971): 524.

17. Paul Theroux, *Book World*, May 28, 1972, 4.

18. Roger Sale, *Hudson Review*, Winter 1974, 635.

19. Michael Mewshaw, review of *Love Feast*, *New York Times Book Review*, September 22, 1974, 3.

20. Frederick Buechner and Lee Boltin, *The Faces of Jesus* (New York: Simon & Schuster, 1974), 14.

21. Horton Davies, "Frederick Buechner and the Strange Workings of Grace," *Theology Today*, July 1979, 192–93.

22. Revelation 22:21.

23. B. M. Firestone, *Library Journal* 102 (June 15, 1977): 1403.

24. Christopher Lehmann-Haupt, "Enough Is as Good as a Feast," *New York Times*, September 25, 1974, 34.

25. Margaret Wimsatt, review of *Love Feast*, *America*, October 19, 1974, 219.

26. Julian Moynahan, "Saint? Charlatan? Both?" *New York Times Book Review*, October 30, 1977, 15.

27. Mark Twain, *Following the Equator* (New York: Harper & Bros., 1897), 101.

28. Walker Percy, *Signposts in a Strange Land* (New York: Farrar, Straus & Giroux, 1991), 359. Hereafter cited as Percy.

29. John 1:1.

30. Kathy Ewing, "Book of Revelations: Frederick Buechner's *Telling Secrets*," *Cleveland Edition*, February 7, 1991, 1.

31. John Skow, *Time*, July 3, 1972, 63.

32. Personal correspondence, June 26, 1986.

33. Personal correspondence, June 26, 1986.

Chapter Seven

Losing and Finding

Godric

In a note stuffed into the archival copy of the manuscript copy of his ninth novel, Buechner describes his entanglement in the life of a character beside whom even Leo Bebb waxes pale: "If I were to be remembered by only one book, this is the one I would choose. In every way it came unbidden, unheralded, as a blessing" (Archive, IV A 9). I have recorded here some of Buechner's stunning achievements reaching back to that summer in Maine when he and Jimmy Merrill decided to be writers, but the thirty-year apprenticeship yields an unquestionable masterpiece in 1980. *Godric* is one of those great books, the kind where we prolong the reading, dread turning that last page, because the journey has been so musical, the reverberation so complete as to rearrange the chords of our inner lives, the kind of book that makes you want to run up to strangers and ask them if they've read it.

The success of this novel is all the more surprising, as it is the most difficult read of all of Buechner's books. Those readers looking for neat chronology, for example, will be thwarted. From the opening page of the novel, Godric is unsure about time, wonders if he's "got time straight for once,"* and readers are plunged into a muddle of past, present, and future—a stream of consciousness that steers clear of mannerism as it reflects the mind of a very old man (*Godric* 3). Godric tells his story "from both its ends at once," covering his more than a century without much regard for orderly chronology (*Godric* 165). Students coming to *Godric* for the first time must deal with a Faulkner-like array of episodes arranged more or less randomly. The second challenge of the narrative comes with

Frederick and Judith Buechner
Circa 1980

the language. Buechner re-creates a Saxon feel for his novel, a twelfth-century visitation featuring pre-French-Latinate vocabulary. Although the Anglo-Saxon language is often archaic, context usually provides the sense, and most readers settle into the prose as part of the pleasure of the book. From the major news organs to book review pages all across the country, readers were remarkably effusive in their acclaim, and *all* of them mentioned the language as part of the triumph. The praise for *Godric* rivaled that which surrounded *A Long Day's Dying* thirty years before. No doubt the experimental narrative style and the era-appropriate diction were among the features drawing admiration from the Pulitzer Prize reviewers who made *Godric* a finalist for the award in 1981.

One of the ironies of *Godric* is that the book comes at a time of personal stress in Buechner's life, specifically during the early stages of a daughter's anorexia and "the attendant fear and frustration" her illness created for the whole family (Archive, IV A 9). In his memoirs Buechner records the terrible phone call that informed him of her hospitalization, the appalling news that "unless they started feeding her against her will, she would die" (*TS* 24). Caught up in his daughter's starvation, Buechner begins to recognize his own hunger. His dilemma this time is much deeper than it was when the critics panned *The Seasons' Difference* or when they were shrill about *The Final Beast*. The shadows are more ominous even than they were when he faced the feelings of irrelevance around the writing of *The Entrance to Porlock*. This time, he contends, he was "in hell," and the darkness he

Buechner's daughters
Left to right: Katherine, Sharman, Dinah

describes is not only that of the family tragedy (*TS* 25). He fears the loss of a daughter, yes, but also has, in some inexplicable way, almost lost himself as well. In midcareer, successful and productive, Buechner loses his way in a Dantean wood, and it is Saint Godric who helps him through—the "hard time" becomes a "fearsome blessing" (*TS* 24). His daughter slowly recovered herself, and Buechner limped back to life as well.

The dedication page of *Godric* yields one clue as to the crises of the time beyond his daughter's illness. The epigraph, which Buechner says, "excited him enormously" (Archive, IV A 9), reads: "*IN MEMORIAM PATRIS MEI ET AD MAIOREM DEI GLORIAM ATQUE SANCTI GODRICI*" (*Godric* vi). "In memory of my father," Buechner writes, as he returns to thoughts of his father, pondering still the conundrum of that suicide. Though he offers the dedication in Latin, in part as a way of coming at the subject obliquely, keeping the secret, as he puts it, he seems now to have learned that "although death ended my father, it has never ended my relationship with my father" (*TS* 22). Writing this new novel, his tenth, may well have saved Buechner's sanity in a dark time, he admits (*TS* 21), and the saving has as much to do with working out his father's absence as working through his daughter's illness. He's caught up in the issues of parenthood, looking both backward toward his father and forward toward his daughter. In retrospect Buechner notes that "nothing I've ever writ-ten came out of a darker time or brought me more light and comfort." Then he adds that the book also "brought me a sharper sense of the cru-cial role my father has always played in my life" (*TS* 21).

It is intriguing to note the progression of comments about *Godric* from Buechner. In *Now and Then*, written only two years after *Godric*, Buechner devotes only a few pages to the novel and makes little reference to auto-biographical forces that may have driven the work. Eight years later, in *Telling Secrets*, Buechner seems to have reflected more fully on the role of his personal circumstances in the creation of the novel. *Godric* is thus one of those books that outruns authorial intention, a book that "was not only a word *from* me," Buechner explains, but "also a word *to* me" (*TS* 21). A book about his daughter and about his father, *Godric* is also a canvas on which Buechner paints his preoccupation with his own aging, "trying on various ways of growing old and facing death," as he puts it in his 1983 memoir (*NT* 107). The character Godric became "a metaphor for growing old and facing the approach of one's own death," according to McCoy: "Godric presents a pattern for aging and dying that makes them acceptable, even creative" (McCoy 98). Can there be any doubt that wrestling with his father's untimely death, dealing with desperation at a daughter's tragedies, and reflecting on his own mortality propel Buechner toward a new summit as a novelist? "From old Godric I learned much about how to bear loss, great pain, and about faith in the face of despair and something like joy in the midst of great sadness and anxiety," Buechner concludes (Archive, IV A 9). Amid the new problems, there still looms the old fixations—laughter and tears and whether or not faith is a leg on which to stand.

Buechner often alludes to other events of the time, "providential events," he calls them, that swirl about in the writing of *Godric* (Archive, IV A 9). Godric is born out of Bebb; perhaps he "was actually Bebb in an earlier incarnation," Buechner admits, citing a notion abandoned along the way, though one that helped him to get started with the novel (*NT* 106). Godric takes Buechner into waters that he has not heretofore charted. He happened upon Godric, not in a barbershop as with Bebb, but while leafing through a Penguin paperback on saints. Coming upon an entry for Saint Godric, Buechner knew that "he was the one" (Archive, IV A 9). What Buechner seems to admire in Godric, what draws him from the start, is the "feet made very much of clay."[1] Fascinated by the brief paperback summary of Godric's life, Buechner had stumbled on a story shot through with shadows and complications, yet also a story through which God found a way to move. His Godric is reminiscent of the better-known Saint Augustine. An Augustinian tone perks in Godric's account of life on the run from God. Godric is no plaster saint, no model of piety. He is, like most of us, more bumbling than masterful, more miserable than devout. But to be touched by him is nonetheless to be transformed.

"A saint is a life-giver," Buechner says, and surely Buechner is drawn to Godric because he wants life for himself and those around him in this troubled time (Zinsser 120). The novel is not merely a book about miracles; it is something of a miracle itself. Like the first of the *Bebb* novels, *Godric* "came so quickly and with such comparative ease that there were times when I suspected that maybe the old saint himself was not entirely uninvolved in the process" (*NT* 106). Buechner sometimes describes the process as "mysterious" and claims that he "can't feel entirely responsible" for *Godric* (Zinsser 126). But many writers speak of the way the creative process outstrips their rational attempts to keep up, and Buechner may well simply be describing the way subconscious struggles work to produce art. Yeats had it that "the quarrel with others" produces rhetoric, while the "quarrel with ourselves" produces poetry.[2]

In Buechner's struggle with himself, the first stroke of providence was the paragraph on an obscure saint. The second surprising coincidence came in the pursuit of Godric's life. A copy of the original manuscript of the story was easy enough to procure via interlibrary loan from a nearby university, but Buechner's excitement over the project must have dimmed a bit when he opened the thin book to discover that the *Life of Godric* by Reginald of Durham had never been translated from its medieval Latin into English. As Buechner's study of Latin dated back more than forty years to his high school days at Lawrenceville, Reginald's prose presented an unanticipated obstacle. Within a day or two, Buechner recalls, his daughter Dinah, then a student at Groton School, phoned about bringing guests home for the weekend. Among the visitors, quite unexpectedly, was Hugh Sackett, then chair of the classics department at Groton. The translation was complete within two days.

Treating these events with characteristic ambivalence—maybe providence, maybe fortune—Buechner recalls the way being prepared for *Godric*. In the memoirs he wonders "if there are such things as accidents in matters like this" (*NT* 105–6). In a speech at the New York Public Library in the winter of 1987, Buechner records his discovery of Godric as "entirely by accident, or by grace, or by luck."[3] Thus Buechner hints that the story of Godric—"my saint," he calls Godric—is part of some divine drama that involves not only a rendering of a medieval character but also a rendering of Buechner himself (*NT* 106). He writes that Godric "came alive" for him, and one suspects that Buechner came alive for Godric as well (*Belfry* 23).

I am convinced that the confessions of Godric and the lessons he brought to Buechner influence the loosening of the tongue that breaks forth in Buechner's increasing willingness to reveal his own story. A most productive period for Buechner, the late 1970s saw the publication of both *Telling the Truth* (1977) and *Peculiar Treasures* (1979), and *Godric* was soon to be followed by the first of the many memoirs, *Sacred Journey* (1982). From *Godric* on, the memoirs proliferate—*Now and Then* (1983), *The Wizard's Tide* (1990), *Telling Secrets* (1991), *The Longing for Home* (1996), *The Eyes of the Heart* (1999), and various collected pieces in such volumes as *A Room Called Remember* (1984) and *The Clown in the Belfry* (1992). But Buechner's maturation as a novelist and as a thinker becomes most apparent in the theological position that mediates the story of Godric. With *Godric* Buechner focuses on a version of faith that opens to the possibility of transcendence without closing in on dogmatic propositions.

With the advent of the culture wars, we have forgotten nuance, this middle way. Buechner seems more than ever preoccupied with issues of faith as he writes of his saint, less inclined to hiddenness on matters of religion. This is, of course, partly because for half his life the historical Godric was an ascetic, a man pursuing a religious vocation. But beyond that obviously fertile territory, Buechner seems to want to talk openly about a faith that, fundamentally, allows room for doubt while, simultaneously, taking the God business quite seriously. While Horton Davies labeled Buechner "an imaginative apologist for the Christian faith" (HDavies 186), and many have tried to make of Buechner a spokesperson for Christianity, everything depends on what version of the faith Buechner is being assumed to represent. If the Christianity Davies referred to is that version that shows up on American television debates and radio talk shows, it just won't wash. What Buechner does speak for is an option somewhere between the hard-to-swallow tenets of evangelicalism and the hope-destroying fundamentals of abject secularism.

I might even go so far as to predict a growing readership for Buechner on these grounds alone. He represents a full-bodied alternative for literalist Christians as well as for unbelievers. As the shades of their walls turn from black and white to gray, both camps may find in Buechner a refreshing and helpful voice. I am speaking here of neither so-called liberal Christianity, a relatively meaningless bromide, nor New Ageism, an easy target for derisive laughter. Categorizing Buechner's theology in *Godric* as "psychological spirituality," Victoria Allen cited what she calls the "use of psychotherapeutic dynamics to convey spiritual truths" as the key to *Godric* (Allen 110). I am more comfortable saying that what Buechner represents in *Godric* is a robust take on faith, akin to mysticism perhaps and marvelously difficult to pin down. (Allen's summary of *Godric* as "the most telling example of the artist's unconscious conflicts producing art" was useful, although I think she may violate her own warnings against reducing a novel *merely* to an image of a writer's psychological conflict. Nonetheless, her understanding of the importance of therapy to what Buechner will produce after *Godric* is insightful and well taken.)

Godric is Buechner's clearest faith statement to this point in his career. Offering a way of faith that does not rest on an acceptance of improbable dogma, while keeping the door open to a glimmering possibility of divine action in the puzzle of human existence, Buechner rejects biblical literalism, doctrinal exclusivism, and pietistic moralism, while holding to the possibility that "the voice of silence calls," as one of Godric's mentors will put it (*Godric* 70). *Godric* calls forth applause on many fronts—the narrative voice, the diction, the point of view, the poetry—and Buechner senses the success. He becomes preoccupied with saints from this point on in his career. Although I have given considerable space here to the early work as the logical entryway to understanding the imposing edifice of a career, I concur with Buechner's own belief that it is by the later books that he'll stand or fall.[4] He often refers to the early books, especially *A Long Day's Dying* and *The Seasons' Difference*, with embarrassment, labeling them "juvenilia," and speaking of how they make him "cringe."[5] Asked to read the *Bebb* books for a 2004 recording, he speaks of his "near mortification" that he had written such books, created such scenes.[6]

If ordination gave him his subject, as he argues, then surely the discovery of the saints helped him to focus that subject.[7] He will revisit the theme of clay-footed saints in many versions, from Brendan, another historical saint, to the biblical Jacob in *Son of Laughter* and the Apocryphal Tobit in *On the Road with the Archangel*. He also has had countless, so far incomplete, runs at a version of the life of Mary Magdalene. Somehow, sainthood is the core subject he has been working toward all along. With *Godric*, he begins a new era.

Although *Godric* is not really a historical novel—Buechner is more interested in people than in history—Godric is a historical figure. The novel is woven from the cloth of the life of a twelfth-century saint. Buechner imagines his way between the lines of the historical sketch, choosing Godric from among the thousands of saints. Or did the choosing, as with Leo Bebb, perhaps run the other way? Peter Lewis, in the *Times Literary*

Supplement, called Buechner's approach to the hagiography "a stylistic tour de force."[8] Lewis admired the idiom that is "neither ancient nor modern but a bit of both cleverly combined" (Lewis 278). Although Lewis seemed not to notice the poetry, the iambic pentameter cadence that echoes in Buechner's prose and adds to the "mood of Lear on the heath,"[9] critics were quick to notice what one called "Chaucerian exuberance."[10] Peter Prescott, in his substantial review for *Newsweek*, understood the daring nature of the language as well as the subject: "Buechner has risked much in attempting to define the ambivalences in the life of a saintly man, and risked even more by adopting a language that could easily have become overwrought. . . . Godric glimmers brightly."[11]

Buechner's method is to alternate between the story of the saint as the aged Godric himself remembers it and the official biography as written by Reginald, the young Durham monk sent by Ailred, abbot of Rievaulx, to pen Godric's history. Buechner mixes in translations from Reginald's Latin and evokes an Anglo-Saxon atmosphere, creating, as the critics almost unanimously agreed, "a true work of art."[12] Officially, Godric, reputedly the first English lyrical poet, was born in Walpole (Norfolk), England, around 1065 and died at Finchale, near Durham, in 1170. His life breaks roughly into two parts: half a century of worldly pursuit and another half century as a cloistered ascetic. Beginning as a con artist, he bought a half share in a ship and sailed as a merchant, spending roughly sixteen years at sea. Some historians believe he is the *Gudericus Pirata* with whom Baldwin I sailed to Jaffa in 1102. Touched by an account of the life of Saint Cuthbert, Godric was apparently converted to Christianity around the same time. During a pilgrimage to Jerusalem, he was baptized in the Jordan River. Forswearing shoes from that day on, Godric served for a time as a house steward for a wealthy landowner, until he learned of the nobleman's immoral treatment of the tenants. After two more pilgrimages, one to Provence and one to Rome with his mother, Godric turned more exclusively to a religious calling.

Around 1105, he renounced his earthly possessions and home, joining the hermit Elric near Durham. At Durham he attended school with the choirboys and acted as bellringer for the Church of Saint Giles. Finally, he settled at Finchale on the lands of Bishop Runulf Flambard, along the river Wear. Practicing the austere life of a religious hermit and leaving Finchale only three times in the more than fifty years before his death, Godric survived on berries and roots and wore a hair shirt beneath a heavy iron breastplate—all part of his penance. He lived under the guardianship of the prior of Durham, Ailred of Rievaulx, who assigned the monk Reginald to the daunting biography. His life once threatened in a flood and later by brigands, Godric lived mostly alone, though he was said to have been a confidant to Pope Alexander III as well as to Thomas à Becket. Godric's sister, Burcwen, also shared his hermitage for a time before becoming a nun at a hospital in Durham.

In his later years, he became widely renowned as a holy man and healer, attracting pilgrims and gaining a reputation as a seer. His miraculous gifts were said to include discourse with animals, even snakes, which he treated as pets until they distracted him in his prayers. Reginald includes four lyrics in his account, songs that Godric claims to have heard in a vision. They are the oldest surviving English lyrics. Soon after his death in 1170, his tomb became a shrine where miracles were reported. Like many ancient saints, Godric was never formally canonized, though the Cistercian order adopted Godric early on as a symbol in their attempts to reform the church.[13] That is the back story, a sketchy history that is simple enough to tell. Buechner's novelistic version, however, resists paraphrase.

Although Buechner may "take his readers by surprise"[14] with the "daring departure"[15] of *Godric*, the novel is, despite the Chaucerian language and medieval aura, only a step away from the *Bebb* novels. In a vision Godric, like Tono, discovers his name, but Godric, unlike Tono, thinks he knows the source and implication of the revelation. In a picture reminiscent of Tono's dream, Godric describes his vision: "His face was the holiest face I ever saw. My very name turned holy on his tongue. If he had bade me rise and follow to the end of time, I would have gone. If he had bade me die for him, I would have died. When I deserved it least, God gave me most. I think it was the Savior's face itself I saw" (*Godric* 144).

The operative phrase in Godric's visitation, however, is "I think." Godric is never quite sure of himself or his God. Like Antonio Parr, Peter Cowley, and Theodore Nicolet, Godric is another of Buechner's God-haunted heroes, and Godric's life, as imagined by Buechner, resounds with the ambiguous mixture of human frailty and saintliness. In a substantial interview with Buechner in 1989, Harold Fickett took Buechner to the crucial question that has dogged the heels of O'Connor, Percy, Greene, and a host of others who have tried to write from faith or about faith. Asked if "having a dogma to which you ascribe" is a "limiting thing," Buechner answers, "I don't feel it limiting at all. I think my faith, the effect it's had on my imagination, the effect it's had on me, is that it has made me open my eyes much wider and kept my ears much more acute than anything else I ever got involved in. If the God I have faith in really is, then who knows where I may not find him, and that's a lot of what my fiction is about"

(*Image* 55). So it is not just the story of the erstwhile saint that attracts the novelist here; it is also the territory of faith, the inquiry into belief, toward which Godric's story opens.

Another way to consider Buechner's career as the 1980s open has to do with his evolving role as interpreter of a lost religious vocabulary. Anticipating such books as *The Alphabet of Grace* (1970) and *Wishful Thinking* (1973), Buechner's 1966 sermon collection, *The Magnificent Defeat*, includes a note about the meaningful words of the Christian faith: "There was a time when such words as *faith, sin, redemption*, and *atonement* had great depth of meaning, great reality; but through centuries of handling and mishandling they have tended to become such empty banalities that just the mention of them is apt to turn people's minds off like a switch" (*MD* 111). *Godric* becomes another venue in which Buechner can furnish those significant religious words—especially such words as *sin* and *forgiveness, guilt* and *grace*—with sharper colors and shocking contrast in a narrative that, despite the archaisms, has astonishing relevancy. Indeed, a surprising number of the critics made the point that Godric was "like all of us . . . remarkably human."[16]

"Five friends I had, and two of them snakes," reads the captivating first line of Godric's tale, and Buechner gets quickly to the poetic rhythm of his prose, the wildness of tone, and the mysteries of his central character (*Godric* 3). In the opening pages of the novel, Godric flits about in his past, remembering his five friends and the coming of the bothersome Reginald. He also signals something of his efforts to conquer lust. The presentiments at the outset suggest that Godric's problems have something to do with sexuality, as he speaks of sitting in the freezing river Wear "to teach a lesson" to "old One-eye" (*Godric* 3). The river becomes a character in the novel, the place of Godric's hermitage, the site of his penances, and the symbol of time that carries everything away. When he is very old and feeble, he will have the river brought to him in the form of a small pool in which he continues his self-chastisement. Meandering into a narrative flow that accurately reflects the atmosphere of the mind—past, present, and future all surging into one jumbled current—the old man speaks wistfully of Fairweather and Tune, his companion snakes, who lived long years with him until he banished them for disturbing his devotions. They are the first two friends. Roger Mouse is the third, a disreputable brigand with whom Godric sails as a pirate, though "Mouse's sin smacked less of evil than of larkishness the likes of which Our Lord himself could hardly help but wink at when he spied it out in whore and prodigal" (*Godric* 4). Thus Godric gives himself away, reveals his essential compassion, remembering his friends to absolve them, to pray for them.

The fourth friend, Ailred, the abbot, has done Godric only one "bad turn," and even that was "from love," Godric admits (*Godric* 6). "He sent me Reginald," Godric mutters, and the plot immediately thickens (*Godric* 6). Commissioning the inexperienced monk, Reginald, to put Godric's life "on parchment. . . . To unbushel the light of your days," Ailred brings about a central complication of the novel, the tilt between Reginald and Godric (*Godric* 6). Godric's response to Ailred's scheme bespeaks his whimsy as well as his deep regret about his actual history: "Did he but know where Godric's path has led or what sights his light has lit, he'd bushel me back fast enough. I've told Mother Reginald tales to rattle his beads and blush his fishbelly tonsure pink as a babe's bum, but he turns it all to treacle with his scratching quill. I scoop out the jakes of my remembrance, and he censes it all with his clerkish screed till it reeks of mass" (*Godric* 6). With the reference to "jakes," Buechner returns to a debate that reaches back at least as far as *The Final Beast*. Godric's cry is another excremental lament; his life, he thinks, is mere waste, sewage, and Reginald is turning it into sweetness, mawkishness.

From here, the novel swings on the question of which reporter we should believe—Reginald, the official biographer; Godric, the one who lived the life after all; or some third story that we intuit for ourselves, a story suspended in the space between the two versions recorded here, Buechner's version, perhaps. For Godric, "nothing human's not a broth of false and true," a line I early on underscored as pivotal to both Buechner's novelistic career and his theological positions (*Godric* 31). In memorable prose, Buechner fastens on the problem of truth, realizes that any story has many versions; all perspectives are limited and partial. The tension of the novel, then, fixes on the expurgated saint's life Reginald is writing and Godric's own earthy and guilt-ridden story. Godric, as he sees himself, deserves no regard: "Know Godric's no true hermit but a gadabout within his mind, a lecher in his dreams. Self-seeking he is and peacock proud. A hypocrite" (*Godric* 21). Yet this worldly Godric has a fifth friend, Gillian, an angelic presence, who appears to him during his journey from Rome and who somehow inspires the rugged, unlettered Godric to reach for something beyond the pain of his own life.

Buechner manages to pull readers into the story of his saint and the odd collection of friends not only through the rhythm of the prose and the marvel of the language, but also through a distinct humor. When Godric claims that he has forgotten his father's face and will "by God's mercy" someday forget Reginald's face, we get something of the comic interaction that provides part of the delight of the novel (*Godric* 7). But Gillian,

Godric claims, he will "not forget" (*Godric* 7). The five friends have left marks on Godric, Gillian more than the others. It is their absence that Godric remembers as he drifts from first-person into third-person terms—"When Godric banished Fairweather and Tune, they all three bled for it,"—not when *I* banished . . . (*Godric* 7). Sometimes it is as if Godric has already died and is being described from afar. Buechner finds a way to combine narrative techniques. Godric is Tono *and* Leo, Nick Carraway *and* Jay Gatsby. But the marks of his friends translate into those human marks we all bear.

"What's friendship, when all's done, but the giving and taking of wounds?" Godric mutters in one of those pithy Buechnerisms that remind us that the author is still around somewhere, and the story of an obscure hermit is actually our story as well (*Godric* 7). The opening chapter sets up the whole scheme—friends won and lost, Godric's doubts about himself, and his suspicions of Reginald, earthiness and holiness in dramatic mixture. Godric ends the chapter with a prayer for mercy for his five friends, himself, and even Reginald, if God's beneficence can "reach so far" (*Godric* 8).

The unexpurgated version of Godric's life includes little fear of the divine or the human. "He wenched and broiled. He peddled, gulled and stole," Godric reports (*Godric* 48). His confession, early in the novel, both reveals and conceals:

> I started out as rough a peasant's brat and full of cockadoodledoo as any. I worked uncleanness with the best of them or worst. I tumbled all the maids who would suffer me and some that scratched and tore like weasels in a net. I planted horns on many a goodman's brow and jollied lads with tales about it afterward. I took up peddling as my trade. I cozened and tricked the way a baker yeasts his loaves till they are less of bread than air. I passed off old for new. I let out pence at usury. I swore me false. A flatterer I was. A wanderer. I thieved and pirated. I went to sea. Such things as happened then are better left unsaid. (*Godric* 20)

The part left "unsaid" here is, of course, the mystery that drives the plot. Just what is it that Godric has done? What has driven him to such extremes of remorse? Why does he think himself beyond the reach of divine mercy? The early pages of the novel record Godric's days as a peddler and thug, but he always seems to be holding something back, sparing Reginald "things far worse" as a way of "sparing Godric," he admits (*Godric* 21).

Having introduced his friends, Godric turns to family in the second section of his story. (Buechner divides *Godric* into brief chapters with headings more or less summarizing the material of each section. The method not only conjoins perfectly with the picaresque style of the narrative, but it also reflects the chaos of Godric's mind, his inability to sustain one memory for very long. The jumbled order of the memories and the switching points of view suggest senility, and the random paging through the book of Godric's life is perfectly reflected in the way Buechner divides the narrative.) When Godric speaks of his father, Aedlward, he is speaking of a dimly remembered presence, lost before he was known, not unlike Buechner's own memories of his father. "If Aedlward and Godric meet in Paradise, they'll meet as strangers do and never know," Godric confesses (*Godric* 10). But Aedwen, his mother, is another matter indeed. Reginald describes Aedwen as "Friend of Blessedness," and Godric agrees that "she was a friend to all" (*Godric* 11). A presence throughout the novel, Aedwen contributes basic wisdom to her son. We most often hear her laughing, or is she weeping? "Laugh till you weep. Weep till there's nothing left but to laugh at your weeping. In the end it's all one," Godric believes (*Godric* 11). That's Aedwen's kind of wisdom.

Then there's a brother and a sister. William is "owlish," backward and innocent. "Words were the line that moored him to the world," Godric observes, drawing consistently on the nautical imagery that would be natural for the ancient mariner he is (*Godric* 13). The talkative William is half of a "wry pair" (*Godric* 12). The other half is the sister, Burcwen—"merry and mad" (*Godric* 12). Burcwen and William are still children when Godric, a young man in his twenties, nearly loses his life to the sea. Battling a porpoise, Godric finds himself pulled far from shore and at the mercy of the tide. What happens then may be, Godric thinks, a miracle. He wakes with Burcwen's breath bringing him back his own. Having narrowly escaped drowning, he's learned that "the sea's a killer," that "Burcwen's heart was his," and—most surprisingly—"that it was Jesu saved him from the sea" (*Godric* 16). Two currents at least flow from here through Godric's story: the deep connection to Burcwen and the enduring question as to what Jesu may have been up to by saving him.

The comedy of *Godric* turns out to carry the novel's most potent points, and the laughter seems to emerge most in the moments of sparring between Godric and Reginald over the meaning of the snatches of his life Godric reveals. Reginald will make a great deal of the near-drowning narrative, of course, and Godric often objects to Reginald's spin on the past. For example, when Reginald parses the meaning of "Godric" as Saxon for

"God's reign," Godric argues that "ric" is Erse for "wreck"; thus his name signifies "God's wreck." He explains, "God's wreck I be, it means. God's wrecked Godric for his sins. Or Godric's sins have made a wreck of God" (*Godric* 17). Reginald interprets Godric's anger about the name to be an aspect of saintly humility, as Godric rants on about the Welsh translation of Godric being "not fit for monk's ears" (*Godric* 18).

Actually, Godric in the Welsh probably means "God's mirror," but the argument about the name stands for much here. Buechner intimates that even the most saintly are, if truth be aired, full of "dead men's bones,"[17] regrets, and unloveliness. But Godric's ugliness is not the last thing. Just as Bebb earns the grudging attention of Antonio, Godric's worst cannot negate the direction of his life—the hope toward which he has aimed himself. "As a man dies many times before he's dead," Godric quips, "so does he wend from birth to birth until, by grace, he comes alive at last" (*Godric* 99). Buechner's words here sound like those of C. S. Lewis, who also spoke often of the possibility of rebirth. "This world is a great sculptor's shop," according to Lewis: "We are the statues and there is a rumour going round the shop that some of us are some day going to come to life."[18] Godric's faith is the best of fairy tale, and he reiterates it in the lines Buechner uses as the last words of one volume of memoirs: "What's lost is nothing to what's found, and all the death that ever was, set next to life, would scarcely fill a cup" (*Godric* 96). The sentence is an accurate summary of Godric's hope, as well as a succinct version of Buechner's theology—death acknowledged and more than death embraced.

Godric has left home in search of God knows what, and he understands more about the lostness than the foundness of things. Young Godric bids farewell to his family to go in search of a door that may or may not be "heaven's door," and he has to tie Burcwen to a tree to keep her from coming along (*Godric* 24). Voices from Godric's long-ago adventures crowd into the story as Godric recounts his first professions—peddling nuns' hair and, later, selling false relics dipped in cat blood. Taking advantage of the gullible religious folk proves easy enough until he is ordered out of the territory, but the human zeal to embrace the miraculous, this vulnerability to deception, sets up as another of the considerations running through the novel. In his latter years, Godric will himself become the object of hope for pilgrims who want merely to touch his gnarled hands, his ragged robe. He will be more sympathetic with their longing at the near-end of his days but no more sure of where God is as they spill their prayers for healing.

Restless still, full of longing, the young Godric moves on to the Isle of Farne, where he meets Saint Cuthbert. Is Cuthbert a dream, a ghost, or a vision? Godric admits any of these possibilities, since Cuthbert has been long dead when Godric meets him on the lonely island. Godric's longing speaks in his first words about Cuthbert, words with a certain Tono-like ring of familiarity: "His lips were still, but had he opened them to speak my name, I think that I'd have followed to the world's far rim" (*Godric* 35). Godric is desperate for someone to tell him the secret of things, the meaning of his survival in the sea, the meaning of his homesickness, and Cuthbert translates his emptiness for him. When Godric claims that he came to Farne "by chance," Cuthbert tells him that "When a man leaves home he leaves behind some scrap of his heart" (*Godric* 37). Thinking of Burcwen and his father, Godric understands that easily enough. Then Cuthbert claims, "It's the same with a place a man is going to. Only then he sends a scrap of his heart ahead" (*Godric* 37). When Godric inquires about where this place might be, Cuthbert can only say, "Until you reach it, every other place you find will fret you like a cage" (*Godric* 37). Having listened to an explanation of his spiritual homesickness, having seen a spirit of holiness, and having heard of the possibilities of providence, Godric kneels before Cuthbert to confess, weeping with shame. Cuthbert tells him, "Do good" (*Godric* 38). But Godric has just begun his career as a reprobate. Falling asleep beside Cuthbert, he wakes to Roger Mouse, and we are off on more misadventures.

Pulled back for a moment to the present, we see the demeaning picture of the aged Godric being tended by the lackey, Reginald. Buechner seems to consider the cruel joke that "inside his wrecked and ravaged hull, there sails a young man still" (*Godric* 40). The old man's memories and dreams nearly overwhelm his prayers. We never know, in fact, when Godric is dreaming, so lost is he in fleeting images from the past and startling snapshots of the future. He is never quite sure himself. Word of his sanctity has spread afar, but Godric knows about religious delusion. He admits to having kissed a leper but will not investigate the stories that leper was cleansed—"pride lies one way, rue the other," he knows (*Godric* 42). There's the Buechnerian mix, always the blur of tragedy and comedy, lost and found, yes and no. When pilgrims come craving his touch, Godric sees the irony: "Could I but touch the churlishness within myself or kiss old Godric clean!" (*Godric* 42). He gives grace to others but cannot extend it to himself. His sins are more than God can bear, he thinks, and in his dreams he takes us back to Roger Mouse on the deck of the *Saint Espirit*. With Mouse, Godric piles up treasure while ignoring Cuthbert's bidding that he "do good." "Goodness was not Godric's meat," he confesses (*Godric* 44). He even goes so far as to deny his proper name—Godric becomes Deric, the "good" or the "god" omitted.

Reminiscent of Augustine's testimony of "licking the stinking sore" of the flesh, Godric's account of his villainy with Mouse reeks of an abandonment to the worst in himself (Augustine 32). Their crimes run to the bilking of pilgrims, rape, and more. Taking advantage of gullible pilgrims in need of transport to holy sites, Godric and Mouse provide the ship and take turns leading the pirate gang that attacks their own passengers. They are even known to add a surcharge to their transportation fees before the pilgrims can get from the anchorage to shore. Godric speaks of his riches piling up "like dung" and summarizes his state with the line, "He feared God little, men still less" (*Godric* 48).

Godric plays the prodigal, far from home, but there's an "And yet. And yet" (*Godric* 49). Sometimes he does go back to his holy place, the Isle of Farne, where he first saw Cuthbert. He goes to bury his ill-gotten treasure. Once he even catches a glimpse of Cuthbert, whose face seems to be "full of grief" (*Godric* 49). Something is gnawing at Deric. The treasure, of course, is an allusion to Christ's words about one's treasure and one's heart.[19] The question now is who will win this battle, Deric or Godric, Roger Mouse or Cuthbert? It must be said as well that, even in the years of profane roistering, Godric learns much from Roger Mouse and will be fond of him to the end. Godric sees Mouse's death in a vision many years after they've quarreled and parted. What Godric will remember are Mouse's characteristic words, "LIVE! LIVE!" (*Godric* 44). "He lived and gave me lessons in the art," Godric says (*Godric* 44). So Godric searches for capital-letter life, occasionally turning from the jakes of his false treasure to dream of some other treasure that he cannot name.

He finally turns his feet toward home, but not toward repentance. He carries in his heart only "an empty place," as he puts it (*Godric* 51). At home he discovers that his father has died. "It's like a tune that ends before you've heard it out," Godric mourns, and Buechner manages to capture his own longing along with that of his old saint (*Godric* 51). Back with the remnant of his family, Godric finds only a "snarl of false and true," awkwardness with Burcwen, anger at the father's absence, and a mad proposal from Aedwen that they go on pilgrimage to Rome to pray Aedlward on his way (*Godric* 54). Interrupting himself again, Godric delays the story of Rome to flit to other memories, among them the story of his rescue from a flood and a wonderfully comic scene of Ailred and Godric perched on top of the church Godric has built beside the Wear.

We also get here the first mention of Perkin; neither friend nor family but somehow more than either, Perkin is the boy who serves Godric, the mischievous lad whom old Godric loves, an image of the son Godric has

never had, the life he's not to have. When Buechner does readings from
Godric, he often turns to a passage where Perkin has convinced Godric to
carve out his own coffin and convinces Godric to climb in to check the fit.
Suddenly, Perkin clambers in beside Godric, and Godric knows that his
tomb "will be less lonely for knowing that my boy once lay there too"
(*Godric* 98). Godric's attachment to Perkin certainly captures the wistful
reality of the missing connection with Aedlward and probably shines some
light on Buechner's own pensiveness about what might have been with his
own father. Godric's memories all drift together. He wonders, "Am I daft,
or is it true there's no such thing as hours past and other hours still to pass,
but all of them instead are all there at once and never gone?" (*Godric* 57).

So Godric heads off at the behest of a dead father, who never did much
for Godric in life. And Rome is a disappointment. The Godric who heads
to Rome is a hollow emptiness trying to carry the burden of the ugliness
he has seen without and felt within. Farne is far away. And God seems not
to be in Rome, though Ailred will say, years later, that "God's never gone. . . .
It's only men go blind" (*Godric* 61). Maybe God was there, but, for the still
young Godric, Rome is "a corpse without a shroud" (*Godric* 62). Buechner's take on Rome calls to mind James Joyce's similar observation: "Rome
reminds me of a man who lives by exhibiting to travelers his grandmother's corpse."[20] Even the pope who passes through the crowd seems
to be looking for the absent God. In a tumult of religious noise, the genuine article is submerged.

The real power of the pilgrimage turns out to be the trip home. Having
reached the point of his deepest desolation in Rome, where God turns out
to be blind and deaf, Godric can find no words to even try to speak to this
God. Then he has another vision. In his dream, he watches as a bear gorges
himself on sweet fruit and then "voids all that sweetness out its hinder part"
(*Godric* 66). It is friend Gillian who explains the vision and is herself part
of the vision. Godric is the bear, of course, turning "to dung the precious
fruit" of "Christ's sweet grace and charity" (*Godric* 66–67). Like Chaucer's
troupers, Godric and Aedwen join other pilgrims on their return journey,
but it is Gillian's few appearances that make all the difference. She is his
angel, his conscience, his call to repentance. Godric complains to her of
the great quiet in Rome. "I prayed to him in Rome," Godric cries; "It was
like praying down an empty well" (*Godric* 70). When Gillian answers that
some voice may be calling in the silence and urges Godric to listen more
carefully, Godric confesses his "thirst," his great longing (*Godric* 70).

Readers often recognize Godric's admission of need as one of several
conversion moments in this narrative. Although I grant the point, I am

somewhat wary of that suggestive word, "confession." Godric has not suddenly stepped from darkness into light. Despite the biblical allusions and the saintly subject, Buechner insists on a rendition of the restlessness that never goes away as much he insists on a respite for longing in the soul. Godric's biographer is quick to pounce on the confession, of course. Reginald is the first to hear of Gillian, apparently, as Godric has kept her a secret until the end. One suspects that his chronicler at two removes, Buechner, who writes through Reginald, has a similar feeling about the dangers of trying to speak of miracle. "I've never told a soul of Gillian," Godric confesses, "for fear to breathe her forth into the world with words would be to risk the world's wind blowing her away" (*Godric* 75). Gillian is Godric's hound of heaven, and her coming means death for Deric. Godric's two stories move closer to an intersection.

When he renounces earthly pursuit, he returns to his original name and to some of his original innocence, but his failings do not evaporate. Although he renounces his guilty past, Godric still epitomizes the dual nature of humankind. He learns the difference between seeming and being in a metaphorical lesson taught him by Hedwic, the distraught child-wife of Falkes de Granvill, the Norman noble in whose service Godric spends some years. Directing Godric's gaze to a floor of the magnificent manor house, Hedwic points out the festal decorations, the sweet herbs and fresh rushes strewn about on the floor. "What's underneath is turds of dogs and grease and bits of bone. . . . The part you see is fair and fresh. The part you do not see is foul," she explains (*Godric* 85). Hedwic concludes that the floor reminds her of her own bitter life. The metaphor might well serve as a microcosm of the entire novel. Reginald's story is the seeming; Godric's version claims to be the being. The reader gets to decide if truth is in there somewhere.

Godric eventually closes the door on life and becomes a hermit, not so much to save himself from temptation, he admits, as "to save the world from me" (*Godric* 158). Like Greene's whiskey priest, who claims that loving God is "wanting to protect him from yourself" (*Power* 173), Godric is another failed priest; he is overwhelmed by guilt and remorse even in those moments when he recalls the miracles that have sprinkled through his days. Reginald wants to record that Godric leaves the nobleman's service for a spiritual vocation. With that notion ringing false in his ears, Godric tricks Reginald into stooping and catches him with a kick, a moment of slapstick in the midst of a grim story of Godric's service to the cruel lord. Falkes de Granvill's motto is "Base-born folk, like willows, sprout better for being cropped," and it is Godric who, as overseer, must

Buechner
Circa 1985

do most of the cropping (*Godric* 82). When he steals away in the night, he abandons not only the oppressed folk who must still serve the brutal lord but also Hedwic, for whom Godric feels something more than pity, if not love. Reginald doesn't buy Godric's version. "Thus like a child that fashions poppets out of muck, a monk makes saints of flesh and blood," Godric fears (*Godric* 88). Maybe Godric agrees to participate in Reginald's infuriating project as a way of getting the truth spoken at least, if not recorded. It is "a bitter brew" that Godric wants poured out (*Godric* 81).

Even late in his life, when the supplicants line up for a blessing or a touch from the revered holy man, Godric feels only his unworthiness. Remorse and doubt cloud all visions of holiness for him, and he prays: "Dear Father, see how these thy children hunger here. They starve for want of what they cannot name. Their poor lost souls are famished. Their foolish hands reach out. Oh grant them richer fare than one old sack of bones whose wits begin to turn. Feed them with something more than Godric here, for Godric's no less starved for thee than they" (*Godric* 122–23). Godric wants his story told with the "grief and ugliness," the doubt and resistance included (*Godric* 132). His story must encompass both his longing for God and his failure to follow God's will. He occasionally dares to hope that he will be remembered "not for the ill I've done but for the good I've dreamed" (*Godric* 105). Such a wish strikes a universal note about the distance between the ideal and the actual. Robert Browning goes after the same idea: "What I aspired to be, / And was not, comforts me."[21] Godric asserts the necessity of making public the seedy and shocking side of his history, even as he still withholds something of the tale from Reginald.

Buechner perceptively explores the human reality of how low the prodigal has to plunge before he can really turn toward home. Buechner also demonstrates his strong grip on the subtle, almost intuitive, connections and misconnections that determine the course of human relationships. If Gillian's appearance on the road from Rome was to be Godric's Damascus road moment, then we must conclude that Godric is much slower witted than was Saul of Tarsus. Godric flees Hedwic and Falkes de Granvill, not for Christ but for Roger Mouse. When Deric and Mouse reunite, "there was . . . a sadness that hid in all we said" (*Godric* 90). Something has changed for Godric; he and Mouse are no longer of the same stuff. Although Godric cannot speak Gillian's name to Mouse, her wind is blowing in Godric's sails. After the rascals have helped King Baldwin I to save the port of Jaffa, they quarrel over the mistreatment of pilgrims, Godric's conscience having grown so large as to be unable to brook their usual schemes.

As they use their fists to express their rage at the broken friendship, the long silences, the divided path, Buechner makes another pass at the subjects of sin and grace. First, Godric tells Reginald that "through a pair of ragged Saxon rogues, God's will is done"—they've been on the right side for once (*Godric* 92). Then follows Mouse's scheme to bilk the pilgrims. "Sin and grace go hand in hand," Godric believes (*Godric* 92). We are back to the mix of good and evil, the ever-wed impulses that define human nature. The theological proposition on which all of this rests is that of the creation and fall paradigm. Made in the image of God, humans are flawed; redemption is possible, though holiness remains elusive. But beyond the doctrinal supposition, the real strength of *Godric* is the truth it tells about us. This is Noah making a fool of himself after being delivered from the flood. This is Elijah hiding in a cave after bringing down fire at Mount Carmel. This is King David again and again turning away from his best instincts—holiness and sinfulness inextricably bound. These craggy Old Testament folk would find good company in Godric, and the complexity of King David's story—the repeated episodes of success (Goliath) followed by episodes of failure (Bathsheba)—actually works as a stronger allusion for Buechner's novel than does the New Testament parable of the Prodigal Son, though there's plenty of prodigal in the young Godric. Godric is each of us, bound in the conflict between what he is and what he might be.

Shedding Deric for good this time, Godric heads back to Jerusalem. In Rome he'd found only "the broken bones of ancient times" (*Godric* 101). If Rome is "a city men had built," then "Jerusalem is God's," he says (*Godric* 101). Maybe it is only that Godric has changed. Toting his burden of sins to the Jordan, he manages a baptism reminiscent of those I imagine performed by Christ's cousin John—a rugged and joyful dunking. Whatever happens at the river, "the Godric that waded out of Jordan soaked and dripping wet that day was not the Godric that went wading in" (*Godric* 105). Though quick to admit that he has many times fallen away from "the holy mirth and madness" of the time, Godric is transformed (*Godric* 104).

Remembering the moment in the last days of his life, he prays for a return to the wonder of it, the madness, the wild joy. He has tried to leave his burdens at the Jordan, with little success, as it will turn out, but he can get rid of the dung that has piled up on Farne, the visible poison of his misspent years. Cutting the lines to his old life, Godric abandons Deric's treasure on the altar of a stone church, and there he also meets Elric. An anchorite at Wulsingham, Elric anticipates the life of a hermit that Godric will himself live in later years. For now, Godric plays the role that Reginald will someday play for him. He is Elric's student and factotum for two years. And what a job this one is. Elric is obsessed with demons. "Shadows he saw everywhere, but never light," Godric argues, though the point seems somewhat lost on Godric (*Godric* 117). Though he can see a certain vacancy in Elric's approach to faith—"I feared that when his time for bliss came round at last, he'd find he'd lost the art," Godric says—he never seems to realize how much he is like Elric, dwelling in the gloom of his failure more than in the joy of the Jordan. Since "El" is the Hebrew word for God, we might legitimately see Godric as twin to Elric, a suggestive similarity in more than their names. Elric's motto—"Scratch fair, find foul"—could just as easily be Godric's own (*Godric* 114). When Elric dies, Godric moves off toward his own hermitage, a place he has seen only in a dream, and the novel moves to the strangely full years of inaction.

The last sections of the novel increasingly feature the aged Godric passing in and out of sleep, sometimes telling his story to Reginald and often telling it merely to himself in the recesses of a memory grown sharp as death approaches. Sometimes he thinks he has already died and only dreams that he is living. He dreams of the robbers who cursed and beat him for his poverty. "Did they but know, the only treasure old men have lies buried deep in graves," he concludes (*Godric* 127). One of those graves is Burcwen's. Long neglected but never absent from the narrative, Burcwen's part is soon to be spoken. When Reginald wants to know how she died, Godric responds with striking bitterness, "She died of that which slays us all. They call it life" (*Godric* 126). Buechner insists on black bewilderment at the two graves Godric stands over, his father's and Burcwen's. God misses a good many chances in this narrative. This reminder of unanswered prayers sets up the movement toward the darkest of Godric's secrets.

Recalling his words to Burcwen, spoken over her grave on a trip to Durham, where the bishop has trotted him out for Christmas mass, Godric speaks of "shame" and "darkness" and "that night you came" (*Godric* 126). When he begs her to pray for him and wishes her "peace at last," readers begin to get a glimmer of the sin that Godric has withheld from Reginald (*Godric* 126). There remains only one more foray into the prehermit years, the record of his days as a bellringer and door-minder at Saint Giles School. Godric learns his letters with the children while serving the parish as general custodian and disciplinarian. The schoolboys love his stories of the *Saint Esprit*, even though Godric edits his life to make it fit for their ears. So he has understood Reginald's dilemma better than he lets on. "How seemly is a life when told to children thus, with all the grief and ugliness snipped out. I suppose it's how monk Reginald will tell of mine," he complains (*Godric* 132).

Godric graduates into the service of Bishop Flambard and another kind of education. Flambard anticipates the renaissance man, full of predictions of a new world and busy building bigger barns. "With wit we'll make a new and wondrous world as God made this one long ago that now grows old and stinks," he proclaims (*Godric* 136). Fifteen years later, Flambard will be dead, his "wondrous" world still distant, but Godric will have found his place at last. When he first spies Finchale along the Wear, Tune and Fairweather are already there. "I knew that here was where I'd live whatever years were left, and here I'd die," Godric announces, feeling as if he's almost home at last (*Godric* 138). Disappointed because he thought Godric might rise "to serve the King," Flambard nonetheless agrees to give Godric the spot for his hermitage. Godric merely responds by saying that he does indeed intend to serve "the King" (*Godric* 138).

Godric's life is barely half gone when he moves to Finchale. He will leave his hermitage only three times over the next fifty years. "By the reckoning of men," he figures, "one half my life has been an empty box" (*Godric* 139). By Godric's reckoning, however, it is the first half that was empty. Buechner seems fascinated by the years of prayer and the pulsing guilt that defines his character, and he manages to pull his readers into that fascination. How does the hermit fill his life? "Three things I've filled it with: *what used to be, what might have been*, and, for the third, *what may be yet* and in some measure *is* already had we only eyes to see," Godric notes (*Godric* 139). He prays for "daylight mercy" on his "midnight soul" (*Godric* 140). He reviews his life as a kind of "tilt" between good and evil (*Godric* 141). He shoots prayers like "shafts into the dark," hoping that they strike some mark, but never certain if they do (*Godric* 142).

Like Elric, he battles demons. "How useless is my life. My flesh is ever prey to lust and pride and sloth. I let folks call me Holy Father though I know myself to be of all God's sinful sons most foul," he owns (*Godric* 143). He is, he thinks, chief among sinners. Like Greene's disheveled priest, who believes that, if anyone at all is bound for hell, it is surely he. Godric is submerged in his sense of unworthiness. Reginald will call it humility, but it mostly resembles the torpor of unbearable guilt. The hermitage turns out to be no retreat from the battle but the locus of an intensified struggle within Godric. There are moments when something breaks through, even a vision in which Godric thinks he sees Christ himself and hears his own name spoken. But like his encounter with the porpoise, his pleas before Gillian, his moments with Cuthbert, and his glow at the Jordan, this miracle too passes quickly, and life at Finchale is a riot of despair and anguish. Faith seems to be mostly a sporadic possibility.

The spiritual warfare at Finchale takes a twist when William, Burcwen, and Aedwen turn up. Burned out by "rogues and thieves" and ostracized by nasty neighbors who hint of something untoward in Burcwen and William's relationship, they've come looking for a place near Godric (*Godric* 146). Like her son, Aedwen loves the river, whose song she understands. Long after the river of years has borne her away, Godric remembers her description of the song: "He sings that all things pass. He sings that winter passes. Then comes spring. The old king dies, they crown a new. Pink-cheeked lads and lasses shrivel up like apples on a shelf. There's not a man alive today but time, like Wear, will carry him off too" (*Godric* 147).

When Godric responds, "It sounds like a sad song then," she is dumbstruck: "What? Are you daft? Can't you hear him chuckle while he sings?" she asks (*Godric* 147). Godric will remember her wisdom at his own end, and Buechner resurrects that central image of laughter and tears in an irresolvable mixture.

Most readers have by now seen what's coming—at least part of it. Poor Reginald could not have been prepared for such a story, if such a story was ever told him. Despite all his attempts to chastise "the ape that gibbers in our loins," the lust that years and austerities have not quenched, Godric sees Burcwen bathing in Wear and burns as King David once burned for Bathsheba (*Godric* 153). The story emerges with Godric's shudder, and readers share his revulsion at the memory. As the two consummate their years of longing, speak of all that has been unsaid over the decades, William searches for Burcwen, upon whom he has become entirely dependent. Distraught in the darkness, William falls into Wear and drowns. "So, Reginald, when you come to write out Godric's sins, be sure, although he struck no blow himself, to set down murder with the rest," Godric instructs Reginald (*Godric* 157). The secret is out—incest and murder—a saint's life indeed. Godric offers only one brief explanation: "Reginald, when you sit down to write my life, write this. The worst that Godric ever did, he did for love. Nor was it of an earthly sort that seeks its own but love that gives itself away for the beloved's sake, and thus, when all is said and done, the love that God himself commands" (*Godric* 155).

And what are we to make of this? Buechner's guess about his saint's dark secret introduces a question about how great a sin can be covered by God's grace. Can we possibly believe that the confidence man—the pirate, the lecher, the murderer—somehow becomes "a man after God's own heart"? Godric's conviction is no less remarkable than David's who, after all, was the first to wear such a label. Despite Bathsheba and the rest, it is David who claims that he will "stay in the house of the Lord forever."[22] Godric is not quite as good as David at climbing out of the muck and walking back toward God, but he is of the same family. Wracked by their guilt, Godric and Burcwen "could not speak for shame" (*Godric* 159). Burcwen retreats to a nunnery, and Godric will see her only once more, and that from a distance at a mass in Durham. Godric seeks to save the world from the horror of his sin, bolting the door on the world and flogging himself. As the years pass, Godric's reputation for sanctity spreads, though he only aims "to tame the beasts" within himself (*Godric* 164). Like Saint Francis, Godric addresses nature in personal terms, has an affinity with animals, goes unshod, suffers self-imposed asceticism as a way of castigating his temporal preoccupations, experiences various visions and visitations, and even builds a little church when he is eighty. But Godric's journey is no simple, Francis-like step into piety. For all his love of God, Godric is a sad man. His second sight gives him glimpses of deaths to be—Flambard's untimely demise and Perkin's death in battle, the sadness of death piling up around him as his many regrets crowd in as well. Even at the end, no saintly glow surrounds the rugged old man.

Godric has pretty much had his say by now. Buechner gives the last pages to Reginald. The biographer who has played Boswell to Godric's Johnson, the nosy innocent who has edited the rough-and-tumble story Godric has doled out over months, finally gets his say. And Godric is anything but pleased. Buechner juxtaposes Reginald's sanitized version with Godric's salty heckling. When Reginald speaks of Godric's "worldly circumspection," for example, Godric mutters, "Write worldly greed if you would better hit the mark" (*Godric* 167). "This life you've written down will be the death of me," Godric cries to Reginald, and he's right this time (*Godric* 167). When Reginald refers to him as "this saint," Godric cries, "This SAINT!" and apparently suffers a stroke in his outrage. His final words are "Blasphemer! Fool!" (*Godric* 169). Reginald's attached "last word" is strikingly anticlimactic to Godric's last thoughts as he awaits death in Perkin's arms. He wishes he could beg forgiveness from Reginald, he hears Wear laughing in the night, he recalls a joke from Aedwen's girlhood, he looks with gratitude on Perkin, and he thinks, "All's lost. All's found. Farewell" (*Godric* 171).

Godric's last thoughts summarize the novel in one memorable line. Flannery O'Connor argued that "the artist penetrates the concrete world to find at its depths . . . the image of an ultimate reality" (O'Connor 157). *Godric* sure enough gets at the tangible world, the earthly mire, the stench, the suffering, and incompleteness. The novel moves relentlessly from shock to shock, from human cruelty to crippling spiritual battles. But with Buechner the "ultimate reality" is somewhere beyond the morass that threatens his characters. All is lost, but that is only the penultimate word. *Godric* is Buechner's most sophisticated statement of his hope that faith can survive failure. Godric summarizes in words that Buechner says speak for him as well: "Praise, praise! I croak. Praise God for all that's holy, cold, and dark. Praise him for all we lose, for all the river of the years bears off. Praise him for the stillness in the wake of pain. Praise him for emptiness. . . . Praise him for dying and the peace of death" (*Godric* 96). Godric sees only dimly, no doubt, but he bets his very life that everything is going somewhere in particular.

In the last pages of *Now and Then*, written more than two years after *Godric*, Buechner speaks of a walking stick on which he has carved the phrase "*vocatus atque non vocatus Deus aderit*," which he translates, "in the long run, whether you call on him or don't call on him, God will be present with you" (*NT* 108). To the question of what he would be willing to bet on, Buechner answers simply "That life is grace" (*NT* 108). From the tentative Tristram to the dreaming Cowley to the almost lost, then found, Nicolet; from the Bible-banger to the rude hermit, Buechner's novels show forth "the endless possibilities of its [life's] becoming transparent to something extraordinary beyond itself" (*NT* 108). As Tim Murray argued, "At the heart of his books is an idea that mystery and knowledge are bound up so tightly in some way that without one, the other can have no meaning."[23] Buechner speaks of hints, intimations, suggestions, glimpses, possibilities—never of dogmatic certainty.

Labeling Buechner's novels as "theologically-tinged"[24] is useful only if one remembers the scrupulous fluidity of his theology. His novels are a "kind of whistling in the dark," he admits, and then explains:

> To whistle in the dark is more than just to try to convince yourself that dark is not all there is. It is also to *remind* yourself that dark is not all there is, or the end of all that is, because even in the dark there is hope. Even in the dark you have the power to whistle. And sometimes that seems more than just your own power because it's powerful enough to hold the dark back a little. The tunes you whistle in the dark are the images you make of that hope, that power. They are the books you write. And in the same way, faith could be called a kind of whistling in the dark. (Zinsser 128).

"Seeing too much to deny and too little to be sure"[25] is the way Pascal described the essential human dilemma, and it is the tension in which we live that Buechner manages to tap in Godric. It is the tension between "In this world you will have trouble" and "I have overcome the world."[26] It is the tension of singing one's song in a foreign land, the drama that Yeats's Crazy Jane gets just right:

> Fair and foul are near of kin,
> And fair needs foul . . .
> But love has pitched his mansion in
> The place of excrement."[27]

Such is Buechner's métier.

Always interested in that "dim little whisper of providence from the wings" (Zinsser 108), Buechner draws a distinction between "faith," the word I've most generally used to talk of Buechnerian religion, and "the-ology": "Faith is different from theology because theology is reasoned and systematic and orderly, whereas faith is disorderly and intermittent and full of surprises" (Zinsser 111). He goes on to argue that faith is different from mysticism, too, and ethics, suggesting that worship might be the most appropriate analogy—"a response to God" (Zinsser 111). But he concludes with a strikingly unsystematic take on the whole business, "Faith is homesickness. Faith is a lump in the throat. Faith is less a position *on* than a movement *toward*—less a sure thing than a hunch. Faith is waiting" (Zinsser 111). Buechner claims that, as a novelist, "you fashion your story as you fashion your faith, out of the great hodgepodge of your life—the things that have happened to you and the things you've dreamed of hap-pening" (Zinsser 114). This speech in which he tries to explain the ways in which faith and fiction come together for him sheds considerable light on what Buechner offers in *Godric*. He has tried to follow the hodgepodge of Godric's days as he follows his own, not imposing meaning on them but listening for what meaning might reside there.

Thus we return to another of those Buechner fundamentals that define his career—paying attention. Theology, fiction, and memoir become one pursuit in Buechner's theory of writing, because they are each about pay-ing heed to the passing moments, probing them for some "mightness," some fertile possibility. A year or so after *Godric* appears, an interviewer asks Buechner to summarize the unifying theme of his work: "What would you say is the one sermon you're working on?" Buechner responds, "Lis-ten to your life" (*Radix* 9). In another place he adds, "As a summation of all that I've ever had to say as a writer I'd settle for that" (Zinsser 129). He implies that developing a sensitivity to one's own experience may lead to a deeper perception of spiritual matters. Yet there remains a smiling sad-ness in much of Buechner's work. Even his most powerful affirmations are often spoken with a lump of doubt in the throat. The grace is amazing enough, but the suffering and desolation always have their say. Pascal summarizes the position: "The nature of man may be viewed in two ways: . . . he is great and incomparable . . . he is abject and vile" (Pascal 131). Neither imposing a religious system nor offering a simplistic plan, Buech-ner celebrates the potential for greatness despite the clutches of inevitable misery. "There's always room for doubt," he insists, "in order, perhaps, that there will always be room to breathe" (Zinsser 116). In this precari-ous breathing space, Buechner seems to be aware of both poles. In recent years, we have seen a proliferation of the happy-ending stories from writers like Janette Oke, Phillip Gulley, Ann Ross, and Jan Karon. Their attempts to write of goodness are worthy of notice. Overwhelmed by the dark, we no longer know how to speak of light. Surely some of the serious writers of happy stories are in part reacting against an older generation that canonized the opposite of goodness, a voice like Hemingway's, for example: "Our nada who art in nada, nada be thy name."[28] But Buechner comes down in the middle ground.

Godric is a miracle for Buechner, and in bringing the venerable saint alive for himself, Buechner brings him alive for readers as well. *Godric* has assured him a larger audience and discovery by a new generation of readers. The novel is showing up on college syllabi and being listed with the great books of our time. Buechner's place as a novelist of consequence is assured with *Godric*. Stacy Thompson argued that neglect of Buechner's writing derives from his explicitness: "The issues are always clear and direct, even if the resolution of these issues is problematic. Contemporary spiritual malaise is the issue, Buechner suggests, laying all his cards on the table" (Thompson 156). But "spiritual malaise" is the issue for many modern and contemporary novelists. If Buechner is more "direct" than Walker Percy, Flannery O'Connor, Graham Greene, or John Updike, he is, at least, of the same family. Whether Buechner's fiction embodies theological truth or fairy-tale dreams is finally irrelevant. The tension between belief and unbelief, between hope and despair—the heart of Buechner's work—will endure as the vital center of his career. You can almost hear Wear chuckling there.

Notes

1. Personal conversation, October 19, 1989.
2. William Butler Yeats, "Anima Hominis," in *Mythologies* (New York: Macmillan Co., 1959), 331.
3. Frederick Buechner, "Faith and Fiction," in *Spiritual Quests: The Art and Craft of Religious Writing*, ed. William Zinsser (Boston: Houghton Mifflin, 1987), 123. Hereafter cited as Zinsser. An edited version of this essay also appears in *The Clown in the Belfry*.
4. Personal correspondence, December 14, 1987.
5. Personal correspondence, December 14, 1987.
6. Personal conversation, November 13, 2004.
7. Personal correspondence, November 12, 1981.
8. Peter Lewis, "Lives of the Saint," *Times Literary Supplement*, March 13, 1981, 278. Hereafter cited as Lewis.
9. Edmund Fuller, "Fascinating Views of the Monastic Life," *Wall Street Journal*, October 6, 1980, 11.
10. *Booklist*, November 15, 1980, 442.
11. Peter S. Prescott, "Holy Man with a Past," *Newsweek*, November 10, 1980, 114.
12. P. L. Adams, book review, *Atlantic*, December 1980, 96.

13. Buechner's novel has, ironically, popularized the story of Godric and spawned several renderings of Reginald's *Life of Godric*. See, for example, Robert McNamara's "Saints Alive" Web site at www.stthomasirondequoit.com, Katherine Rabenstein's "Index of the Saints" Web site at www.saintpatrickdc.org, and the entry for "Reginald of Durham" in *Sources of British History*. Buechner's own "Historical Note" appended to the novel provides valuable insight into the history and legend into which Buechner is imagining his way.

14. Steven J. Curley, *Library Journal*, January 15, 1981, 164.

15. John R. May, "Public Concerns," *America*, April 25, 1981, 348.

16. Randall H. Balmer, "Saint with Feet of Clay," *Reformed Journal*, June 1981, 28.

17. Matthew 23:27.

18. C. S. Lewis, *Mere Christianity* (New York: Macmillan Co., 1960), 140.

19. Matthew 6:21.

20. James Joyce, *Letters* (New York: Viking Press, 1966), 2:165.

21. Robert Browning, "Rabbi Ben Ezra," ll. 41–42.

22. Psalm 23:6.

23. Tim Murray, *Best Sellers*, December 1980, 309.

24. *Kirkus Review*, July 1, 1980, 849.

25. Blaise Pascal, *Pensees* (New York: Modern Library, 1941), 78. Hereafter cited as Pascal.

26. John 16:33.

27. William Butler Yeats, "Crazy Jane Talks with the Bishop," in *The Poems*, ed. Richard J. Finneran (New York: Macmillan Publishing Co., 1989), 259–60.

28. Ernest Hemingway, "A Clean, Well-Lighted Place," in *The Short Stories of Ernest Hemingway* (New York: Charles Scribner's Sons, 1925), 383.

Chapter Eight

Navigating Sainthood

Brendan

A nd what to say of Brendan, who follows Godric in Buechner's career, even though he comes centuries before Godric in the stream of time? In the summer of 1981 Buechner tells Marie-Helene Davies that *Godric* is "the distillation of everything" (Davies 67). An estimable achievement, *Godric* set a high standard, and the next novel was around several bends in the river, seven years away, seven years of important passages in Buechner's life. The 1980s featured an increasingly empty nest on the farm in Vermont, and the daughters' departures for schools and marriages were thorny days for their father, the house full of "emptiness" (*TS* 55). Time in the study—the Magic Kingdom Buechner calls the place—turned more and more to memories and memoirs. *The Sacred Journey* appeared in 1982, and *Now and Then* followed soon after in 1983. Buechner supposes that "they helped let a little light and air into the dark place where I was imprisoned" (*TS* 47). The memoirs illustrate Buechner's theory of what he calls the "sacred function of memory"—the obliteration of the artificial designations of past, present, and future in order to reinhabit and reunderstand the moments of our lives (*TS* 35). The novels of the 1980s, *Godric* and *Brendan*, certainly exemplified this theory of memory, as did the grab bag of occasional pieces *A Room Called Remember*, which includes sermons and reviews alongside a commencement address, essays on books, and the text of a speech, "The Speaking and Writing of Words," which summarizes core elements of Buechner's theory of language (*RCR* ix).

The decade was also rich with the rising acclaim of new readers coming to Buechner via *Godric* and *The Book of Bebb*. Honorary degrees and invitations to deliver speeches also took Buechner out of the study more regularly. There's an unspectacular stint at Harvard Divinity School in

1982, and I think he must have shocked even himself when he agreed to spend a semester at Wheaton College, an evangelical Christian college in Illinois, in the fall of 1985. The time at Wheaton might be labeled spectacular; surely pivotal in the pause between *Godric* and *Brendan*, it epitomized the new constituencies coming to the writer who had worked in relative quiet since the move to Vermont in the mid-1960s. Other notice was coming, too, in the form of books and articles devoted to studying his work. About this attention, he was and is ambivalent. He hears of such work with "a mixture of pride, embarrassment, surprise, apprehension, and who knows what else," he says.[1] And somehow in the comings and goings of the times, Buechner managed yet another novel, his eleventh, another "form of dreaming, of deepest remembering," to use Buechner's own words on the writing of novels (*TS* 66). In a 1986 letter he commented on the book to come: "In May Atheneum is bringing out a novel about a fifth century Irish saint known as Brendan the Navigator. I thought it was terrific while I was writing it, and now it depresses me to think about it."[2] A certain fragility, Buechner's typical uncertainty about what he may or may not have written, rings in his feelings as *Brendan* makes its appearance in 1987.

As with *Godric*, there was a personal connection. Of Brendan, Buechner notes, "He was a haggard sort of man as I pictured him, in many of the ways that I also am haggard, a loose-footed sort of red-headed, inhibited, nimble-tongued, miracle-working man" (*TS* 87). Looking into Brendan becomes another way of looking into himself. At Wheaton in 1985 Buechner delivered a lecture, "Faith and Fiction," later to be reworked for a lecture at the New York Public Library in 1987 and anthologized in William Zinsser's collection, *Spiritual Quests*, and in *The Clown in the Belfry*. Material from the speech/essay shows up in many forms and as the core of Buechner's stump speech through the late 1980s and early 1990s. His thoughts about the connections between faith and fiction surfaced during the very time when his imagination was beginning to brim with *Brendan*. Buechner first notes that both faith and fiction circle on plot, on the notion that "events are somehow leading somewhere" (Zinsser 112). "They both start with a leap in the dark," he adds, and goes on to talk about the dangers of starting a story with the end already in mind (Zinsser 131). What writers are trying to do, he argues, "is less to impose a shape on the hodgepodge than to see what shape emerges from it" (Zinsser 114). Finally, he argues, "In both faith and fiction you *fashion* out of the raw stuff of your experience" (Zinsser 115). To suggest that either *Godric* or *Brendan* is an autobiographical novel would be, in some sense, a dramatic stretch. Buechner nonetheless insists that his central subject is tied up even in these excursions into the far past: "Everything I write is about the presence of God in this patchwork quilt of a world—telling my story, looking for Him in my story as I look for Him in my life."[3] *Brendan* grows out of the soil of Buechner's most sophisticated thinking to date on the intersections of personal faith and the writing of a novel.

Another preliminary thing to say of the new novel is that it is not a simple remake of *Godric*, although connections are obvious enough. Both books carry readers to distant worlds, and they each resist paraphrase in their unique style and use of language. Indeed Buechner turns to historical sources again and is caught up in another hagiography, but *Brendan* is a very different book from *Godric* on many counts; the narrative voice, the deeper foray into mythology and fantasy, and the consideration of a collision between the old religions and the new are all marks of a singular book. Where the diction made all the difference in *Godric*, it is the syntax in *Brendan* that proves the tour de force. The research into Celtic mythology helped, but the real masterstroke, Buechner says, was the discovery "that one of the great devices in Irish writing is the simple business of reversing the usual position of adjectives. Instead of saying the little black dog ran into the room, they say the black little dog ran into the room, and it's all the difference in the world" (*Image* 43). Of the language and style of the two books, Chris Anderson argued that both *Godric* and *Brendan* featured "a Hopkinsesque, pseudo-Saxon speech in which all our Latinate, sing-song rhythms for Christ are sprung, broken into new patterns" (Anderson 16). Buechner will express his debt to Hopkins in *Speak What We Feel*, but Hopkins is certainly already present here. And the style of *Brendan* conjures another time, surely.

Thematically speaking, much of the masterfulness of *Brendan* has its source in Buechner's imagining the resounding clash between paganism and Christianity in the youthful days of the Christian faith in Ireland. He will consider a similar subject from a slightly different angle in the 1993 novel *Son of Laughter*, the story of Judaism's youth. Yet, with the several explorations into new territories, essential Buechnerian themes such as the mixture of false and true and the possibility of God's involvement in human experience remain in *Brendan*. One working title for this novel was *A World of Crowns*, a phrase suggestive of Buechner's long-term preoccupation with laughter, or possibility, at the heart of things (Archive, IV A 12). He discovered the idea in Chesterton and cites it as an epigram for *Brendan*: "In the very shape of things there is more than green growth; there is the finality of the flower. It is a world of crowns."[4]

If Chesterton was right that regal glory resides in all things, then everything depends on how well we see. Saints are people who are overwhelmed by a world the rest of us barely notice. It is like being on a fast train on a dark night and passing through a city, Buechner explains: "Even the saints see only an occasional light go whipping by, hear only a sound or two over the clatter of the rails. The rest of us aren't usually awake enough to see as much as that" (*WT* 22). Brendan is one of the wakeful ones, an exemplar of fortissimo, an example of life in capital letters. Again the issue is attentiveness.

Many of Buechner's long-term readers were disappointed when Buechner turned to the saints. Maybe they'd been hoping for more of the Bebbish, but Buechner tried other subjects—an alchemist, a novelist, a dishwasher in a Vermont restaurant, an old lady in a nursing home. None of those worked. He kept finding himself back in the stories of saints. Not just a turn in the career, the preoccupation with saints is a pivot point: "After Bebb, only saints really interested me as a writer, and I've spent my life since then writing about them. There's so much life in them. They're so in touch with, so transparent to, the mystery of things that you never know what to expect from them. Anything is possible for a saint. They won't stay put or be led around by the nose, no matter how you try" (Zinsser 123). With the exception of the 1998 novel *The Storm*, Buechner has stayed true to his commitment to the saints' lives. His saints are "ribald, roaring, God-defying, God-loving, put-up-your-dukes saints," as Mitch Finley saw it.[5] Even if his saints are unlike our usual stereotypes of such people, Buechner has stayed with hagiography. I think he hopes to sneak into the saint club, maybe in the back row, but in the club. He writes about saints because he longs to be one.

Again, the emphasis is on attending to life and being willing to risk everything on one throw of the dice—"only a life given away for love's sake is a life worth living," Buechner posits in the *Wishful Thinking* entry for "Fool" (*WT* 28). Martha Stout believed that Brendan is another of "Buechner's fools for Christ,"[6] a preoccupation apparent in Buechner at least as far back as *The Final Beast*. Also present is that long-felt Buechner subject relating to the craving in the human heart for news of the more-than-this; the spiritual longing that characterizes so many of his characters drives this novel as well. Finally, too, this book is another hefting of grace and guilt and the wondering out loud about the vagaries of the faithful—their words and their realities. In this regard, *Brendan* is another book whose territory is today, even if it is set in a time out of mind and memory. On one of his adventures, Brendan tries to interpret the sound of a whale's roar and comes up with "God is just? God is jest?"—the old mix of false and true, fair and foul, yes and no, the conundrum that broods at the center of the Buechner corpus (*Brendan* 116).

I once heard Buechner talk about his sense of where *Brendan* came from, and he began by speaking of "literary saints." He referenced the "crazy saints" of Flannery O'Connor, along with Dostoevsky's Father Zossima, Salinger's Seymour Glass, and Greene's whiskey priest, who, he said, has had the "most lasting effect" for him.[7] He went on to trace his interest in saints back to 1973 and the book *Wishful Thinking: A Theological ABC*, where he mulls over the much-worn words of faith, and the 1979 *Peculiar Treasures: A Biblical Who's Who*, where he finds new ways to look at the shop-worn stories of the Bible. From there, the steps to *Godric* and on to *Brendan* were short ones. Much of what brews in the memoirs to which Buechner turns with increasing frequency in the 1980s is a meditation on saints and sainthood. *The Sacred Journey* is even dedicated to saints "remembered and forgotten" (*SJ* v). He celebrates the saints of his own experience, while wondering about what saintliness he might bring to others. Clearly thinking of his own nearly sixty years as *Brendan* takes shape on the accumulating manuscript pages, Buechner studies the inconstant Brendan for clues to his own meandering way. Asked if he reads the circumstances of his life in a way that incorporates providential possibilities, Buechner answers, "Yes. . . . I don't know that I could even go on doing what I do if I didn't have that feeling" (*Image* 57). Readers are off on another Buechnerian journey, this one dating all the way back to the fifth century and to yesterday, and another novel puzzling toward the hints of providence.

Apparently there really was a Brendan. According to Buechner's historical note, the man was born in 484 in what is now Tralee, Ireland, and died ninety-four years later at Anaghdown, Ireland. Brendan's adventures turn up primarily in *Navigatio Sancti Brendani*, a tenth-century version of his life that had wide popularity for its medieval lore and was translated into many languages. Buechner uses the *Navigatio* as well as Katherine Scherman's *The Flowering of Ireland*, Robert T. Reilly's *Irish Saints*, and Tim Severin's *The Brendan Voyage* as basic research sources in the writing of the novel (*Brendan* 243). Educated by Bishop Erc and Saint Jarlath, Brendan not surprisingly became a builder of monasteries himself as well as an evangelist for the new faith. He helped establish one of Ireland's first Christian kings, Hugh the Handsome, and converted the pagan bard MacLennin, who eventually became a saint himself.

But Brendan's primary fame derives from his voyages in search of Tir-na-n-Og, the Celtic otherworld, an imagined paradise. According to the legends, Brendan may have sailed as far as Florida in his questing after the place of peace. In any case, his many journeys as a bard for Christ make perfect material for a picaresque depiction of medieval cultural conflicts and human longings. The missionary, Brendan, is living off the seed sown by Saint Patrick a generation or so before. While Europe is still dark, Ireland is alive with the new faith, but the old gods are not finished just yet. Buechner takes the conversion of Ireland and Wales as his subject, the book growing from a scene he imagines, a moment of great violence, where Brendan brings down his club on a fertility idol. Playing like a film in his imagination, that germ leads Buechner to find his way beyond Brendan's history and into his inner life.[8]

The most critical departure of *Brendan* has to do with the narrator, the unflappable and irascible Finn. Brendan's childhood friend and loyal disciple, Finn tells all of the story, except for one memorable chapter where Brendan himself takes the reins. I suspect a subtle backhanded tribute to Mark Twain in Buechner's Finn. Buechner speaks often of his regard for Twain: "Mark Twain is one of my great heroes—less as a writer, perhaps, than as a human being whom I find endlessly touching and somehow strengthening."[9] He calls *The Adventures of Huckleberry Finn* Twain's "undoubted masterpiece" and especially notes the truth that Twain's tale gets at: "He had written it [*The Adventures of Huckleberry Finn*] out of the deepest truth of who he was and in doing so had come to terms with the shadows that all his life haunted him" (*Speak* 59). The connection to Twain is more than just the appropriation of a name, even if the name is the best known of all American literary monikers. The deeper connection has to do with the trouble of telling the truth. Huck Finn gets right to the business in the first paragraph of Twain's novel when he talks about "stretchers" and how almost everybody stretches the truth now and then.[10] Huck establishes his credibility quickly, and Twain's novel, of course, turns on the reliability of the truth Huck tells.

Buechner's method is similar; his Finn insists on a straightforward recounting of Brendan's adventures. "The sights I saw with my own eyes only are the ones I've set down. I've neither added nor taken away any or made them more wondrous than they truly was," he asserts in a restrained phrase with biblical echoes (*Brendan* 101). Brendan's claim matters, because the legends about his travels threaten to overwhelm the actual facts. Such is Buechner's dilemma, of course. As with *Godric*, he is forced to cut through the accretion of legend to the what-might-have-been. Finn's anxiety about the truth embodies Buechner's dilemma as storyteller. Expecting a dubious readership, Buechner anticipates their doubts by allowing Finn to embody their incredulity. Finn is especially skeptical on those occasions when he is asked to accept Brendan's version of events. "There's no way of telling either if it all fell out like he says or if that's just how he wished it had," he complains (*Brendan* 102). Just as readers had to negotiate *Godric*, choosing between Godric's rendition of things and Reginald's, so here we must decide which version to trust.

Yes, we have another Tono reporting on Bebb, another Nick Carraway telling Gatsby's fantastic tale. The difference this time, however, is that Finn is never very impressed with Brendan. Oh, he loves Brendan, that's true, but Finn knows him too. Julia O'Faolain in her *New York Times Book Review* piece captured something of the critical importance of Finn. Noting Finn's combination of "naïve joy in miracles" alongside his "earthy skepticism," O'Faolain suggested that Finn may be the "true saint" here.[11] There's something to that. Finn is Brendan's sidekick in a way that calls up Sancho Panza. Like Sancho, he is practical and sacrificial in the face of the wide-eyed idealisms of his master. They each pay a heavy price for the mad schemes of the dreamers they serve. And they no doubt strike audiences as more credible than the larger-than-life madmen they follow. Smarter than we first thought, Finn navigates the navigator's tale, insisting on a version of truth that, we suspect, may be close to the real facts. And, like Huck, Finn knows that truth telling is complicated. "Nor is plain truth the only truth there is either any more than what you see with your own two eyes is all there is to see," Finn declares with his characteristic mixture of brilliance and ambivalence (*Brendan* 102). Finn's tale of life among the Druids and the hair-raising exploits of Brendan often returns to the simple insights gleaned along the way. Finn's lessons learned become our own, his version of the truth the one we generally lean on. He offers the light that we see by in the tale.

If Finn establishes some of the departure that is *Brendan*, the plunge into the Dark Ages, a fifteen-hundred-year removal, also adds to the novel's originality. Where *Godric* was Old Testament, *Brendan* is Old Norse. *Brendan* is a stew of Dante and Homer, the northern mythologies, and even a dash of Malory and Tolkein. There is much more here of the fanciful and fantastic. *Godric* had its miracles, yes—a dream here and a vision there, maybe a leper healed. But *Brendan* has magic as much as miracle, fantasy writ large. Buechner likes the mix of genres—the Tolkein alongside the Baum. "The one reminds us of the chaotic, the chthonic, the primitive, which, from within if not from without, threaten always to overwhelm us. The other speaks to us of curious promises, which, for all our sad skepticism, may even once above a time be kept," Buechner explains (*RCR* 163). On one of his voyages in search of the otherworld, Brendan comes across a suffering Judas, the real Judas apparently, and the extremity of his torment rivals those ordeals pictured by Dante.

Odysseus's travails on his perilous trip over the sea have little on Brendan's adventures as he deals with his own versions of Scylla and Charybdis, Circe, Calypso, and the Cyclops. The ancient Celtic religions bubble here in the fascination with Tir-na-n-Og, the paradise where time loses all power, and the holdover gods of the Druids move in and out of the narrative as well. Perhaps Buechner's months at Wheaton rubbed off in his Tolkein-like Bishop Erc, a wizard to rival Gandalf, and a rendition of Arthur and Camelot comprises one of Brendan's last adventures, a foray into the unhappy time after Arthur's own vision of paradise has tumbled.

With all that, Buechner manages to crowd in such contemporary subjects as feminism, homosexuality, and wayward priests. *Brendan*, in fact, made its appearance just as the televangelist scandals of the mid-1980s were beginning to play out on the television news. Brendan has something in common with Jimmy Swaggart, I suppose, and Leo Bebb too, truth be told. Brendan is one more of those larger-than-life evangelists who can tame all the world but cannot tame himself. But in one sense, Brendan is indeed Godric revisited. Like Godric, Brendan has little notion of his goodness; it is rue that fills his mind, his dark deeds on which he meditates day and night. Brendan's last words, "I fear the sentence of the judge," illustrate his sense of guilt even at the end of his life (*Brendan* 240). The reader feels he needn't have feared so much.

In addition to the renewed foray into guilt, *Brendan* forces us to think again about miracles, nothing new for Buechner, but the miracles this time are flashy indeed. More than branches clacking or the shadow of a face in a dream, Brendan's world is alive with the fabulous. Partly, it is the age in which the novel is set that shapes the miraculous material in the book. Explaining the contexts of the miracles, the religion and the magic intertwined in *Brendan*, Buechner observes: "Those ancient Celts saw crocodiles as monsters and were wrong. Nonetheless, their very innocence and primitiveness allow them also to see things that we don't see which are *right*. In other words, they were open to being deceived and open to superstition, but also open to the truly miraculous, truly wondrous" (*Image* 44).

This novel allows Buechner room to explore the wonders more than before. He believes that "Christianity blew like a warm breeze through Ireland" in part because of this tendency to belief (*Image* 45). "The Druids prepared them to believe in the reality beyond the reality they can immediately see," he asserts (*Image* 45). Readers of Buechner's work would immediately see why such a historical moment might interest him—it is the deeply embedded preoccupation with the possibilities beyond the appearance of things that has driven his career. But Buechner's honesty persists as well. Although he enjoys the fairy-tale quality of the times themselves, he claims that, as with *Godric*, he takes pains in *Brendan* "to leave room for the possibility that there may not have been a miracle, that there is a natural phenomenon that might have had the effect of a miracle upon those who witnessed it" (*Image* 43). We've seen this before; maybe Brownie was just out cold in Knoxville. "It is faith that sees miracles," Buechner believes (*Image* 44). Miracles do not create faith, as Buechner sees it, so the miracles, as entertaining as they are, are somehow beside the point. True or not true, who knows?

Once again it is the territory of ambiguity that Buechner insists upon, even as his subject takes him on holy excursions into stunning deeds done for Christ. In another of those speeches of the mid-1980s Buechner contends that "that no man's land between the Yes and the No, that everyman's land, is where faith stands and has always stood. Seeing but not seeing, understanding but not understanding, we all stand somewhere between the Yes and the No" (*RCR* 22). But in that in-between land, Buechner finds room to speak of nobility and virtue, words he appropriates from Anthony Trollope:

> For a novelist to speak of himself as a preacher of sermons puts everybody off. But when Trollope—than whom I believe there is no greater novelist in English—says that the calling of a writer is to teach virtue and nobility, and when he expresses the hope that people will learn from his words that true manliness, true humanness, is to be found not in falseness and flashness but in truth and a gentle spirit, that is something else again. (*RCR* 179)

It is not too much to say that *Brendan* is the precise playing out of just such a theory. Brendan is another of Buechner's characters who taught him something, and he seems to hope that Brendan's instructiveness will extend to readers.

Whatever we make of the assorted jumble that is *Brendan*, Buechner's notion of mythology rests as a foundation beneath his story:

> The raw material of a myth, like the raw material of a dream, may be something that actually happened once. But myths, like dreams, do not tell us much about that kind of actuality. The creation of man,

Adam and Eve, the Tower of Babel, Oedipus—they do not tell us primarily about events. They tell us about ourselves.

In popular usage, a myth has come to mean a story that is not true. Historically speaking that may well be so. Humanly speaking, a myth is a story that is always true. (*WT* 65)

Brendan begins with myth, a miracle—"Erc said the night the boy was born he saw the woods by the boy's house catch fire" (*Brendan* 3). Or maybe the fire was just one of those things that happen. Either way, it is the human story into which Buechner entices his readers with a name that sounds like a stutter or a linguistic slip and an image that prefigures a life of startling fortune. Erc is the bishop who comes to claim the child Brendan, taking the baby from the parents, Finnloag and Cara, followers of the new faith Patrick has brought to the isle. "A great cairn of a man," Erc has been "weaned from druidry by no less than the sainted Patrick himself" (*Brendan* 4). Perhaps the burning wood is a sign. Erc thinks so. In any case, Brendan is to be "raised to the glory of the new and true grand God" (*Brendan* 5). Another cause for amazement accompanies the child's arrival. He is fed his milk from the teat of a "skittish lovely hind" that mysteriously shows up every day (*Brendan* 6). Finn is dubious on this point. "That is the way they tell it," the waffling Finn observes, leaving room for other versions (*Brendan* 6).

Erc soon carries Brendan away to Abbess Ita and her school in the foothills of Sliabh Luacra. Many years later, quizzed by Finn about the story of the hind that fed the baby, Ita attests that she did not send the hind. She *was* the hind, she claims. "I don't know to this day if it was truly a joke she told or if the joke she told was the truth," Finn grumbles (*Brendan* 7). The legends of Brendan's first months are bewildering for his chronicler. He knows there's true miracle floating around in the story. He believes, for example, that Ita has actually saved starving children by offering them her fingers and toes to suckle. Less a believer than the Reginald who tells Godric's story, Finn nonetheless tries to keep an open mind. From the schooldays at Ita's, Finn will at least have the advantage of the eyewitness, because it is at Ita's that his story first joins Brendan's own.

Finn understands early on that the companion of Brendan's intensity is a propensity to exaggeration. "He made every villain he ever met more villainous and every gray wave that ever heaved him wilder," Finn admits (*Brendan* 9). Like Leo Bebb, Brendan is the charismatic weaver of tales, making big stories out of little ones. From their youth, though, it seems Finn and Brendan have their roles to play. Brendan is arms thrown wide.

Finn is arms crossed. Ita teaches the boys about the new Christian God, but she has a good bit to say about the old ones too. Another of Buechner's teachers who teach mostly themselves, Ita advises simplicity, charity, and steadfastness. She is the "plain truth" on which her charges will build lives (*Brendan* 12). When Bishop Erc moves him on to Abbot Jarlath's school, Brendan proves to be a good student, adept at Latin and at Scripture. Sitting on the cliffs above the school, Brendan watches the water roil, and there he catches a vision of Tir-na-n-Og, "the land of the Ever Young" (*Brendan* 15). Is it a spiritual dream that fixes him that day, or is it simple wanderlust that has invaded his soul? Brendan himself will puzzle over such questions.

Life at Jarlath's sounds every bit as barren as life in such a time and place probably was, but Brendan at least has the companionship of his sister, Briga, and the tomboy, Maeve, his companions at Jarlath's odd school. "Jarlath taught him heaven," Finn clarifies, and "Erc taught him Earth" (*Brendan* 17). From Briga, Brendan learns something of the family love otherwise denied him, and from Maeve he learns of sexuality that he will step fearfully around for all his days. Like Godric, here is another monk-ish stray haunted by sexuality as the territory of "mortal danger," as Jarlath warns (*Brendan* 22). Brendan will be more successful than Godric at controlling his lusts. Whether that's a good thing or not is left to the reader, though Maeve and Brendan would have been some kind of pair. All of his life as a celibate, Brendan seems to be wondering how it might have been different had he acted on his impulses with Maeve.

In his crisis of having seen more of Maeve than he ought, Brendan prays to the new God and to Dagda and Mac Oc, as well. The old and new gods clamor in his head, but Brendan gets no relief from any of the gaggle on either side. Praying for mercy, he gets only "emptiness and darkness like God had gone off altogether" (*Brendan* 24). Brendan is like Godric praying down the empty well in Rome until, according to Brendan's report, the feverish prayers produce a miracle in the form of musical angels. "Their singing was itself the mercy of God," Brendan remembers (*Brendan* 24). From this time forth, Brendan forswears the company of women. He also carries waxen earplugs, reversing Odysseus, to avoid hearing any music that might taint the remembrance of the heavenly chorus he now hears in his mind.

Finn's entanglement in Brendan's story soon resumes as Brendan is to be sent on a mission as a prelude to his ordination as a priest. Although he has not been privy to all of Brendan's adventures firsthand, Finn is to go along. So two boys, barely twenty and innocent of the ways of the road, nonetheless go forth to do Jarlath's bidding and carry a blessing to the new king to be crowned at Cashel. "Me and Brendan wasn't what you might call friends at first," Finn summarizes in something of an understatement (*Brendan* 37). Finn is a plain fellow looking out at the world in the usual way. Brendan, on the other hand, is "turned around the other way to peer in at his own secrets" (*Brendan* 37). Brendan is "full of brags," the lucky one, the "darling of the world" (*Brendan* 37). Finn is the guy who does most of the work.

Their first adventure is almost their last, as they are set upon by a band of "old ways" believers (*Brendan* 40). Unimpressed by the bishop's ring meant to guarantee safe passage, the Druids take Finn and Brendan to their king, one Bauheen, an aged but still menacing presence. There in a Stonehenge-like world of stone and mist, Brendan works several wonders. Even Finn cannot figure how Brendan came up with Bauheen's name, but the wizardry impresses the king. "I'm Christ's man," Brendan tells a stunned Bauheen; "I make old things as good as new" (*Brendan* 44). Bauheen's conversion is more to Brendan than it is to Christ, perhaps; Brendan's is the best magic he's yet seen. His fealty is assured when Brendan restores strength to his old legs by speaking boldly, "In the name of the true Christ walk" (*Brendan* 45). If the Christlike triumph over infirmity isn't enough, the startling scene that Finn recounts next is not so much the baptisms of Bauheen and all of his kindred as the picture of Brendan taking a club to the "stone pizzle," the fertility symbol at the center of the old ways (*Brendan* 48).

Finn cannot resist noting that Brendan's club leaves little mark on the stone, just as he also notes that Bauheen has to be helped to his feet when the deed is done. Finn is mercilessly honest in his testimony. But puzzle as he might over the currents drifting through his own account, Finn acknowledges the wonder of the old ways giving way to new. Brendan has remarkable gifts, and readers can almost see Finn watching out of the corner of his eye as, with the reader, Finn is wondering if this Brendan is the real thing or a magnificent imposter. As Brendan spreads the news of Christ to the poor folk they meet on the journey to Cashel, Finn observes, "It was like flirting or courting the way Brendan did it" (*Brendan* 50). Brendan manages to tell the tales of Christ with humor and drama, while connecting the tales to real lives. He makes his listeners laugh and cry, and he gives them a bit to eat, too. And so on to Cashel.

A castle right out of the storybooks, Cashel rears up as a fearsome mossy stone, a place of feasting, warriors, painted women, Druids, and bards. "Lastly at Cashel there's heads," Finn details, and what he points to are the shriveled heads decorating the walls and hanging helter-skelter around the castle, heads of the king's enemies, maybe even the heads of some of the king's friends (*Brendan* 51). With the grisly images of the chance they are taking ever before them, Finn and Brendan meet Crosan, the kingdom's clown. Riddler and jokester, Crosan is like Lear's fool, whose indirection finally leads somewhere. The news they eventually learn from Crosan is that the kingdom is up for grabs. A new king is to be named, and the choosing is momentous. Will it be Hugh the Black, handsome and haughty and of the old faith? Or will it be Hugh the Handsome, ironically plain and humble and of the new faith? Crosan believes that Hugh the Black is a shoo-in. His "proud manner" impresses the men and flusters the women (*Brendan* 56). Surely Buechner is smuggling into this scene some comment about the nature of political power in this picture of the charismatic and effusive Brendan. Crosan observes that "There'll need be someone sent straight from Heaven itself to change their minds if we're to get a Christly king over us," and Brendan responds, "Heaven sent me" (*Brendan* 56).

Two Hughs may sound like comedy, but the stakes are high as the coronation approaches. Black Hugh has not only the advantages of his looks but the effective services of the bard MacLennin, a singer of songs and general blackguard. The savage tone of Cashel is evident in the games that precede the choosing of a king. The gladiatorial contest leaves one man impaled, a spear through his chest, and Brendan rushes to the dying man. When Brendan announces, "I worked it," we suspect another miracle, though Finn seems unsure again (*Brendan* 63). The fallen man restored to life, miracle enough, the real amazement is reserved for the warrior who appears on the scene. It is Maeve, the grown-up tomboy, who has abandoned the nunnery for the sword. The Amazon-like Maeve is still an eyeful, though Brendan manages to look away this time. With Crosan and Maeve, Brendan begins to plot an ascension to the throne for Hugh the Handsome. Although Mitch Finley argued that Buechner's *Brendan* is "a page-turner,"[12] up to this point in the narrative, I'd disagree. But the wind really fills the sails with the story of how the little band of Patrick's loyalists plant another outpost for Christ.

Maeve brings news of a rumor that Black Hugh "wants one of his two stones" (*Brendan* 67). Everybody knows that one of the inviolate laws of the place is that the king must be unblemished, whole. Anything less would be bad luck for the crops. An infertile king would be unthinkable. They carry the rumor to Handsome Hugh, and a plan emerges to test the truth of the matter. Maeve will sacrifice herself on Black Hugh's couch "to uncover by starlight the naked truth of him" (*Brendan* 67). Nearly unhinged by the lewdness of their plans for Maeve, Brendan waits with the others. He has probably already seen about as much of the real world as he can stomach, Finn thinks. Maeve returns to confirm the rumor, though, to Brendan's joy, she gets her information by wrestling Black Hugh to the ground, not by bedding him. Overwhelmed by the indignity of his weakness with Maeve and seeing the way of the wind, Black Hugh agrees to a lesser role in the administration.

A Christian king is crowned despite the grotesquerie of the pagan fertility rituals that he performs before the people. The juxtaposition of the pagan and Christian not only gives the novel much of its edginess but also opens intriguing doors into a credible version of Celtic history. Buechner captures the spirit of an age here and marvelously relates it to our own. For all the talk of bards and Druids, the human issues—the longing for understanding and the inadequacy of earthly power—swirl at the center of the text. MacLennin, the bard of the old ways, is taken short by Brendan's claim that Christ was a bard, "a song himself you might say" (*Brendan* 76). Brendan baptizes MacLennin into a new name, Colman, and heads back to Jarlath along with Finn, Crosan, and the psalm-quoting new convert. "Christ is my druid, I shall want for nothing," Colman sings, and the old and new conjoin (*Brendan* 82).

Back at Jarlath's, Brendan's education continues, especially when Erc drops in with his tales of Saint Patrick and stories of all varieties of martyrs, especially the "curragh martyrs," the ones "scouring the blue storms of the sea for the peace of God" (*Brendan* 86). Tir-na-n-Og has many names—"the land of the Blessed," "the country of the Young," and "Hy Brasail" (*Brendan* 86). Other mythologies celebrate El Dorado, Atlantis, Avalon, *Mag Mell*, *Götterdämmerung*, and Ragnarok, all conjurings of the end times and what might come after, if anything. The dream Erc plants in Brendan is an old one indeed. When Erc pauses to catch his breath, Brendan gets in some of his own yarns as well. Finn notices that Brendan tells the story of Bauheen "straight pretty nearly" but lets other reports of their journey "boil out however it suits his fancy" (*Brendan* 87).

Here the Buechner hero emerges most completely; Brendan is, like Bebb, like Godric, another truth teller of an odd sort. Brendan proves to be as much politician as preacher. It is that old mix of false and true again. "Maybe it was to glorify Christ Brendan told it like that, yet it was to glorify his own self as well surely," Finn admits (*Brendan* 88). Who can tell? But Brendan is a priest now, and legends are already emerging—some say "he'd raised a man from death" (*Brendan* 89). Finn would like to believe it, along with all the fine words at Brendan's ordination. When there's talk of light overwhelming darkness and fear being banished, Finn confesses his own desire for faith: "I never heard a tall tale I'd sooner have true than that tale" (*Brendan* 90). But he cannot ignore either "the old gods whistling through a chink in the stones," so he goes along to keep an eye on things (*Brendan* 90). Just as Tono is mysteriously drawn to Bebb, so Finn is drawn to Brendan. The real story begins with Erc's death and Brendan's restlessness for "fresh sights to fill his eyes" (*Brendan* 92). Brendan dedicates himself, finally, to being a curragh martyr, vowing to "scavenge the watery desert storms for the peace of God" (*Brendan* 94). He plans to "outpatrick Patrick" in search of the Land of the Blessed (*Brendan* 94).

Buechner uses one of his research sources, Tim Severin's *The Brendan Voyage*, to describe the building of the curragh, the boat that is to carry Finn, Crosan, Colman, and Brendan in search of the dream. After they have named the craft *Cara*, in honor of Brendan's mother, two more of Jarlath's monks show up, longing for adventure. Dismas and Gestas bring the number to six. For all the talk of sailing for "the glory of God," readers suspect there's a good bit of sailing for other reasons at work here too (*Brendan* 94). Finn hints that the ancient human yen for adventure is somewhere in the piously posed intentions of these sailors. Brendan is following his "heart's desire," and Finn wonders how Christ "would fancy that" (*Brendan* 100). Ironically, however, Finn will not get to find out as he falls overboard in a squall before the boat is well away, and we are left to Brendan's version of events, knowing how reliable those may be. So Brendan sails off with the burdens of Finn's supposed death, the memories of parents he'd meant to visit, and the besetting dreams he can only dimly speak. Curled in the tossing hull of the fragile, leather-hulled ship, Brendan thinks of himself as Jonah. "I cry Jonah's cry out of the belly of hell," he laments, and this time we do not have the mitigating humor of Finn to soften the words (*Brendan* 102).

This is the crisis we've seen before, from Peter Crowley to Nicolet, from Tono to Godric. Brendan faces up to his "vainglory and self-seeking" as he confronts Finn's unnecessary death (*Brendan* 103). Despite the days of fire and miracle, Brendan is now convinced that he has been abandoned by God, "cast out." Praying for a chance to return to grace, Brendan beseeches God to remember that he was once marked "precious" (*Brendan* 103). Maybe it is the height of the waves that drives his prayer; maybe he has loved Finn more than we'd guessed.

Finn's absence shows in the very typeface of the novel—Buechner offers Brendan's chapter in italics; thus readers are constantly aware that this account is not Finn's. The italics also work to underscore Brendan's words, capturing something of his intensity, something of his tendency to hyperbole. The sailors serving Father Brendan catch his sadness "like yawning" (*Brendan* 106). The ragtag bunch sails only where the wind takes them or where God has willed they go, as Brendan would have it. Brendan's inward adventures are many—he worries over his countless sins, he rues the abandoning of his parents, and he prays that he will be able to forgive their abandonment of him. But the Homeric echoes come with the extraordinary happenings on and off the *Cara*. There are mysterious monks on remote islands. Just when the sailors are near death from hunger, some savior or another will turn up; but there are also monsters in the deep, dangers by which even Finn may have been impressed. It is Dismas who first calls the *Cara* "a ship of fools" (*Brendan* 112). Grumbling and dissension break out on the little boat going God knows where.

The search for a "Land of the Fair Hope" looks increasingly like chasing after the wind, a vanity, especially to Dismas (*Brendan* 112). Peevishness gives way to panic when, thinking they've landed on an island of safety, they discover they have perched on the back of a gigantic whale, "the first and foremost of all the whales" (*Brendan* 116). They've mistaken his eye for a pool of refreshing water, and they've built a fire on his hump. The giant sea monster "is forever trying to bring his tail to his mouth," Brendan reports, and Buechner nods toward the Norse myths of the Midgarth Serpent encircling Yggdrasil, or Earth, and portending doom when he gets his tail to his mouth.

But Buechner's whale turns out to be less ominous, because Brendan can speak with all manner of creatures. The whale's name is Jasconius. Their conversation consists in a phrase to be variously translated—"Just *is it? Jest is it? God is Just? God is jest?* (*Brendan* 116). The scene is part hilarity and part hallucination. Desperate for meaning in his voyage as in his life, haunted Brendan hears in the sounds of the whale deeper messages from afar. "CONE!" becomes "Come to me ye heavy-laden," and "YUSS!" becomes "Yes," as in "the start of all things," and "the end of all things" (*Brendan* 116). Escaping Jasconius, the adventurers try to care for their leader, the navigator, their wounded Jonah, who drifts in and out, talking to the birds as often as to his men. Like the aged Godric, who loses track of when he's talking to Reginald and when to himself, Brendan dreams of the land Erc has planted in his imagination, asks the birds if he's likely to find the place. His spiritual restlessness registers with every beat of his heart—"Thrashing inside me like a caged bird," he cries (*Brendan* 118). Brendan comes out of his delirium just in time for hell. "Forty days out we sighted Hell," he records, though a volcano seems more likely. I'll bet that's what Finn would have seen.

More Dante now than Homer, the narrative moves to a crisis as the *Cara* moves too close to the burning slag. Dismas is lost in the burning sea. There's more guilt for Brendan in this, of course, but the remorse sharpens as we learn of the special friendship between Gestas and Dismas. "Maybe the best Dismas ever did with all his years of monkery was win the heart of his friend. Maybe the best Gestas ever did was lose his heart to Dismas," Brendan figures (*Brendan* 122). In any case, the burden to be borne now is not just a death but a living death, as Brendan watches Gestas go quiet with grief, "like a carved man" (*Brendan* 123). Suddenly, Brendan's gaze is drawn from Gestas to "a shaggy man" sitting motionless on a whale-size rock (*Brendan* 124). Brendan tries to steer the *Cara* by the hideous figure, hoping that he is "only a troubling dream," but the waves push them close (*Brendan* 123). The stranger's tale of woe captivates the sailors, especially Gestas. The rock, it turns out, "is paradise" compared to the man's usual condition (*Brendan* 124). Most days he boils in a pot; the rock is his Sabbath respite. He is in hell for his sin. Gestas blanches when he hears that the man's sin was "the kissing of a friend by moonlight" (*Brendan* 124).

What happens next is the center of this novel and certainly the nadir of its hard look at matters of faith. The tormented man, Judas, of course, wakes Gestas from his torpor. It is not Judas who is the fiend, Gestas argues; "The fiend is God himself" (*Brendan* 126). Everyone freezes as Gestas shakes his fist at the heavens, though, as for that, "he could almost as well have been waving at a friend" (*Brendan* 126). Buechner keeps both lines in view, but Gestas's rage is indelible when he shouts to the heavens, "Thou holy bleeding God, I piss for spite into your lovely eyes" (*Brendan* 126). Readers need a pause here, and Brendan does too. "The whole world held its breath," he says (*Brendan* 126). Judas may have been a dream, but Dismas's death was surely not, and neither is Gestas's loss of faith, another weight to bear. So who has it right, Gestas, the doubting Thomas, or Brendan, the priest in search of paradise? Brendan's chapter ends abruptly in a land that first appears to be Tir-na-n-Og but turns out to be a land of garden-variety cannibals. Gestas is full of glee.

Brendan returns home to deaths—his mother and father have passed away, Jarlath has died, and the five years have been freighted with dismay, though the one death he'd expected, Finn's, is yet to be. "The death that struck him least," though, Finn laments, was the death of Finn's son, born into the world and gone out of it while Brendan sailed the seas (*Brendan*

130). Finn had named the boy Brendan. We are glad to have Finn back at the helm. Though he is sadder, he sees quite clearly as he resumes Brendan's story and his own. Finn suspects that Brendan turned priest not so much to save others as to try to save himself. And Finn recognizes his own "Hellworthiest thing" in his desertion of his wife to follow Brendan, this time on a mission to found monasteries (*Brendan* 131). Buechner maintains the poise between his missionaries as laudable and liable. They carry faith to distant places. They cause considerable pain at home. To be fair, Finn's wife is, like Sancho's, a bit of a shrew. She thinks he should give up the service of mad monks and find his own fortune in the world. Finn knows by now that she's probably right, but he follows Brendan as one who cannot quite seem to control his own steps. Gestas has run away, and Brendan has changed, according to Finn's report. Brendan's face is more of "a closed door" than before (*Brendan* 132). Though Brendan tells many a tale, Finn is sure that he keeps locked away many more that are "crueler, lovelier" still (*Brendan* 132). The aging Brendan, like the aged Godric, has become a man of secrets and haunting memories.

Off to Abbess Brigit to learn something of the building of monasteries, Brendan gets a lecture full of remarkable ideas about women. Abbess Brigit makes little of gender distinctions. Lecturing Brendan, she opines, "Higgledy piggledy, woman and man. . . . Is God either one of them, think you? Neither if you ask me. Or both" (*Brendan* 134). Whatever Brendan learns, he throws himself into the monkery business with a fever that Finn tries to fathom. Maybe he did it for Erc, Finn thinks, and Jarlath, and even "to make up for the terrible curse that crazed man cried out against God," Finn argues, referring to Gestas (*Brendan* 136). With less conviction, Finn notes that Brendan no doubt does it all for God. Plumbing the depths of the matter, however, Finn probably gets closest when he reports that "Brendan never would have worked so hard if he hadn't the notion tucked in the back of his red pointed head that someday God in his glory would reward him for it" (*Brendan* 136). Reliable Finn recognizes that Brendan is driven by some deep sense of sin. Unlike Reginald, who can never see the truth of Godric, Finn sees something of the truth of Brendan and follows him anyway. Admirable fellow, loyal Finn.

Brendan proves very good at attracting monks to his company. His rule is relatively easy compared to the usual operations of such places, but the real magic of serving under Brendan is in getting to hear his stories. The tales of his voyage have stretched a bit by now. The *Cara* has become a ship for sixty, not six, and the sailors were, in his memory, compassionate toward one another, sacrificial, and ever holy. Brendan tells of islands where the mice were as big as sheep and grapes as big as apples. His exploits sound marvelous, parsed thus, and the monks warm to the legends of Brendan's saving his men by walking on water and other derring-do. So is it too harsh to say that Brendan builds his monasteries on lies? Even Finn is puzzled. Remembering a night of tales when the rapt listeners are beset by stinging gnats, Finn tells of how Brendan "bade them be gone forever" (*Brendan* 141). "Just like that," Finn testifies, "they were gone or we was so lost in the glory of his words we forgot them" (*Brendan* 141). With Brendan, you just never know.

Up to now, I must admit that Brendan's obsession with guilt seems self-indulgent. What is it that could be worth so much regret? Now Buechner takes us into that universal human arena, the interplay between the brothers that leads some to be admired and others to be despised, some to be the butt of jokes and others to be venerated beyond all common sense. One can almost imagine the shuffling of chairs as Brendan does his best to avoid some of the more annoying of the brothers, especially Malo, a "wrathful" man, and Beothacht, "a cow-eyed priest" (*Brendan* 142). Sent by Brendan to guard the *Cara*, Malo is nearly trapped by rising flood-waters. Beothacht bothers Brendan about heading off to rescue Malo. The flame-haired Brendan's generally controlled temper explodes in his words, "If you've got that much pity, you ninny, go drown in his place yourself and be damned" (*Brendan* 142).

Drown he does, of course. Brendan is inconsolable. Finn registers his own inadequacy. "I was never much comfort to Brendan," Finn confesses, though the reader suspects that Brendan just hasn't noticed the comfort Finn proffered. "You need somebody bigger than yourself to comfort you," Finn adds, and the reader thinks that Finn may be bigger than he knows (*Brendan* 144). To all his many indiscretions and missteps, Brendan can now add a capital letter crime—murder. Beothacht is dead, and Brendan blames himself. Malo is the one they save from the flood, so Brendan is doubly cursed by the plaguing presence of the bitter man, "a thorn in Brendan's foot" (*Brendan* 148). Brendan will learn that Malo's spewing hatred is really aimed at Christ. Thus Brendan bears the brunt, because he's "the closest to Christ of anyone he [Malo] knows" (*Brendan* 164). When Finn explains that Brendan ought to be honored "to take Christ's blows for him," Brendan is scandalized (*Brendan* 164). Like old Godric, Brendan cannot bear any talk of his own sanctity.

Although his very name suggests something of his evil, Malo is another of Buechner's intriguing villains who turns out to have a story to mitigate the villainy. The price Malo has paid for his conversion to Patrick's Christ has been the horrific murder of his wife and two children at the hands of their own kindred. The scene of their butchering, among the most graphic passages in the novel, explains Malo's wretchedness. Brendan is nearly done in by what he's done to Beothacht. Finn wants to ease Brendan's pain by trying to make him understand that "we all have hearts made the same way," but Brendan is never easily consoled (*Brendan* 150). In their grief and misery, Malo and Brendan now become a curse on one another—for Brendan, a penance, for Malo, an expression of torment. Off to Ita's for counsel, Brendan picks up another disciple for his motley band, a blind one this time. Mahon will be along for the remedy Ita recommends, "a second go at Tir-na-n-Og" (*Brendan* 153). The navigator does it up right for the second voyage—a crew of fifty and a real ship that he dubs *Bishop's Joy* in memory of Erc. Crosan returns for the trip; Malo and Mahon are there along with Brendan's brothers and a notable stowaway. A yellow-haired monk turns out to be Maeve in disguise, Maeve in search of some part of paradise herself. Brendan leaves the steering to others this time, though he does set the direction—true west.

Brendan has no patience for adventures this time. He longs only for the hope that Tir-na-n-Og represents. Finn imagines that Brendan is mostly peering inside himself "to find how he'd look washed clean of all his nastiness" (*Brendan* 158). Mahon teaches him chess, but Brendan mostly reads metaphor into the game. Everything he sees is about his failure, his distance from what he might have been. Protecting the king, for example, is like protecting God. "It is ourselves above all we must keep him safe from," Brendan mumbles in words out of the mouth of Greene's whiskey priest (*Brendan* 159). Is this a profound love of God or a profound despising of self? Brendan's second voyage is mostly into himself, where, Buechner believes, "the real news is" (*TS* 2). Brendan does come on deck when they catch a glimpse of Jasconius, his old friend from the first journey. The central challenge on this voyage is probably boredom, at least until they finally reach the balmy day when the raven flies back with a leaf in her mouth. Brendan is now Noah coming close to the end of the journey. The draggle-tailed crew of *Bishop's Joy* scrambles ashore to a reception of "brown-limbed women and men both with feathers in their hair or flowers" (*Brendan* 167). Brendan has lived so long with his dream, is so sure of what he wants to see, that he is certain that he has arrived at last in the land of the blessed. A jokester of an old man, the only one who speaks their language, makes matters worse. Brendan tremulously asks, "Hy Brasail? . . . Is it true then?" The old man, Tara, answers, "There's not a doubt of it in the world, my dear" (*Brendan* 177).

Readers have already had a doubt or two. So has Finn. Saint Patrick turns out to be a pet monkey, and the old man is the only survivor of a company of monks who came to this place long ago, only to be eaten by a monstrous pig that the monk has named Para, short for Paraclete. "He's got eleven holy ghosts tucked away in his tum somewheres," Tara declares, and the humor turns dark indeed (*Brendan* 181). Although Brendan takes some convincing that the blessed land is not *the* blessed land, the dream has pretty well gone up in smoke. Circumventing the silly Tara, Brendan seeks out the tribe's wizard, hoping for directions to "the souls of the blessed," and the sailors are all in on the dream by now, all "thinking of some blessed soul he'd be every bit as glad to find as Brendan to find Erc" (*Brendan* 189–90). Adventures crowd close: Maeve is exposed in all senses of the word, and Brendan, of all people, holds her for a moment; the king's daughter, the beautiful Etain, leads a band of six on the final reach of the journey; Crosan is dying; Maeve is doubting; Malo is Malo.

Maeve has come along to learn "if there's a God at all" (*Brendan* 194). Like Brownie, at the end of the sprawling *Bebb* chronicles, Maeve has tried to hang on to the faith she's seen in the nuns and monks. The earth is shifting beneath her feet; "I've never seen so much as a print of his shoe myself though I've looked sharp many a year," she groans (*Brendan* 194). Maeve's loss of faith becomes merely one more weight on Brendan's load of guilt. What's worse, the pilgrimage ends on the bank of a river, the edge of the world for Etain and her people, and Brendan knows that, like Moses, he is not to see the promised land. This is the big moment; Brendan's whole life is in the balance. Yet Finn notices the irony—Brendan "looked less like a man defeated than a man with a load off his back" (*Brendan* 197). Brendan has finally grown past the need for certainty. Maybe the hints of heaven are enough. To know for sure would be to risk annihilation. Maybe Brendan doesn't try to cross the river because he fears the anger of the king on the other side. Or maybe he simply fears that the only thing on the other side is another shore. "Suppose not even there could Maeve make out so much as the print of God's shoe?" Finn asks (*Brendan* 197). They only get close enough to the river to bury Crosan in it—death so near the place of eternal life.

Buechner might have stopped the story here, the great voyages over, the life of Brendan at its ebb. But there's more. Brendan retreats with Malo, Mahon, and Finn into a hermitage to add up the score, catalog his sins. There's Dismas to call up and Gestas's curse. There's Maeve's dead faith and Beothacht. There's years of hard travel to no apparent end. "My believing is as muddled as my hearing," the old man Brendan concedes, not sure himself what to make of what he may or may not have seen across that river. Folks back home believe Brendan found paradise, indeed, and they rush "to feast their eyes on him" (*Brendan* 204). Before fleeing their adulation, Brendan declares, "I'll tell you about my voyages, then. . . . They never did anybody a bit of good least of all Christ" (*Brendan* 206). Here's Leo Bebb and Saint Godric all over again, convinced of the ineradicable stain of sin, sure that their lives have been a vacancy. "Rue and shame was the winds that drove him," Finn explains (*Brendan* 207). Saved by a woman again, this time by Brigit, who comes to shake Brendan from the stupor of despair his guilt has brought on him, Brendan rouses enough to tell her that his sights weren't "worth the price" (*Brendan* 211). Brigit tells Brendan that the hermit business is not for him. With his knack for preaching, he should be "harvesting souls for Christ," she argues (*Brendan* 210). Ancient Brigit "called Brendan out of the grave that day," as Finn understands the episode, and we are glad enough that Buechner didn't leave Brendan's story back there on the shore of the promised land (*Brendan* 212).

Where does it end? In Wales, surprisingly enough, a land where the legends of Brendan's deeds have yet to stretch. More new characters await in this cast of hundreds, the first being Gildas the Wise, though Finn submits that "Gildas the Sour fitted him better" (*Brendan* 213). A bookkeeper for Christ, Gildas is carefully recording his neighbor's sins, just in case Christ has missed a few. "Gildas was so steeped in the badness of things he was as blind to goodness as he was blind to the sunlit meadow" (*Brendan* 214). Where have we heard all this before? Gildas is attentive in all the wrong ways, but he points Finn and Brendan to Artor and the last great adventure of the novel.

The Brendan of the novel's final pages is a wiser man, offering solid advice to Gildas and thinking deeply into his own scattered life. Brendan tells Gildas that the busywork Gildas is performing for God may not be what God "truly wants" (*Brendan* 216). When Gildas turns the question back to him, Brendan is forced to answer it for himself. "He wants each one of us to have a loving heart. . . . When all's said and done, perhaps that's the length and breadth of it," Brendan concludes (*Brendan* 216). Buechner's novels are stocked full with cripples—fluttering eyelids, blind men, bodily decrepitude, and, especially, lameness. We are all of us "poor naked wretches," as the hapless student in Tono's class summarized it in *Open Heart* (*Bebb* 179). Buechner speaks of his own "crippling secret" in the memoirs and keeps a stock of walking sticks and canes at his back door (*TS* 33). All of us are "crippled as the dark world," Brendan figures out, and the only respite is "to lend each other a hand when we're falling. . . . Perhaps that's the only work that matters in the end" (*Brendan* 217).

For all his desire to make a big splash for Christ, what Brendan seems to have learned is the power of the small acts. Most days in Wales, Brendan goes off to visit a poor widow with whom he plays a board game. He is nobody famous to her, but his being there is everything to her. The scene is reminiscent of a chapter in Buechner's own life where he played Aggravation regularly with an elderly woman near his Vermont home. "You'll never know the good you do me," Olwen, the widow, tells Brendan, and we can hear another voice saying the same words. Here's a new version of Christianity, not about the blaring big thing, but about the personal small ones. Brendan visits the naked and the hungry. He exemplifies the message of Christ's last parable, the one about sheep and goats and visiting the prisoners and clothing the naked. He has learned much, has Brendan. Maybe he didn't bring them heaven, but at least "he brought them himself," Finn believes (*Brendan* 220). And surely that counts for something. This is not to say that Buechner is waxing homiletical or has become, as McCoy would have it, a "novelist/theologian" (McCoy 98). Buechner is as open-ended in *Brendan* as always—ambiguity and darkness still having their place on the stage.

More forgetful now of his own wretchedness as he looks outward again, Brendan hears of a great need in Caerlon where Artor, the famous king who "saved the Welsh land from pillage and rape," has fallen into despair at the betrayal of his queen and the evil machinations of a bastard son. Brendan's visit causes Artor to "take heart," though he will die soon after in battle. Ironically, it is Finn who blesses the old king before Finn and Brendan head back to Gildas. Surely Finn has had his own reversals toward wisdom. News of Artor's death stirs Brendan to think of his own. He plans one last voyage, the one toward home. Frustrated by wars and rumors of them in his own time, Buechner slips in a take on the idiocies of war via a return to Cashel, as Brendan tries to mediate a peace between King Hugh of Cashel and the king of Connacht. When Hugh explains that he has "given them leave to war for the sake of peace," Brendan realizes something of the convoluted tangle of human affairs (*Brendan* 228). "It's the way of a dark world," he decides (*Brendan* 229). But this particular bloody time is averted when Brendan calls up a thick mist, a cloud so thick as to bring "dimness to their eyes" and "confusion to their feet," as Brendan prays (*Brendan* 231). Finn offers no other explanation for the mist. Maybe this miracle was just what it seemed to be.

Adventures give way to memories and reunions in the final pages of the novel. Maybe simple survival is "at the heart of our remembering," Buechner argues, and Brendan has survived indeed (Zinsser 7). Brendan decides to burn his parchments, though he cannot burn the parchments of his mind (*Brendan* 234). Remembering his failures, Brendan conjures up Dismas, Judas, and the others. "I've seen hell," he cries to Finn (*Brendan* 233). Finn tells him that he's "looked on the fair shores of Heaven as well," but the hopeful side seems to have little weight for Brendan (*Brendan* 233). Perhaps he gets some peace when he runs across an aged Gestas, the monk whose blasphemy and flight had caused Brendan so many sleepless nights. Finn is struck by the peaceful aspect of Gestas, "the one that had cursed God," as opposed to the look of "a man in torment" on the face of Brendan, "the one that had spent his whole life long serving God" (*Brendan* 237). "Maybe it was God's jest," Finn concludes, and Buechner carries us back to that incalculable mystery at the core. Even Malo has mostly forgiven God by now; having lived for so long in the pity and regard of Brendan, Malo has been transformed. When Brendan prays for mercy, it is Malo who utters "Amen" (*Brendan* 238). And Finn chimes in, too. "I said amen myself even," he tells us (*Brendan* 238).

Finn's transformation, though subtle, speaks not only in his attempts to record Brendan's life but also in what he tells us of his own. He has forsaken almost everything to follow the gadfly Brendan, and in the end Finn gets the joke. "It was like the jest had grown riper and sweeter," Finn says of Brendan's cackling over Saint Patrick as a red monkey, and Finn will have the last word on his friend (*Brendan* 239). Brendan dies, words of fearfulness on his lips, and "the whole land mourned him" (*Brendan* 240). "As to the sentence of the judge," Finn summarizes, "I'm not the one to know nor even if there be a judge at all" (*Brendan* 240). Finn maintains his neutrality on matters of faith right to the end. But readers can hear that Brendan has turned out all right as far as Finn is concerned. If he were the judge, he concludes, he'd want Brendan to know that he "won't be alone" if there really is a "Country of the Young" (*Brendan* 240). And, most importantly, Finn wants Brendan to know that, despite his having becoming so snarled in Brendan's life as to have little room for his own, "it was worth it" (*Brendan* 240). Finn finishes, "I'd tell him he has my pardon anyhow" (*Brendan* 240). Finn prays to his friend for mercy on himself and his listeners; then he whispers "Amen" one more time.

Like most of Buechner's heroes, Brendan gets everything wrong and yet, somehow, gets the one big thing right. Given a few pages to focus *Brendan* in the memoir *Telling Secrets*, Buechner goes to the scene where

Finn and Brendan realize that Gildas the Wise has only one leg. "I'm as crippled as the dark world," Gildas confesses (*Brendan* 217). "If it comes to that, which one of us isn't, my dear?" Brendan answers, offering that word of affection, "dear," in the way of Erc and Jarlath and the monks of his youth (*Brendan* 217). Thus Buechner reads his own book as underscoring incompleteness and need. But he also adds something of the lesson Brendan is slow to learn. "'The kingdom of God is among you,' Jesus said—the Land of the Blessed. . . . It is not beyond the western horizon that the Kingdom lies but among you, among ourselves, within ourselves and our life together," Buechner writes (*TS* 88). He refines a long-standing preoccupation with *Brendan*. I suspect that it was at Wheaton, where he read or reread C. S. Lewis's *The Last Battle*, that he begins to ponder the further implications of his many pages on the business of listening, paying heed. In the memoirs, he recalls the scene of Lewis's dwarves "huddled together in what they think is a cramped, dark, stable." In reality, of course, they are standing in "an endless green meadow" (*TS* 89). Such is Brendan's dilemma too. *Brendan* is a novel, finally, about misunderstanding. And the one most misunderstood is one who moves only dimly in the background—God himself. The wind of this theme will fill Buechner's sails now for voyages into the Old Testament and into the Apocryphal book *Tobit*.

Notes

1. Personal correspondence, June 26, 1986.
2. Personal correspondence, June 26, 1986.
3. Frederick Buechner, quoted in Renni Browne, "The Power of Fiction," *Christian Retailing*, November 15, 1989, 17.
4. Frederick Buechner, *Brendan* (New York: Atheneum, 1987), 1. Hereafter cited as *Brendan*.
5. Mitch Finley, "The Oddball Saints of Author Frederick Buechner," *Our Sunday Visitor*, March 26, 1989, 1.
6. Martha Stout, "Tale of a Saint," *Eternity*, November, 1987, 50.
7. Frederick Buechner, speech in Iowa City, Iowa, October 16, 1989.
8. Frederick Buechner, speech in Iowa City, Iowa, October 16, 1989.
9. Personal correspondence, November 12, 1981.
10. Mark Twain, *The Adventures of Huckleberry Finn*, ed. Henry Nash Smith (Boston: Houghton Mifflin Co., 1958), 3.
11. Julia O'Faolain, "St. Patrick Monkeys Around," *New York Times Book Review*, August 9, 1987, 15.
12. Mitch Finley, book review, *St. Anthony Messenger*, July 1988, 50.

Chapter Nine

Managing Mirth

The Son of Laughter

The trouble with Bible stories is that we've already heard them, heard them so often that we've stopped listening. In the early 1990s Buechner decides to take on Genesis, tell us a tale we already know. The book that appears in 1993, *The Son of Laughter*, might be a novel, or a retelling, or what the *New York Times* reviewer labeled a "novelization."[1] In any case, *The Son of Laughter* is the story of the biblical patriarch Jacob, a man we thought we knew. We've seen the paintings that celebrate his midnight struggle with an angel. We remember the humor and the horror of those years he spent fruitlessly laboring for the wrong wife. We've probably seen flannel board versions of the famous coat of many colors that, to his regret, he gave to a favorite son. We've read about the tricks that he played on others and the tricks that were played on him. Noting the familiarity of the story, Calvin Miller suggested that Buechner "has a way of telling us what we already know, so that we are glad we know it."[2] Buechner makes the "predictable intriguing," Miller added (Miller 52).

In an interview with Wendy Herstein, explaining his move from historical saints to biblical patriarchs and remembering the genesis of his plunge into Genesis, Buechner hearkens all the way back to *The Power and the Glory*. There, he intimates, he "became interested in the notion of a saint as a human being who's just as much clay-footed and full of shadows as the rest of us, but who is used nonetheless by God."[3] He then goes on to survey his own career as a preoccupation with saints. The *Bebb* novels, he suggests, are about a man who is "a religious crook" and "a bearer of grace." Godric is "a lecher and a scoundrel" but "also a saint," he adds (Herstein 308). There's Brendan too, of course. But describing the route to *The Son of Laughter*, Buechner records a striking moment: "Suddenly, I thought, 'My God, there's Jacob.' Absolutely made to order—a man who was all that he was, a rascal, a cheater of his father, a cheater of his brother, and, at the same time, was the father of the twelve tribes and the bearer of the promise. So Jacob was a natural next step for me" (Herstein 308).

Buechner finds his way into the gaps of the Jacob record in much the same way that he had imagined his way into the lesser-known histories of Godric and Brendan. He breathes new vitality into familiar stories this time, managing to find remarkable relevance in those tales we've heard from childhood, though I'm inclined to agree with Mark Twain in wondering about the good sense of parents who allow their children access to stories like Jacob's. Many critics noted the contemporariness in the new novel, using words like "universal" and "archetypal."[4] Buechner finds relevance in the ancient narratives, sure enough, but the most interesting word in the reviews is "surprise." George Garrett struck the chord when he argued that "Buechner's career as a novelist has been a string of surprises" (Garrett 293). Looking back over the hundreds of reviews of Buechner's novels, I am surprised by all the surprise. Buechner takes a certain pleasure, I think, in catching reviewers and readers off guard. He is a staid and reserved man, but I've long suspected a mischief beneath the exterior; there's fun for him in raising readers' eyebrows. Central themes persist, but the way of approaching those themes is as different as Leo Bebb and Peter Cowley. *The Son of Laughter* is yet another departure, the surprise this time in how Buechner makes Jacob's story our own.

This period in Buechner's career also features other red-letter moments, especially the loss of his mother, who died in 1988. Katherine, or "Kaki" as the family called her, had in some way shut her son's mouth with her "fury" at the oblique references to herself in her son's 1958 novel, *The Return of Ansel Gibbs* (TS 10). Her notable absence in *The Sacred Journey* renders that book partial, a story of a son with his mother omitted. Now comes a loosening of the tongue, a veritable flood of new angles into the story of a disrupted childhood. *The Wizard's Tide: A Story* appears in 1990, and *Telling Secrets: A Memoir* follows in 1991. *The Wizard's Tide* is often grouped with Buechner's novels, but that is a problematic classification, since the short book is so directly autobiographical. Buechner clearly defies simple categorization. I prefer William Pritchard's word on the relationship between the memoirs, fiction, and nonfiction: "these categories infuse one another."[5] *The Wizard's Tide* is a novel infused by memoir, or is it a nonfiction infused by fiction? In any case, Buechner ran into some difficulty when shopping the manuscript of *The Wizard's Tide*, not only because it was his only foray into writing for a young adult audience,

Buechner's mother
Circa 1968

but also because that market is uneasy about the sort of subjects Buechner features in the tale. The book is, as he labels it, "A Story," but it is decidedly his own story, a thinly veiled revisiting of Buechner's own childhood. *The Wizard's Tide* should be located with the memoirs and should be read as an important moment in Buechner's self-analysis, an introspective tour that also produces his most telling memoir, *Telling Secrets*. Taken together with *The Son of Laughter*, the two memoirs establish Buechner's preoccupation with filling in the gaps in his own story, gaps remaining even after several excursions into autobiography. What he finds in the gaps—most notably the coming to terms with a father, the tragedy of a family's dysfunctionality—spills over into the biblical excursion that will produce the big novel of these years. In all of these books of the early 1990s, Buechner is making peace with the past. Although the memoirs have found a significant readership and have served Buechner well as they weave in and out of the novels, his career will stand or fall on the fiction. He admits as much in a 1983 interview; asked what he would like to be remembered for, he answers, "I would choose the fiction."[6]

The interplay between the fiction and the nonfiction provides a fruitful consideration for approaches to Buechner's work, and we must detour into the rich background work of the 1990s to understand the frame in which *The Son of Laughter* ultimately rests. Buechner claims his nonfiction is the place where he is "trying to be as honest as I can to my own experience—my own experience of God, my own experience of the absence of God."[7] In the fiction, he says, "I find myself saying things that are more than I know and better than I am" (*Door* 12). Most readers of, say, *The Sacred Journey* and *The Son of Laughter* will naturally wonder about the connections between the two, because the novel of the life of Jacob would seem at first glance far removed from Buechner's own life.

The question is not so much about how much of his personal story finds its way into the novels, though that is a legitimate inquiry, and I do contend that Buechner is an autobiographical novelist in the richest sense. His novels are not a record of the events of his life, but they are a record of *the* life. More basic still, however, is the question of what influence the nonfiction, especially the memoirs, has on the fiction. Buechner cites *The Alphabet of Grace* and other such early attempts at memoir as teaching him "to trust the sound of my own voice."[8] That is, the memoirs allow him to be funny, to relax, and the turn to first-person narration in *Bebb* is surely related to the accumulating pages written in the decade of the 1970s in his own voice and out of his own experience. The memoirs and the other nonfiction undoubtedly fuel the fiction. That much we can say with confidence.

The year before *The Son of Laughter* also sees Buechner's appearance on a famous lectureship program in New York and San Francisco. The 1992 Trinity Lectures featured Buechner with Maya Angelou and James Carroll. In those lectures and in *The Clown in the Belfry: Writings on Faith and Fiction*, a collection of essays and sermons also appearing in 1992, Buechner visits his memories as a way to speak of the same mysteries for which his novels have become celebrated. His many takes on autobiography include an attempt to see from a child's perspective in *The Wizard's Tide*, a book that tells Buechner's story with the names changed—Buechner becomes Schroeder, Freddy becomes Teddy, and Jamie, Buechner's brother, James, becomes Bean. Some details shift in the fictionalization, but *The Wizard's Tide* is essentially the first chapter of *The Sacred Journey* revisited from a new angle and with heretofore withheld parts of the story included. As he has done before with *Godric* and *Brendan* and as he will do with *The Son of Laughter* and *On the Road with the Archangel*, Buechner turns the material of *The Sacred Journey* fifteen degrees, juggles it in his now older hands, peers at it from a freshened perspective.

The Wizard's Tide is another take on the central event of Buechner's life, his father's suicide, and Mark Twain's voice sounds again in the second sentence—"It is a mostly true story," the narrator claims—but the voice is Buechner's too.[9] To announce that the tale is "mostly true" is to caution the reader about the difficulty of actually getting at the truth while also claiming the high ground of veracity. Duly warned, we learn in the second paragraph that the subject here is the grown-up Teddy, who is conducting a kind of self-therapy, trying to solve "the mysteries about his childhood" (*WTide* 1). The narrator clarifies Teddy's intentions: "He told it [his story] because it helped that child inside himself to solve at least some of those mysteries at long last and because—who knows?—maybe it would clear up a few mysteries for other grown-up children too, or even some real children if any of them ever happened to get around to reading it" (*WTide* 1). The premise here is the same as that which drives *The Sacred Journey*, in which Buechner explains the motive behind the memoir: "My assumption is that the story of any one of us is in some measure the story of us all" (*SJ* 6).

The Wizard's Tide is primarily another way to get at his own story on the way to recommending the process to others. Buechner's real life experience is only lightly disguised in *The Wizard's Tide*, and the fact that Buechner wrote the book in the months after his mother's death in 1988 is of some consequence. What this version of the story adds has mostly to do with the mother, the "very pretty" Mrs. Schroeder (*WTide* 3). "She never learned to be kind and generous and unselfish because she never had to," the narrator tells us, and Mrs. Schroeder comes off as superficial and shrill, deeply implicated in the irresponsible behavior of Teddy's father and in the drama of a family falling to pieces (*WTide* 4). In painful observations about his own mother, Buechner surmises that she "really survived all the bad things that happened in her life by simply denying them, and she couldn't bear to touch on anything painful" (Brown 37). Apparently there were fights that made Teddy "afraid that the very ground they were standing on would split apart like an earthquake and they would all be swallowed up in it" (*WTide* 14). Teddy's insecurity here directly echoes that which Buechner details in *The Sacred Journey* when he confesses, "I knew that hurt, loss, darkness, death could flatten that house in seconds"

(*SJ* 36). The house is his childhood home, and in both versions of the story, the house is flattened, indeed.

The Wizard's Tide includes many of the more graphic outtakes from *The Sacred Journey*. In one scene, for example, Teddy is forced by his mother to be the custodian of his father's car keys. Mr. Schroeder has been drinking, and the boy has to play an unbearably adult role. Buechner recounts this scene in an essay, "Adolescence and the Stewardship of Pain," in *The Clown and the Belfry*, speaking of it as part of the bewildering hurt that he filed away—"cast it off together with many other painful scenes like it"— only to have to deal with it later in such books as *The Wizard's Tide* (*Belfry* 90). And the deepest problem in this family is that "when bad things happened, nobody ever talked about them" (*WTide* 56). Buechner tells the story again in the Trinity Lectures and in *Telling Secrets* without the fictional mask. "Don't talk, don't trust, don't feel," is, Buechner notes, "the unwritten law of families that for one reason or another have gone out of whack" (*TS* 10). Buechner's mother presided over the family secrets "like Victoria over the British Empire" (Kendrick 901). Even when Teddy's father dies a suicide, nobody wants to talk about it.

Thus *Telling Secrets*, *The Wizard's Tide*, and *The Son of Laughter* all come in a period when Buechner is exploring the psychological dimensions of his family history, and it is, therefore, understandable that Victoria Allen concluded that "*The Son of Laughter* represented Buechner's most conscious use of psychological dynamics to reveal and explain spiritual truths" (Allen 144). To say, as Allen did, that Buechner sees the Christian faith "through the lens of a psychologically-informed spirituality" is merely to speak a truism (Allen xvii). All good writers are by definition, I suppose, psychologically astute. And who of us in these therapeutic times is not at least shaded by psychology in one way or another? Buechner clearly does see memory, heeding one's experience, as a key to recovering from the slings and arrows of our various misfortunes. In *Telling Secrets*, he concludes, "memory makes it possible for us both to bless the past . . . and also be blessed by it. If this kind of remembering sounds like what psychotherapy is all about, it is because of course it is" (*TS* 33). But Buechner doesn't stop with that: "I think it is also what the forgiveness of sins is all about—the interplay of God's forgiveness of us and our forgiveness of God and each other," he adds (*TS* 33). Buechner's work of the early 1990s reflects his ventures into psychotherapy; his own experience of therapy clarifies much for him as a human being and as a writer.

The therapeutic model, however, does not replace Christian faith. The nonfiction continues to be "unabashedly Christian," as Frank Levering

Buechner
Circa 2004

noted.[10] *Telling Secrets*, Levering believed, was "a meditation on the connection between knowing and sharing secrets and discovering the reality of a loving and merciful God" (Levering 7). Frederick Buechner has been touched by the recovery movement, by Adult Children of Alcoholics sessions, by therapy, and more. Buechner has had extraordinary impetus to explore those regions of the psyche that might explain and address his personal pain. This exploration shows up in the work of Buechner's career, and the territory of psychology can elucidate many passages in the Buechner corpus. It does not follow, however, that Buechner's lifework can be explained simply in terms of therapeutic models. The most recent, book-length treatment of Buechner's work, *Listening to Life*, Allen's study, was helpful in the way she opened Buechner's preoccupation with shame, guilt, memory, and forgiveness, but her focus on "psychological spirituality" works only partially as an approach to Buechner's work.

That said, *The Wizard's Tide* is a book in which Buechner explores not just his past but also his psyche. It is a book where bad things happen, an unusual book for adolescents, as the publishers must have thought—a kid's book about suicide? Two publishers rejected the book as "too grown up" (Brown 41). But the bad things need to be told, if truth is what we're after. A wrenching story, *The Wizard's Tide* is one more way for Buechner to remember his father and come to terms with his father's absence, even though he can face the details only by cloaking them beneath the veneer of a fiction. Teddy "wanted to remember everything about him [his father] that he could remember so someday he could tell about him to other people who had never even seen him," we hear in the novelist's voice (*WTide* 103). The memories are clouded by the pain, the dysfunction that ruled the days, but Buechner finds impetus in that subject that will carry him from his own story to one of the most dazzlingly dysfunctional families of all time, the family of Abraham. From the old man himself, willing to butcher his son at God's whim, to the fearful son Isaac, whose name means "laughter," to the trickster Jacob, who will one day be called Israel, their story of fathers and sons is one of unbearable collapse and unspeakable joy. So is Buechner's story.

Telling Secrets is another wondering out loud about the meaning, or lack thereof, in any human experience. "Have I concocted a plot out of what is only a story? Who knows? I can only say that to me life in general, including my life in particular, *feels* like a plot, and I find that a source of both strength and fascination," Buechner remarks in the introduction (*TS* 2). As Timothy Jones noticed, "More than anything Buechner has written, *Telling Secrets* is full of *becauses*. He is eager not just to tell but to understand."[11] So what is the plot in a father's suicide or a daughter's anorexia? Buechner explores such questions in his own family history. *Telling Secrets*, originally entitled *Family Secrets: The Life Within*, is an untangling of those family connections as well as a study of the price of denial, an attempt to order apparent chaos. The implicit notion is that good can come from keeping track, and Buechner will carry that conception over from his own experience to his imaginative encounter with Jacob's experiences.

Buechner even includes a poignant scene in which, on the advice of a therapist, he writes "about those distant days" with his left hand (*TS* 98). "It was as if some of my secrets had found a way of communicating with me directly," he writes (*TS* 98). The moment is pivotal in the memoir and in the career. Writing with his left hand apparently had the effect of suspending the writer's brain and allowing the more "artless and basic . . . awkward scrawl" of the child to have dominion (*TS* 98). The scene is a bidding farewell, a coming to grips, that spills over into the novel of the time, the continuing reconciliation with painful memories. Having reached his sixties, Buechner is reconciling with his own past as he walks the aged Jacob through a similar reconciliation.

Buechner also speaks in *Telling Secrets* of his involvement with Al-Anon, where he met with groups whose families had been afflicted with alcoholism, apparently part of the problem in his own family history. He admires their attempts at revealing their secrets and making peace, and he compares such groups to churches, which often display what he calls "an uncomfortable resemblance to the dysfunctional family" (*TS* 93). What churches could learn from Al-Anon, he thinks, is to be more honest and basic—"Hello, my name is Joe; I am a sinner." Maybe church should start there. *Telling Secrets* is a confession, a revealing, and a statement of hope in which Buechner can say, "I have bumbled my way at least to the outermost suburbs of Truth that can never be told but only come upon" (*TS* 106). But fundamentally *Telling Secrets* is about telling secrets—talking right out loud about that dismal day in November and all that followed from it. It is "a complicated story and certainly a sad story," Buechner allows, "but in other ways it's, I think, a very hopeful story" (Fickett 59).

The hopefulness is in the potential consequences of confession, the conjecture that revealing the secrets may well lead to forgiveness, even healing. Since the early 1990s, Buechner's work has been increasingly preoccupied with the airing of secrets, and the idea turns up again in the 2006 collection of sermons and essays *Secrets in the Dark*. The premise that the releasing of the secret can lead to hope and healing, the assumption of some schools of psychotherapy, is at the heart of Buechner's theological assumptions. It is a theology that begins with a sense of failure, inadequacy, and incompleteness, a theology that David Crumm summarized as "All of us are charlatans."[12] I think Buechner would prefer Will Campbell's version: "We're all bastards, but God loves us anyway" (Brown 85).

Although it may seem like a long journey from a suicide in 1936 to the larger-than-life patriarchs of Old Testament lore, Buechner manages a fusion of the two in *The Son of Laughter*. The tales of Jacob have offered inspiration and fascination to many artists. Allen mentioned Ernest Hemingway and Marianne Moore as examples. She might also have included writers as diverse as Virginia Woolf, Joel Yanofsky, and Katherine Paterson. Buechner was apparently attracted to Jacob almost from the beginning of his writing career. In his first sermon, delivered in May of 1954 at

Lawrenceville School, well before seminary and ordination, Buechner cites the Genesis version of Jacob's ladder and employs the story as a metaphor for all our longing: "What we want is always missing. The only way we can be sure that it exists at all is that we miss it, that we are born with a longing for it in our hearts."[13] Buechner authorized publication of the sermon in 1990, saying, "though I might put it differently these 36 years later, there's nothing in it I still wouldn't sign my name to" (Sermon 12). Remarkably, the core of Buechner's theological position is in place early on, and Jacob is on the scene, his midnight brawl with an angel the perfect image for Buechner's dream of encounter with the divine, as well as his sense of how enigmatic such visitations remain.

Buechner further reveals a fascination with Jacob in the 1979 book *Peculiar Treasures* and returns to the story in many of his published sermons. In "The Magnificent Defeat," for example, he characterizes Jacob as a "shrewd and ambitious man who is strong on guts and weak on conscience" (*MD* 15). Displaying his penchant for name play, Buechner translates Jacob's Hebrew name as "he who supplants" or "the go-getter" (*MD* 13). Dating from the late 1960s, "The Magnificent Defeat" emphasizes Jacob's rascality, but by 1979, with *Peculiar Treasures*, Buechner's view of the story will have ripened toward humor. "The book of Genesis makes no attempt to conceal the fact that Jacob was, among other things, a crook,"[14] he gibes there. The whimsy of Buechner's take and the rich potential of such a character as Jacob are apparent already in one sentence. The theme of the novel is already in his head, too, as he concludes his entry on Jacob: "God doesn't love people because of who they are but because of who he is. *It's on the house* is one way of saying it and *it's by grace* is another, just as it was by grace that it was Jacob of all people who became not only the father of the twelve tribes of Israel but the many times great grandfather of Jesus of Nazareth" (*PT* 58). This summary of the meaning of the Jacob story is intriguing in part because of the way Buechner avoids such summaries in the novels. In the homiletical material, lessons are OK. In the novels, lessons are anathema, the jokes are never explained, and the themes never delineated in any overt way. Nonetheless some part of that reevaluation of God is in the mix of the book, as Buechner seems again to be weighing his own thoughts about the supernatural as he engages Jacob's struggles.

Buechner's rendering of Jacob, the Old Testament trickster who came to be known as Israel, emphasizes the humanness of the father of nations—his loves and jealousies, his humiliations and bewilderments. Buechner imagines his way into the soaring faith and plunging despair of this rich character. Along the way, Buechner paints the weariness of day-to-day survival and offers a vision of an Old Testament world that adds color and depth to our assumptions about the times and the places. As with most of Buechner's stories, however, the main character finally gets to be the reader, as Jacob's struggles mirror our own. As the old man Israel tells his story, moving back and forth over it, telling it from both ends at once, as old people often do, Buechner underscores his belief in the power of remembering. Jacob has plenty he'd like to forget—the betrayals and failures and hurts—but at the center of *The Son of Laughter* is the promise, a runaway blessing, careening down through the generations. Sometimes it looks more like a curse. But always there: "I will be with you. I will make of you a great people" (*Laughter* 269). Jacob sees the blessing as the central reality of his life and understands the privilege and the terror of being chosen. *The Son of Laughter* is a lively and grisly story that mixes Old Testament flavors with contemporary ones.

Jacob tells his own story, though he cannot tell it straight. Flitting between the famous episodes and scenes Buechner has more or less dreamed up, Jacob casts about in his life in the clouded way of an old man, half remembering, half dreaming, Godric-like. As usual, Buechner finds the lacunae most interesting as he imagines the human emotions and conundrums implicit in the Genesis version of the stories of the patriarchs. Playing fast and loose with Bible stories is bound to cause trouble somewhere, and a few minor demurrals appeared here and there in the criticism. Buechner treats as fluid that which some readers prefer to think of as firmly etched on stone tablets. His take was near-blasphemy for a few. But the overwhelming tone in the criticism and the reviews rang with words like "masterpiece."[15] Noting that hagiography is "a notoriously failed genre" that "gets high marks in boredom and dishonesty,"[16] Eugene Peterson praised Buechner's effort in *The Son of Laughter*, understanding that Buechner was turning the genre on its head, coming up with something both "accessible and honest" (Peterson 608). Jill Baumgaertner also noticed Buechner's accomplishment in a genre that is "neglected and abused."[17]

But the praise Buechner most valued was Annie Dillard's. Her review, which Buechner "much liked,"[18] called the work "inspired"—"writing that sounds as though the writer is holding onto a lightning bolt."[19] Dillard celebrated more than style in her admiration for *The Son of Laughter*: "With profound intelligence, Buechner's novel does what the finest, most appealing literature does: It displays and illuminates the seemingly unrelated mysteries of human character and ultimate ideas" (Dillard A15). I'm sure Buechner admires the review, one of the few he keeps around, because Dillard recognized the deeper currents, the universality, implicit in the exploration of the conflict of the natural and the supernatural, the material and the spiritual. Buechner also thinks well of *The Son of Laughter*, placing it behind only *Godric* in a 2002 interview, though he characteristically admits, "if you asked me tomorrow I might say something quite different" (Kauffman 29). The novel also was honored as the Book of the Year by the Conference on Christianity and Literature, a group that had awarded Buechner its Belles Lettres prize in 1987. In the speech announcing the award, Joseph Sendry mentioned Buechner's psychological acuity, but concluded that *The Son of Laughter* reaches further—toward "the challenge of showing the intrusion of the divine into human life."[20]

Buechner begins with Laban, showman and shyster, a character so large that he, as Dillard saw, "almost steals the show" (Dillard A15). Jacob's narrative starts with Laban's gods, the fertility symbols reminiscent of those in *Brendan* and the clash of cultures there. This time the collision is between the pagan and the Jewish, the gods of the land versus this interloper God of the nomads—Ashtoreth, Baal, and Dagon versus the God of Abraham, Isaac, and Jacob. Although he'll have more to say later about the twenty years with Laban, Jacob first remembers the flight from Laban with his servants, wives, children, and cattle stretching "as far as the eye could see" (*Laughter* 4). It is a drama that opens up a life, fresher in the old man's memory than his most recent meal. Rachel, his most beloved, has stolen her father's gods. Maybe she thinks the idols—stone, wooden, and silver—will provide extra protection on the journey to God knows where. Learning of her thievery, Jacob will eventually bury the figurines in a pit along with whatever talismans and charms his entourage has toted out of Haran: "It was for the Fear's sake I did it," Jacob proclaims in his own defense (*Laughter* 6).

Buechner accomplishes much by simply translating Jehovah into "the Fear." Buechner not only enjoys wandering around in the meaning of names like Isaac and Jacob, but he fiddles with the vowelless name itself. As Logan Jones put it, the God of this novel is "mysterious, present and absent, friend and foe and bringer of hope and terror."[21] The constant wrangling between the patriarchs and their God emphasizes the "friend and foe," and "the Fear" gets at both "terror" and reverence. To think of Abraham, Isaac, and Jacob serving Fear is to understand something of the burden of the promise they pass from father to son. This is no El Shaddai, no Father of ease but a force of dis-ease, closer perhaps to the unnameable YHWH. For Fear Jacob flees Laban, for Fear he buries the old gods, for Fear he quakes and hopes: "The Fear came to me in the night and whispered words of hope into my ear. He told me that he loved me as he had loved Laughter, my father, before me and Abraham, my grandfather, before that. He repeated the ancient promises that never fail to frighten me with their beauty just as the Fear himself never fails to frighten me" (*Laughter* 6). The God of Jacob is not a warm and gentle presence by a long shot; nonetheless Jacob tumbles the gods into a pit beneath an oak tree and puts all his bets on Fear. But he is careful to keep open the possibility that Rachel's hidden figurines have power: "Who knows about the gods? Maybe they have seen every step I have taken since," he admits (*Laughter* 7).

Although most critics admired the quality of Buechner's research and historical accuracy in *The Son of Laughter*, this nod to Jacob's respect for the moon gods and the rest sparked some controversy. Assuming that Buechner paints Jacob as polytheistic, Ken Ristau, for example, protested, claiming that Buechner had done Jacob a "disservice" and argued that "there is little basis" for the claim in Genesis."[22] But Ristau has simply misread Buechner. Jacob nods toward the gods of the land, partly out of courtesy to his neighbors, but mostly out of a human instinct to cover all his bases. He's knocking on wood. He believes in the Fear, but he is also superstitious, haunted by doubts, capable of faith in fits and starts. He is one of us. Jacob will be the narrator, but the ominous force beyond and within everything will be the Fear. *The Son of Laughter* begins in doubt and potent memory, again the mix of false and true.

The central story of Jacob's life turns out to be the one handed down to him from Isaac, his father. Jacob is the son of Laughter, after all, and Laughter has carried all his days the specter of those trembling minutes on an altar beneath his father's knife. Buechner tells the familiar story of the almost-sacrifice of Isaac without recourse to the usual facts—the where and what. He doesn't even mention Moriah, for example, the setting for the sacrifice that almost happened. Instead, he opens the story through the eyes of the child, now an old man, who lived it. It is not a story about Abraham's loyalty to Fear's demands as much as it is a story about a child's bewilderment with such a father, such a God. Buechner taps into what Michael Aeschliman called "our revulsion at Abraham's God-intoxicated fanaticism."[23] When the story is unsanitized and moved off the flannel board, Buechner indeed opens the possibility that Abraham's act might be viewed as horrific, especially by the parent Isaac will one day become.

The entries from *Peculiar Treasures* that got the most play in the years after that book appeared were no doubt those treating Abraham, Sarah, and Isaac. Musicians like Michael Card and Daniel Amos wrote songs based on the humor and contemporary themes Buechner finds in the

Genesis account. His attraction to the tale is not unique; the story of Isaac's near escape, the ram caught in the thicket, has bewildered and intrigued many, from Kierkegaard to Nietzsche to contemporary sermonizers and theologians. Add Jacob to Oz, Lear, and the lives of saints as a particular point of absorption for Buechner. What Buechner sees is how such an event may well have played across succeeding generations and how the event relates to his own exploration of fathers and sons in his memoirs. There's the story of how Isaac got his name, a reference to the uproarious laughter of his parents at the news that they were to have a son. "They laughed because they knew only a fool would believe that a woman with one foot in the grave was soon going to have her other foot in the maternity ward," Buechner writes in *Wishful Thinking* (*WT* 25).

That part of Isaac's story fuels Buechner's attention to one of his core preoccupations: "Nobody claims there's a chuckle on every page, but laughter's what the whole Bible is really about. Nobody who knows his hat from home-plate claims that getting mixed up with God is all sweetness and light, but ultimately it's what that's all about too," Buechner concludes (*PT* 153). Like Brendan, Isaac is born in miracle, but the trip into the mountains of Moriah, those terrifying moments on an altar, give the story shadows that add nuance to the notion of laughter at the heart of all things. In *The Son of Laughter* Buechner ponders how a promise can be a burden, how a blessing can be a blight, how the fervid light in the old man's eyes that day on the mountain may have burned a fearfulness into his son. Aeschliman suggested that Buechner's great success in *The Son of Laughter* related to his "catching some of this sense of election, of chosenness, of uniqueness, and of its incipient absurdity and terror" (Aeschliman 306). Aeschliman entitled his commentary "Blessing and Bane," an underscoring of another of those paradoxes of which Buechner is so fond.

The narrative of Isaac's trip up the mountain with his God-obsessed father is the pivotal story in the lives of three generations, much as the suicide of Buechner's father is the pivotal moment in his family history. Laughter tells his son, Jacob, stories of Grandfather Abraham, a man who talked with the Fear "the way a man talks to his friend" (*Laughter* 10), and Jacob grows up with a heady heritage, a chronicle of being chosen "to breed a lucky people who would someday bring luck to the whole world" (*Laughter* 11). The promise is, however, couched in ambiguity. Isaac cannot recount the tale of his mysterious walk into Moriah without breaking into tears. The moment on the mountain has left him addled in some way; like Godric and Brendan, he is one of Buechner's cripples.

Buechner also reads much into the Old Testament account of Sarah's death following soon upon Abraham's trip with Isaac. Laughter leaves it to Jacob and the reader to decide if the account of what happened on Moriah actually led to the death of Sarah. "When my mother heard what Abraham had nearly done to her son, she was dead within the year. What killed her? You tell me," Laughter answers (*Laughter* 19). Characteristically, Buechner imagines the human side of the spectacular and familiar story. Ristau suggested that Buechner's version of events here echoes a common Midrash (Ristau 3). I suspect, however, that most readers of *The Son of Laughter* would be surprised by the intimation that Sarah dies as a result of her son's near sacrifice. In Buechner's hands, the famous story of faith becomes also a story of tragedy passed along. "Perhaps it is because his father tried to kill him once when he was a boy that he has never been like other men," Jacob theorizes as he tries to justify his father's tears (*Laughter* 51). Although most of the critics commented on Buechner's fidelity to the Genesis text, a few, including Allen, realized that Buechner's focus on Jacob's doubts and supposed shame was a significant deviation from the biblical narrative.

The early chapters of the novel juxtapose guesses about Jacob's childhood against the familiar background stories. We learn that Jacob's nickname is Heels, for example, a reference to his having been born holding the heel of his twin, Esau. Does Buechner like the translation as it plays off the notion of Jacob as *a heel*? Esau is Laughter's "Heart's treasure" while Jacob is his mother's darling. Although Esau is always out hunting while Jacob "is quiet and stays at home," it will be Jacob who plays the prodigal's role (*Laughter* 14). Buechner considers Laughter's supposed favoritism as mostly bluff and bluster, I'd say. Jacob is a treasure too. But the boys are of disparate fabric somehow, and we are set up for the famous episode where Jacob steals the birthright from the rightful heir. A simple and practical fellow, Esau is presented as fundamentally different from his father, a man of disturbing memories and a longing for the filling of an unnamed emptiness. By contrast, like Laughter, Jacob is never satisfied. Esau can be bought off with a plate of red beans. Esau is also oblivious to the conniving spirit of his brother. Jacob is smarter, yes, but also driven, like his father, by notions of the promise, a sense of destiny. When Esau, or Hairy, as Jacob calls him, gives away his inheritance, the rights and promises of the elder brother, Jacob is not sure as to "which of them got the better of the bargain" (*Laughter* 28). But the old man, Jacob, who tells the story, is sure of his shame at having so deluded his brother.

The chapters that work best in *The Son of Laughter* are probably the ones based on lesser-known episodes in the biblical accounts. "The Two Stones," for example, features a speculation on how the patriarchs may have heard the voice of their God. Jacob recounts the awe-full story of going into a smoky tent with his father and watching the casting of the six-sided stones in which Laughter somehow reads Fear's will. The weeping, the hysteria, and Isaac's chest bloodied from his tearing at himself in a fit of religious frenzy leave Jacob trembling with the thought that Isaac is about to re-create something of that long-ago scene where Abraham held the knife over Isaac. Surrounded by the pagan gods and their worshipers, Jacob must have witnessed human sacrifice in the cause of abundant rains and plentiful crops. Besides, Jacob is sure the stones will reveal his duplicity with Esau, lay bare Fear's anger. "I had dared meddle with the fire the Fear was trying to start with us and the plan he had for starting it," Jacob explains (*Laughter* 33). But the stones merely speak of the famine they've been enduring, and the scene features a call to move on to another land. In the smoky tent, Jacob has learned the secret name of Fear and the great risk of doing business with him, though Fear seems to have little regard for the youthful shyster at this point. Jacob has also confessed, at least to himself, his guilt about Esau, and he has begun to understand something of the silence that dominates his family. Rebekah, Jacob's mother, knows about the deal with Esau. Laughter doesn't know. It is a family increasingly defined by its secrets, its silences.

Despite the rampant dysfunctionality, Laughter's family prospers in the new land, Gerar, to which the Fear has directed them. Abimelech, the king, offers hospitality, but everything here is based on another secret. Isaac has lied to the king, fearing that his wife's beauty might be a motive for the king to put Isaac out of the way. Echoing a lie of his famous father, Isaac tells the people of Gerar that Rebekah is his sister. Buechner understands that such a lie would have many enormous consequences, one of which is that Isaac comes to hate the people of this land. He cannot "look into their faces without being reminded of his cowardice" (*Laughter* 45). Lots of enmity gets started just this way, no doubt. Gerar is an increasingly strange land; the people are seafaring types, and their god is a "great fish," probably some version of Dagon, though Jacob, from faith and superstition, refuses to speak the name (*Laughter* 52). Laughter begins to fret about the mingling that is bound to bring a confusion of the gods. Even Esau has married outside the clan. It is the promise that drives Laughter, apparently, a hunger that Jacob dimly understands. "Who knows what your father is starving for?" Rebekah asks Jacob (*Laughter* 51).

When his mother speaks of his father's "strangeness" and "folly," Jacob recognizes that his birthright is somewhere in that hodgepodge, a word that Buechner likes, as it captures his sense of the mixture of things (*Laughter* 53). Jacob too is borne along on strange currents.

While Esau takes wives, Jacob is tending sheep and watching the burgeoning prosperity of the clan. But they are a timeless family, these descendants of Abraham, reminiscent of families everywhere in all times. Laughter is despairing about Esau's marriages, and Rebekah is happy to tell him tales of the wives' indiscretions. Jacob's increasing blindness complicates matters, but he stands up to Abimelech in the conflicts over wells, water being the most important commodity in that place. Laughter's people have worn out the hospitality of Gerar. They are resented for their "cleverness," Abimelech claims (*Laughter* 60). Disputes are breaking into open conflict, and Laughter is glad enough to escape the strange gods of Gerar, especially the horned fish with the crooked teeth and the painted priestesses who serve him. At Beersheba Laughter builds an altar and has another dazzling encounter with the Fear. When he repeats Fear's words renewing the promise "for my servant Abraham's sake," Rebekah is unimpressed: "He [Isaac] should stand up like a man and demand his just due" (*Laughter* 64). Her cynicism is part of her legacy to her favorite, Jacob, and she has grown weary of her husband's concessions to the mysterious Fear. "It is because Abraham offered to slit your father's throat in honor of him that he loved him so," she whispers to Jacob, and the long-term implications of the aborted sacrifice continue to play out. Buechner details Isaac's leadership skills, and readers get some sense of the research involved in the novel in the scene of Laughter's departure from Gerar. In the graphic scene of the two old men, Abimelech and Isaac, grasping one another's genitals in an oath to brook no strife between their peoples, Buechner reminds us of the primitiveness of the historical era. In this particular rendition, Buechner is, ironically, more accurate than the King James Bible which uses euphemisms like "loins" or "thigh" and thus obscures the actual record.

Reading *The Son of Laughter* is like watching a movie you've seen before. Some parts you remember; other scenes seem brand new. Buechner gets to another of the well-known snapshots in Jacob's photograph album with the stealing of the blessing from the blind and dying Isaac. But this is no gentle laying-on of hands, no simple matter of reciting some ritualistic mumbo jumbo, nothing for a photograph album, come to think of it. The blessing here is almost a physical thing. It has a terrifying and staggering materiality. Rebekah warns Jacob that his father is about to "speak a word of great power to Esau." If Esau gets the blessing, she judges, "everything will be lost" (*Laughter* 74). How should we understand her duplicity in inspiring Jacob's ruse with Laughter? Jacob simply posits love as the core issue: "She didn't want Esau's face to shine like a god's face. She wanted my face to shine like a god's face" (*Laughter* 75). First, we notice the power of the blessing, the long reach of Abraham; next we wonder over the ways of a mother's mysterious love for a child.

Jacob confesses that, in his youthful ignorance, he worried only about getting caught, not about the injury to Esau, the insult to his father, and the great risk he was taking before the Fear. The older Jacob who tells the story is full of the horror of what he's done. But he was a young man when he "fouled the Fear's name" with the lie that he was Esau, and Buechner lets considerable air into the story by weighing the possibility that Laughter, despite his blindness and weakness, actually knows what is happening with the charade: "I do not know to this day if he believed me. I will never know. Maybe he himself did not know. Maybe he knew all along I was Jacob. Maybe though it was Esau he loved, it was Jacob he believed in his heart would be the luckier luck bearer and he only pretended to believe me" (*Laughter* 82). Knowing the way of families, the reader can only echo, "Maybe."

The blessing introduces another name for Fear—the Shield of Abraham—and other prayers that go back even before the time of the great patriarch (*Laughter* 84). Jacob, however, recognizes that he is not up to such glorious callings and promises. "My face did not burn with light like a god's. Shame was what burned it," he confesses (*Laughter* 85). So the undeserved blessing becomes a curse that will drive Jacob in something like the way his father's childhood experience on Moriah drove him: "It was not I that ran off with my father's blessing. It was my father's blessing that ran off with me" (*Laughter* 86). The curse means that Jacob will have to flee the anger of both his father and his brother. It is as a fugitive that Jacob will arrive in Laban's land. If you've ever wondered why Jacob would be so docile as to work twenty years for his duplicitous uncle, maybe it is simply because he thought he was only getting what he deserved. The toil with Laban is something of a penance, perhaps. Saying goodbye to his mother, whom he will never see again, Jacob hears her own confession that she's only getting her just deserts for the "meddling and scheming" (*Laughter* 90). The episode smacks of what Susan Lovell called "the human reality of mothers and fathers and sibling rivalries."[24] Jacob hies to Haran with his eyes "fixed only inward" (*Laughter* 90). Like Brendan, who sails inner seas of remorse and doubt as he travels to an unknown land, Jacob is plumbing the depths of all he has thrown away and wondering about the blessing that has turned his life inside out. From Fear, however, he gets only silence—"emptiness that had no end"—the price of his iniquity, he thinks (*Laughter* 91). But everything is about to change.

On the road to Haran, Jacob dreams of a stone stairway climbing into the heavens. From the top of the stairs comes a voice, not the voice of Fear, but "Light's voice" (*Laughter* 94). The words are the ones Laughter has prayed down on Jacob, the words of promise. "I am with you, Jacob," the voice announces (*Laughter* 94). Such are the words we all want to hear. Everything will be all right—the happy ending. They are the last words of Buechner's left-handed conversation with his father in the memoirs: "Everything is going to be all right" (*TS* 100). The words are at the core of the Jacob story. The trickster, the liar, the fallible son, Heels, will make it home in one way or another. Like so many Buechnerian heroes, Jacob turns out all right in the end. He may even be something of a saint. "Jacob holy?" Peterson asked, and answered, "Yes. An earthy, flawed, confused, deceitful, scared saint. A holy life" (Peterson 607). All is okay. And if Jacob has a chance, maybe we all do. Such ideas move at the center of Buechner's work. He claims to have "sensed the presence of a presence . . . felt a promise promised," and he's tried to speak of the experience without imposing it on others, tried to witness to it through his telling of stories like Jacob's (*TS* 106). Like Jacob here and like Godric before, Buechner is also telling his own life from both ends and from many angles at once.

The story of Jacob at Laban's is a tale of romance, children, family tensions, and—beneath it all—the simmering sense of being the "bearers of the earth's best luck and blessing" (*Laughter* 98). Buechner makes quick work of the chronicle of four wives and thirteen children, the familiar names of the twenty-year sojourn in Laban's shadow. But Rachel he cannot pass by. Buechner plays Jacob's arrival among the uncircumcised men of Haran with a spectacularly extrabiblical guess. Weary and disheveled, bewildered by a strange language and the suspicious eyes of strangers, Jacob spies Rachel coming toward the well. And what does he do but embrace and kiss her? In Genesis, that kiss had always struck me as an innocent sort of traditional greeting of the time and place. Buechner sees it from a different angle. Who can say that the kiss was not emblematic of more than a routine greeting between kinfolk? How else to render that special love, the first-sight kind, that will make Rachel his favorite for all his days? With that kiss, "the door of the years opened" (*Laughter* 103).

In those passages where Buechner reminds the reader that a very old man is telling this story, we hear how the blessing has by now stretched to sons and grandsons. "The runaway blessing careens down the years," is

Jacob's attempt at describing the ineffable presence of the divine (*Laughter* 105). At Haran the fun was just beginning, and Jacob describes his dealings with Laban as "a dance" (*Laughter* 106). The dance Jacob describes is not unlike the one many families dance, not the seven years' labor for first one daughter and then another, perhaps, but certainly the rivalry between Rachel and Leah, the dubiety of the father, the desires of Jacob, the conniving running in all directions. Laban, the con man par excellence, pulls off the Leah debacle via a technicality or two. He never said "which daughter," he claims, and he certainly never swore by any gods— "I am not a blasphemer," he complains (*Laughter* 114). Jacob means to kill Laban, but settles back into harness for love of Rachel. The subsequent plots to wrangle wealth from Laban seem easily justified by the dastardly swindle Laban has perpetrated. The settling of scores runs deep. Jacob avenges himself on Leah by managing to keep her childless, which is, of course, also a vengeance on Laban, as he is denied heirs. But most surprising is the "revenge upon the Fear" that Jacob records as "sweetest" (*Laughter* 118).

As it turns out, Jacob is most angry with God, the one who has made promises but stayed hidden, the one who "did not choose to let me see him" (*Laughter* 119). The gods of the land, Sin and Dagon and the rest, are to be seen everywhere, but the Fear seems to exist only in the mad eyes of an old man and in the starry stairway of a dream. Withholding his seed from Leah's womb is a way for Jacob to make jest of the Fear's talk of many nations, a way to say just what he thinks of the whole covenant business. Fear will, as usual, have the last laugh. When Jacob finally marries Rachel, she is barren. "Terrible are the ways of Fear and more cunning even than mine," Jacob concludes (*Laughter* 120). Thus we have another Buechnerian doubter. Jacob's struggle with God at this point is reminiscent of Mark Twain's rage or Voltaire's doubt—not so much an atheism, a denial of God's existence, as an enraged sense that God indeed exists and is malicious. As bad as Jacob can be, God is worse, as Jacob sees it.

Michael Aeschliman examined this slippery territory of Jacob's occasional rage at the heavens. Aeschliman admitted that "terror, contempt, disgust, or hatred" might well be legitimate responses to the story of Abraham's near-sacrifice of Isaac (Aeschliman 302). Outlining a history of sentiment against the Old Testament portraiture of Jehovah, Aeschliman included not only Voltaire and Twain but also Thomas Jefferson, Samuel Butler, Anatole France, and others as skeptical of Jewish monotheism, viewing it as ethnocentric, fanatical, and superstitious (Aeschliman 302). What Aeschliman caught in Buechner is an ability to live with that skepticism. He is more like Tertullian or Kierkegaard, Aeschliman argued, in his ability "to rejoice in the paradox of faith." Buechner, Aeschliman added, "looks at and then through sin, vice, folly, and weakness to the Spirit that defines them *as such* in the first place" (Aeschliman 303). What this critic understood is that Buechner, like his characters, "is haunted by the sacred" and driven by the possibility of something beyond suffering (Aeschliman 305). Moreover, Buechner's fascination with the spiritual sees both the fearfulness and the blessedness in the idea.

As we have seen repeatedly over the course of more than thirty books, Buechner finally comes to wager everything on the blessedness. Laughter is the best word, the perfect word, for this novel with a very-much-not-funny character named Laughter and for the whole Buechner corpus. For Buechner, this laughter has to do with incredulity: "There is a kind of laughter in the Bible, and I don't mean the kind of laughter that preachers put in sermons to warm up the audience—but a deep, joyous laughter" (*Radix* 8). Such is the large preoccupation that Buechner returns to in *The Son of Laughter*. Jacob's wrangling with the Fear seems always to end with a return to the promise. His outrage and doubt never quite become the last word. Despite the darkness of so many days, a flickering light continues to shine. Jacob is all about getting up out of the mud, wiping himself off as best he can, and walking back toward the light.

Buechner entitles one chapter in the Laban section "A Storm of Children," and this little world is stormy, to be sure. "We were all of us at odds with each other," Jacob remembers (*Laughter* 121). Always the deal-maker, Jacob figures that maybe Rachel's barrenness is a consequence of his mistreatment of Leah, a quirky God's justice. Maybe there is some genuine compassion in the mix as well, and Jacob is lonely, just plain lonely. The children who eventually begin to arrive do nothing to soothe the family fractures or his loneliness: "There is no telling the wretchedness and turmoil of those child-begetting years," Jacob confesses (*Laughter* 125). So great is the hatred and rivalry between the sisters that they force their maids into their husband's bed. Rachel organizes the union with her maid, Bilhah, out of her longing for a child to elevate her status beside the now-productive Leah. When Leah can no longer conceive, she forces her maid, Zilpah, to join the insane competition. Jacob will have ten sons and one daughter by Leah and the two maids, but the price is chaos and tension instead of joy. Just when we've about given up on Jacob, hopelessly deceiving and being deceived, he manages a moment. One day, right in the thick of the family exploding all around him, he realizes that his children are "the Fear's promise" (*Laughter* 127). Somehow, he had forgotten this elemental fact of his life. We all forget similar rudimentary things, Buechner suggests, as he returns to another of his preoccupations—wakefulness. Jacob wakes up just long enough to catch a glimmer of the depth of the Fear's promise. Rachel gives it language. "I thought he had forgotten me, but he remembered me," she prays. When Joseph is born, Jacob returns to a conversation with the Fear.

Rachel's barrenness finally gives way, perhaps a magic worked by the Fear, or maybe it was the mandrakes brought home by one of Leah's sons. Or maybe the mandrakes were Fear's way at "the hidden root of things" (*Laughter* 131). Buechner writes of a Jacob who keeps all possibilities in play—providence and chance always in tension. Family strains have by now passed from mothers to sons. Jacob's rambling family is the usual mixture of favorites and outcasts, remembered wrongs and frustrated hopes. Laban has grown weary of Jacob's success. According to Jacob's view of Laban's disgruntlement, it is the "cunning" that Laban "could not endure" (*Laughter* 142). The flocks have multiplied to Jacob's advantage by the time he decides to head back home. Fearing Laban's anger, Jacob tries to sneak away with his wives, children, servants, and herds—an entourage sure to raise dust. When Laban catches up with them, a violent dispute seems sure. But Rachel hides the stolen gods, and Jacob and Laban swear peace. After a twenty-year dance with Laban in Haran, Jacob heads toward Esau and another possible confrontation, and he goes with the memory of Laban's farewell kiss. It started with a kiss. Now it ends with another.

The road to Esau is fraught with worry over what rage awaits. Even his beloved Rachel knows that they may be marching to their deaths. That's why she's stolen her father's gods. Jacob asks them for help but hears only silence in response. To him, the way seems to be lined with angels, the whole journey mysteriously linked to the Fear's promises, but, in characteristic trepidation, he deploys his minions in such a way as to save his immediate family in the event of an attack. Jacob always hedges his bets. The messengers he's sent ahead to Esau are no help. They return with an ambiguous message. "Tell him I have never forgotten him!" Esau charges (*Laughter* 152). Jacob sees this can still fall out either way. Maybe Esau will massacre them all. Destruction is what he deserves, Jacob knows. Maybe Esau will welcome them home. Jacob beseeches the Fear for the first time in months, but even there he gets silence. He sends gifts and herds ahead, in part to slow Esau's revenge if that is indeed what waits at the end of this road.

At the river Jabbok the whole momentous adventure comes to a crisis for Jacob: "I knew what lay behind me. I did not know what lay ahead of me" (*Laughter* 157). Sending his entourage across the ford, Jacob stays behind to take stock. Alone in the land between wakefulness and sleep, he remembers the sweetness and ugliness of Haran, clearly wondering if maybe he should give up this mad quest for home. Suddenly, out of his dreams, he is attacked. Is it the god of the river? he wonders. No, it must be Esau pinning him, throwing him, bringing him to the terror of his eminent death. Through the night they battle "like fighting in a dream" (*Laughter* 159). Finally, miraculously, it is Jacob who, just at daybreak, gets the upper hand. His opponent begs to be freed, but Jacob refuses; "I will not let you go unless you bless me," he shouts (*Laughter* 160). Jacob probably gets more than he bargained for when the muscled figure asks him his name. Winded and wounded, Jacob hears the stranger's pronouncement—Jacob is to be renamed. "Now you are Israel. You have wrestled with God and with men. You have prevailed. That is the meaning of the name Israel," his enemy proclaims (*Laughter* 161). The blessing comes, though Jacob cannot remember the words or even if there were words.

He longs to know the stranger's name, but the dark shape balks at that: "He never told me his name. The Fear of Isaac, the Shield of Abraham, and others like them are names we use because we do not know his true name. He did not tell me his true name. Perhaps he did not tell it because he knew I would never stop calling on it" (*Laughter* 161). Thus Jacob gives away just who he thinks it was that he wrestled with that night on the river bank. The one glimpse he's had of the stranger's face reveals an aspect "more terrible than the face of dark, or of pain, or of terror. It was the face of light. No words can tell of it" (*Laughter* 161).

This is the climax of Jacob's life, the moment toward which all things have worked. Buechner makes it the pivotal scene of the novel as well, a scene that captures precisely the Buechnerian principle of the mixture of hope and despair. Old Jacob wonders still about the meaning of his long night's struggle: "Sometimes I cannot believe I saw it [the face] and lived but that I only dreamed I saw it. Sometimes I believe I saw it and that I only dream I live" (*Laughter* 161). Did he actually do battle with an angel? With God himself? Or did he simply dream? As usual, Buechner keeps several possibilities open and again shows his fascination with dreams and dreamers, his resistance to easy readings and clear interpretations. But we can be sure that the Jacob who wades the river to rejoin his family and his life is not the same man who had made his bed the night before in a land suspended between past and future. Because of his midnight brawl, Jacob is lame. "From that day to this I have moved through the world like a cripple," he reports (*Laughter* 162). Here's another character with a painful limp, but Jacob also has a new name. He is Israel, and he has been blessed. Crippled and lucky, too. Buechner's theology of paradox.

Because Jacob has clutched holiness so close, we might expect a brave and noble Israel in the scene that follows, the reunion with Esau. Instead, we get a return to cowardice, the sort of thing we saw with *Godric*, the jumble of sacred and profane. Esau approaching, Jacob arranges his family with Rachel and Joseph closest to him and orders Bilhah and Zilpah to move to the front with their broods. "Everyone understood my meaning," he says (*Laughter* 163). Leah has by this time become a kind of friend to her husband, a confidante really, so her grief is palpable when she is told to take her children into the position behind Bilhah and Zilpah. Such favoritism for Rachel and Joseph will surely be remembered if they all survive this day.

At the last, to his credit, Jacob does ride on ahead to face his brother. There's Esau with his flash of red hair. He is holding a spear. Everything hangs in the balance. With their kinfolk and servants looking on, amidst the bleating of the cattle that Jacob has sent ahead to seek Esau's kindness, the brothers grasp one another, reuniting with kisses of mirth and sadness. Is it Jacob or Israel who speaks the words: "To see your face is like seeing the face of God" (*Laughter* 166)? The luck has held; the promise is alive. Though his mother has died, Jacob is almost home at last, and he has managed to find favor again with the rugged Esau. Beset by all the what-ifs of his life, Jacob lives the whole reunion scene as a kind of dream, the residue of his encounter at the river.

On the fringes of the land of promise, Jacob sends Esau on ahead, as the children and the herds make for a slow passage. Near Shechem, on the slopes of Mount Ebal, Jacob talks to the long-dead Abraham of the new griefs that have befallen his family as they approach home. Imagining his grandfather staring at the same landscape, Jacob can almost feel the old man's obsession: "It was the Fear that Abraham thought about. What else, with the Fear's hook tearing at his mouth?" (*Laughter* 170). Jacob knows something about that hook. He too has puzzled over the promise and the twists in the road toward it. He has sought the Fear and been sought by him as well, and he is somewhat the worse for the wear of the seeking: "Abraham knew the nethermost caverns of grief if any man had ever known them" (*Laughter* 171).

And Jacob tells the story of his own sorrow, the story of Dinah, his daughter, and the unfortunate Shechem, named for the city he was to rule after his father, Hamor. The horror is easily told, though the memory becomes another of those haunting old Jacob. Shechem has fallen in love with Dinah. Maybe, Jacob thinks, "their beauty took each other by sur-prise" (*Laughter* 171). But Dinah's brothers, Simeon and Levi, see only lechery in the story. It is an ancient version of a timeless story, a virginal sister defended by headstrong brothers. When Hamor comes with his son to explain the situation—Shechem and Dinah have already been together as husband and wife—Jacob can imagine the loveliness and innocence of their breaking all the rules. Dinah's brothers, however, can imagine only rape. Simeon and Levi concoct a plot, demanding that the Shechemites be circumcised as a penalty for the dishonoring of Dinah and as a gesture of peace. Jacob yields to his sons, but he has no knowledge of the horror to follow. Made vulnerable by the circumcisions, the men of Shechem are easy prey for the swords of Simeon and Levi. The brothers' rage spills into a massacre of unspeakable proportion. "By the time Simeon and Levi's work was done, there was not a house in the city where there were not women with ashes in their hair beating their breasts and wailing," Jacob remembers as he describes his own shock at what his sons have done (*Laughter* 178).

Raging against his sons, Jacob binds the two boys to a tree until they are near death and is only brought back to his senses by Leah's words, "It is yourself you are killing" (*Laughter* 179). He thinks again of Abraham. "Was it himself he was killing when he raised his knife over Laughter bound like a beast to the dry sticks?" (*Laughter* 180). For that matter, "By command-ing Abraham to do it, and to die of doing it, was it the Fear himself that the Fear was killing?" (*Laughter* 180). Jacob has told no one yet of his encounter at Jabbok, but it is as Israel and as Jacob that he weeps for his boys, "for all the sadness there is between fathers and sons" (*Laughter* 180). Thus Buechner jerks his readers back to now. The sons are freed, but the family moves on under a curse because of the butchery at Shechem: "Everything they touched" was fouled by the blood of Hamor's people. The effects of the sin sweep through the whole clan. Dinah is silent, soul-wounded, forever lost in sadness and bewilderment. His people "an abom-ination," Jacob wonders how they can ever return to the promise—always the curse and the blessing tied up together (*Laughter* 182).

The purging of the Shechem carnage reminds readers of the surpris-ing customs of the times. Jacob forces his sons to drink sludge—a combi-nation of ashes, water, and blood—until they retch out their uncleanness. His "unlucky, luck-bearing boys" are both "cruel and cleansed" (*Laughter* 183). The other part of the cleansing is the decision to finally be done with Laban's gods. "It was to cleanse our hearts of every other trust but trust in the Fear," that Jacob orders the burial of the idols. "The gods took their revenge soon enough," Jacob recollects, so maybe he did believe in them as much as he disbelieved (*Laughter* 185). The oldest of Jacob's entourage, Deborah, who was, years before, Rebekah's nurse, dies along the road, the first victim of the revenge of the gods as Jacob reads it. They bury her at the foot of the pillar Jacob had set up twenty years before to mark the place of his dream about the stone stairway into the stars, a place that will later be called Bethel. The second death is hardest of all. Jacob's beloved, Rachel, dies giving birth to Benoni, "Son of My Sorrow" (*Laughter* 189). Here Buechner finally introduces at some depth the other great figure of these stories from Genesis, Jacob's darling, Joseph. The dying Rachel charges Joseph with the keeping of Benoni: Joseph must "teach him to say his name" (*Laughter* 191). The "thoughtful, inward-looking boy," Joseph, assumes a certain gravity from this moment on, a seriousness that will cause him no end of trouble in days to come. Rachel's death comprises Jacob's "deepest sorrow," she who was his "deepest delight" (*Laughter* 193). Although he will change Benoni's name to Benjamin, "Son of the South," a "name with hope in it," he will never be able to look at the boy without remembering the death that gave him life (*Laughter* 192).

It is a shattered Jacob who stumbles on toward Esau, his family in shambles. Rumor has it that Reuben, his eldest son, has taken Bilhah with a man's desire. Does he wish to oust his own father? Among the boys there is grumbling that Simeon and Levi have brought down an ineffaceable curse because of Shechem. Or maybe it is Jacob's burying of the gods that they're all lamenting. The family is leaderless as Jacob wanders in the bitter desert of his sorrow and regret. Where is the promise leading them, he wonders. He remembers how the Fear has told him to "Arise" (*Laughter* 199). Israel probably speaks for Abraham and Isaac before him when he asks, "Did he know in all his high heavens the weariness of rising? Lord as they say he is of all the living, can he guess at the bitterness of death and dying? . . . Can he without shame bid a man go and then cripple him for going?" (*Laughter* 199). Jacob's question is everyone's question, and Buechner relentlessly foregrounds the bitter question, making it prominent in the narrative. Many readers praised Buechner's portrait of Jacob on this point of his doubt. James Cook, for example, admired what he calls the "flesh-and-blood portrait" implicit in this novel, and Buechner has achieved more than an accurate portrayal of the sights and sounds of the era and the realistic depiction of sibling rivalries and the currents that drive mothers and fathers.[25] He has also painted the despair of a world in which humans feel abandoned to their own meanness, an anguish so rich as to fill the mouth with curses.

Full of joy at his brother's coming home at last, Esau nonetheless has more bad news. Isaac is dying, another death to set beside those of Rachel and Deborah. "Grief follows grief like sheep through a gate," Esau summarizes, in a metaphor beyond his usual reach. Isaac floats in the netherworld between life and death, reunited with a son he thought dead, a scene that Jacob will one day visit in his own senility. Isaac wonders if perhaps the dead aren't "the lucky ones" (*Laughter* 201). The tone stays relentlessly dark here as Isaac carries to his grave the memory of his bound arms and legs as he was lifted onto the altar by Abraham all those years before. Isaac's gibes at the end are about the Fear who was "Abraham's friend." The joke is that "Maybe Abraham would have been better off friendless" (*Laughter* 203). Unsure what it all meant at the end, Isaac passes along the Two Stones, one black and one white. "They say they are the Fear's lips, if the Fear has lips," Isaac quips (*Laughter* 202). Jacob seems to have little use for the stones; maybe some of the power of them has diminished since Abraham held them. Along with the stones comes the fulfillment of the blessing. Isaac's flocks and herds, his slaves and servants, all come to Jacob along with the mantle that had been Abraham's. Thus Esau, with only his six sons compared to Jacob's twelve, must be the one to move on this time. Jacob will never see him again save in his dreams.

One more memory stirs in the old man's mind in that part of the story he calls "The Promising," the story of the son to be savior. The final chapters of the novel are Joseph's chapters, as Buechner turns to another Old Testament superstar, another set of familiar scenes. The angle of vision is still Jacob's, however; he dreams his way into what might have been, what must have been, in Joseph's story. Buechner forces the reader to imagine along with Jacob, make some guesses, and look at the worn tales in new ways. Rachel's joy at Joseph's birth, for example, explains Jacob's special love for the boy: he is "Fear's richest gift," so Jacob cannot help "making him gifts" (*Laughter* 206). Those gifts, like a silver ring and a robe bedecked with scarlet stripes, set off peevishness and dissension among the other children. Jacob knows that he should have known better. To make matters worse, Joseph is a dreamer. Is it his remarkable egotism or his remarkable innocence that motivates him to interpret his dreams for his brothers, dreams about his ascendancy and their diminishment, at least as he reads their meanings? Joseph speaks as one touched with the obsession of Abraham and the other illustrious patriarchs, speaks as if he is merely reciting some supernaturally derived word. Abraham, Isaac, and even Jacob have talked to the Fear, we know, but theirs was a conversation set in purgatory, a wrestling, torn flesh in smoky tents. Now this whippersnapper, Joseph, effortlessly conjures messages from the Fear out of his dreams. His mad bent gets him a beating or two before one of the boys finally brings the news that Joseph is dead. Jacob's old age begins as he holds the bloodied and torn robe, all that remains of his beloved son. All the rest he will call "The Dreaming."

The doddering old man who narrates Joseph's adventures is probably not the most reliable sort. The Jacob of these pages is like the aged storytellers Godric and Brendan, characters in whom Buechner plays out his own thoughts on aging. Jacob has lived so long with the promise and with his memories of a stone staircase and a midnight melee that talk of Egypt and the rest seem far-fetched, figments of his daytime dreams. Some of Joseph's tales Jacob has heard from his sons, some he will hear from Joseph, but the picture has gone fuzzy as he approaches it with an imagination shaped by years of struggle with his family, himself, and the Fear. Somewhere in his dream is a picture of a boy, bound at the hands and ankles and thrust into an abandoned well. The violence this time comes from brothers and not from the father, but it is again a scene of cruelty. Joseph's story opens on the scene of the rage of his brothers. The pit is "a strange mercy," because they had meant to kill him straightaway until Reuben talked them into simply leaving him in the well (*Laughter* 216). As the brothers wrangle over what to do with the gentle boy, who comes to his rescue? "Does the Shield of Abraham shield him?" Jacob asks—a rhetorical question indeed (*Laughter* 216). When their murderous rage has cooled to mere greed, the brothers agree to sell Joseph as a slave to a band of merchants who happen along at the right moment. Is this part of some providential design? Who knows? Buechner keeps the possibility in play that Fear is behind even these evil machinations. But the price is twenty pieces of silver.

So Joseph is carried to "the Black Land," Egypt, the land of Ra (*Laughter* 219). In Jacob's dreams, Egypt is like Haran, another milieu with alien gods, a place where "Gods swarm like flies at their harvest and planting" (*Laughter* 219). He even has a dim memory of standing before Ra and being asked his age. "Few and evil have been the days of the years of my life," he has apparently answered (*Laughter* 220). Explaining the phrase and speaking of himself in the third person, he notes, "By few he means many that seem few. There are times when his whole life seems a single day that he has been dreaming. By evil he means full of grief and waiting" (*Laughter* 220). The grief is obvious enough—Rachel, Isaac, and now Joseph, all gone. There's grief too over Laban and Esau and Rebekah and Shechem and more. It must feel like all grief to the old man, and waiting for the Fear to keep his promise must have long since turned to gall.

The most daring chapter of *The Son of Laughter* is the part of Jacob's dream that treats Joseph's days as servant to Potiphar, a friend of Ra. The shepherd boy grows toward manhood as a favored slave in the household. And what a household. A high official in the government, Potiphar is decadent and corrupt. One scene even hints of Potiphar's sexual appetite for Joseph, who is still a boy at the time. Buechner further tinkers with the biblical narrative in the episode between Joseph and Potiphar's wife. In Buechner's hands, the famous story takes surprising turns. Lore Dickstein in *The New York Times Book Review* analysis of Buechner's novel focused on this scene as the epitome of Buechner's "meddling" with Scripture. Dickstein argued that Potiphar's wife "here becomes a ludicrous character in a soft-core romance novel."[26] Joseph's encounter with Potiphar's wife has long been a standard in the moral training of children. In that version, Joseph resists temptation, endures unjust condemnation, and emerges, finally, victorious because of his steadfast faith.

Buechner, through Jacob, cannot quite imagine the scene that way. First, Potiphar's wife is not the vixen of the moral allegory. She is "full of sorrow" (*Laughter* 226). No doubt some of her sadness is the superficial vanity of an aging and empty woman. She is in love with the boy, and Buechner paints her in surprisingly sympathetic colors. The seduction scene here is no simple attack and rejection. Joseph is at least half-willing as he understands something of the older woman's loneliness. He does flee just in time, his clothing left behind, but Buechner lets human nature into his take on the ancient story. Maybe for a minute Joseph saw a possibility that he might find something like home in the warmth of this woman. What follows is universal too. Potiphar suspects the real truth of the matter but cannot allow himself to speak it. So we have another wrecked family, one riven by secrets and silences, denials and desperation.

Joseph's education continues in prison. Buechner finds a way for some humor even there by depicting Joseph's cellmates, Ra's butler and baker, as "a towering bony man with a stammer" and a dwarf whose "forehead bulged like a melon" (*Laughter* 234, 235). Their sleep troubled by dreams, the mismatched pair turn to the young dreamer for help. Joseph thinks he hears "the voice of Fear" in their dreams (*Laughter* 237). That is to say, Joseph still holds to some notion of the Fear's direction, even in this foreboding place and despite the downward turn in his fortune. His interpretation of their dreams proves to be on the mark; the butler lives, and the dwarf is hanged. His friends gone, Joseph makes his way in the prison, gaining the trust of his jailers, until he is called before Ra himself. Troubled himself by inexplicable dreams, the king has sought out Joseph on the advice of the butler. Goodness will out, we are tempted to say, as Joseph gets these dreams right too. Egypt is to have seven years of abundance to be followed by seven years of famine. His reading of the king's dreams "changed the whole course of the Black Land's life from that day forward and the whole course of the king's life as well, and of the boy's life and of the life of their peoples" (*Laughter* 242).

In *The Eyes of the Heart*, Buechner speaks of his fondness for the two great narratives of Genesis—the exodus, which captures something of the human instinct for freedom, and the exile, which also speaks of universal human longing. Buechner asks "if there are any of us who do not feel the sadness and loneliness and lostness of being separated from where we know in our hearts we truly belong, even if we're not sure either where it is to be found or how to get there, if there are any of us who do not yearn, more than anything else, to go home" (*EH* 76). Such is Joseph's dilemma. Forced to sing the Fear's song in a foreign land, Joseph becomes an ideal character for Buechner's thoughts on providence, the preoccupation always brooding just behind the appearance of things in Buechner. So much of Buechner's work seems a testing of the truth of the claim that God moves in human reality. In an early sermon, Buechner catches the conundrum: "However inanely and blindly we are seeking the kingdom of Heaven, and in the damndest places literally, it is also seeking us" (*MD* 122). Thirty years later, with Jacob and Joseph, Buechner seems still to be hefting the proposition.

Joseph's star begins to rise again with his insights into Pharaoh's dreams. He ascends to prominence in the king's administration after explaining that the Fear is the inspiration behind his gift for reading dreams. When Pharaoh asks why Joseph refers to his god as the Fear, Joseph answers, "It is his promises that I fear, and I fear his favor." Joseph's ambivalence sounds even louder when he adds, "I am afraid of the dreams he sends" (*Laughter* 245). Clearly Joseph has inherited his forefathers' sense that knowing God is not always a comfortable thing. He already knows much about the tortured path toward the promise. Joseph's plan to store up grain for the famine to come wins him the job of carrying out the plan, and thus he becomes powerful in the kingdom, especially when the famine does come as he has predicted. The king gives Joseph a new name, Zaphenath-Paneah, "which means in the tongue of the Black Land, The God Speaks and He Lives, though which god is meant the name does not say," Jacob notes (*Laughter* 248).

Abraham, Isaac, and Jacob had each been rechristened by the Fear himself. Joseph comes by his new name more conventionally, though the name suggests something of the testimony to the power of his god that Joseph's rise to prominence marks. In one of his talks with Pharaoh, Joseph makes clear the difference between his god and those of the Egyptians. "My god is a god of those who are alive," he tells the king (*Laughter* 250). For better or worse, Joseph seems to have this part right. There's also a new wife in the package and two sons. The first of the boys he christens Manasseh, "Making to Forget"—"The Fear made him forget all the griefs of his youth" (*Laughter* 252). In all the drama of Buechner's reprise of the familiar stories, one might easily miss a most stunning sentence: "She made Joseph a good wife" (*Laughter* 252). Her name is Asenath, and the marriage seems to be a happy one in Buechner's version. The Genesis text merely mentions that she bore him sons. Having wondered why the biblical narratives rarely record whether or not the subjects of their stories were happy, I like Buechner's account. Maybe the curses are winding down at last. Six simple words suggest that the blessing may be taking hold.

And the promise is heating up, too. For all his happiness in his adopted land, the complex Joseph feels the loss of home still. He keeps memories alive because, he thinks:

> The remembering was better than the forgetting because to forget the griefs was to forget also the gifts born out of the griefs like the life of his brother Benjamin born out of his mother's death, and his own rise to great power born out of the pit where his brothers had cast him. The Fear had two hands, he thought, one of them a hand that takes away and the other a hand that gives to a child he has brought to sorrow. (*Laughter* 253)

Joseph seems to be the first of his line to live in an open embrace of the sadness and the laughter, the remembering and the forgetting. "The Lord gives, and the Lord takes away; blessed be the name of the Lord," is the way Job puts it.[27]

Joseph has not forgotten his brothers when they are paraded before him, visitors from a starving land looking for respite. Unrecognized by his frightened and bedazzled brothers, Joseph asks for news of home and develops a strategy that will eventually bring Jacob and Benjamin to Egypt. Benjamin has become Jacob's favorite after Joseph's supposed death. We learn of Jacob's feelings for Benjamin in a scene that echoes Twain again. Twain's famous runaway slave, Jim, tells Huck the moving story of the time he mistakenly punished his daughter Elizabeth, a story that establishes something of Jim's dignity and humanity in Twain's novel.

Jacob, like Jim, has unjustly struck his child. Thinking Benjamin is dishonoring him by mimicking his limp, Jacob slaps him, only to learn that the limp, like his own, is real. "From that day forward, I always kept him close to me and favored him as I had favored Joseph before him," Jacob remembers (*Laughter* 259). Benjamin is another of the Fear's cripples, and Jacob is wretched at the idea of losing this last son. Weeping as Isaac wept when he spoke of Abraham and Moriah, Jacob cries over the misery and shame of it all: "My tears were for all the sadness there ever was between sons and fathers, fathers and sons" (*Laughter* 260). Buechner keeps that point of tension taut to the end.

The disquiet of the last few pages of the novel has mostly to do with whether or not Joseph will soften his heart toward the brothers who have treated him so cruelly. We know what's coming, of course, but Buechner fills in the gaps of Joseph's human struggle with his instinct to revenge. "Some madness in him" stops his mouth just when he wants to confess his identity and embrace his family (*Laughter* 263). It is the madness of unforgiving, of course, the hardness of the human heart: "He was the hound-headed god weighing their hearts and searching them. It was his own heart as well that he was weighing and searching, sifting through his love and his anger till one or the other came uppermost" (*Laughter* 263). In the pivotal moment when Joseph is about to send the brothers back to Jacob and imprison Benjamin in Egypt, Joseph studies these men who, in their youth, had given way to their worst. "They were the seed of Abraham, the bearers of luck and blessing. Their luck lay scattered about their bare feet in steaming mounds like the dung of the horses. Where was their blessing?" he asks (*Laughter* 264). And here the irony of the generations emerges. Joseph is the blessing. The promise lives with his declaration: "I AM JOSEPH!" (*Laughter* 265). One might even call it a happy ending.

Jacob hears the Fear's voice one last time, this time on the road to the Black Land. The voice speaks the same sort of things Jacob has heard before—"Do not be afraid" and "I will make of you a great people" (*Laughter* 267). Jacob will live on for seventeen years in Pharaoh's strange land, listening to Joseph's tales and trying to forgive his sons. "Perhaps their evil was only a dream of evil which they had waked from," he concludes. After all, "it was through their evil that the Fear had worked the saving of us all," he adds, pondering still the meaning of "I will be with you" (*Laughter* 269). In the last days, Jacob passes the blessing, not to Joseph, but to Manasseh and Ephraim, his grandsons. We can almost see the twinkle in his eye when he crosses his hands and gives the greater blessing to the younger of the two. The joke continues. Jacob knows that

Joseph will carry him home to the cave where Abraham and Isaac both lie buried. And, he predicts, "Joseph will bury me, not as Jacob, but as Israel because Israel is the name that the Fear himself gave me the night he blessed and crippled me" (*Laughter* 273).

Jacob's long wrestling almost over, Buechner returns to a dialogue between Joseph and Ra. The builder of pyramids and leader of a people who pay great attention to death has asked Joseph about his god's after-life. "He makes promises about life," Joseph notes; "I do not know what he promises to the dead if he promises anything" (*Laughter* 273). Such a response might well bewilder a king, if not all of us. How could one be expected to believe in a deity who cloaks himself in silence on such a sub-ject? Joseph has something of an answer: "He speaks to us sometimes in dreams that are like torches to light our way through the dark. He gives us daughters and sons so our seed may live after us and the promises he has made may be kept to the world's luck and blessing" (*Laughter* 273–74). The reader echoes Jacob; "perhaps that is enough" (*Laughter* 274). Buech-ner ends this novel on the tentative note of such words as "may" and "per-haps." "Is his promise only a dream?" Jacob wonders at the end. Or "is it in our dreaming that we glimpse the fullness of his promise?" (*Laughter* 274). Faith is the dream that brings us to those intermittent moments of blessing, those intimations of more and more.

At the end of this day, what Buechner seems to have learned is to pre-fer the given, as he comes, like Dante, to "the end of all desires."[28] An older man's wisdom simmers in *The Son of Laughter*, the wisdom of accept-ing what comes and watching for those glimmers of hope, those sugges-tions of possibility. Buechner has read well passages like the one in Psalms: "Even before a word is on my tongue, O LORD, you know it completely. You hem me in, behind and before, and lay your hand upon me. Such knowledge is too wonderful for me; it is so high that I cannot attain it."[29] He understands that the word "wonderful" here could contain terror as much as serenity, fear as much as faith, and *The Son of Laughter* rests on the back and forth, the up and down of faith and fear, promise and dread.

Buechner will return to the acceptance theme in the novel to come four years after the Jacob novel, *On the Road with the Archangel*, in which his pen-chant for capturing Hebraic style will serve him well again. Both books are praised for their stylistic innovation. Buechner has an ear for "the likely sounds of speech from a distant time and place," one critic argued.[30] Irv-ing Malin underscored Buechner's use of "simple sentences which, in effect, mirror the Hebraic style."[31] Some readers even lamented the loss of Buechner's own voice, the *Bebb* voice, so successfully has he submerged

Buechner
Circa 1995

himself in Jacob's storytelling. He manages a pleasurable prose style while also capturing the crudity and rawness of the times. Particularly from *The Book of Bebb* on, Buechner's prose is startlingly sensual. Auchincloss noted that the reader of *The Son of Laughter* can "almost smell" Esau (Auchincloss 95).

The Son of Laughter becomes yet another of Buechner's novels to wear the label "masterpiece" (Auchincloss 95). But the remarkable success of the novel has more to do, I think, with the increasing clarity of Buechner's themes, his way of keeping the paradoxes in order—natural versus supernatural, guilt versus forgiveness, doubt versus faith—and the way in which his characters and their questions are like his readers and their questions (Garrett 299). Although he has yet to receive the respect he deserves in literary circles, Buechner takes another step toward rarefied company with *The Son of Laughter*. Malin nominated Buechner as "at least as important as Flannery O'Connor and Walker Percy," a bold claim but one supported by the weight of the work (Malin 27). In a review comparing the Buechner novel to a book on Joshua by Joseph Girzone, John Bookser

Feister said that the move from Girzone to Buechner was like the move from the "literary minor leagues to the majors."[32]

Whatever the book turns out to mean for his literary reputation, Buechner's foray into the psychology of Jacob ends up as an invitation to readers. His portrayal of the fathers and sons and mothers and daughters of the biblical record becomes, finally, a portrayal of all of our families and a consideration of what gets carried along from one generation to the next. In those early 1990s, Buechner speaks often of his attempts to write from a "deep source": "I believe there is within us this image of God. . . . There is something deep within us, in everybody, that gets buried and distorted and confused and corrupted by what happens to us. But it is there as a source of insight and healing and strength. I think it is where art comes from" (Brown 44). Writing into and from this inner source, Buechner seems to have found healing and grace. And the results of his journeys, the many books, offer something of the same to readers. We all of us walk with a limp.

Notes

1. Lore Dickstein, "Jacob: The Novel," *New York Times*, September 19, 1993, 3.
2. Calvin Miller, book review, *Southwest Journal of Theology* 36, no. 2: 52. Hereafter cited as Miller.
3. Wendy Wise Herstein, "Never beyond Reach," *The World & I*, www.worldandi.com, April 1993, 308. Hereafter cited as Herstein.
4. John Bookser Feister, "Authors Weave Sacred Yarns," *National Catholic Reporter*, May 28, 1993, 37.
5. William Pritchard, "Buechner's 'Secrets' Most Telling," *USA Today*, March 8, 1991, 5D.
6. Kenneth Gibble, "Ordained to Write," *United Presbyterian A.D.*, March 1983, 17.
7. Richard A. Kauffman, "Ordained to Write: An Interview with Frederick Buechner," *Christian Century*, September 11–24, 2002, 27. Hereafter cited as Kauffman.
8. Stephen Kendrick, "On Spiritual Autobiography: An Interview with Frederick Buechner," *Christian Century*, October 14, 1992, 900. Hereafter cited as Kendrick.
9. Frederick Buechner, *The Wizard's Tide: A Story* (San Francisco: Harper & Row, 1990), 1. Hereafter cited as *WTide*.
10. Frank Levering, "Painful Family Secrets Point the Way to Faith," *Chicago Tribune*, February 10, 1991, 7. Hereafter cited as Levering.
11. Timothy Jones, "Secrets He Tried to Forget," *Christianity Today*, February 11, 1991, 63. Hereafter cited as TJones.
12. David Crumm, "Buried Truths," *Detroit Free Press*, February 3, 1991, 9P.
13. Frederick Buechner, "A Sermon," *Testament*, Fall 1990, 14. Hereafter cited as Sermon.
14. Frederick Buechner, *Peculiar Treasures: A Biblical Who's Who*, illus. Katherine Buechner (San Francisco: Harper & Row, 1979), 56. Hereafter cited as *PT*.
15. Douglas Auchincloss, "*The Son of Laughter*," *Parabola* 18 (Winter 1993): 95. Hereafter cited as Auchincloss.
16. Eugene Peterson, "*The Son of Laughter*," *Theology Today* 50, no. 4 (January 1994): 607. Hereafter cited as Peterson.

17. Jill P. Baumgaertner, "*Son of Laughter*," *Christian Century*, August 25–September 1, 1993, 826.

18. Personal correspondence, July 20, 1993.

19. Annie Dillard, "The Ancient Story of Jacob, Retold in a Passionate, Exalted Pitch," *Boston Sunday Globe*, May 30, 1993, A15. Hereafter cited as Dillard.

20. Joseph Sendry, "1993 *CCL* Book Citation Award," *Christianity and Literature* 42, no. 2 (Winter 1993): 378–79.

21. Logan Jones, "*Son of Laughter* Makes Bible's Jacob Come to Life," *National Christian Reporter*, July 23, 1993, 20.

22. Ken Ristau, "Characterization, Customs, Theology," www.anduril.ca, 5. Hereafter cited as Ristau.

23. Michael Aeschliman, "Blessing and Bane," *The World & I*, www.worldandi.com, April 1993, 302. Hereafter cited as Aeschliman.

24. Susan Lovell, "Buechner Deserving of a Shelf in Your Library," *Grand Valley Advance*, December 7, 1993, 21.

25. James Cook, "A Torch to Light the Way," *Perspectives*, January 1994, 21.

26. Lore Dickstein, "*The Son of Laughter*," *New York Times Book Review*, September 19, 1993, 32.

27. Job 1:21.

28. Dante Alighieri, *The Divine Comedy*, trans. Charles Eliot Norton (New York: Houghton Mifflin Co., 1920), 3:253.

29. Psalm 139:4–6.

30. Linda-Marie Delloff, book review, *Lutheran*, June 1993, 61.

31. Irving Malin, "Words Fail Me," *Commonweal*, July 16, 1993, 28. Hereafter cited as Malin.

32. John Bookser Feister, "Authors Reweave Sacred Yarns," *National Catholic Reporter*, May 28, 1993, 37.

Chapter Ten

Revisiting Jehovah

On the Road with the Archangel

I suppose every group has its salivation words, telltale litmus tests that reveal positions and proffer a way of defining others as in or out. Buechner has often provided fodder for groups attempting to divide the sheep from the goats. In the late 1980s, for example, he mentioned a fondness for Matthew Fox's *The Coming of the Cosmic Christ*, which set certain mouths to watering (Brown 45). Read New Ageism and relativism for Matthew Fox. In the late 1990s it was Marcus Borg's *Meeting Jesus Again for the First Time* that Buechner endorsed, which got him pigeonholed once again (*EH* 75). One of the conveners of the Jesus Seminar, Borg is a public liberal on matters theological, and Buechner is often himself painted into that dreaded corner. (Borg even provides a blurb for Buechner's *The Eyes of the Heart*.) Others, of course, applauded Buechner's position between the literalists and the secularists. Noting Buechner's admiration for Borg, Lauren Winner, for example, marveled at the unlikely attraction of evangelical Christians to Buechner's work. She answered her own puzzlement by arguing that "no matter how many news stories penned by the cultured despisers painting evangelicals as smug, unquestioning, unthinking puppets, Christians themselves know that Buechner is right."[1] What Winner applauds is Buechner's insistence that the issues are more complex, the doubt more palpable, the encounter with God more ominous, than many institutions of religion are attesting. Many thoughtful Christians are indeed finding consolation in Buechner's books, books in which they hear the truth of things. My own position that Buechner's work will continue to grow in popularity is based partly on a similar supposition about his faith-based readership. Most believers are not glib about issues of faith, the stereotypes of the popular media notwithstanding. Buechner offers substance to a subculture wrestling with what belief means in their day-to-day lives. I think too that many so-called secularists, attracted to Buechner's literary style and storytelling, may find a certain solace in his suggestions about meaning. So Buechner is not so much between the two worlds as he is embracing the two worlds.

In the general discourse these days, the word "liberal" is commonly associated with other words—"bleeding heart," "wacky," "spineless," "waffler," and the like. A recent letter to *Newsweek* capsulizes the debate: "So-called liberal Christianity does not stand up under fire. Either you believe that Jesus was, and is, the King of Kings and the Lord of Lords, or you must consider him a phony. Many theological liberals like a lot of things Jesus Christ taught ('love thy neighbor,' etc.), but can't accept miracles and any talk of the judgment to come."[2] It is precisely Buechner's rejection of an either/or point of view that has made room for his art. As we have seen, the maybe space, the commitment to paradox, and the admission of doubt fuel the novels. Noting how Buechner "elegantly sidesteps" the nasty disputes about the Bible—inspired truth or mythology?—Wesley Sheffield claimed that Buechner "faces this highly-charged debate by calmly substituting the category of 'faith' for that of 'truth.'"[3] Sheffield found that substitution helpful; others are not so sure. A reviewer in *The Bookstore Journal*, while admiring the "good writing" of *The Sacred Journey*, lamented Buechner's failure "to hint of the need to trust in a historical Jesus Christ for salvation."[4] In another of the commentaries, this one a review of *Telling Secrets* in *Christianity Today*, Timothy Jones acknowledged Buechner's significance but framed his praise in a distinct suspicion: "Many readers will wish Buechner's voice, when it comes to faith, was more certain. We could wish that Buechner was a more unabashed apologist, saying more about the transforming power of Christ" (TJones 64).

No. No. No. We can wish no such thing if we want art. Some observers like the word "ecumenical" as a tag for Buechner. Robert Taylor, for example, argued that Buechner's mix of mysticism and Christianity is "ecumenical in spirit."[5] Better than "liberal," I suppose, but "ecumenical" is also too weak a word. Like all good artists, Buechner is impossible to place at one pole or another. He encompasses poles.

Buechner's work of the mid-1990s continues his preoccupation with infusing the old stories with new vitality, wondering about the lives of near-saints, studying ambiguity, admitting mixed feelings, and exploring still the flow between memoir and fiction. *The Longing for Home: Recollections and Reflections* comes along in 1996, another grab bag collection including memoir, essay, and even some poetry. *On the Road with the Archangel* follows in 1997, a novel based on the Apocryphal book of Tobit.

In *The Longing for Home*, Buechner's "vision is rounding into an orbed peace which holds a promise for the rest of us still struggling with those then what? questions," according to Virginia Stem Owens.[6] Although Buechner struggles as ever with the big questions, Owens did get at what I mentioned in the discussion of *Son of Laughter*—the quiet wisdom of the now seventy-year-old writer. The take on Tobit will display his ongoing preoccupation with the Job-like questions, the questions that reach all the way back to the beginning of his career. From *A Long Day's Dying* to *Secrets in the Dark*, Buechner has studied the improbable presence of grace in the mundane day-to-dayness of human experience. The work continues here in fiction and in memoir. The novel could be said to be about the unmarked presence of God. The memoir focuses on homesickness—a construct we've observed throughout the Buechner oeuvre. Dedicated to the Buechners' grandsons, *The Longing for Home* parses "home" in two directions—"the home we knew and will always long for, be homesick for" and "the home we dream of finding and for which we also long" (*Longing* 2). We have seen how Buechner often uses the nonfiction as a way to reflect on earlier works of fiction. So *Open Heart* shows up in *Telling the Truth*, and *The Wizard's Tide* and *Treasure Hunt* show up in *The Longing for Home*. Buechner refers to the WELCOME HONE sign from *Treasure Hunt* both to explain his methodology as a writer and to discuss again his central preoccupation with the meaning of human longing. The sign, Buechner remembers, was no literary contrivance but a gift "from some deep place within," the same place dreams come from (*Longing* 18).

Buechner's argument that his art emerges from sources he only dimly understands complicates the argument that, as a believer, he has a thesis in his pocket when he sits down at his desk to write. "I am simply letting an empty place open up inside myself and waiting for something to fill it," he claims (*Longing* 22). Robert Olen Butler labeled this literary commonplace, "listening to the voice of the characters" (Brown 59). I've discovered that writers as diverse as Ernest Gaines and Jon Hassler make similar claims about the ways in which their stories emerge. No outliner, Buechner concurs with these others. He speaks often about the surprising turns his novels take, wonders about lines and ideas that seem to come from wells deeper than any he had suspected in himself. The masterstroke of HONE, of course is that it is partial, a word with "something small but crucial missing" (*Longing* 18). In the memoir, Buechner discovers that, like his character, he too longs for a place with nothing missing. The memoir seems to fuel an interest in family history that will spill over into another visit with his grandmother, Naya, in *The Eyes of the Heart*. He will fiddle with the idea of spiritual yearning in *On the Road with the Archangel,* and it will be a driving force in his 1998 novel, *The Storm,* where Kenzie Maxwell on the last page dreams of a home he might someday find "if he kept his eyes open and his nose clean and his powder dry."[7]

The *Christianity Today* reviewer of *On the Road with the Archangel* got it right this time. Arguing that Buechner's "distinctive gift lies in giving voice to the streak of ambiguity that runs through human existence," David Stewart nonetheless concluded that "amid the ambiguity that is our lot, the Almighty is at work, quietly and profoundly."[8] That's precisely the right note for Buechner's work—God works, yes, but just how or to what ends, we can never be sure, and *On the Road with the Archangel* carries us right back to that territory. Patricia DeLeeuw summarized the novel as another where Buechner finds "his favorite theme in an ancient source."[9] Many critics attempted connections to the earlier work, especially to *Godric, Brendan,* and *Son of Laughter.* Some similarities are obvious; we are indeed into an encore visit to several of Buechner's concerns—theories of God, notions of grace and forgiveness, the weightiness of guilt, and the need for acceptance.

But the venue for the thorny issues is once again a surprise. Although another perusal of an ancient text, *On the Road with the Archangel* has a fairy-tale quality that is new in Buechner, a lightness that seems a break from the three preceding novels. Buechner's own explanation of the surprising turns from novel to novel is that each book is "a sort of vacation from the book that preceded it."[10] Alfred Corn in his *New York Times* review caught some of the shift when he spoke of Buechner's style as "based on contemporary speech" and of Buechner's "turn of mind" as "ironic."[11] The original Tobit was probably excluded from the sixty-six-book canon because of its folktale quality, and Buechner manages to exploit the fun of the genre even in the muddle of Job-like questions and situations. Some might find the comparison to Job a stretch, but I would argue that Job's questions are Tobit's indeed: Who is this God? Why is this happening to me?

This novel is Buechner's happiest, despite plenty enough ugliness to go around. The take on faith issues in this novel reminded me of a line from Doris Betts: "Christian writers must decide whether their works should whisper or shout their message."[12] Although Buechner usually whispers in the fiction, he gets closer to raising his voice this time. The *Kirkus Reviews* reader was probably right to say that Buechner was "playing down suffering, playing up faith" in *On the Road with the Archangel.*[13] (What he gives here, he will, however, take away in the next novel, *The Storm.*) George

Garrett said this one "sings and dances" as he pointed to the laughter Buechner manages to find in the Tobit tale.[14] Garrett venerated Buechner, saying he is "as good as we have" (GGarrett 10). Judith Moore went further, claiming that Buechner's achievement made the reader "want to fall on your knees and kiss the damp earth, you're just so glad to be alive."[15] Well, maybe she was a bit over the top, but I think she caught the infectious aura of the little book that plays big in the Buechner corpus.

In a surprisingly candid interview about *On the Road with the Archangel*, Moore gets Buechner's own words on the impulses behind the book:

> I had my seventieth birthday two summers ago, and I began thinking about things people write when they get to be old codgers. I thought about Shakespeare. I thought about how at the end of his life he wrote these wonderful sort of fairy tale plays like *The Tempest* and *The Winter's Tale*, and everything ends up wonderfully, and it's sort of too good not to be true. I cast about for something like that kind of fairy tale, and something drew me to the *Book of Tobit*, which I'd read before, and I'd decided it was not my thing. But all of a sudden it was. It would be my sort of *Tempest* or *Winter's Tale*. (Moore 65)

A happy story toward the end, perhaps. The original Tobit might well be described as a moralistic fable, a didactic tale "to show the value and reward of serving God faithfully," as one commentary put it.[16] Some even think the original document was intended to comfort the Jews after the destruction of the temple. Actually, Tobit is much like Jonah, a book that did make the A list. Both narratives are about second chances and misunderstandings of God; both stories have a fairy-tale dimension and end in irresolution. As far as I can tell, the only other writer to make literary fodder of the tale is Edward Albee in *A Delicate Balance*. Albee, of course, inverts the Tobit narrative. Buechner tells it straight.

Buechner dedicates *Archangel* to "the memory of James Merrill," whose death in 1995 was another marker along Buechner's way.[17] Penning the dedication after the book was finished, Buechner realized that Merrill's Ouija board poems have several conversations with an archangel in them "that may also have played a part in the genesis" of *Archangel*.[18] In his introductory note, however, Buechner makes it clear that the book of Tobit is his starting place, though he admits a certain haziness in his foundational materials. The anonymous author was "more interested in telling a good story" than in getting his facts straight, Buechner thinks, and concludes that "so, through the Archangel's lips, was I" (*Archangel* ix). As he has done in *Son of Laughter, Godric,* and *Brendan,* Buechner listens to Tobit's story for clues to fill in the gaps, and the first stroke of the novella is to let Raphael himself tell the story.

As one of the seven archangels, Raphael's job seems to be carrying prayers to "the Holy One" from all petitioners, especially those "who don't even know that they're praying" (*Archangel* 1). From the first paragraph, we have yet another Buechnerian angle on God. Surely the debate about the very nature of God is one of the preoccupations of Buechner's small book. Raphael calls him "Holy One" or "the Presence" (*Archangel* 14). But Raphael is about to enter the story of Tobit, a man who lives with the same unease as that of a child dreading punishment. Tobit keeps his head down, sure that all the evils of his days are deserved retribution for his sins. God is Scorekeeper for Tobit—"ill-tempered and irrational and vengeful" (*Archangel* 14, 130). Tobit's God, something like Jacob's Fear, proves incomplete when set beside Raphael's version, but the God who gets confused with luck is deeply entrenched in Tobit's mind. Buechner assumes that confusion about the nature of God might well be a contemporary issue too.

For Raphael, who has inside information, these human misunderstandings often move him to laughter, though he seems capable of a certain compassion for the agonies of the creatures whose prayers he totes to the Holy One. He assures us at the beginning that the story he is to tell is one of the funniest of them all, one that makes him "shake with laughter" (*Archangel* 2). Is this narrator reliable? Although he admits that he tends to "lose track of the details," Raphael rather quickly establishes himself as not only omniscient but also as wise and involved: "The things that the world fills time with are enough to turn the heart to stone, but the goodness of time itself is as untouched by them as the freshness of a spring morning is untouched by the yelps from the scaffold" (*Archangel* 3). Raphael is a kind of doting father, shaking his head over the stubborn blindness of humanity, but the shake is sympathetic. Almost everybody misses the goodness of time, he thinks; "not even the most devout understand this for more than possibly a day or two out of the entire year" (*Archangel* 3). Thus he arrives at the consistently inconsistent Tobit, and thus Buechner returns to a favorite theme—paying attention, getting it.

We meet Tobit at his worst. He really is blind, and he's had it up to here. We'll learn the story of his blindness later, but the curtain rises on a scene full of sad humor. The reader can imagine Buechner reading the passage to his wife after a day of writing in his study. He and Judith would "both roar with laughter," he recalls (Moore 65). The scene features a hapless dog, a shrewish wife, and a bewildered Tobit. Angry with Tobit over some slight, Anna storms around the house like one of the Furies. She calls her husband a "fool," and Tobit "suspected that she might be right and that the Holy One agreed with her" (*Archangel* 3). When Anna trips over the dog and overturns a table loaded with dirty dishes, Tobit concludes that "she was in the process of adding to her insult by pulling down the house around their ears" (*Archangel* 4). So Tobit heads for the outhouse. (In the original manuscript, Buechner has marked through "courtyard" and substituted "outhouse," an edit suggestive of his move toward comedy in this novel [Archive, IV A 17].) In his retreat, Tobit prays to die, and Raphael dutifully carries the plea to the Presence. From an outhouse in Nineveh, Raphael flits to a woman in a town some miles away who, as it happens, is praying a prayer almost identical to Tobit's, she too being blind to the goodness of time. "It is with those two prayers for death that the story begins," Raphael comments, though he immediately moves to the back story of two dysfunctional families.

Always quick to revise villainy, Buechner, through Raphael, lets us know soon enough that Anna is no battle-ax. Tobit and Anna are actually fond of one another, "though neither of them would ever have thought to mention it, least of all to each other or even to themselves" (*Archangel* 5). They are another of Buechner's suffering families, though some of their tribulation derives from their status as captives. King Sargon has carried them off to Nineveh along with many other Jews from the northern kingdom. Forced to live under Sargon's hard rule, Tobit has nonetheless kept his music with him. Still young and sighted at the time of the exile, Tobit is known for a conspicuous eccentricity: "In moments of distraction, he had the habit of conducting an imaginary group of musicians" (*Archangel* 6). The image of Tobit chopping the air in rhythm to some unheard melody indeed seems ludicrous, but the practice produces a certain harmony in the man who is often morose and unsettled. Buechner's own lifelong habit of humming a tune just under his breath—"Seventy-six Trombones," of all things—echoes Tobit's routine.[19] Tobit's orchestra and Buechner's show tune are all the more remarkable as Tobit and Buechner are serious-minded men often given to fretfulness and melancholy. It is as if the music suggests another side to things—that old mix of comedy and tragedy—a laughter in the well, the goodness of time in the badness of time. Thus Buechner finds something of himself in this character emerging from the Apocryphal text.

Tobit's strange habit brings him the fortunate notice of the king. Suspecting that Tobit may be a lunatic, which would mean entertainment and good luck, King Sargon will learn that Tobit is merely an honest man. Entrusted with some of the king's mercantile business, Tobit settles into a relatively auspicious life in the foreign land. The problem is his instinct toward charity. Ever mindful of his compatriots, Tobit feeds and clothes the less lucky Jews. He pushes the envelope by going so far as to bury the discarded corpses of the many who are executed by the cruel king and his vicious son, Sennacherib. The captor's practice is to toss the bodies of dead Jews on a garbage heap or simply leave them lying in the streets, a symbol of their disgrace, and Tobit risks everything to steal and inter the bodies. Although he narrowly escapes his own execution, he does endure the scoffing of his family. They believe he risks too much. Even the dog hides his eyes when Tobit goes off on one of his missions to the dead. Buechner brings comedy to a most weighty situation, and Raphael adds to the laughter with a dramatic line in his characteristic spare and whimsical style: "Now enter the sparrows" (*Archangel* 12). Tobit's luck is about to change.

Asleep in the courtyard after one of his midnight excursions, Tobit manages to catch sparrow droppings on his uncovered face. When he awakens, he is blind. More fecal imagery from Buechner, of course, but this time with a tragic-comic force, a bizarre calamity that carries, as Corn argued, "all the flavor of a folk tale" (Corn 23). So Tobit winds up sitting around in his own stew, sightless in every way, while Anna keeps the family afloat by sewing for their wealthier neighbors. Tobit blames God. Raphael laughs at the way Tobit falls into the belief that his sins or those of his ancestors have brought this visitation of blindness. Unable to endure Anna's insults any longer, Tobit seeks release. "You have made a laughing stock of us all," Anna rants, sounding for all the world like Job's wife (*Archangel* 16).

Buechner's voice emerges from the narrative in Raphael's summary of the situation when Tobit prays for death: "Like the rest of the devout, he was incapable of understanding that the Holy One's face is never turned away but constantly looks down on all creatures with a beneficence that they are too busy apologizing for their unworthiness and performing their good works and assuring Heaven of their unfailing devotion to notice" (*Archangel* 16). The contemporary note rings as Buechner makes clear his preoccupation with misunderstandings of God.

Another narrative folds into the noisy tale of Tobit, Anna, and their calamities—a story of a beautiful young woman, Sarah, the daughter of Raguel and Edna in Ecbatana. The fairy-tale quality continues, especially with Edna, a wicked stepmother type who speaks in clichés reminiscent of Flannery O'Connor's Mrs. Hopewell. Edna wants her daughter married off, because Sarah "was as much admired as Edna was shunned like the pox" (*Archangel* 19). Raphael admits that there's a bit of love in Edna's machinations to get her daughter a beau, even if the love is of a sort twisted by several human currents. For her part, Sarah wants none of it. She cannot fathom betraying her father to the harangues of her mother just as she cannot imagine "the embrace of a virtual stranger" (*Archangel* 20). So Sarah makes a deal with the devil, or at least one of the devil's minions. His name is Asmodeus, which, Raphael explains, means "the Destroyer" (*Archangel* 20). In an interesting aside, Raphael wonders "why the Holy One permits such creatures to exist" (*Archangel* 20). Attempting an answer to his own question, Raphael says, "Perhaps the light of his glory casts shadows whose very darkness bears witness to its brilliance" (*Archangel* 20). Finally, Raphael gives up the query. Even the angels must bow to mystery. If we were expecting ultimate answers from the archangel, they will not be forthcoming—even archangels are not in on the whole picture.

Surprisingly, Asmodeus is moved by Sarah's fears of marriage. He is more than a little taken with her beauty as she is more than a little taken by his. Buechner, thereby, complicates another villain. Raphael wonders if "not even the lords of darkness are entirely bereft of some glimmer of the radiance they abhor" (*Archangel* 22). In his *Wishful Thinking* entry on "Hell," Buechner quips that "Maybe not even Old Scratch will be able to hold out against him [God] forever," exactly the sort of universalistic rhetoric sure to set mouths watering in some quarters (*WT* 38). Despite his spark of goodness, however, Asmodeus proves capable enough at the grim business of doing away with Sarah's husbands, and Edna's careful conniving merely wrangles up a bridegroom who will be found dead on the morning after the wedding.

Despite her resistance to marriage, Sarah seems helpless before her parents' wishes and almost grateful when the corpse puts a damper on the whole business. But even Sarah is thoroughly distraught when the story repeats seven times. Seven dead husbands. You can imagine the neighbors' whispers. At first, folks think that Sarah's bridegrooms have been overcome by amorous bliss. A few begin to reason that "something unearthly was surely involved" by the time the seventh rigid body is toted out of the bridal chamber (*Archangel* 23). Others think that Sarah is herself the murderer, a fact she is hard pressed to refute, since she has indeed put Asmodeus on the job. Her honor at stake, not to mention her future, Sarah unsuccessfully tries to hang herself before praying that the Holy One will simply take her life. Her prayer in his left hand and Tobit's in his right,

Raphael does his duty as intermediary with the Most High only to be ordered to "Set everything right" (*Archangel* 26). Thus the plot thickens.

Tobit's son Tobias, whom Raphael describes as "a slow-talking, sleepy-eyed young man with a shy smile," now emerges as an important character in the narrative, and "slow" may be just the right adjective for Tobias (*Archangel* 9). Fully expecting his prayer to be answered, Tobit prepares for his coming death by delivering certain instructions to Tobias. He is to look after Anna, of course, and "remember the score is always being kept" (*Archangel* 29). "Never forget for one instant that the eye of the Holy One is upon you," Tobit tells Tobias and thus passes along his neurotic faith (*Archangel* 29). Tobit's goodness is in the mix, too, when he commissions his son to remember "the ones who are worse off than you are," but the reason for the call to charity seems to be mostly related to the score being kept (*Archangel* 31). Tobias hears his father's wisdom while being distracted by one of the many women who always seem to be hanging around him. Like Sarah over in Ecbatana, Tobias is beset by a good many feelings he doesn't very well understand. Both of them are bewildered when it comes to talk of love and romance. Tobit advises Tobias to be sure to seek wise counsel from his cousin Ahikar, who has considerable influence with the king, and the reader senses Tobit's dubiety about Tobias's cerebral powers. Lovable Tobias, though not "soft-headed or anything like that," has "always been somewhat slower to understand things than most people," Tobit tells him in a Polonius-like speech that is to send Tobias on his destiny-filled trip.

The reader is unsurprised by the news that Tobias is a bit slow off the mark (*Archangel* 30). The surprise is in what follows. Tobias tries to pull his eyes away from the seductive woman in the doorway as his father tries to tell him a story about a treasure. On a job for the king in a place called Media and fearful of the dangers of the time and place, Tobit has apparently left a small fortune, two sacks of silver, with a friend, Gabael. Tobias's charge is simple enough. Taking along his father's receipt for the treasure, he must find his way to Gabael and the silver and return the treasure for the sustenance of the family after Tobit's sure demise. How the fuzzily focused Tobias is to perform such a feat is part of the mystery and humor of the narrative. Ironically, Tobit, whose luck has run out, nonetheless trusts fortune for his son's journey: "Someone is bound to turn up to show you the way," Tobit believes (*Archangel* 33). Maybe the dog will help, the dog who has been known to take Tobias's hand in his mouth and lead him here and there.

Much has been entrusted to Tobias, and readers may fear that such trust is perilously placed. Raphael, however, keeps insisting that Tobias "was not a fool" (*Archangel* 35). Raphael's fondness for Tobias no doubt inspires the defense. With a fatherly love not unlike Tobit's, Raphael prefers to think of Tobias as distracted and innocent: "Much of the time his mind was simply absent somewhere else" (*Archangel* 35). The truth is that Tobias is a young man with great imagination—his dreams make him appear simple. When the king and his entourage pass by, for example, Tobias may well forget to bow. He is not being disrespectful; he is simply caught up in a reverie about royalty: "kings were only men very much like himself when all was said and done. They worried themselves sick when someone they loved was in trouble. They kept dogs. They stubbed their toes on the way to make water in the dark" (*Archangel* 37). Such imagination endears Tobias to Raphael and the reader and also manages to connect the ancient story to contemporary lives. Indeed, Buechner aficionados will recognize in Tobias that familiar figure of doubter/believer. Taught that the score is being scrupulously kept, Tobias figures the whole business is "a complicated game," and he wonders how "to tell whether you were winning or losing, or how you were supposed to play it right" (*Archangel* 38). Here is another Jacob, another Peter Cowley, another Antonio Parr—aware of ambiguity, and longing to believe somehow. Wasn't it his own father's good deeds that brought down the house? And now this mission to go in search of a treasure. We finally see where all this is going, how two stories will become one, when Tobit delivers his final punch. "It would be nice," he quips to his son, "if somewhere along the way you could find yourself a wife" (*Archangel* 39). Uh-oh.

Who is to assist poor Tobias in his bafflement? Raphael, of course. The dog sees through the disguise immediately when the archangel shows up as a traveler, Azarias, who knows the way to Media, is familiar with the Jewish community there, and even knows a fellow named Gabael. Tobias "marveled at this unforeseen stroke of luck" (*Archangel* 43). The lineaments of fairy tale firmly in place, Raphael, now Azarias, dreams up a family connection and passes muster with Tobit, so the mismatched pair are off on their odd pilgrimage. Buechner's own empty-nest anxiety sounds in the farewell. Mocking Tobit's mad scheme, Anna wonders what the house will be like without their boy in it. "Have you stopped to consider that he is the mortar that holds our lives together and the bright star in our sky?" she asks (*Archangel* 47). Another contemporary note. Afraid he has been too tough on Anna, Raphael here revises our understanding of her. Like most of us, "her heart was at bottom no less tender for the way she kept it most of the time hidden" (*Archangel* 48). Tobit assures her that "the Holy One, blessed be he, will send a good angel to attend him" (*Archangel* 48). The irony is not lost on Raphael, who knows that Tobit doesn't really believe his own cliché. Like most humans, Tobit cannot imagine a deity who cares as much as he does for his wife and son. He speaks the right words but still cannot see the benevolence hovering all around.

The comedy, a fertile mix of *Bebb* and Chaucer, now turns to the picaresque. Adventure comes soon enough, an opportunity for Tobias to show his mettle, demonstrate his worthiness. Breaking from their journey alongside the Tigris River, the footsore travelers set up camp for the night. (Raphael never quite explains why Azarias would have trouble with sore feet.) While Azarias fishes for their supper, Tobias swims in the ancient river. Lurking in the deep waters is a gigantic fish, one that threatens to reverse the dining arrangements. After Tobias wrestles the monster to death, Azarias instructs him to cut the heart, liver, and gall from the venerable fish. The dog distrusts the whole business, but Azarias suggests the offal may prove useful. The motley travelers, now tested in adversity, trek on to Ecbatana, which turns out to be a kind of ancient vacation community, a place, Azarias warns Tobias, "for a young man like yourself to steer clear of because it is full of frivolous people who would do you no good" (*Archangel* 54).

I wonder if Buechner is thinking of the snowbirds he sees flocking every year to Florida where he and Judith have spent part of their winters for more than a decade. He will most certainly use some of that Florida vacation community in the next novel, *The Storm*, and even here he seems to be thinking of the spectacle of such places. In an aside in his own voice, for the moment abandoning the Azarias guise, Raphael concedes that there is more to Ecbatana, "much there that struck me as charming, and the Holy One too if I may presume so far" (*Archangel* 54). What Raphael realizes about the Ecbatanans is that they "at least saw that the world was created for their delight," and he concludes that "they came closer to living their lives as the Holy One intended than those who were continually apologizing for their unworthiness and trying to avert the wrath of the One who, had they but known, wishes the world only well" (*Archangel* 55). Buechner, I think, feels the same fondness for his Floridian neighbors. In any case, the wondering about the personality of God bubbles on. Would God prefer delight or fear? Such is the enduring inquiry in Buechner's books, although this book will be much closer to answers than to questions.

Unlike Buechner's other novels, *On the Road with the Archangel* is not a story of digressions and hidden complications, at least not many. Azarias and Tobias head straight to an acquaintance of Azarias for their first night in Ecbatana, and who might that turn out to be but Raguel, the father of

the unfortunate and beautiful Sarah. All the way back in Nineveh, Tobias
has heard something of Sarah's tribulations. When Azarias suggests something of his design—that Tobias is to be Sarah's eighth attempt at marriage—the boy is a bit shaken. To his credit, Tobias thinks of Tobit and
Anna, imagining their sadness at losing their only son. Azarias reminds
him of the stinking bag of fish entrails that he carries and promises to
"make sure you're absolutely safe" (*Archangel* 58). But it is the promise,
reminiscent of those sobering Abrahamic covenants, that Azarias delivers
that has the most weight for Tobias. Told that Sarah will bear him children, Tobias's face "went all soft and helpless," and Azarias knows then
that Tobias "would have loved her even if she had not been beautiful"
(*Archangel* 59). But this is a fairy tale—easy enough to make her beautiful.

The marriage contract is now coming fast; readers will have seen it coming long before. The unanticipated turn, however, is the story that frames
the union of the star-crossed Sarah and the fluff-headed Tobias. Raguel and
Edna are unbelievers. Perhaps we should have expected such; after all,
given the corpses they've carried away from the marriage bed, these people have had good reason to doubt the benevolence of the universe. Their
unbelief is of a sort that rings universal: "It was not that they believed necessarily that the Holy One didn't exist. They took the position that maybe
he did and maybe he didn't and were more than willing to leave the final
say-so to professionals" (*Archangel* 61). All that sounds innocent enough
until Raphael adds, "even if it could be proved conclusively that the Holy
One was indeed enthroned somewhere in the clouds the way it was
claimed, they felt it would make no more difference to them than if it could
be proved conclusively that there was indeed a blue camel with seventeen
legs living somewhere in the desert" (*Archangel* 61). Theirs is a practical
atheism. They go about their days assuming that even if the Holy One is
out there somewhere, he doesn't give "a tinker's dam for the world he was
said to have created" (*Archangel* 62). Here Buechner drops a serious note
into a hilarious story. Like Tobit, who misunderstands the nature of his suffering, Edna and Raguel are about to experience a dramatic challenge to
their assumptions about the indifference of the Holy One.

Among the many consolations readers find in Buechner's work, surely
one of the most obvious is his insistence that God is not put off by doubt.
Maybe God even respects doubt, Buechner intimates here and there.
Raphael gets this:

> Surely he [the Holy One] knew also that Raguel and Edna had long
> since written him off, and why they had too, but unless I miss my

guess, he didn't for a moment hold it against them. I would go so far as to say that it may even have caused him to think the more highly of them because their unbelief grew from a far more honest view of the wretchedness of things than the belief of the devout who see only what they choose to see and turn a blind eye on the rest. (*Archangel* 63)

Such a passage is consonant with Buechner's penchant for turning our usual assumptions on their heads, especially our conjectures about religious practice. "Whether your faith is that there is a God or that there is not a God, if you don't have any doubts you are either kidding yourself or asleep," Buechner writes (*WT* 20). Many readers might find great solace in the assertion that doubt may be integral to faith, perhaps even a necessary part of wakeful living.

In spite of their unbelief, Edna and Raguel have held to the rudiments of tradition and hospitality. Willingly enough, they invite the travelers into their home, and a Romeo-and-Juliet moment follows when Sarah enters the room to greet the guests. The dog sees her first. Stunned as Tobias is to learn that Tobit and Raguel are of the same family, he is speechless at the sight of Sarah. After a resplendent supper, he will find enough voice to ask for the marriage contract. Although Edna and Raguel might have kept their mouths shut about Sarah's history, they bravely tell what they know of the dangers. Is it faith or foolishness that keeps Tobias from being discouraged by their tale? Finally, Raguel takes their hands and blesses them "in the name of the One in whom he did not believe for a minute" (*Archangel* 69). "And thus they were wed," Raphael sums up: "that was all there was to it in those days" (*Archangel* 69). The most complicated character here, and surely the most interesting of the human contingent, is Sarah, who goes to the bridal chamber that night both afraid that Asmodeus will show up and afraid that he won't show up. At least some of her heart belongs to the demon.

You've probably guessed that demons have an aversion to the smoke of burning fish entrails. Demons "have their own problems just like everybody else," Azarias assures Tobias, as the smoldering concoction magically exposes the demon's true aspect (*Archangel* 75). Seen for what he is, Asmodeus loses power and creeps away. Thus Sarah turns to "the husband who had delivered her from an unspeakable horror" (*Archangel* 79). Alone in the bridal chamber, the newlyweds first pray for mercy, innocently reversing their parents' commitments to unbelief, then fall to other matters. They don't even hear the racket of Raguel digging a grave outside their bower. Convinced that another corpse is soon to be available, incapable now of belief in a happy ending, Raguel is only hoping that this time he can conceal the tragedy from the neighbors.

The feasting that follows the morning's revelation of a live bridegroom is infected with the amazing idea growing in Raguel and Edna that "possibly the Holy One existed after all" (*Archangel* 85). In the joy of Sarah and Tobias and the dissolved family curse, the other story line has almost disappeared. What of Tobit's treasure? In some ways, Buechner seems to be addressing his own innate pessimism in this book. Tobias's legacy is a kind of distrust, an assumption that the worst is the most likely. "You forget that as often as not what happens is a very good thing," Raphael cautions him, and Tobias decides to trust Azarias with the mission to Gabael. Perhaps the spectacle of a dwindling demon and the presence of a wondrous wife have pushed Tobias toward trusting his luck. In any case, the party continues while the archangel dispatches his errand quickly. Gabael turns out to be a fantastic character who adds to the sensation in Raguel's neighborhood when he shows up to join the celebrations and add two bags of silver to the treasures that Tobias will carry toward home.

Back in Nineveh, however, doubt and worry are having their way, the party in Ecbatana contrasting mightily with the deathwatch in Tobit's household. Tobit is fretting over his son's long delay. Anna is sure that Tobias is dead. Hiding behind a head scarf, she goes everyday to the gates of the city where, with the peddlers, beggars, and ne'er-do-wells, she watches for some sign of Tobias. "For hours on end she would watch the road for some glimpse far in the distance of the boy and the dog coming home," Raphael reports in an image that conjures the prodigal and the anxious father of the New Testament parable (*Archangel* 95). Back in Ecbatana, the celebration winding down, Raguel and Edna begin to dread the day of their daughter's departure.

Buechner's own thoughts of absent children and inevitable aging crowd into his narrative now. Such is the human stuff that makes this little book an important contribution in the array of Buechner's various books. Raguel and Sarah speak of what was and what will be, of old lives and new ones, of the games of Sarah's childhood, things that make Raguel feel young again and things that make him fear he will be an old man when she leaves with her new husband. In the bittersweet sadness, Raguel finds himself thinking more often about the Holy One, about the meanings of his life. Maybe the Holy One is not so remote after all, he thinks, but, even in this time of great happiness, shadows persist—always the profound mixture that Buechner insists to the front of his reader's minds. When the newlyweds are all loaded up for the return to Nineveh, a distinct sorrow invades the scene. Tobias has his bags of silver, an impressive dowry of gifts from Raguel, and the greatest treasure of all, Sarah herself, there beside him when Edna speaks a blessing. "May the good angels watch over you both," she prays, and adds, "If there *are* good angels" (*Archangel* 101). Raphael doesn't comment on that line.

The Jewish community of Nineveh knows more about Tobias's adventures than Anna and Tobit could guess. Despite Anna's disguise, they know she is watching at the gates, they know he is overdue, and they suspect all of this matters very much. The journey from Ecbatana to Nineveh takes much longer because of the throng of servants and the baggage-laden beasts that Tobias and Raphael have in tow. Finally, they decide to ride ahead to assuage the fretting of Tobit and Anna and to prepare them for the arrival of their daughter-in-law. At the moment of reunion, even Raphael has to avert his eyes. Like the more celebrated reunion in the prodigal's parable, this one is also beyond words' ability to tell. The first business, of course, is to finish the miracle of the fish entrails. Tobit is stupefied when his son, at Azarias's prodding, rubs the fish gall on his blind eyes. As the blindness clears, Tobit speaks to the Holy One. "You afflicted me because my unworthiness deserved affliction," Tobit prays, "and now you have restored my sight because your nature is always to be merciful to those who please you" (*Archangel* 107–8).

One sharp prong of the novella gets succinct summary in Raphael's response to Tobit's prayer: "He was totally wrong on both counts, of course. The Holy One does not go around afflicting people, and although his nature is indeed above all else merciful, Tobit was a good man and in no more need of mercy than a two-year-old child. What he needed was simply someone who understood the therapeutic powers of fish gall" (*Archangel* 108). This is more than Buechner's usual insistence on offering various explanations for apparently supernatural interventions. At the center of *On the Road with the Archangel* is an argument about the nature of God. Buechner seems to think we have underestimated God's laughter and overemphasized his judgment. Impressed by the songs of praise now pouring out of Tobit's household, Raphael nonetheless realizes that "by and large the world believes in him [the Holy One] for all the wrong reasons and . . . it disbelieves in him for all the wrong reasons too" (*Archangel* 108). Every Buechner book has a line or two that somehow becomes the fulcrum supporting the whole business. Raphael gets the words in *Archangel*.

Weighty themes cannot, however, mute the fall-down-laughing humor of the novel. There's the blind beggar who is the first to see Tobias on the horizon as he returns to Nineveh. The con man who needs no healing is also the first to spot Sarah and her entourage as they arrive for more weeks of feasting and celebration. The poor dog still moves around unregarded, still has no name. Cousin Ahikar comes along to the parties. He is now second in power to the new king, Esarhaddon, but a fit of the king's rage has cost him his left hand. Now the king refers to Ahikar as "his right-hand man" (*Archangel* 112). Tobit and Anna are genuinely glad to have Tobias back and Sarah to boot. The silver and Raguel's gifts are welcome too. Tobit goes back to his charitable ways among the poor, hoping that the Holy One has forgotten that outhouse prayer. Tobias spends some of the treasure on a new house for his folks, though Buechner takes pains to underscore their position as a captive people. As with most of us most of the time, all is well enough, but all is not well. There are the usual niggling problems and the occasional sense of not belonging. The Assyrians regard Tobit and his people with "a combination of fear, condescension, and guilt," the usual potpourri of emotions that constitute race suspicion and fear of the outsider. Finally finding a place outside the city, Tobias settles the family and that would seem to be that.

But there's still Azarias, of course. His mission mostly accomplished, apparently, he is still hanging around. He does make it clear that there are six other archangels to take care of all necessary business, and he even suspects that the Holy One could get along without the lot of them in a pinch. Raphael seems to have one more thing in mind, and his moment comes when Tobias offers him half of the treasure as payment for his guidance. We have seen that Tobias has more questions than answers when it comes to matters theological, and Raphael concludes that "Tobias had never given much time to religious speculation" (*Archangel* 120). His gratitude toward Raphael speaks well of his instinct to charity, of course, and he is clearly a good man, if not a particularly religious one. Now, Raphael thinks, is the time to clear up "false pretenses" and maybe jog Tobias's attitude toward the Holy One as well (*Archangel* 120).

Like Raphael, Buechner has one more note that he wants to strike here. Raphael's unveiling, less dramatic than the revelation of Asmodeus, nonetheless gives Raphael an opportunity to offer a bit of advice to his stunned traveling companion, Tobias. Having witnessed the banishment of Asmodeus, Tobias is more confused than impressed by Azarias's transformation into Raphael, but he manages to hear Raphael's counsel that he should follow his father's example in charity. Tobias confesses that he's always avoided those streets where the beggars hang out, and Raphael tells him to "try other streets" (*Archangel* 121). That is, once aware of being blessed, one has a certain responsibility to bless. The instinct to withdraw from the earth's ills has long haunted Buechner. He speaks in *The Sacred Journey* of his instinct to fearfulness, of his need for self-protection against the assault of need in the world (*SJ* 105). Referring often to his introspection and anxiousness, Buechner has long known the dangers of the private world of his writer's study—the Magic Kingdom he calls it. He knows that genuine engagement with the problems of our culture is required. "We are involved. We can't help it," he offers (Brown 49). All of this broods in Raphael's words to Tobias, a notion that involvement is a consequence of blessing.

Raphael's parting message extends beyond Tobias to the reader when Raphael encourages Tobias to tell his story: "I am thinking about all the things he [the Holy One] has done for you and your family, for instance. Tell people about those things and never forget them yourself. Tell them how even on the darkest stretches of the road to Ecbatana, he was always at your side if you'd only had the eyes to see him" (*Archangel* 122). Tobias's new mission is to become a witness to a revised vision of the divine that has dropped into the lives of these several families. Raphael finally reveals enough of his glory to make the point: "What they saw of me was about as much as a child's hand can hold of the sea" (*Archangel* 124). Even the dog, who has been a cheeky enough presence throughout the narrative, shields his eyes at the specter of the resplendent angel.

In one of the early manuscripts, Buechner has scribbled out the word "fear" as the response of Tobit's family to Raphael's unveiling, and substituted in its place the word "wonder" (Archive, IV A 17). The slight shift in connotation captures something of the heft of *On the Road with the Archangel*, a book more about the embrace of God than the silence, more about God's compassion than his justice. *Son of Laughter* is about the Fear; this new book is about the Holy One. Overcome by awe, heavy with blessing, Tobias and the others, we suspect, will turn out all right. Yet the happy ending is not unmitigated. Tobit's mind keeps flitting to the unholy mix of things—a "blind beggar who can see farther than a hawk," a cruel king who chops off hands over trifles, the poor people by the river, and his own Jewish people carried off to "a godless land" (*Archangel* 126).

God as Scorekeeper is so deeply ingrained in Tobit that he cannot dream of speaking to the Holy One "like the friend one would have hoped he knew him now to be," and Raphael chuckles at "the heart-wrenching absurdity" of Tobit's prayers (*Archangel* 127). Tobit speaks to the Holy One in third-person clichés still, carries his piety carefully as if afraid of breaking it. He goes back to his frequent set-tos with the flies, a metaphor Buechner has borrowed from Twain, I suspect. Tobit "liked to believe that the Holy One might decide to spare him" for the same reason that he sometimes spares a fly here and there (*Archangel* 128). Tobit's vast misunderstanding of the divine persists as he assumes it was the Holy One's decision to scatter the Jews, to bring this oppression. Their iniquity is the problem, Tobit thinks. They are only getting what they deserve. But the dark stuff has little impact in this joyous little book. For Tobit, everything depends on doing "just two or three things a day right when the Scorekeeper's eye was upon him" (*Archangel* 130). If he can just do enough to soften the heart of the Holy One, then maybe the luck will persist for his family. "*If* was the hinge that the fate of the whole world hung on," as he sees it (*Archangel* 131). What Tobit seems to be struggling toward is the kind of wisdom that Buechner has brought increasingly to the fore in the novels of his seventies—simple acceptance. Jacob got there. Tobias will get there. Tobit is on the way.

In fact, Tobit's gloomy thoughts are not to be the last word here. Even he can imagine better. Now and then, "wild and hopeful conjectures" bloom even in the shadows of his doubt (*Archangel* 130). Maybe his children and grandchildren will "live to see a day when the Holy One decided to love them for what they were instead of to afflict them for what they were not. Who could guess what glorious things he might do for them once he got started in a new direction?" (*Archangel* 131–32). The Apocrypha begins here to give way to the New Testament. Raphael applauds when Tobit's wild imaginings start skirting, at least, something of the truth of things. This startling new version of the Holy One dimly understands that the Holy One "wishes the world and its creatures nothing but well" (*Archangel* 135). He is no swatter of flies. Thus we circle back to laughter. Distrustful of happiness, Tobit lives on in the back-and-forth of doubt and hope. To the end of his 148 years Tobit hopes there is some afterlife where his iniquities will be overlooked. But "he was ready to go when the time came," though the dog goes first (*Archangel* 141). Tobias's grief is doubled by the death of his beloved dog and by his father's dying wish that Tobias will move the remnants of the family out of Nineveh. Tobit has heard something of Jonah, but he dies with the music still in his head, amazed "at how when he had prayed to the Holy One for death, the Holy One had given him instead not only life but the lives of all these other people" (*Archangel* 147). Anna follows soon after, and Tobias gives them magnificent farewells complete with elephants and noisy ceremonies before packing up Sarah and the children and leaving Nineveh. "It was true that they had no Azarias to make sure they took the right roads or get them through unforeseen disasters like the fish, but even though they were aware of nothing more than occasional unexplained flicker of light in the air as they went, they were of course never altogether on their own," Raphael asserts (*Archangel* 147–48).

Years later, now himself an old man, Tobias will weigh everything, remembering even the dog, "who was a native Ninevite" (*Archangel* 149). No mention of the Scorekeeper now, Tobias dies "certain that he could feel him [the Holy One] taking his hand in his mouth in order to lead him wherever it was he might be going next" (*Archangel* 149). DeLeeuw posited that "the rueful, loving and forgiving acceptance of what is—from sparrow's dung to human failure—is Buechner's lesson and gift to his readers. When we recognize that our lives are God-touched at particular moments in the corners of our experience, this speaks to our limits, not to God's boundless grace" (Deleeuw 27). Although I dislike the word "lesson" and the attempt to summarize Buechner's novel as simply about this or that, Deleeuw's review was among the best on *Archangel*, because she understood how Buechner tangles again with the intrusion of the supernatural into the ordinary. So much depends on what humans do and do not see. The persistent presentiment that Something is trying to get through in the midst of the muddle of our day-to-day lives consistently eddies in Buechner's work. John Gardner was right in his conclusion that "Didacticism inevitably simplifies morality and thus misses it," and Buechner again misses the didactic trap by keeping the mixture, the many possibilities, in play. A feckless dog and a wry angel help too.

We have long relied on Buechner for a good story, and again he has not disappointed. It would be a shame to overlook this book because of its brevity and fairy-tale dimension. *On the Road with the Archangel* is another of those animations of old stories we've filed away. Buechner has done this before in books like *The Alphabet of Grace* and *Son of Laughter*, and other texts, like *Wishful Thinking* and *Whistling in the Dark*, have demonstrated his uncanny ability to reenergize religious words and familiar stories in ways that help readers encounter them afresh. Following Gardner's dictum that "critics would be useful people to have around if they would simply do their work, carefully and thoughtfully assessing works of art, calling our attention to those worth noticing," one might simply conclude that *On the Road with the Archangel* is a good story indeed, one worth the trouble (Gardner 127). In our contemporary penchant for thrillers and soon-to-be-a-movie blockbusters, little books like this one are easily missed.

As with almost everything Buechner has written since his ordination in 1958, this book is contemporary. Through these ancient characters, Buechner raises the familiar questions of belief and unbelief. Almost everyone in this cast has completely misunderstood God's nature. Alfred Corn argued that "no Job-like depths have been plumbed" in this novel, a point with which I have quibbled (Corn 23). Caught up in the shallows of humor, we are sometimes apt to miss the deeper currents of wisdom. Corn did, however, wrap up his look at *Archangel* with a penetrating take: "the conclusion's lightly borne sweetness works to justify the ways of God to man by implying that adversities are sometimes remedied, and that curses can never rival the steadying power given us when we praise being" (Corn 23). I'd say that's a depth indeed. Aesop's fables and Shakespeare's histories notwithstanding, literary folk argue on about the role of thesis in fiction. Unfortunately Buechner has been sometimes tarred with that feared epithet—didacticism. The only thesis he maintains has to do with the integrity of ambiguity. Though no thesis mars the force of this book, the large idea that happiness, even optimism, may be legitimate as we rest in the assurance of ultimate benevolence is an insight worth the testing. As Raphael travels among the frail creatures of these ancient households, he repeatedly wishes these mortals knew the immortal better. We too, I presume.

The real-life questions that Buechner has a penchant for turn up here again and again: the emptiness of a household where the children have departed into their own lives, the problem of the poverty and pain of so many, the honesty of unbelief, and the terror of faith. Finally, *On the Road with the Archangel* centers on the question of whether or not there is really a Holy One who looks after the world. Answering "NO" is understandable enough, Buechner understands. He reminds us nonetheless that expecting the worst is easy, but sometimes the best is there for those with eyes to see. Maybe "yes" is the last word after all, maybe even "YES." Maybe the seventy-six trombones are still leading the parade, "marching still, right today."[20]

Notes

1. Lauren F. Winner, *re:generation quarterly*, Spring 2000, 40.
2. Richard Paff, letter to the editor, *Newsweek*, January 10, 2005, 18.
3. Wesley Sheffield, review of *The Clown in the Belfry: Writings on Faith and Fiction*, *Circuit Rider*, April 1993, 13.
4. W.W.B., *"The Sacred Journey," Bookstore Journal*, July 1982, 356.
5. Robert Taylor, *"The Longing for Home," Boston Globe*, August 21, 1996, C3.
6. Virginia Stem Owens, book review, *Image* 17 (Fall 1997): 117.
7. Frederick Buechner, *The Storm: A Novel* (San Francisco: HarperSanFrancisco, 1998), 199. Hereafter cited as *Storm*.
8. David Stewart, "Touched by an Angel," *Christianity Today*, February 9, 1998.
9. Patricia DeLeeuw, *"On the Road with the Archangel," America*, March 28, 1998, 26. Hereafter cited as DeLeeuw.

10. Personal correspondence, January 6, 2005.
11. Alfred Corn, "God's Mailman," *New York Times*, October 26, 1997, 23. Hereafter cited as Corn.
12. Doris Betts, "Everything I Know about Writing I Learned in Sunday School," *Christian Century*, October 21, 1998, 966.
13. Book review, *Kirkus Reviews*, August 15, 1997, 2.
14. George Garrett, "Informed Opinions," *Washington Post*, December 7, 1997, 10. Hereafter cited as GGarrett.
15. Judith Moore, "Reading," *San Diego Weekly Reader*, December 4, 1997, 65. Hereafter cited as Moore.
16. Philip Schaff, ed., *A Religious Encyclopaedia: Or Dictionary of Biblical, Historical, Doctrinal, and Practical Theology* (New York: Christian Literature Co., 1888), 1:103.
17. Frederick Buechner, *On the Road with the Archangel* (San Francisco: HarperSanFrancisco, 1997), v. Hereafter cited as *Archangel*.
18. Personal correspondence, January 6, 2005.
19. Personal conversation, November 13, 2004.
20. Meredith Willson, "Seventy-six Trombones," 1957.

Chapter Eleven

Finding a Better Seat

The Storm

*O*n the Road with the Archangel, a kind of valedictory piece, was not to be the final word from Buechner. The words keep coming as the millennium turns: *The Storm*, another novel, in 1998; *The Eyes of the Heart: A Memoir of the Lost and Found* in 1999; and *Speak What We Feel (Not What We Ought to Say)*, a 2001 nonfiction reflection on the faith quotient in literature and life via ruminations on Mark Twain, Gerard Manley Hopkins, G. K. Chesterton, and William Shakespeare. By now, the career stretches over fifty years, and the books continue to be rich and varied. For the 2004 book *Beyond Words: Daily Readings in the ABC's of Faith*, Buechner tinkers with three earlier collections of definitions—*Wishful Thinking*, *Whistling in the Dark*, and *Peculiar Treasures*—editing former entries and adding some new ones, to produce a daily devotional reader along the lines of *Listening to Your Life*, the 1992 collection that has become one of his bestsellers.

Buechner is a writer. Well past the usual retirement markers, he keeps at it, still finding his way into his study, the Magic Kingdom, almost every day to see where the words might take him. In *Eyes of the Heart* Buechner reprints part of a letter he received from the former dean of an English Cathedral on the occasion of the death of Princess Diana: "Only the young die good. We live by myths and fairy tales" (*EH* 180). Buechner remembers how the letter helped him reflect on his long life and his avowed inadequacies. The reference to "myths and fairy tales" is especially salubrious for Buechner, as he has amassed a body of work that moves from one myth to another, from ancient stories into the story of himself, offering readers the burgeoning wisdom of his days. The wisdom continues in these recent books with an undertone of goodbye, a kind of joyous sadness that percolates through the very different books, a way of summing up.

Judith and Frederick Buechner

Taken together, the three books of this period can be seen as a ringing finale. The four writers of *Speak What We Feel* have been, as Bruce Wood noted, "allusive presences" throughout Buechner's work.[1] In Buechner's now old-fashioned way of looking at literature as clarifying of life, their books have given him a vantage point from which to weigh his own experience; they are what Robert Neralich called "lenses through which readers gain an enhanced appreciation of their personal and collective lives."[2] For the title of this book, Buechner adopts Edgar's words from the last lines of *King Lear*, words spoken on a stage littered with corpses. Edgar admonishes an obedience to "the weight of these sad times,"[3] a truth telling about the tragedy. In his mid-seventies by 2001, Buechner's life is also littered with corpses. Speaking to his long-dead grandmother, Naya, in *The Eyes of the Heart*, Buechner will enumerate some of the deaths—his friend, James Merrill; his brother, Jamie; his mother, his father, and more. Kenzie Maxwell in *The Storm* is caught up in thoughts of his own coming death and spends much of his time composing a letter to his long-dead love, Kia. Yet somehow none of the books is ultimately sad. They are valedictory but "not gloomy," as James Yerkes noticed.[4] What Buechner manages is a consideration of the weight of his own sad times, through an encounter with those of Twain, Hopkins, Chesterton, and Shakespeare in *Speak What We Feel*; through conversations with and about the dead in *The Eyes of the Heart*; and in the grief and exuberance of the septuagenarian Kenzie Maxwell in *The Storm*. But the stunning conclusion is that he achieves "not just a kind of temporary release, but a kind of unexpected encouragement" (*Speak* 161). What he learns and offers the readers of all three books is "Fear not. Be alive. Be merciful. Be human" (*Speak* 161).

From Hopkins, Buechner learns "that the profane is not always the antithesis of the sacred, but sometimes the bearer of it," and it is precisely this insight that shapes Hopkins's "religious resonance," Buechner believes (*Speak* 19). Buechner's career-long preoccupation with the God who may move in the mire thus reemerges in his esteem for Hopkins. But the Twain chapter is the strongest one here. Buechner identifies with Twain in several ways, I think. Twain had a certain sense of inferiority, a distrust of self and celebrity, that Buechner shares. Furthermore, both writers experience a deep disjunction with the age in which they live. Twain, of course, labels his "the Gilded Age." Buechner too has an eye for the excesses and crudities of the twentieth and twenty-first centuries, especially for the shallowness of our political life. Buechner understands that Twain's greatest creation, the sound-hearted, strangely lonely Huckleberry Finn, is an icon of hope in a desolate landscape, an expression "written out of the deepest truth of who he was" (*Speak* 59). Huck represents Twain's struggle with the shadows, his "lover's quarrel," in Robert Frost's phrase.[5] Buechner has long fought much the same battle.

Relating to Chesterton's sense of living in a time when doubt has overtaken everything, Buechner applauds Chesterton's attempt to hold the line of faith. In an obscure poem that Chesterton dedicated to Richard Bentley, Buechner discovers a spirit that might be ascribed to Chesterton himself: "Not all unhelped we held the fort, our tiny flags unfurled; Some giants laboured in that cloud to lift it from the world" (*Speak* 117). Though he would balk at being placed in such company, Buechner too has resonated with Chesterton's "shrug of skepticism about skepticism," words that Chesterton spoke of Robert Louis Stevenson. Chesterton argued that Stevenson's "real distinction is that he had the sense to see that there is nothing to be done with Nothing" (*Speak* 119). When Buechner submits that the same can be fairly spoken of Chesterton, the reader can only add that the same can be fairly said of Buechner as well. In an 1899 letter Chesterton summarized himself in the third person, another description that might straightforwardly apply to Buechner: "All his passion and longing, all his queer religion, his dark and dreadful gratitude to God . . . the joy that comes on him sometimes (he cannot help it!) at the sacred intoxication of existence . . . the unconquered adoration of goodness, that dark virtue that every man has, and hides deeper than all his vices!" (*Speak* 121). Hasn't all of Buechner led to this tenuous hope that goodness wins in the end?

Finally, there's the indebtedness to Shakespeare, all the more current as Shakespeare's *The Tempest* is the allusive force behind Buechner's late work and especially the novel of the period, *The Storm*. In *Speak What We Feel*, Buechner turns again to *King Lear*, this time to puzzle over Shakespeare's dramatic reversal of the way his sources had presented the last episodes of Cordelia and Lear's lives. Reading Edgar's "not what we ought to say" as Shakespeare's sense that, "like all these predecessors, he ought to have ended it [*Lear*] in a way to suggest that good ultimately triumphs over evil in this world and that, all in all, life makes sense. But that is clearly not what Shakespeare *felt*" (*Speak* 133). Here again, meaning, even hope, emerges from an unblinking admission of hopelessness. Of Gloucester, Buechner argues that it is his blindness that helps him see his own sons and his situation. "It is not with the eyes of his head that he has seen it," Buechner notes, "but with the eyes of his heart—another kind of seeing, another kind of light" (*Speak* 141).

This other way of seeing is what interests Buechner most in the twilight of his own career. Nobody in Shakespeare's greatest work is precisely what he or she seems to be, Buechner concludes: "What is Shakespeare saying in all this about the weight of time's sadness? He seems to be saying that more often than not people are blind not only to each other, including the poor naked wretches of the world, but also to themselves, the best as well as the worst" (*Speak* 146). Reading the play as Shakespeare's gloss on Paul's words in 1 Corinthians—"God chose what is foolish in the world to shame the wise; God chose what is weak in the world to shame the strong; God chose what is low and despised in the world, things that are not, to reduce to nothing things that are"[6]—Buechner extols Shakespeare's refusal to "view life as either tragic or comic, or as sometimes one or the other" (*Speak* 153). What Shakespeare understands is what Buechner's own stories have tried to exemplify: "Life is continually both [tragic and comic] at once is what his obedience to time's sadness led him to say, and what he *felt* about it and opened his veins to make his audience feel along with him was that it was precisely that quality that constituted the richness of it, and the terror of it, and the heartbreaking beauty of it" (*Speak* 153). The mix of comedy and tragedy, the inseparable collusion of false and true, is what Buechner has long since set his felt-tipped pen down upon. Although *Speak*

What We Feel reveals a good bit about four literary greats, it reveals even more about Buechner himself; the small volume is a litany in praise of kindred spirits, another mirror in which Buechner reveals his own take on literature, religion, writing, and being.

Appearing just months after that calamitous day in September of 2001, *Speak What We Feel* rings with a deep sense of something beyond the darkness. Sharing our shock, Buechner describes the nightmare: "It seems the hounds of hell have been unleashed. There's always been evil in the world, and sometimes it has been on our side as well as the other side."[7] But finally, he adds, "good wins out" (JBuie 2). Hope is where he hangs his hat. In the stories of these four writers who emerged from dark struggles to offer masterpieces of possibility, Buechner himself arrives at what David Stewart called "the culmination of a lifetime."[8] Having lived his life in the shadow of his father's suicide and temperamentally inclined toward sadness, Buechner meditates on the anguish of others and comes to a reappraisal of his own suffering. The movement again is toward grace. It would be a mistake, however, to read Buechner's conclusions as sentimental. The poignancy and melancholy are palpable, but, as Helen Harrison said of *The Eyes of the Heart*, "there is an underlying joy and love."[9] Such are the deepest reaches of each of the recent books. In an echo of the final lines of *Godric*, Buechner gives the summary to Naya in *The Eyes of the Heart*: "No one is ever lost. Nothing is lost" (*EH* 176). Then he appropriates her words in his own conclusion: "If it is true about God, then . . . there is nothing to worry about, not even death, not even life, not even losing the ones you love most in the world because, as Naya told me, no one is ever really lost" (*EH* 181).

The Eyes of the Heart takes its title from Paul's prayer in Ephesians that others may receive "a spirit of wisdom and revelation" from God "so that, with the eyes of your heart enlightened, you may know what is the hope to which he has called you, what are the riches of his glorious inheritance."[10] But, as Buechner tells Gustav Niebuhr, he is not "pitching propaganda." He is writing now to point toward "the elusive presence of the holiness of God."[11] In this latest book of memories, Buechner fills in gaps, observes a kind of frame going all the way back to the beginning of his career. His angle of vision informed by decades of thoughtfulness and experience, Buechner plunges more than before into the possible pattern of his journey. Dedicated to the three latest grandchildren and his recently deceased brother, Jamie, the memoir opens with a detailed description of Buechner's "haven and sanctuary," the Magic Kingdom (*EH* 1). His guest, Naya, dead since 1961, takes the tour with her grandson, a tour, really, of

Buechner's grandchildren and one of his daughters
Circa 2004

his life. Naya's role seems to be mostly to listen, though she does have star-tling, if succinct, things to say about her life since 1961. To her grandson's need for an explanation, she merely responds, "It is the *world* that passes away" (*EH* 12). She also asks just the right questions to give her grandson a chance to explain himself. He tells her that he's been thinking about dying. "Sometimes the sadness is lost in wondering what will come next. If anything comes," he says (*EH* 8). And Naya's ghostly presence seems at least a partial answer to his questions. He tells her that he wonders if this memoir will be his last book. She tends to her knitting as he talks of being "a hopelessly religious person" who nonetheless wonders what she can tell him of the afterlife (*EH* 11). Naya carries on with the knitting, speaks obliquely of being "astonished" by her death—"nothing could have been more peaceful," is about all she says (*EH* 13). So Buechner moves on to the other passings that haunt his memory.

The first death they pause over is that of Buechner's mother, who died in 1988. Although Buechner has spoken only obliquely of the strains between himself and his mother, readers sense a good bit of the complexity of that relationship going all the way back into Buechner's perilous childhood. In the weeks before her death, his mother has, uncharacteristically, asked her son if he really believes that "anything *happens* after you die" (*EH* 14). Because of her deafness, his answer is a shouted "YES" (*EH* 15). In a letter that tries to elaborate on his answer, the son testifies to his mother that his faith is based on "a hunch"—"if the victims and the victimizers, the wise and the foolish, the good-hearted and the heartless all end up alike in the grave and that is the end of it, then life would be a black comedy, and to me, even at its worst, life doesn't *feel* like a black comedy" (*EH* 16). In words that connect the strands of much that Buechner is saying in his latest books, he tells his mother that life "feels like a mystery. It feels as though, at the inner-most heart of it, there is Holiness" (*EH* 16). Thoughts of his mother lead him, of course, to his father: "I suppose one way to read my whole life—my religious faith, the books I have written, the friends I have made—is as a search for him" (*EH* 23–24). Thus we return to the core again, the lifelong attempt to understand the inexplicable.

The other death of the early pages of this memoir is that of James Merrill, Buechner's lifelong friend, who died in 1995. Buechner ponders the puzzle of his friendship with Merrill, realizing that he and Merrill were, in that famous summer of 1948, not unlike the characters in Buechner's early novels, beset by an inability to speak the truth of themselves, because that truth was only just beginning to make itself known to them. Of those first novels, Buechner seems to recognize that their context was lostness but that something in them was reaching toward God knows what. And how do we understand the trajectory from the emptiness of the full days of Buechner's youth to the splendid wisdoms of the mostly quiet days of the grandfather writer? The Magic Kingdom itself is part of the answer. The books have helped. As he pauses in the room with Naya, the books, read and unread, are mostly silent:

> Shakespeare is not saying anything, and neither is L. Frank Baum. The Duc de Saint-Simon, the Buddha, Dostoyevski, and Paul Tillich are all holding their tongues. Not a peep out of Abraham Lincoln, Meister Eckhart, or Emily Dickinson. Even Walt Whitman and the prophet Jeremiah are for the moment speechless. The air of the Magic Kingdom is electric with the silence they are keeping. What would I have been if I had never heard them break it? What would I have failed to see if they had not pointed it out to me, and what would I never heard without their ears to hear it through? (*EH* 50–51)

The Magic Kingdom

As he has done in *Speak What We Feel*, Buechner remembers his debts to those whose testimony has helped him keep his oars in the water. Here is a paean to voices that have helped keep the music going.

Among the books and mementos lining the shelves of the Magic Kingdom, Buechner is apt to point out several gray boxes of family papers, a collection that commemorates family—photographs, marriage certificates, diplomas, and stray pieces of days dimly remembered. Shuffling in those papers, Buechner shows Naya a manuscript of his first literary tome, not yet sent along to the archives, "The Voyage of Mr. and Mrs. Cloth," which young Freddie apparently penned in Washington, D.C., at the age of six. Most of the memories in the gray boxes, however, lead in one way or another back to a childhood in which Buechner was "constantly terrified" that the family was about to collapse (*EH* 52). Although the family papers, like the books, rest innocently enough, gathering dust, Buechner realizes that "even in their silence they are always present" (*EH* 60). The books have left their marks, and so have the contents of the gray boxes. "My father has been dead for more than sixty years, but I doubt that a week has gone by without my thinking of him. In recent years I doubt that a day has gone by," Buechner adds, and we hear something of the incredulity and mystery that still drives the writer (*EH* 60). But the weight of the journey through pleasant and painful family memories seems finally, this time, to be forgiveness. Somehow Buechner forgives them all, blesses the past, and perhaps receives something of their forgiveness in return.

The religious book section in the Magic Kingdom lets Buechner loose on personalities like Tillich, Barth, Borg, Pedersen, and Niebuhr, revealing, simply via the names, a good measure of his theological persuasion. He speaks as well of his days at Union Seminary and quizzes Naya about the whole religion business, which they, apparently, more or less ignored when she was alive. The terms Buechner chooses to speak of his faith, always interesting, this time take on a certain melancholic twist. Preachers, he argues, should make us "recognize in our lives all the ways that, like Israel, we too are in bondage, if only to our shadows and shallowness, and need above all things not to be forgiven, but to be set free" (*EH* 76). The theological note for Buechner in these works of recent vintage centers on a new way of seeing, a way informed not by facts but by intuition, not by creedal declarations but by confessions of longing. His discovery of the line about the eyes of the heart in Ephesians—"'O altitudo!' as Sir Thomas Browne would have said—to find such words where I never found them before and just when I needed them"—spills in many directions (*EH* 165). To see with the eyes of the heart is to see his grandchildren, his past, his future, and all of life with hope. In a 2004 sermon, Buechner conjectures that seeing this way is what led Thomas to say, "My Lord, my God." "He'd seen with the eyes of his heart, and there was nothing more he could say, nothing more he needed to say," Buechner claims.[12] Such a proposition could never be reduced to a three-by-five card, a tract, or a thesis. Living in mystery and hope is the most Buechner can offer, and the memoir is a story of reaching toward such a life.

Buechner goes on in *The Eyes of the Heart* to speak of the novels he's tried to write, especially the Mary Magdalene story that has fascinated and eluded him in various manuscripts over the years. He has even considered a novel about the Christ, one focusing on the memories of those who surrounded the Messiah. In one discarded manuscript, he has a character say, "I do not tell of the look of him, but only the look of the shadow he cast" (*EH* 85). That is, we see only darkly, indirectly, via something more felt than understood. There in the Magic Kingdom, above the desk where Buechner writes, is an etching of Rembrandt's *The Return of the Prodigal Son*, signed and dated by Rembrandt in 1636. What Buechner underscores in the picture is the emotional heft of coming home. The prodigal has returned, but "it hardly matters which is the father and which is the son," Buechner judges. "They have both come home," he concludes, as he considers his own homecoming with Naya (*EH* 92). As is usual with Buechner, however, the point of the memoir is not the vanity of telling one's own story so much as the encouragement to his readers to recognize that "each family on earth is a magic kingdom, and the spells that it casts are long-lasting and powerful" (*EH* 100). The explorations into the lives of the four literary giants of *Speak What We Feel*, the revelations of Buechner's own meandering way in *Eyes of the Heart*, and the disclosures of Kenzie Maxwell's history in *The Storm*—all are calculated to inspire a similar opening in the lives of readers. It is "the vocabulary of the heart" for which Buechner is reaching as he commends us to the same business (*EH* 107).

Interviewers always ask authors about their favorite reading, and Buechner aficionados will find great joy in Buechner's survey of his shelves in *The Eyes of the Heart*. There's the Baum, of course, but who would have expected the Henry James, the William Maxwell, and the Salinger and Melville first editions? Fans will also enjoy the personal revelations here. We learn, for example, that Buechner signs his books by first marking through his name on the title page, a habit he borrowed after watching T. S. Eliot perform a similar operation on a visit to Princeton in the late 1940s. But the real power in the tour of the Magic Kingdom is in the memories that explode in all directions, the connections into the meanings of things. Buechner worries about what will happen to the books and the mementos. Imagining buyers perusing the booklists in some future sale, Buechner can say only that "the catalogue will tell them nothing about the real treasures" (*EH* 113). Who could appreciate, for example, the signed photograph of Anthony Trollope? Buechner calls Trollope "one of the immortals" and unearths memories of the many readings of Trollope, including one where he and Judy became hopelessly lost in Boston traffic while he read aloud from *The Prime Minister*. Does Buechner fear that, like Trollope, he has been misunderstood? Opposed to the popular conception of Trollope, Buechner regards him as an explorer into "the labyrinthine depths of the human spirit" (*EH* 143). Somehow Trollope's musical prose, his instinct to affirmation, his close look at domestic life, led to his being shunted into a side room of the palace of literature. Buechner knows something of such shunting. Everything Buechner says of Trollope could be spoken into a mirror. "Incapable of creating real villains," Trollope was undermined by his own deep understanding of the flawedness of us all, Buechner argues (*EH* 145). Trollope's autobiographical confession of what he calls a "certain weakness" of character, "a crav-

Buechner's brother, Jamie

ing for love," strikes Buechner as the real secret of Trollope's gift (*EH* 145). Buechner has the same problem with villains, and surely his mining of the human longing for connection has some relation to his enduring success as a writer.

A final remarkable moment in the reflection comes when Buechner's praise of Trollope is interrupted by news of another death. It is July of 1998, *The Storm* is now out on the bookstore shelves, and Buechner is brooding over this new memoir when he learns that his brother, Jamie, has died. Another voice has fallen silent, and for the brother left behind "the earth itself has to be bulldozed and shifted around and reshaped" (*EH* 147). Jamie's death occasions more journeys into the past. Buechner remembers the scene, first recorded in *The Sacred Journey*, where months after the suicide he comes upon Jamie "crying about our father" (*EH* 154). He recalls changing one of the two central characters of *The Wizard's Tide* into a little girl as a way of protecting his brother's privacy. He thinks of all the contrasts between them, all the connections. He looks toward the mantelpiece and the blinking cross, "the horizontal beam marked OPEN, and the vertical one marked HEART," a gift from Jamie to commemorate one of the *Bebb* books (*EH* 157). One brother who could never brook direct questions and another who could never stop asking them. Jamie "never went to church except once in a while to hear me," Buechner remembers, and adds, "he didn't want a funeral . . . too much like a direct question, I suppose" (*EH* 163). The nub at the end, as Buechner puts it, is, "I hope that it is true about God. I hope it is true about Jesus. I hope that maybe it is true even that Jamie and I haven't seen the last of each other" (*EH* 167). He could easily have added Naya, his mother and father, Grandmother Buechner, James Merrill, and more to that summary.

He could have added his father, whose words from the dream in *Telling Secrets*—"I know plenty, and it's all good"—Buechner will return to in the final pages of this memoir (*EH* 171). "Can it be true what I've seen with my heart's eyes?" he wonders (*EH* 171). Has he truly seen the last of Jamie? Of his father? "Well, I can tell you that at least you haven't seen the last of me," Naya jokes (*EH* 171). Speaking sharply to her grandson when he considers the possibility that she is "only a vision . . . only a dream," Naya scolds, "Why say *only* a vision, my poor ignorant child . . . *only* a dream—you of all people?" (*EH* 172). Maybe it is through just such visions and dreams, through memory and imagination, that the mysteries of God are opened to us. It is as close as Naya gets to preaching. All Buechner can say is, "Let it be true because I want it to be true. I feel in my bones that it is true" (*EH* 177). The benediction here is one that reaches through Buechner's entire career. He admits that in the nonfiction he has tended "to understate because that seemed a more strategic way of reaching the people I would like to reach" (*EH* 180). Exactly the reverse of what is usually said of Buechner—overt in the nonfiction and subtle in the fiction; his confession here suggests that he has restrained himself when talking of his encounters with the divine. On the other hand, he says that "it is only in my novels that I have allowed myself to speak unreservedly of what with the eyes of my heart I have seen" (*EH* 181). And Buechner provides the gloss on those thirty-plus books of his own, copies of which are stored there in the entryway to the Magic Kingdom:

> When old Godric makes out the face of Christ in the leaves of a tree and realizes that the lips are soundlessly speaking his name; when Antonio Parr has his vision of Christ as the Lone Ranger thundering on Silver across the lonely sage and then covers himself by adding that it may be only a silvery trick of the failing light; when Brendan as a scrawny, hollow-chested wreck of a boy sees angels spread out against the sky like a great wreath and hears their singing as the mercy

of God; when every once in a while even on the warmest, most breathless days Kenzie Maxwell feels a stirring of chill air about his nostrils or sees a snow-white bird circling around and around in the air over him as he takes his pre-breakfast walk on the golf course— they are all of them telling my story. (*EH* 181)

Such are the insights that Buechner wants to offer about his own books— intimations of "thoughts that do often lie too deep for tears."[13] He has "caught a glimpse" of something and tried to say so (*EH* 181).

Finally Buechner claims, "What is magic about the Magic Kingdom is that if you look at it through the right pair of eyes it points to a kingdom more magic still" (*EH* 183). The Magic Kingdom alludes to a peace, a coming to terms, a spiritual possibility, that perks in the "miniature epic," the "quiet marvel," that is Buechner's most recent fiction, *The Storm*.[14] Like his creator, Kenzie Maxwell is a writer. He's had a piece in *The New Yorker*, published a collection of stories that he calls "the story of my life," and written a novel, *A Fine Frenzy*, that has shocked his friends and created a stir (*Storm* 4). *A Fine Frenzy* is "a book of saints," and Kenzie admits that he's "lost his heart to them" (*Storm* 6). Late in life he's been "struck by the passion that they all seem driven by" (*Storm* 7). It is as if they're all pointing at something in the sky that he cannot see, so Kenzie decides to "find out for himself what all the excitement was about" (*Storm* 8). He starts going to church, of all things. His wife, Willow, believes he's gone "off the deep end" (*Storm* 8). But Kenzie does succeed in "catching at least an occasional glimpse of what all the shouting was about" (*Storm* 9). Kenzie's glimpse echoes the last pages of *The Eyes of the Heart*, in which Buechner speaks of his own intimations of immortality. An intriguing phrase banging around in the memoir first comes up in a strange, half-frivolous scene of Ouija-board play with Jimmy Merrill and another friend. Thinking they've made contact with their recently deceased English teacher from their prep school days, the young men ask him if his views on issues of religious belief have changed. The enigmatic reply, spelled out on the makeshift game board, is, "Have a better seat now" (*EH* 170). The mystery deepens when, a few pages later, Naya uses exactly the same phrase, "I have a better seat now," to describe a revolution in her attitude toward spiritual things. "From where I am now," she says, "I see farther, and the farther I see, the more I come to understand how much more there is to see beyond that" (*EH* 175).

More than an inscrutable summary of the mysteries of the afterlife, the phrase—"Have a better seat now"—suggests a new angle of vision that is the keynote of Buechner's focus in these recent books. Age and experience have yielded up a new perspective, an angle from which Buechner seems more than ever convinced of the truth of the promises of Christianity. One critic even called *The Storm* "a contemporary tale of redemption."[15] Just past seventy, Buechner writes *The Storm* with a protagonist closing in on the same age. Buechner recalls that he actually looked forward to the event: "Turning seventy seems to be some kind of benchmark—then you can really be old if you feel like it. I think you *do* get wiser in some ways. I have found it easier to be myself" (*Door* 13). For Buechner, aging has meant the freedom to speak with less restraint about the miracles and madnesses that his imagination and memory suggest.

So has the old Buechner disappeared, the one always so consistent about giving voice to doubt? Another critic, Maude McDaniel, "ambivalent about Buechner's ambiguity," couldn't help but notice that Buechner's fifteenth novel was "arguably the most ambiguous of all his books."[16] McDaniel noted that "ambiguity has become Buechner's stock in trade . . . and is probably the key to his success as a religious writer in the studiedly nonreligious culture of the last half of the twentieth century" (McDaniel 278). Although she admired *The Storm*, she worried that Buechner's penchant for ambiguity served to "water down the true problem of evil" (McDaniel 281). Her protestations at least establish that Buechner's position between the sacred and the profane remains much the same. Letters between Buechner and his agent, now tucked away in the archives, indicate a certain concern about the first manuscript version of the novel. Buechner's agent fretted that Kenzie Maxwell might be too much "a monster, a bad man" (Archive, IV A 16). His literary agent even suggested that Buechner might rewrite passages to make Kenzie "more appealing," and, though he does make a few edits in that direction, Buechner cannot offer up an unadulterated good man, a simple story of forgiveness and salvation (Archive, IV A 16). His angle of vision has not changed that much.

The angle on Kenzie that Buechner's agent worried about shows up in the first line of the novel: "They say that Kenzie Maxwell married Willow because she was the only woman he still knew at the time who could afford him" (*Storm* 1). He's been married twice before; maybe he's even married Willow—both of them in their sixties—for her money and social status. Maybe it is her still girlish beauty that wins the day. The ambiguity of the arrangement is also complicated by early hints of some scandal hanging in the background. The plot of *The Storm* is driven by Kenzie's disreputable past, a life sidetracked by a sordid affair that has threatened to crush him into nothingness. Once a promising writer, Kenzie now carries a "burden of sadness and shame and loss that lay beneath everything he did to conceal it" (*Storm* 72). Twenty years before the time period of the novel and "increasingly apprehensive himself about where his life was taking him, if it was taking him anywhere," Kenzie has had a midlife crisis that spiraled into an immense transgression. The residual guilt is a troublesome load not unlike the burden old Godric kept toting around (*Storm* 17).

This time, the story is quickly told. Feeling the need "to go deeper off the deep end," Kenzie has volunteered at a rescue mission for abandoned people in the South Bronx (*Storm* 10). For the Alodians, an organization for which Kenzie's older brother, Dalton, acts as the chairman of the board, Kenzie pens a newsletter. He fusses around the place, mostly listening to the painful and poignant stories of the young people, the "poor naked wretches" Buechner can never quite ignore. Buechner takes a mere three pages to tell the story of how Kenzie's instinct toward goodness is thwarted. The girl is only seventeen, a street waif, a graffiti artist. Kenzie knows that a relationship with Kia would "stink to heaven," but he falls in love in spite of himself (*Storm* 20). Their union is brief, mostly an affair of desperation on both sides, but the child of their forbidden lovemaking will be real enough. Hiding her pregnancy from Kenzie, Kia endures the premature birth in a cold-water flat. "There was a lot of hemorrhaging and a high fever, and within the week Kia died. The baby lived. It was a girl" (*Storm* 21).

Thus abruptly, Buechner moves to the consequences. Left with a daughter, Bree, and a "frayed black sneaker," the only possession Kia leaves behind in his flat, Kenzie must try to find a way to navigate both the sorrow and the scandal (*Storm* 20). His personal hell is exposed by his own brother, Dalton, who publishes Kenzie's private letter of confession in the mission newsletter, an unforgivable violation, as Kenzie sees it. For twenty years, Kenzie has tried to take care of Bree while writing a rambling journal to Kia, the waif he cannot forget, the love he cannot decipher; and he has not spoken to his brother in all those years.

The good Samaritan winds up a pariah, and it is this mixed and mixed-up man whose story Buechner tells in a third-person narrative, perhaps as a way of maintaining some distance from the sordidness of the tale. Willow and Kenzie are a mismatched pair in most ways. As they approach their seventh decades, she believes in nothing, and he believes "in everything" (*Storm* 3). Like Bebb before him, who also proclaims, "I believe everything" (*Bebb* 143), and like Buechner himself, who admits, "I am a hopelessly religious person" (*EH* 11), Kenzie is moved by things he cannot see. None of them ever declares that such belief is easy, however. Critic Bill Ott summarized Kenzie's belief as "an oddly ambiguous, utterly human kind of faith—characterized not by certainty but by good-humored irony, even world-weariness, and above all, by a profound sense of quiet."[17] Kenzie himself thinks of his faith as a kind of *"tendresse oblige,"* a remarkable tenderness that his failures have opened him toward (*Storm* 4).

The tricky temptation here is to think of Buechner as Kenzie—both of them aging writers with a proclivity "to imagine almost anything," both of them haunted by memory and given to faith (*Storm* 4). Again, the autobiographical dimension is oblique and elusive. There's the study of dysfunctionality in families and the specter of the endearing sinner, themes that Buechner has turned to repeatedly. As Philip Yancey understood in his chapter on Buechner in *Soul Survivor*, Buechner has made a text of his own life in much the same way that Annie Dillard finds a text in nature.[18] That is not, however, to say that the events of Buechner's novels can be simply viewed as memoir. The text of his life that Buechner explores has more to do with imaginings and ideas than with the facts of experience. The driving idea this time is, as Gwenette Robinson put it, "forgiveness."[19] Will Kenzie Maxwell recover from his disgraceful plummet? Will he forgive Dalton? Will he forgive himself?

Readers of *The Storm* are persistently reminded that Buechner is hanging this novel on a Shakespearean backdrop. The play this time is *The Tempest*, that late Shakespeare that Buechner thinks of as a valedictory offering. The fact of the play as a romance, the movement toward a happy ending, infects Buechner's novel with a sense that, despite the merciless storm, everything may turn out well after all. Steve Van Der Weele's contention that the "kinship" between Buechner's novel and *The Tempest* "has a common base in the wisdom of the gospels" is worthy of a look.[20] The isle of Buechner's fiction is Plantation Island, an upper-class resort community not unlike Hobe Sound, where Buechner often winters. Plantation Island is ruled by Violet Sickert, another of Buechner's almost-villains, who endures Kenzie's scandalous presence only because of his connection to Willow. The cast extends to Willow's son by an earlier marriage, Averill, a forty-year-old hippie who seems to live on another planet entirely. Averill is Ariel, an Ariel "transformed into a New Age windsurfer, complete with ponytail," as one critic puts it.[21] Prospero is Kenzie, the compromised magician. Bree is Miranda. Miss Sickert (Sycorax, the witch mother of Caliban) has discarded her angry servant, the usually drunk handyman Calvert, who is to play something of the Caliban role. The brooding Calvert is rumored to be Miss Sickert's own illegitimate son, the ne'er-do-well in line to inherit the whole island. Dalton is Sebastian, though the link seems tenuous, and Dalton's stepson, Nandy, fits into the formula as Ferdinand, the son of the king of Naples. One critic went so far as to label the novel "a paraphrase" of Shakespeare, an "entirely wonderful" rendering.[22]

My own sense is that the Shakespearean connection is much more artfully employed than was the Oz backdrop in *The Entrance to Porlock*. As with the flickers of Graham Greene's *The Power and the Glory* that inform *The Final Beast*, the lines to Shakespeare are held loosely in *The Storm*. Shakespeare is at the table, but he mostly keeps his peace. The allusiveness provides readers and critics a pleasant jolt, a shared moment of literary consonance, and Irvine was right to say that matching up the characters from Buechner to Shakespeare is "part of the pleasure" of *The Storm*, but the novel works dramatically at a level quite apart from Shakespeare's tale (Irvine 129). Many reviewers actually read the novel successfully without resort to the Shakespearean connection. The central plotline of the novel moves toward a birthday party that is to celebrate Kenzie's seventieth year, a party that will prove to be the occasion for a denouement of sorts. Everyone is coming to Plantation Island—Dalton, ostensibly to draft a will for Miss Sickert; Nandy, to meet his stepfather, with whom he is on uncertain terms; Bree to celebrate with Kenzie. All the residents of and visitors to the beautiful isle, the rich and the poor, are to pass through a storm, a metaphorical one and a startlingly real one.

Like a good many of Buechner's characters before him, Kenzie Maxwell is a better man than he knows. Working among the homeless and abandoned, he thinks "of the absurdity of trying to salvage them when he was himself so in need of salvaging" (*Storm* 14). Yet the wisdom he offers at the rescue mission is poignant and powerful. He tells his world-weary audience that "even street people usually had something beautiful about them, and beautiful people, if they were honest, sometimes admitted that they felt like street people inside and just happened to look beautiful" (*Storm* 15). His fascination with the saints seems genuine enough as well. He dreams of some outlandish, saintly act—kissing a leper, as Saint Francis is reputed to have done, or sitting on a sixty-foot column for Christ, as Simeon Stylites is said to have done. But Kenzie's act of passion ends up being a furtive tryst with a seventeen-year-old whose last name he doesn't even know.

How could such a wise and compassionate man wind up in that place? Part of it is his desperation, what might be called his crisis of meaning. Part of it is Kia's desperation, her spiritual lostness, her economic plight. Kia spray-paints her name all over the city. She needs to be somewhere, longs for connection and identity. Does Kenzie simply take advantage of her vulnerability? Or is there in his embrace of her some simple response to their mutual desperation? No character in the novel will grant authenticity and meaning to Kenzie's days with Kia. Given our revolutionary understanding of sexual relationships and power, contemporary readers are also unlikely to extend mercy in this situation. It is the most predictable of all clichés—pitiful older man makes a fool of himself over a pretty younger woman. The fact that twenty years later Kenzie is still composing his letter to Kia, still trying to understand what happened, suggests that the affair may have been more than an affair, the issues of the heart more complex than the cliché allows. Buechner has offered up this time a deliciously complicated present-day situation. In his bewilderment, Kenzie reminds me of the pastor's wife in Robertson Davies's *Fifth-Business*, who, when caught *in flagrante delicto* with a passing tramp, can only comment, "he wanted it so badly."[23] In his confession to Dalton, Kenzie can only cite an obscure poem of Thomas Ford's: "I did but see her passing by . . . And yet I love her till I die" (*Storm* 23). Dalton doesn't get it.

In Kenzie's letter of resignation from the Alodians, he acknowledges the gravity of his sin and accepts responsibility for the child. He confesses that he hopes for God's forgiveness and for the child's forgiveness too (*Storm* 24). He says he loved Kia. But his confession carries little weight when Dalton publishes the letter. What Kenzie finds unforgivable is not the injury to himself; he is only getting what he deserves, he thinks. But what Dalton has done is "vilifying the memory and the name of Kia, the name that she had so daringly painted up in so many impossible places like a kind of battle flag whose wild colors and flamboyant curlicues she had hoped might make up for losing the battle itself as she had always known she would lose it" (*Storm* 26). Even the craziest of saints could not forgive such a violation. So Kenzie lives on in his cloud of disgrace, a shattered man, an angry man, and yet a man softened by his own failures. Approaching his seventieth birthday, Kenzie, like Tobit, still has a discernable music about him, a longing for miracle, a capacity for faith.

But Kenzie is strikingly unfinished, an outsider even at home. The only mark he has made at Willow's place on Plantation Island is in the books, particularly the Andrew Lang fairy-tale volumes, which almost slip us back to the Magic Kingdom. Maybe Willow has married Kenzie simply to escape the meditating vegetarian, Averill, who, though in his forties, still lives with his mother, constituting a bothersome if unobtrusive presence around the place. Despite his status as a pariah who must endure the deadly social cuts administered by the indomitable and bitter Violet Sickert, Kenzie has had a moment. At one of Miss Sickert's intimidating suppers, Kenzie has noticed her sitting, as usual, alone. Approaching her on an impulse, he grabs one of her hands and kisses it. Readers can almost imagine the air going out of the room. Maybe Saint Francis did kiss the leper. But we are unsurprised when Miss Sickert wrangles Dalton into visiting the retreat on the same weekend as Kenzie is to celebrate his birthday. Willow thinks the invitation is most likely further evidence of her malicious spite. Kenzie is not so sure. Maybe "nobody could know the full truth about Miss Sickert's motives or anyone else's," he says (*Storm* 40). In his letter to Kia, he writes, "Nothing is entirely black. Not even the human heart. Maybe not even my own" (*Storm* 40).

So many sad people populate *The Storm*, and Kenzie is chief among them. He's lived a long time to know so little, he thinks, as he marvels at the computer his stepson has given him to put "the whole world at my fingertips" (*Storm* 42). Revealing more than he knows, Kenzie notes, "I prefer to keep the world at arm's length" (*Storm* 42). Like Bebb at the end, like Godric, Kenzie looks at his life as something missed. "It is like having lived nearly seventy years and wondering about all the wonderful things you might have done with them if you had only known how" (*Storm* 42). He's lived with arms folded, for the most part, with fists clenched. Closing himself to hurt, he has also closed himself to healing.

He's done the best he could for Bree, establishing her with his older sister, Norah, in a rambling farmhouse in Massachusetts and visiting often, answering her questions as best he can. He worries over Bree, tells her about the books he has written and about the time he thinks he may have seen an angel fly into a park. Like "a benevolent stranger," he takes her on educational trips to Boston and remembers her birthdays, but his guilt stymies him. He is like Godric, who edits his past for Reginald. Kenzie omits more than he reveals in his talks with Bree (*Storm* 46). When he learns that Averill has caught the drunken Calvert peeping outside Bree's room on one of her visits to the island, he is enraged but still can't fire Calvert who, dismissed by Miss Sickert, is the jack-of-all-trades around Willow's place. Kenzie remembers that he too has spied on a sleeping child. His guilt and compassion staunch his anger. When Bree writes to say she is coming in for the birthday fete, she asks, "What are *you* going to do, Kenzie dear, now that you're so old?" (*Storm* 54). His answer is in the letter to Kia:

> I will continue to do penance, that's what I will do. . . . I will continue to live on my wife's money. I will continue to attend the eight o'clock service Sundays in my hooded blue sweatshirt and try to hear the voices of the saints through the Frog Bishop's amiable bromides. In

short, I will go on, as I have for years, the feckless has-been they take me for with my unmentionable past and queer ways. That is my sack-cloth and ashes. (*Storm* 55)

Condemned to life, Kenzie faces his birthday marker full of the wistful "If only . . ." (*Storm* 56).

Kenzie's brother has had his battles too. Having retired from his post at the law school, Dalton has carefully structured a life of routine. "Fearing disorder above all things," Dalton is shaken by Miss Sickert's summons (*Storm* 58). He's managed to push the whole business of his life—Nandy, Norah and Bree, and even Kenzie—to the margins. He's never seen Bree, and he is "mystified about why for all these years he and his brother had remained totally estranged" (*Storm* 59). It is Jacob and Esau all over again. Dalton has dreamed of being a writer too. His book is to be a history of Central Park, because "to tell the history of anything was, if you did it thoroughly and accurately, to end up telling the history of everything" (*Storm* 61). Buechner's sense of the interconnectedness of all things shines through in Dalton's unlikely plan. By his own testimony, Dalton has "gone mad twice in his life," and Kenzie appears in both scenes (*Storm* 60). On the occasion of Kenzie's first marriage, his best man, Dalton, crumbles into unaccountable tears on the way to the church and has to have a stand-in. Years later, after the death of his wife, Dalton is visiting Kenzie and speaking of his plans for the Central Park book when he suddenly starts thinking of ultimate things. From somewhere he hears himself uttering the enigmatic sentence, "If the world hasn't come to an end by this time tomorrow, I'll know I'm nuts" (*Storm* 62). Both times, Dalton winds up in the "Looney Bin" (*Storm* 62).

The intriguing part of Dalton's recounting of his two infamous spells is that "while the madness was upon him he had discovered that everything he saw was incandescent with meaning" (*Storm* 62). He's been just that close to understanding the very essence of his life. Reliving the strange history of his life as Kenzie's brother, Dalton is finally persuaded to accept Miss Sickert's directive, because the trip will also allow him to meet up with Nandy, the troublesome stepson who seems to be constantly drifting up one dead-end street after another. He'll invite Nandy to meet him at the West Palm Beach Airport and drive him on to Miss Sickert's. In his note to his client, Dalton jokes that "pushing eighty," he "could use a young man to make sure he got where he was going" (*Storm* 68). We know it is a joke, of course, because Nandy seems to be the sort of fellow who seldom knows where he's going, and Dalton is certainly the sort of fellow who always knows where he's going. Or thinks he does.

When the news of Dalton's plans reaches Willow and Kenzie, Willow has her own joke: "I don't believe in anything else, least of all God, but I find it nothing short of miraculous not only that that appalling woman would go to such lengths to torment you, Kenzie, but that that appalling man would play along with her" (*Storm* 72). Despite her protestations about believing in nothing, Willow has had her moments too. She knows about Kenzie's never-ending letter and the black sneaker he keeps hidden away. She thinks more deeply than her bridge partners might guess. She remembers her first marriage, a happy one that ended in her husband's untimely death. She ponders her second marriage and now this third one with the unpredictable Kenzie. And despite her unbelief, "she sensed the working of some behind-the-scenes power that now and then made things happen in a way that was different from the way they would have happened otherwise" (*Storm* 74). Though they have "virtually nothing in common," and she cannot really enter Kenzie's world of maybe-angels and wacky saints, Willow, nonetheless, "believed in the capacity of whatever the power was to work an occasional miracle, either darkly or otherwise as the fancy took it, but she didn't believe things made sense" (*Storm* 76). The sadness and misconnection of these characters combines to remind us of Buechner's preoccupation with the realities of sorrow and loss, but Willow and Kenzie have that human penchant to hope for the moment when all things will be tumbled inside out, maybe even made new.

Miracle, then, is surely one of the Buechnerian subjects up for a revisitation in *The Storm*. Kenzie can find one just about anywhere. "Even on the warmest, most breathless Sundays he sometimes felt a stirring of cool air about his nostrils," Kenzie remembers as he tries to talk about what happens to him in church (*Storm* 78). Unlike his creator who, though he acknowledges "I *owe* the church so *much*," finds himself struck by a general "drabness and "unexcitedness" in the institution (*Door* 13), Kenzie finds church sometimes to be "the right place at the right time" (*Storm* 79). But Kenzie sees miracles in car license plates that, providentially, he thinks, display his very own initials, and there are the white birds on the golf course and a particular tree that he meets every day on his walk about the island. All of these maybe-miracles will sound quite familiar to readers of Buechner's memoirs. He too has an eye for the possible deeper meanings of apparently random events. Kenzie calls them "small miracles"—"fragile and ambiguous" (*Storm* 80).

Kenzie has also had one rather remarkable miracle, though this one too is shrouded in maybe. Just before Willow's guests are to arrive at one of her outdoor cocktail parties, a storm has blown up. Directing Calvert to begin hurriedly the work of moving everything inside, Willow is halted by her bathrobe-bedecked husband, who raises his hands to the sky and chants, "Rain, rain, go away, little Willow wants to play" (*Storm* 81). And just that quickly, the storm passes. A lucky guess? Who is to say? Kenzie puts it in his letter, but he knows that his miracle pales before the one that would be needed to work reconciliation between the Maxwell brothers.

Family dysfunctionality reaches new proportions in the eddy of multiple marriages, stepchildren strewn about here and there, and grudges simmering in the pages of *The Storm*. Just as Kenzie has farmed out Bree to Norah Maxwell, Dalton has trusted his stepson, Nandy, to the care of the housekeeper, Mary O'Brien, who teaches Nandy to read, tells him stories, takes him to school, and the like. The Maxwell brothers do not warm the heart on the issue of fatherhood. Dalton presses Nandy to make something of himself, but Nandy is a college dropout. He's taken a summer to ride his bike across the continent, and now he works as part of a golf course maintenance crew. Not the life Dalton had imagined for him. Sorry to have been "such a continual disappointment," Nandy, nonetheless, feels a certain fondness for his stepfather (*Storm* 90). When Dalton calls to ask how he's doing, Nandy usually responds, "I'm easy," an answer that irritates his stepfather (*Storm* 91). "Life wasn't supposed to be easy, especially for a young man with no plans for the future, and not much money, and no apparent ambitions or goals," Dalton thinks (*Storm* 91). The universal unease between parents and children is here magnified by the mother's death and Dalton's two departures into madness. Sensing his father's fragility, the young Nandy has taken on the role of trying to protect his stepfather from the whimsical misfortunes of existence. Now, getting Dalton's call at the golf club, Nandy agrees to the trip to Plantation Island. "One way or another," Nandy thinks, "he would get him [Dalton] where he was going, and maybe in the process get himself wherever in the world he was going too" (*Storm* 95). Two more wounded souls start the journey to Miss Sickert's haunted isle.

If this is to be a tale of redemption, Kenzie and Dalton are going to have to heal the breach somehow. Even Willow sees that Dalton's rumored trip might be the occasion to make it up: "You might as well bury the hatchet," she jibes her husband; "You're too old to do anything else with it" (*Storm* 97). Like most of us, Kenzie has not imagined forgiveness and reconciliation; he's only tried to "make a path around it somehow"

(*Storm* 97). He's put Dalton out of his mind, lived without that relation-ship, but now Willow wants to invite Dalton to the party. And Averill is to deliver the invitation to Miss Sickert's, where Dalton and Nandy will be staying. Known around the island merely as "Willow Maxwell's son," poor Averill is another lost soul in this motley collection, but his unantic-ipated meeting with the chief honcho, Miss Sickert, opens new vistas in our understanding of both characters (*Storm* 101).

Averill is the sort of fellow nobody ever really notices, so when Miss Sickert actually looks into his eyes and asks him questions about himself, surprise reigns. He tells her, "I've got a life," but wonders "if he was telling the truth" (*Storm* 102). Another adult officiously straightening out the children, Miss Sickert responds, "Well, we've all of us got lives. . . . The question is what do we do with them" (*Storm* 102). Averill shifts the shoe to her foot. "What do you do with yours?" he asks (*Storm* 102). Violet takes on new dimensions for us, first by having the good sense to admire Averill's directness, and by way of her answer: "I try to keep this island afloat like a ship, that's what I do. I try to make the journey as well run and attractive and civilized as possible" (*Storm* 102). To his credit, Averill knows the next question: "Where is it journeying to?" (*Storm* 103).

The conversation has suddenly gone metaphysical. Miss Sickert, like the wizard in Oz, pulls strings and manages lives, but there's a hole in the middle of it all. She prefers not to think about the end of the journey. Such thoughts are "depressing," she believes (*Storm* 103). Averill, on the other hand, has thought about the ends a great deal. Maybe there's "a far shore" away from the "ten thousand things" in his family's world, he thinks (*Storm* 103). Into this scene of two isolated souls oddly connecting now arrives Bishop Hazelton. The Frog Bishop, as Kenzie names him, has come by for his regular visit with his most important parishioner. The voice of Christian orthodoxy, the bishop worries that he has capitulated overmuch to her wealth and power. She's instructed him, for example, to clear up the "unfortunate impression" he's left with that sermon about the rich man, the camel, and the eye of a needle (*Storm* 106). Shocked into thoughts of mystery by her exchanges with Averill, Miss Sickert listens as Averill asks the bishop if he has "ever seen God" (*Storm* 108). The good bishop answers that, "Nobody has ever done that" (*Storm* 108). Before he pedals away, Averill shouts, "I have," and even the spiritually blind bishop can dimly intuit that Miss Sickert has "never even found anybody to love and never found anybody to love her either" (*Storm* 108). Thus Buechner sets up another handful of characters longing for more than they can express even as they have spoken of the possibility of God.

Closing in now on the party that is to bring all these people together, Buechner moves to Bree's misadventures on her flight to West Palm Beach. Is it coincidence that she winds up seated next to the uncle she's never met? The turbulent flight inspires a conversation about their mutual fear of flying and their fears of death before she learns her companion's identity. Seeing his name on his engagement book, she lets the cat out of the bag, and Dalton thinks for a moment that he's about to go mad again. He can feel the tears welling up. He fears that all may be "confusion and chaos" (*Storm* 115). Something important happens when Bree takes Dalton's hand to comfort him. With characteristic understatement, Buechner allows the reader to imagine the emotion of the surprising reunions at the luggage carousel. There's Nandy meeting Dalton, and Kenzie meeting Bree. There's a spark when the cousins meet for the first time. There's the "historic reunion" of the brothers (*Storm* 119). Kenzie whispers to Bree, "It wouldn't be a party without you," and we realize something momentous is brewing.

Miss Sickert is less than pleased to hear that Dalton will be going to Kenzie's party. Maybe she's piqued that her nefarious scheme has gone awry; maybe she just dislikes losing control of the situation. In any case, she does her best to avoid Dalton and any talk of the will he's come to review. All that smacks too much of death. She's taken, however, with Nandy. There's something touching about the stepson, something not unlike that which drew her to exchange personal thoughts with Averill. So moved is she by Nandy that she asks him to call her "Violet" (*Storm* 126). Her thoughts are mostly about what to do with her money. She's angry about the rumors, those laughs behind hands that assume that Calvert Sykes is her bastard son. She's still angry at Kenzie and Willow for offering Sykes a place when she banished him. She's angry at Dalton for fussing about the will and for undermining her weekend plots by accepting the invitation to her disreputable neighbor's birthday party. Most of all, she's angry at her lonely life. Maybe she can get even with everyone by leaving all her money and property to Sykes. Doing so, she could get even with her gossipy neighbors, who fail to appreciate all she's done to build their little world. She'd get her own back, too, on Kenzie and Willow and the others. Even the dense Bishop Hazelton, who has failed her at the weekend's opening dinner by not knowing the date of the Feast of the Assumption, would be brought low by such a stunning reversal of fortunes. "It might even serve Calvert Sykes right himself. He could see how he liked being rich and alone with no one he could really call a friend," she thinks (*Storm* 133). The storm is about to blow in, and the elements of potential tragedy are thoroughly in place. In *Telling the Truth*, Buechner has used *King Lear* to establish a line of thought that echoes in *The Storm*:

> Beneath our clothes, our reputations, our pretensions, beneath our religion or lack of it, we are vulnerable both to the storm without and to the storm within, and if we are ever to find true shelter, it is with the recognition of our tragic nakedness and need for true shelter that we have to start. Thus it seems to me that this is also where anyone who preaches the Gospel has to start too—after the silence that is the truth comes the news that is bad before it is good, the word that is tragedy before it is comedy because it strips us bare in order ultimately to clothe us. (*TTT* 33)

The Storm could be read as a gloss on Buechner's words from that 1976 speech. The novel could go either way from here—toward *King Lear* or toward *The Tempest*. The stripping bare has been mostly accomplished by now. We've peered into the fragility of Dalton, the loneliness of Miss Sickert, the lostness of Averill, the bewilderment of Nandy, the unbelief of Willow, and the debilitating remorse of Kenzie. That leaves Bree.

Gabrielle is her real name, though no one calls her that. She's more or less without identity, like almost everyone else in Buechner's cast. Unsurprisingly, she will tell her story to Nandy, who shows up at the Maxwell place already half in love with this cousin he's never met. She tells him about Kia. Kenzie has told her of the Alodians and his love for Kia. Nandy says, "He guessed all families were pretty mixed up, theirs maybe more than most, but then maybe not" (*Storm* 141). Bree has inspected the undersides of bridges and the doorways of abandoned buildings in Kia's old neighborhood, looking for her mother's name scribbled up somewhere. But there's no trace. Bree tells Nandy about the time Kenzie has asked Kia about her last name. Kia claims that Maxwell "was good enough for her too," and Bree thinks of that as the moment they were married (*Storm* 142). She even talks of visits to church, where, at Kenzie's urging, she's tried to pray but found it "hard to believe that anybody was listening" (*Storm* 143). Her scattered memories are poignant, even wrenching, but Nandy simply listens. He has no answers to offer, only himself. Before their retreat is interrupted, Bree tells him of Kenzie's prayers—his prayers for Bree and Kia and for the forgiveness that he's never been able to extend to himself.

The day of the party, Sunday, begins innocently enough. Miss Sickert is off to church, and Nandy has planned a most unusual morning for Dalton, a fishing expedition just off the beaches of the resplendent houses that dot Miss Sickert's isle. In their little rented rowboat, Dalton and Nandy feel the weight of the silence that often persists between parents and children. Dalton tries to avoid the subject of Nandy's aimlessness. Nandy, for his part, seems content to just put lines in the water as his startlingly out-of-place stepfather clutches the gunwales. The inevitable questions finally emerge: Bree's mother? Why the breakdown in the family? The helplessness in Dalton's eyes is answer enough. "God only knows why," Dalton muses, and adds, "Think of all the time wasted" (*Storm* 151). Back on shore, more experienced Floridians have noticed the appearance of an unexpected and strangely ominous cloud. The serious storm assails the tiny boat before Nandy can steer them toward shore. From their house, Willow, Bree, and Kenzie can see the tiny blur of a boat being tossed in the sudden waves. Willow is only half-joking when she accuses Kenzie of conjuring up this terror. "Had he willed it without knowing that he was doing so?" Kenzie wonders (*Storm* 155).

The light satire of a family's domestic tragedies and dysfunctionality has given way to a genuine crisis. Sending Averill and Calvert to search the beach for his shipwrecked relations, Kenzie has to be told, "You are seventy now," lest he run out himself into the pitiless storm (*Storm* 156). Suddenly the weight of it all descends. Kenzie feels "enormously tired" (*Storm* 157). "What does it feel like to be seventy?" is the question that's been echoing around him all day. He decides the answer is that "it felt as if the party was over" (*Storm* 160). The end seems dead ahead, and, although Kenzie still believes it will come "as a friend" and be welcomed, he admits that maybe Willow might be right that death will lead him "nowhere at all" (*Storm* 160). His faith wavering, Kenzie wants to believe that his death will take him "to somewhere so different from anything he had ever been able to imagine," but he also wonders if he'll recognize "what it was when he got there" (*Storm* 160). Thoughts of Dalton and Nandy dead in the sea bring on Kenzie's plunge into a despair, a sadness that dissipates only when Calvert totes in the sodden but living Dalton, who, still tangled in his orange life vest, has washed up on somebody's beach.

Taken into Dalton's thoughts as he recovers from his near-drowning, we realize that, like his brother, he has reached his nadir. Thinking Nandy is dead and that the calamity is somehow his fault, Dalton mumbles in his mind to the long-dead housekeeper, Mary O'Brien. "*Nandy is dead*," he tells her, and adds, "*He has drowned. I saw it. I never took care of him. Take care of him. He had a job that was getting him nowhere. Now he has gotten there. We had nothing to talk about over lunch. We had everything to talk about. You of all people may understand, Mary O'Brien. I have never understood a damn thing*" (*Storm* 162). The italics here seem to be Buechner's way of underscoring the weight of Kenzie's sadness, and Buechner sustains the uncompromising dimensions of the tragedy fully into the final pages. Two heartbroken old men think of the waste, the missed chances, and readers are taken into the territory of the costs of silence, the sad sagas of families gone wrong. And there's still Nandy to worry over. Averill has found him, of course, tossed up along with the wreckage of the boat, a wreck himself. He too is fixated on his futility. "Once again he had failed his father," he thinks (*Storm* 167). All the characters are starkly defined by their sense of having disappointed those they love, by their sure sense of having come to a "lame and impotent conclusion."[24] Ariel's words come to mind, "Hell is empty, And all the devils are here!"[25]

Even the indomitable Miss Sickert is drawn into the tragedy. Kenzie phones her with news of the accident but forgets to call with news of the rescues. Shaken by this latest twist of fate, she unaccountably decides she must get to Willow's house. Bishop Hazelton has similar thoughts. Out in the wet, the two of them slog their separate paths through the remnants of the blast toward God knows what disaster at the Maxwells. Miss Sickert is sick indeed with thoughts of the aborted will and the tragic trap of being alone with all her wealth. The bishop is still mulling over Averill's sharp question—"Have you ever seen God?"—another version of Barth's "Is it true?" (Barth 108). The bishop thinks he should have handled the question more felicitously. Should he have told the boy that sometimes, while droning on in one of his innumerable sermons, he has heard himself say "unfamiliar and unexpected" words that seem to come from "the Spirit itself" (*Storm* 177)? Does he really believe in the grace he has so regularly extended, "an operation of Grace so subtle that not even he had been aware of it" (*Storm* 177)? Arriving finally at the Maxwell's door "with his Disney World poncho billowing about him, he suddenly saw himself as a fool" (*Storm* 178). But is it music that he hears inside the house? Whatever is happy about this ending has been earned. The *metanoia* makes the music work. As Judith Moore rightly saw, "Buechner has put his characters through changes of heart."[26]

Bishop Hazelton stumbles into, of all things, a celebration. Even Calvert is there, off to the side and weeping. "Maybe he was crying, he thought, because he hated them so and because he also hated himself for how much he needed them," we're told (*Storm* 180). Popping the cork from a bottle of champagne, Calvert offers a toast toward Kenzie, "Here's to your seventieth, you old sonofabitch!" and it works (*Storm* 181). The incredulous and now voluble bishop enters the party. Calvert jokes, "This island is always full of weird noises," but for this moment, at least, there seems to be no reason to fear (*Storm* 182). The bishop speaks of golden dreams, Nandy does his hambone act, Dalton applauds, and the merry-making settles into food and drink to commemorate a "raging mercy"— "not the usual way of things in a world that's never been famous for happy endings" (*Storm* 184). The festivities are almost over before a wild-eyed Miss Sickert, soaked and done in, bursts into the room and weeps at the sight of the saved boy and her nemesis, the old man who wants her to think of death. Even the bishop is "more or less speechless" now (*Storm* 187). Before he heads for home, he asks Averill if he's really seen God. Averill's answer—"I am seeing him now"—is as close as Buechner gets to resolution in this novel (*Storm* 187).

It is Prospero who gets the last word in Shakespeare's storm story, words about the inevitability of despair: "Unless I be relieved by prayer" (V, i, 16). Kenzie returns to the computer in Buechner's final chapter. Trying to pour out his "sadness and shame" over the numberless pages, Kenzie has ended with, "*I'm sorry, I'm sorry, I'm sorry*" (*Storm* 190, 191). But now his finger finds its way to the delete key. Erasing his interminable confession, hoping at the last that it will make its way to Kia, Kenzie feels that "a great weight had fallen from his shoulders" (*Storm* 192). The other resolutions are less complete. Nandy will start thinking about what to do with the life given back to him. Miss Sickert will postpone the redrawing of the will. We can dream of Miss Sickert leaving a fortune to Nandy, who will wind up with Bree, but that's mostly vague imaginings. Willow turns back the covers on her bed thinking of that "behind-the-scenes" power who has haunted her days (*Storm* 198). Maybe it was all "some kind of dream" (*Storm* 198). For his part, Kenzie goes to sleep dreaming still about his own homelessness, his mad saints who maybe went "crazy with their endlessly trying, like him, to find where they really belonged" and of his longing for a place that he might "someday" see (*Storm* 199). If *The Storm* is indeed Buechner's valedictory fiction, he has delivered another untangling toward mercy. Kenzie, at the end, is probably more at home among his mad saints than he knows. And Buechner too, who wishes he'd been a saint (*Speak* 161), seems nearer the mark than he knows.

Notes

1. Bruce Calhoun Wood, "Healing Voices," *Presbyterian Outlook*, March 11, 2002, 15.
2. Robert Neralich, "Buechner Delves into Writers' Doubts," *Arkansas Democrat Gazette*, December 1, 2001, 3H.
3. William Shakespeare, *King Lear*, V, iii, 324.
4. James Yerkes, book review, *Christian Century*, December 19–26, 2001.

5. Robert Frost, "The Lesson for Today," in *The Poetry of Robert Frost* (New York: Holt, Rinehart & Winston, 1969), 355. The line also appears on Frost's tombstone in Bennington, Vermont.
6. 1 Corinthians 1:27.
7. Jim Buie, "A Literary Companion along the Way," *Art & Soul: Expressions of the Spirit*, www.episcopalchurch.org, July 17, 2003, 2. Hereafter cited as JBuie.
8. David Stewart, review of *Speak What We Feel*, *Books & Culture*, www.christianitytoday.com, August 14, 2002, 1.
9. Helen Harrison, review of *The Eyes of the Heart*, *BookPage*, www.bookpage.com, 1.
10. Ephesians 1:17–18.
11. Gustav Niebuhr, "An Advocate of Life Off Autopilot," *New York Times*, January 15, 2000, A15.
12. Frederick Buechner, "Seeing and Believing," sermon at Central Reformed Church, Grand Rapids, MI, April 25, 2004.
13. William Wordsworth, "Ode: Intimations of Immortality from Recollections of Early Childhood," l. 203.
14. Michael Harrington, "Miniature Epic of Alienation, Salvation," *Philadelphia Inquirer*, February 21, 1999, 4.
15. Ruth Coughlin, "Books in Brief: Fiction," *New York Times*, www.nytimes.com, January 17, 1999, 1.
16. Maude McDaniel, "An Elusive Grace," *The World & I*, www.worldandi.com, May 1999, 278. Hereafter cited as McDaniel.
17. Bill Ott, book review, *Booklist*, www.ala.org/ala/booklist/booklist.htm, November 15, 1998, 1.
18. Philip Yancey, *Soul Survivor: How My Faith Survived the Church* (New York: Doubleday, 2001), 257.
19. Gwenette Robinson, "Glimpses of Sainthood," *Christian Century*, November 18–25, 1998, 1097.
20. Steve J. Van Der Weele, "Narrative Resonances from Shakespeare's *The Tempest* in Frederick Buechner's *The Storm*," paper delivered at Christianity and Literature Conference, Chicago, March 24, 2001, 4.
21. Joyce Irvine, review of *The Storm*, *Parabola*, Summer 1999, 129. Hereafter cited as Irvine.
22. Larry Swindell, "*Tempest* in a Teapot," *Fort Worth Star-Telegram*, December 6, 1998, P5.
23. Robertson Davies, *Fifth-Business* (New York: Penguin Books, 1970), 48.
24. William Shakespeare, *Othello*, II, i, 160.
25. William Shakespeare, *The Tempest*, I, ii, 214–15. Hereafter cited as *Tempest*.
26. Judith Moore, "Reading," *San Diego Reader*, December 3, 1998, 76.

A Last Word

The clouds seems to be lifting a little.

Academic writing changes few minds. Popular writing tends to attract those already in the choir. Feeling the pinch of that double bind and having said so much about Buechner's work, perhaps I should make one final pass over the "why." In these pages I have surveyed the contributions of those reviewers who have returned to Buechner repeatedly and those critics who have paused for a space over his books. In acknowledging and thanking Nancy Myers, Marie-Helene Davies, Margery McCoy, and Victoria Allen, I am suggesting that, despite a quibble here or there, we are all of us simply trying to say, "Here's a literature worth a look, a writer worth the trouble." Joining the voices of George Garrett, William Pritchard, Roger Sale, Guy Davenport, Judith Moore, Douglas Auchincloss, and the others, I have tried to pay attention to a career of words and ideas, a journey that seems to have led to an increasing awareness of what Buechner calls "sacred moments, the moments of miracle . . . a moment when everything does make sense" (*MD* 87–88). Buechner seems to have more such moments as his career moves along. In speeches and interviews these days, Buechner takes refuge less often in that "Lord, I believe; help Thou mine unbelief" position. I suppose it goes without saying that most of his readers can at least dream of finding such a place.

But Buechner has joined no clubs. Although his career has suffered somewhat in the churning cultural debates that divide us, he has remained scrupulously elusive. Reticent by nature, he is not a book-tour sort of fellow. He is not given to self-promotion. He fits no particular regional category. Is there a Fellowship of Vermont Writers? At home in many

369

worlds, from the secular to the religious, he is at the same time not at home anywhere. Maybe that's one of the points he has tried to make in his novels. His stories, charged with paradox, seem always to push toward the possibility of more, the inevitable inadequacy of now, the amazing hope of then. In February of 2006 a Buechner poem, of all things, turned up in the pages of *Christian Century*. Titled "Miriam," it captures well the gist of Buechner's preoccupations as he closes fast on age eighty:

> Her house was a three year old's drawing
> of a house—two windows on the second floor
> with two below to flank the door.
> On the porch a pair of supermarket tube
> and webbing chairs in case a guest or two
> dropped by plus one where she could lean back,
> a coverlet across her knees when fall
> was in the air or she felt ill.
>
> The shades she always kept exactly so,
> the ones above just low
> enough to hide her on her way to bed,
> the ones below up high to let
> some daylight in. Now that the house is empty
> as a drum, they're every whichway
> like an old drunk's stare,
> and somebody's pinched the supermarket chairs.
>
> Sweet Jesus, forgive me all the days I spotted
> her in one of them and slunk behind the trees
> across the street. A caller on her porch
> for all to see she would have rated
> with her trip to England on a plane,
> or winning first prize for her grapenut pie,
> or the day that she retired from the Inn
> and they gave her a purple orchid on a pin.
>
> Or having some boy ask her to dance,
> or being voted president of her class,
> or some spring morning with her room all warm
> and sunlit waking up in Spencer Tracy's arms.[1]

The sparkling eye for detail still works. The regret for opportunities missed is here, of course, but so is the dream that surpasses all the possibilities of this world.

Buechner
Circa 2005

When Buechner came to Calvin College in 1992 on the evening of what turned out to be an infamous night of rioting in Los Angeles, I introduced him via a translation of Samuel Johnson's judgment of Oliver Goldsmith: *"Nullum quod tetigit non ornavit."* Praising Goldsmith's range, Johnson concluded that Goldsmith "touched nothing he did not adorn."[2] Toiling in so many arenas, Buechner has demonstrated a similar gift. He spoke that night about paying attention. I found him at the television set the next morning, weeping as he watched the reports of chaos in Los Angeles. There, as in the books, I learned something about the cost of attentiveness. When he returned to Calvin College in 2004, I introduced him via the words of Annie Dillard:

Propositioning Freddy

1. Frederick Buechner is my hero, my guide and inspiration. (And, ever since he rose in print to approve a book no one else liked, my beloved friend.)
2. Buechner has likely written so many books because he's plugged in, bless his heart. He has a finger in the socket and can keep it there.

3. The novels are his masterpieces. We must never get too dumbed down to read literary fiction. Nothing else so inspires.
4. Never forget his ribaldry. Love is on earth and in the flesh.
5. He's a great storyteller and a great stylist. His enormous learning vivifies every page.
6. Souls live in the worlds he creates. Souls learn, grow, move! What other novelist's worlds do SOULS inhabit? What other writer gives breathing room to SOULS?
7. Buechner examines his life and sees Divine action. He believes God is poking a finger in, here and there. I don't believe half of it. Yet—here is the point—in the hardest and most unknown regions, such as what life might be like after we're dead, we've hazarded upon identical conclusions. We're both living life and don't see eye to eye on everything; we both know nothing about death and agree in every detail! From this—from Buechner's work and thought—I suspect that assenting to this doctrine or that doctrine doesn't matter a whit. The thing is to stay the course.
8. Do not let this great man leave without telling him you love him.[3]

Dillard's advice makes me hope that I've noticed the right things in these pages.

More tributes have followed. On April 5, 2006, hundreds of readers and friends of Frederick Buechner gathered in Washington, D.C., at the National Cathedral for what was advertised as a "tribute." The dean of the cathedral, Samuel T. Lloyd III, introduced Buechner. Clearly uncomfortable with the attention, Buechner cited Abraham Lincoln's line about the man being ridden out of town on a rail—"If it weren't for the honor of the thing, I'd just as soon walk." Buechner read from his just released book, *Secrets in the Dark*, and then listened to accolades from Barbara Brown Taylor, Thomas Long, and Eugene Sutton. All three focused on the 1977 Beecher Lectures where, Taylor said, Buechner "rearranged the air" for her.[4] Long said that he first came to Buechner in a search for material for his own sermons but came away with the courage to preach from his own story. Sutton focused on that admission of doubt and mystery that so many have found telling in Buechner's work. After the individual tributes, the preachers gathered around Buechner to be led in a panel discussion by Jody Hassett Sanchez, a television producer, but soon Buechner became visibly restless. After several glances at his wristwatch, he finally called a halt. He asked for three minutes of silence. It was as if the words had become an indecipherable cacophony. The panelists and the audience

Fred in the Magic Kingdom
Circa 2005

sat back for a few minutes in the cavernous splendor of the great cathedral, and Buechner then rumbled old Godric's line again—"What's lost is
nothing to what's found, and all the death that ever was, set next to life,
would scarcely fill a cup" (*Godric* 96). Raising his hands, he dismissed the
gathering; "May the Lord bless you and keep you and cause His face to
shine upon you," he said. It seemed like a benediction indeed.

Marie-Helene Davies ended her study of Buechner by noting his "far-
reaching ecumenism" (Davies 189). She was right to recognize the range
suggested by "the liberal Nicolet, the conservative evangelical Bebb . . .
and the lean and ascetic mystic, Godric" (Davies 189). But "ecumenism"
should not be read to mean weak-kneedness. Buechner's middle way
includes the sharp possibility that everything indeed makes sense. John
Updike argued that artists of the twentieth century sought to make art
itself their religion, because they were "confronted with the rubble left
when Darwin, Marx, Freud, and the higher criticism shook Victorian
Christianity to its foundations."[5] The religious instinct was not to be so
easily snuffed out. Despite the "age of disbelief," Updike said, "it remains
curiously true that the literary artist, to achieve full effectiveness, must
assume a religious state of mind—a state that looks beyond worldly standards of success and failure" (Updike 62). Updike also believed that a
"writer's professed religious convictions do not necessarily control the
religious content of his writing," citing Swift, Pope, and Milton to prop
up the point (Updike 61). Updike understood that our own times are different; even our professedly Christian novelists offer "little orthodox
comfort" these days (Updike 61).

Much of the dilemma turns on seismic shifts in audience expectations.
Absent the assumption of a religious sentiment in the reader, the writer
must be, as Ron Hansen put it, "scrupulously honest" or "withdraw from
the field."[6] Buechner might actually be the perfect case study against
which to test Updike's and Hansen's propositions. Buechner has stayed in
the field. Fretting little over popular opinion and literary fads, he has told
his story and his stories with a scrupulousness that is sometimes harrowing, sometimes heartening. Eugene Peterson has written of the essential
dilemma Buechner has had to face for more than fifty years: "Although it
can hardly ever have worked to his advantage either critically or econom-
ically to be known as an ordained minister, Frederick Buechner has never
downplayed the fact."[7] Though Buechner could have "passed," Peterson
added, "he has chosen to be identified with what is generally considered,
in America at least, a vocational underclass" (EPeterson 42). Despite the
tension between the notions of faith and fiction in our time, Buechner has

struggled mightily to wed the two worlds in an imaginative and challenging single narrative. "All of my fiction was written with my life's blood," he claims.[8] In a 2003 article in *Christianity Today* Wendy Zoba concluded, "Perhaps one·day someone will poke through his [Buechner's] work and turn over the rock to find his naked truth . . . looking for clues" (Zoba 59). I don't know if I turned over *the* rock here, but I've turned over as many as I could find. What I have unearthed suggests that Buechner's aim has not been to send messages so much as to raise useful questions. It is what good teachers always do.

I have spent years on Buechner and most of a year on these pages. The journey has been more than worth the trouble. I am grateful to Fred and to Judy, his wife. My thankfulness to them and to my family—Anne, JD, and Gayle. My appreciation to my friends and editors, Jennifer Holberg and James Vanden Bosch, could never be fully expressed. My thanks go also to David Malone, the curator of the Buechner archives, to the many students over the years who have brought to the classroom a curiosity about Buechner and to the festival folks who have inspired my prying into the intersections of faith and literature. Finally, I am grateful to Calvin College for providing the support for this project and to King College for providing the place to do the work. It has been nearly Bebbsian, the most fun I have ever known.

Dale Brown
Grand Rapids, Michigan
June 2006

Notes

1. Frederick Buechner, "Miriam," *Christian Century*, February 21, 2006, 10.
2. Samuel Johnson, "Epitaph for Oliver Goldsmith," *Boswell's Life of Johnson* (New York: Oxford University Press, 1933), 2:59.
3. Annie Dillard, Personal correspondence, February 5, 2004.
4. Barbara Brown Taylor, "The Art of the Sermon: A Tribute to Frederick Buechner," Washington National Cathedral, April 5, 2006.
5. John Updike, *More Matter* (New York: Harper & Row, 1973), 61. Hereafter cited as Updike.
6. Personal conversation, October 21, 2004.
7. Eugene Peterson, "An Exuberant Mishmash," *Christianity Today*, September 14, 1992, 42. Hereafter cited as EPeterson.
8. Wendy Murray Zoba, "Flesh and Blood in the Magic Kingdom," *Christianity Today*, March 2003, 58. Hereafter cited as Zoba.

A Buechner Bibliography

Novels

Abbreviated title used in citations is given in parentheses.

A Long Day's Dying. New York: Knopf, 1950. Reprinted, New Haven, CT: Meridian Books, 1960. (*LDD*)

The Season's Difference. New York: Knopf, 1952. (*SD*)

The Return of Ansel Gibbs. New York: Knopf, 1958. (*AG*)

The Final Beast. New York: Atheneum, 1965. Reprinted, San Francisco: Harper & Row, 1982. (*FB*)

The Entrance to Porlock. New York: Atheneum, 1970. (*Porlock*)

Lion Country: A Novel. New York: Atheneum, 1971. Reprinted, San Francisco: Harper & Row, 1984.

Open Heart: A Novel. New York: Atheneum, 1972. Reprinted, San Francisco, Harper & Row, 1984.

Love Feast: A Novel. New York: Atheneum, 1974. Reprinted, San Francisco: Harper & Row, 1984.

Treasure Hunt. New York: Atheneum, 1977. Reprinted, San Francisco: Harper & Row, 1984.

The Book of Bebb. New York: Atheneum, 1979. Reprinted, San Francisco: Harper & Row, 1990. (*Bebb*)

Godric. New York: Atheneum, 1980. (*Godric*)

Brendan: A Novel. New York: Atheneum, 1987. Reprinted, San Francisco: Harper & Row, 1988. (*Brendan*)

The Wizard's Tide: A Story. San Francisco: Harper & Row, 1990. Reprinted, Boston: G. K. Hall, 1991. (*WTide*)

The Son of Laughter. San Francisco: HarperSan Francisco, 1993. (*Laughter*)

On the Road with the Archangel. San Francisco: HarperSanFrancisco, 1997. (*Archangel*)

The Storm. San Francisco: HarperSanFrancisco, 1998. (*Storm*)

The Christmas Tide. New York: Seabury Books, 2005.

Nonfiction

Abbreviated title used in citations is given in parentheses.

The Magnificent Defeat. New York: Seabury Press, 1966. Reprinted, San Francisco: Harper & Row, 1985. (*MD*)

The Hungering Dark. New York: Seabury Press, 1968. Reprinted, San Francisco: Harper & Row, 1985. (*HD*)

The Alphabet of Grace. New York: Seabury Press, 1970. Reprinted, New York: Walker & Co., 1984. Reprinted, San Francisco: Harper & Row, 1985. (*Alphabet*)

Wishful Thinking: A Theological ABC. New York: Harper & Row, 1973. Reprinted, San Francisco: HarperSanFrancisco, 1993. (*WT*)

The Faces of Jesus. Photography by Lee Boltin. Design by Ray Ripper. Croton-on-Hudson, NY: Riverdale Publishers, 1974. Reprinted, Brewster, MA: Paraclete Press, 2005.

Telling The Truth: The Gospel as Tragedy, Comedy, and Fairy Tale. San Francisco: Harper & Row, 1977. (*TTT*)

Peculiar Treasures: A Biblical Who's Who. Illustrations by Katherine A. Buechner. San Francisco: Harper & Row, 1979. Reprinted, San Francisco: HarperSanFrancisco, 1993. (*PT*)

The Sacred Journey. San Francisco: Harper & Row, 1982. Reprinted, San Francisco: HarperSanFrancisco, 1991. (*SJ*)

Now and Then. Cambridge: Harper & Row, 1983. Reprinted, San Francisco: HarperSanFrancisco, 1991. (*NT*)

A Room Called Remember. San Francisco: Harper & Row, 1984. Reprinted, San Francisco: HarperSanFrancisco, 1992. (*RCR*)

Whistling in the Dark: An ABC Theologized. Illustrations by Katherine A. Buechner. San Francisco: Harper & Row, 1988. Reprinted, San Francisco: HarperSanFrancisco, 1993.

Telling Secrets. San Francisco: HarperSanFrancisco, 1991.

Listening to Your Life: Daily Meditations with Frederick Buechner. San Francisco: HarperSanFrancisco, 1992.

The Clown in the Belfry: Writings on Faith and Fiction. San Francisco: HarperSanFrancisco, 1992. (*Belfry*)

The Longing for Home: Recollections and Reflections. San Francisco: HarperSanFrancisco, 1996. (*Longing*)

The Eyes of the Heart. San Francisco: HarperSanFrancisco, 1999. (*EH*)

Speak What We Feel (Not What We Ought to Say). San Francisco: HarperSanFrancisco, 2001. (*Speak*)

Beyond Words: Daily Readings in the ABC's of Faith. San Francisco: HarperSanFrancisco, 2004.

Secrets in the Dark. San Francisco: HarperSanFrancisco, 2006. (*Secrets*)

Frederick Buechner Sources

Abbreviated title used in citations is given in parentheses.

Adams, P. L. Review of *Godric*. *Atlantic Monthly* 246 (December 1980): 96.

Aldridge, John W. *After the Lost Generation: A Critical Study of the Writers of Two Wars*. New York: McGraw-Hill, 1951. (*Aldridge*)

Allen, Victoria. *Listening to Life: Psychology and Spirituality in the Writings of Frederick Buechner*. Baltimore: American Literary Press, 2002.

Anderson, Chris. "The Very Style of Faith: Frederick Buechner as Homilist and Essayist." *Christianity and Literature* 38, no. 2 (Winter 1989): 7–21.

Auchincloss, Douglas. Review of *The Son of Laughter*. *Parabola* 18 (1993): 95–96. (Auchincloss)

Baxter, Harold Jason. "Touched by Fire and Laughter: The Range of Grace in the Fiction of Flannery O'Connor and Frederick Buechner." Diss., Florida State University, 1983.

Brown, W. Dale. *Of Fiction and Faith: Twelve American Writers Talk about Their Vision and Work*. Grand Rapids: Eerdmans, 1997. (Brown)

————. "A Faith to Live and Die With." *Sojourners Magazine*, May–June 1998, 52–56.

————. "Frederick Buechner: The Sacred Romp." *The Banner*, May 7, 1990.

————. "To Be a Saint: Frederick Buechner's *The Final Beast* and Rewriting Graham Greene." *Religion and Literature* 24, no. 2 (Summer 1992): 51–65.

Bruinooge, Nathan, and Chad Engbers. "Frederick Buechner's Godric: Sinner and Saint Recomplicated." *CEA Magazine* 199: 35–49.

"Buechner, (Carl) Frederick 1926–." *Contemporary Authors: New Revision Series* 11 (1984): 104–10 (interview); 39(1993): 46–51.

"*Christianity Today* 1994 Book Awards: Critics'-Choice Book Awards." *Christianity Today*, April 4, 1994, 41.

Daiches, David. "Widow on a College Campus." *New York Times Book Review*, January 8, 1950, 4. (Daiches)

Davenport, Guy. *New York Times Book Review*, February 14, 1971, 7.

Davenport, John. "Buechner's Fourth." *Spectator*, June 11, 1965, 763.

Davies, Horton. "Frederick Buechner and the Strange Work of Grace." *Theology Today* 36 (July 1979): 186–94. (HDavies)

Davies, Horton, and Marie-Helene Davies. "The God of Storm and Stillness: The Fiction of Flannery O'Connor and Frederick Buechner." *Religion in Life*, Summer 1979, 188–96. (Davies and Davies)

Davies, Marie-Helene. *Laughter in a Genevan Gown: The Works of Frederick Buechner 1970–1980*. Grand Rapids: Eerdmans, 1983. (Davies)

Dillard, Annie. "The Ancient Story of Jacob, Retold in a Passionate, Exalted Pitch." *Boston Sunday Globe*, May 30, 1993, A15. (Dillard)

"Dove on Wires." *Newsweek*, January 25, 1965, 92–94.

Doyle, Paul A. Review of *Lion Country*. *Best Sellers*, March 1, 1971, 54.

Gibble, Kenneth L. "Listening to My Life: An Interview with Frederick Buechner." *Christian Century* 100 (November 16, 1983): 1042–45. (Gibble)

Hassan, Ihab. *Radical Innocence: Studies in the Contemporary Novel*. Princeton, NJ: Princeton University Press, 1961. (Hassan)

Havel, Vaclav. "The End of the Modern Era." Speech reprinted in *New York Times* Op-Ed, March 1, 1992.

Lewis, Peter. "Lives of the Saint." *Times Literary Supplement*, March 13, 1981, 278. (Lewis)

Malin, Irving. "Words Fail Me: *The Son of Laughter*," *Commonweal*, July, 16, 1993, 27. (Malin)

McCoy, Marjorie C. *Frederick Buechner: Novelist and Theologian of the Lost and Found*. San Francisco: Harper & Row, 1988. (McCoy)

Mellin, John O. Review of *The Final Beast*. *Theology Today* 40 (April 83): 103.

Moynahan, Julian. "Writing on Cloth Can Be Tricky." Review of *The Final Beast*. *Book Week*, February 14, 1965, 6–8.

Myers, Nancy Beth. "Sanctifying the Profane: Religious Themes in the Fiction of Frederick Buechner." Diss., North Texas State University, 1976. (Myers)

Nelson, Shirley and Rudy. "Buechner: Novelist to 'Cultural Despisers,'" Review of *Godric*. *Christianity Today* 25 (May 29, 1981): 44. (Nelson)

Ozick, Cynthia. "Open Heart." *New York Times Book Review*, June 11, 1972, 4.

Peterson, Eugene H. Review of *The Son of Laughter*. *Theology Today* 50 (January 1994): 607–10. (Peterson)

Podhoretz, Norman. "The New Nihilism and the Novel." *Partisan Review* 25 (Fall 1958): 576–90. (Podhoretz)

Prescott, Peter. "Holy Man with a Past." *Newsweek*, November 10, 1980, 112–14.

Price, Emerson. "*A Long Day's Dying* Shows Rare Wisdom." *Cleveland Press*, January 10, 1950, 24.

Schaub, Thomas Hill. *American Fiction in the Cold War*. Madison: University of Wisconsin Press, 1991.

Sendry, Joseph. "1993 CCL Book Award Citation." *Christianity and Literature* 42, no. 2 (Winter 1993): 378–79.

Spectorsky, A. C. Review of *The Return of Ansel Gibbs*. *Saturday Review*, February 15, 1958, 21. (Spectorsky)

Tennyson, G. B., and Edward E. Ericson Jr., eds. *Religion and Modern Literature: Essays in Theory and Criticism*. Grand Rapids: Eerdmans, 1975.

Thompson, Stacy Webb. "The Rediscovery of Wonder: A Critical Introduction to the Novels of Frederick Buechner." Diss., Michigan State University, 1979. (Thompson)

Wheaton College Special Collections, Wheaton, IL. Frederick Buechner, Box IV A 1. (*Archive*)

Wilder, Amos. "Strategies of the Christian Artist." *Christianity and Crisis* 25 (1965): 92–95.

Woelfel, James. "Frederick Buechner: The Novelist as Theologian." *Theology Today* 40 (October 1983): 273–91. (Woelfel)

Index

Numbers in *italics* indicate photographs.

813
B9281 ZB

117097